Exam	Prentice Hall Title	MCSE Certification Credit	MCSE + Internet Certification Credit	MCDBA Certification Credit	MCSD Certification Credit	MCP + Site Building Certification Credit	MCP + Internet Certification Credit
70-079	*MCSE/MCSE + Internet: Implementing and Supporting Microsoft Internet Explorer 4 by Using the Microsoft Internet Explorer Administration Kit,* Dell 1999	1 of 2 Elective Requirements	1 of 7 Core Requirements	NA	NA	NA	NA
70-081	*MCSE: Implementing and Supporting Microsoft Exchange Server 5.5,* Goncalves, 1998	1 of 2 Elective Requirements	1 of 2 Elective Requirements	NA	NA	NA	NA
70-085	*MCSE: Implementing and Supporting Microsoft SNA Server 4, Mariscal, 1999*	1 of 2 Elective Requirements	1 of 2 Elective Requirements	NA	NA	NA	NA
70-086	*MCSE: Implementing and Supporting Microsoft Systems Management* Server 2, Vacca, 1999	1 of 2 Elective Requirements	NA	NA	NA	NA	NA
70-087	MCSE: *Implementing and Supporting Microsoft Internet Information Server 4,* Dell, 1999	1 of 2 Elective Requirements	1 of 7 Core Requirements	1 of 1 Elective Requirements	NA	NA	1 of 3 Requirements
70-088	*MCSE: Implementing and Supporting Microsoft Proxy Server 2, Hoffman,* 1999	1 of 2 Elective Requirements	1 of 2 Elective Requirements	NA	NA	NA	NA
70-098	*Core MCSE,* Dell, 1998	1of 4 Core Requirements	1 of 7 Core Requirements	NA	NA	NA	NA
70-175	*MCSD: Designing and Implementing Distributed Applications with Microsoft Visual Basic 6,* 1999	NA	NA	1 of 4 Core Requirements and 1 of 1 Elective Requirements	1 of 1 Elective Requirements	NA	NA
70-176	*MCSD: Designing and Implementing Desktop Applications with Microsoft Visual Basic 6,* Holzner, 1999	NA	NA	NA	1 of 1 Elective Requirements	NA	NA

MCSE:
INTERNETWORKING
WITH MICROSOFT® TCP/IP ON
MICROSOFT WINDOWS NT® 4.0

ISBN 0-13-011251-8

90000

9 780130 112514

MICROSOFT TECHNOLOGY SERIES

KOSTYA RYVKIN
DAVE HOUDE
TIM HOFFMAN

MCSE:
INTERNETWORKING WITH MICROSOFT® TCP/IP ON MICROSOFT WINDOWS NT® 4.0

Prentice Hall PTR
Upper Saddle River, New Jersey 07458
http://www.phptr.com

Library of Congress Cataloging-in-Publication Data

Ryvkin, Kostya.
   MCSE--internetworking with Microsoft TCP/IP / Kostya Ryvkin, David Houde, Timothy Hoffman.
      p.   cm. -- (Prentice Hall series on Microsoft technologies)
   Includes index.
   ISBN 0-13-011251-8
   1. TCP/IP (Computer network protocol) 2. Internetworking (Telecommunication) I. Houde, David. II. Hoffman, Timothy. III. Title.
IV. Title: Internetworking with Microsoft TCP/IP. V. Series.
   TK5105.585.R927   1999   99-21038
   004.6'2--dc21   CIP

Editorial/production supervision: *Vincent Janoski*
Acquisitions editor: *Mary Franz*
Marketing manager: *Lisa Konzelmann*
Developmental editor: *Jim Markham*
Technical editor: *Kirky Ringer*
Manufacturing manager: *Alexis R. Heydt*
Editorial assistant: *Noreen Regina*
Cover design director: *Jerry Votta*

© 1999 by Prentice Hall

Published by Prentice-Hall PTR
Prentice-Hall, Inc.
Upper Saddle River, NJ 07458

Prentice Hall books are widely used by corporations and government agencies for training, marketing, and resale.

The publisher offers discounts on this book when ordered in bulk quantities.
For more information, contact: Corporate Sales Department, Phone: 800-382-3419; Fax: 201-236-7141; E-mail:
corpsales@prenhall.com; or write: Prentice Hall PTR, Corp. Sales Dept., One Lake Street, Upper Saddle River, NJ 07458.

Use of the Microsoft Approved Study Guide Logo on this product signifies that it has been
independently reviewed and approved in complying with the following standards:

- acceptable coverage of all content related to Microsoft exam number 70-059, entitled
  Internetworking With Microsoft TCP/IP on Microsoft Windows NT 4
- sufficient performance-based exercises that relate closely to all required content; and
- technically accurate content, based on sampling of text.

All products or services mentioned in this book are the trademarks or service marks of their respective companies or organizations. Screen shots reprinted by permission from Microsoft Corporation.

Printed in the United States of America
10 9 8 7 6 5 4 3 2 1

ISBN: 0-13-011251-8

Prentice-Hall International (UK) Limited, *London*
Prentice-Hall of Australia Pty. Limited, *Sydney*
Prentice-Hall Canada, Inc., *Toronto*
Prentice-Hall Hispanoamericana, S.A., *Mexico*
Prentice-Hall of India Private Limited, *New Delhi*
Prentice-Hall of Japan, Inc., *Tokyo*
Prentice-Hall Singapore Pte. Ltd., *Singapore*
Editora Prentice-Hall do Brasil, Ltda., *Rio de Janeiro*

CONTENTS

v

3

IP Addressing 47

4

Subnetting 77

5

IP Routing   107

6

Dynamic Host Configuration Protocol   137

7

NetBIOS over TCP/IP   171

8

Implementing Windows Internet Name Service   195

9

IP Internetwork Browsing and Domain Functions   221

10

Host Name Resolution   245

11

Domain Name System   259

12

Connectivity in Heterogeneous Environments 315

ABOUT THE AUTHORS

Kostya Ryvkin, MCSE + I, MCT is a consultant, trainer, and network support engineer. He is multi-lingual, and holds a master's degree and has a solid programming background. He has developed applications and utilities in a variety of programming languages. He provides guidance to customers needing help with network installation, sophisticated Web design and messaging system installation, configuration and support. As a Microsoft Certified Trainer, he has taught these and is adept at developing courseware, student and trainer kits, lab manuals, and test questions.

Dave Houde, MCP holds a master's degree and recently retired from the US Air Force, where he was involved in information technology since the early 1970s as a programmer/analyst and operating system/network support engineer. As a programmer, Dave has delivered mainframe and microcomputer software ranging from simple accounting and database programs to complex navigation and modeling applications. In charge of the local area network for one of the schools of the Air University, he was responsible for making it one of the first to have full Internet access. Dave is a network support engineer and trainer at the Alida Connection, where he provides customers with Windows NT and Microsoft BackOffice network installation, configuration, and optimization. He also provides extensive classroom training in Windows NT administration, support, and networking.

Tim Hoffman, MCSE, MCT, PSS holds a master's degree and often provides consulting, training, and engineering support to assist national-level customer project LAN/WAN implementation. He has designed and implemented databases, taught operating systems, Web design, and systems theory. He is skilled at signals processing, off-line cryptography, high-speed cryptographic secure systems, and satellite communications. His professional experience encompasses over 25 years of telecommunications, and includes systems analysis, protocol definition/information transfer (X.25 and TCP/IP), modeling, certification and accreditation of sites, networks, and systems, as well as systems test.

ACKNOWLEDGMENTS

This book was written for the technical student. Several dedicated professionals at Prentice Hall and The Alida Connection reviewed and coordinated the input to create the final product.

Kostya, Dave, and Tim want to acknowledge the guidance, support, and watchful eyes of acquisitions editor Mary Franz, technical reviewer Kirky Ringer, and our task master, development editor Jim Markham.

Together we encourage the student to learn as much as possible about the technology and wish you well with your certification exam.

#	MCSE Requirement for Exam 70-059: Internet-working With Microsoft TCP/IP on Microsoft Windows NT 4.0	Prentice Hall Chapter/ Syllabus No.	Related Question(s)
1.	Planning Given a scenario, identify valid network configurations.	3/ 3.1	1, 2, 3, 5, 12, 13, 14, 15, 16, 17, 18
2.	Installation and Configuration Given a scenario, select the appropriate services to install when using Microsoft TCP/IP on a Microsoft Windows NT Server computer.	6/ 6.1, 6.2 8/ 8.1 11/ 11.1 12/ 12.2, 12.3 13/13.1	Chapter 14: 16, 17, 18, 19, 20, 21, 22, 23
3.	Installation and Configuration On a Windows NT Server computer, configure Microsoft TCP/IP to support multiple network adapters.	3/3.1 5/5.2	Chapter 5: 10, 11, 14, 20
4.	Installation and Configuration Configure scopes by using DHCP Manager.	6/6.1	1, 4, 10
5.	Installation and Configuration Install and configure a WINS server. Import LMHOSTS files to WINS.	8/8.2	8
6.	Installation and Configuration Install and configure a WINS server. Run WINS on a multihomed computer.	8/ 8.1	7, 9
7.	Installation and Configuration Install and configure a WINS server. Configure WINS replication.	8/8.3	2,3

8.	Installation and Configuration Install and configure a WINS server. Configure static mappings in the WINS data- base.	8/8.2	5,7
9.	Installation and Configuration Configure subnet masks.	4/4.1	1, 2, 4, 5, 7, 8, 9
10.	Installation and Configuration Configure a Windows NT Server computer to function as an IP router.	5/5.1, 5.2	4, 7, 8, 10, 11, 12, 16, 17, 18, 19, 20
11.	Installation and Configuration Install and configure the DHCP Relay Agent.	6/6.2	9, 11
12.	Installation and Configuration Install and configure the Microsoft DNS Server service on a Windows NT Server com- puter. Integrate DNS with other name servers.	11/11.2	2, 5, 11
13.	Installation and Configuration Install and configure the Microsoft DNS. Server service on a Windows NT Server com- puter. Connect a DNS server to a DNS root server.	11/11.2	1, 10
14.	Installation and Configuration Install and configure the Microsoft DNS Server service on a Windows NT Server com- puter. Configure DNS server roles.	11/11.1, 11.3	3, 7, 13
15.	Installation and Configuration Configure HOSTS and LMHOSTS files.	10/10.1 (HOSTS) 7/7.1 (LMHOSTS)	Chapter 10: 1, 2, 4, 5, 6 (HOSTS) Chapter 7: 1, 3, 4, 5, 6, 7, 9 (LMHOSTS)

16.	Installation and Configuration Configure a Windows NT Server computer to support TCP/IP printing.	12/12.2	4, 5, 12, 13
17.	Installation and Configuration Configure SNMP.	13/13.1	2, 3, 4, 5, 6
18.	Connectivity Given a scenario, identify which utility to use to connect to a TCP/IP-based UNIX host.	12/12.1	1, 2, 3, 6, 7, 8 9, 10, 11
19.	Connectivity Configure a RAS server and dial-up networking for use on a TCP/IP network.	12/12.3	14, 15
20.	Connectivity Configure and support browsing in a multiple- domain routed network.	9/9.1, 9.2	5, 8, 9, 11, 12, 13, 15
21.	Monitoring and Optimization Given a scenario, identify which tool to use to monitor TCP/IP traffic.	14/14.1	2, 7, 14, 16
22.	Troubleshooting Diagnose and resolve IP addressing problems.	14/14.3	3, 6, 8, 9
23.	Troubleshooting Use Microsoft TCP/IP utilities to diagnose IP configuration problems. Identify which Microsoft TCP/IP utility to use to diagnose IP configuration problems.	14/14.1, 14.2	2, 7, 14
24.	Troubleshooting Diagnose and resolve name resolution problems.	14/14.4	4, 10, 15

This book is designed primarily for network professionals preparing for exam 70–059 Internetworking with Microsoft® TCP/IP on Microsoft® Windows NT® 4.0. Passing this exam earns the student core credit toward the Microsoft Certified Systems Engineer + Internet certification, elective credit toward the Microsoft Certified Systems Engineer certification, and elective credit toward the Microsoft Certified Database Administrator certification.

This book will also benefit any computing professional who manages Windows-based computing environments, particularly in the enterprise. It is designed to be both a training guide and reference resource.

Who This Book Is For

This book is designed to provide concise and comprehensive information for computer professionals who manage computers running under the Microsoft® Windows NT 4.0 and Windows 95/98 operating systems. Readers of this book should have a working knowledge of a Microsoft Windows operating system, such as Windows 95, Windows 98, or Windows NT 4.0.

What You'll Need

Through the use of numerous illustrations and CD-ROM-based training supplements, we have endeavored to make this book as self-contained as possible. Nevertheless, we acknowledge that there is no substitute for hands-on experience. To fully practice all of the concepts explained in this book, you will need at least two Intel 486/33 (or better) computers with as least 16 Mbytes of RAM (32 Mbytes recommended), 450 Mbytes of free hard disk space, two network adapter cards, two mice (or other pointing devices), two VGA monitors, a CD-ROM drive, a 1.44 Mbyte 3.5-inch floppy diskette drive, and a printer. Optional equipment includes a modem or ISDN adapter and a tape drive. Systems should be running Microsoft Windows NT Server 4.0.

Although the above requirements will permit you to *fully* practice *all* concepts, excellent practice may be obtained with a single computer running any 32-bit Windows operating system (Windows 95/98 or Windows NT). Applicable "hands-on" portions of the text provide advice on how to obtain maximum training benefit from lesser equipment configurations.

How This Book Is Organized

This book is divided into 14 chapters, which cover issues such as addressing, routing, name resolution, browsing, planning, installation and configuration, connectivity, testing, and troubleshooting. Each chapter has numbered sections that correspond to specific MCSE exam requirements, and is concluded with a list of related study questions. Most chapters have hands-on, performance-based exercises in the form of Study Break sidebars that permit you to practice what you learned.

Conventions Used in This Book

This book uses different features to help highlight key information.

Chapter Syllabus

The primary focus of this series is to address those topics that are to be tested in each exam. Therefore, each chapter opens with a syllabus that lists the topics to be covered. Each topic directly corresponds to the Level 1 headings in the chapter. So, if there are six Level 1 headings in a chapter, there will be at least six topics listed under the chapter syllabus. If a syllabus topic and Level 1 heading are MCSE-specific, they will be accompanied by an MCSE icon (see the following icon description). However, there may be instances when topics are not exam-specific. In these cases, the chapter syllabus highlights and corresponding Level 1 headings appear without the MCSE icon.

Icons

Icons represent called-out material that is of significance and that you should be alerted to. Icons include:

 This icon is used to identify MCSE-specific chapter syllabus topics and appropriate MCSE sections in each chapter.

 This icon is used to call out information that deserves special attention; information, in other words, that the reader may otherwise highlight.

This icon is used to flag particularly useful information that will save the reader time, highlight a valuable technique, or offer specific advice.

 This icon flags information that may cause unexpected results or serious frustration.

Study Break Sidebars

These sidebars are designed to test your knowledge in a practical manner. The exercises give you the opportunity to perform actual tasks that will undoubtedly be encountered in a working environment, and simulated in the Microsoft exam.

Chapter Review Questions

Each chapter ends with a series of review questions. These questions are designed to simulate a part of an actual exam and to reinforce what you have just learned. The number of questions will vary depending on the length of the subject matter of the individual chapter. All of the questions are taken directly from the material covered in the chapter, and the author's answers can be found in the Appendix.

About the CD/Web Site

This book is accompanied by a CD-ROM that contains valuable self-paced training material, courtesy of CBT Systems. Please follow the installation instructions on the CD-ROM.

This book is also complemented by a companion Web site on which readers can find additional exam preparation aids and updates to the covered material. It is located at www.phptr.com/hoffman.

Introduction to TCP/IP

This chapter looks at the terminology of TCP/IP, its history, and perspectives. We will describe the installation of TCP/IP on a Windows NT 4.0 computer and briefly cover the major TCP/IP utilities used to test the installation. We will also discuss *Microsoft Network Monitor*, which helps you diagnose and troubleshoot many TCP/IP-related problems.

At the end of this chapter, you will be able to:

- Describe TCP/IP.

- Identify major TCP/IP utilities.

- Install TCP/IP on a Microsoft Windows NT 4.0 computer.

- Test a TCP/IP installation.

- Install *Microsoft Network Monitor* and use it for capturing and viewing packets.

TCP/IP Basic Information

TCP/IP stands for *Transmission Control Protocol/Internet Protocol* and it's an industry-standard suite of protocols designed for wide area networks (WANs). Since the Internet is an example of a WAN, we can say that TCP/IP is the protocol suite for the Internet also. The most common mistake is to think that TCP/IP is one protocol or two protocols (TCP and IP). As you will see, the TCP/IP abbreviation implies several protocols. Among them there are some that you might have heard about: Hypertext Transfer Protocol (HTTP), which is used to navigate the World Wide Web; File Transfer Protocol (FTP), which provides reliable file transfer over the Internet; and Simple Mail Transfer Protocol (SMTP), which supports e-mail communications. Some of the protocols that are included in the TCP/IP suite are quite exotic, for example, ICMP, SNMP, and TFTP.

You might start thinking that TCP/IP is a just-released technology. Although many of the ideas associated with TCP/IP are quite new, the technology itself has been with us for a relatively long time.

Table 1.1 presents some of the major milestones in TCP/IP technology.

Standards and How They Appear

As you can see, TCP/IP has a rich history. Today, TCP/IP is often associated with the Internet. Its architecture and design are closely bound with Internet advances and growth. Since, however, there is no organization that owns Internet, you might ask how this whole system is controlled. There are organizations that are responsible for setting up standards and controlling the advance of TCP/IP technologies. Some examples include *The Internet Society* and *The Internet Architecture Board*.

INTERNET SOCIETY

The Internet Society (http://www.isoc.org/) is a professional membership society with more than 100 organizational and 6,000 individual members in over 100 countries. It provides leadership in addressing issues that confront the future of the Internet, and is the organization home for the groups responsible for Internet infrastructure standards.

INTERNET ARCHITECTURE BOARD

The Internet Architecture Board (IAB) is a technical advisory group of the Internet Society. Some issues discussed in recent IAB meetings (those be-

Table 1.1 *TCP/IP History*

Year	Event
1969	The Department of Defense Advanced Research Projects Agency (ARPA) creates an experimental network called ARPANET. This network provides a test-bed for emerging network technologies. ARPANET originally connected four universities and enabled scientists to share information and resources across long distances. ARPANET continued to expand, connecting many more sites throughout the 1970's and 1980's.
1972	The National Center for Supercomputing Applications (NCSA) develops the `telnet` application for remote login, making it easier to connect to a remote computer.
1973	FTP (File Transfer Protocol) is introduced, standardizing the transfer of files between networked computers.
1974	The Transmission Control Protocol (TCP) is specified in detail in RFC 793.
1981	The IP standard is specified and published in RFC 791.
1982	Transmission Control Protocol (TCP) and Internet Protocol (IP) are established as the TCP/IP protocol suite.
1983	The TCP/IP suite of networking protocols, or rules, becomes the only set of protocols used on the ARPANET. This decision sets a standard for other networks, and generates the use of the term "Internet" as the network of networks, which either uses the TCP/IP protocols or is able to interact with TCP/IP networks. To keep military and non-military network sites separate, the ARPANET splits into two networks: ARPANET and MILNET.
1984	Domain Name System (DNS) is elaborated and introduced.
1985–86	The National Science Foundation (NSF) connects the nation's six supercomputing centers together. This network is called the NSFNET, or NSFNET backbone.
1990	The ARPANET is dissolved.
1993	The European Laboratory for Particle Physics in Switzerland (CERN) releases the World Wide Web (WWW), developed by Tim Berners-Lee. The WWW uses Hypertext Transfer Protocol (HTTP) and hypertext links, changing the way information can be organized, presented, and accessed on the Internet.

tween the July and December 1995 Internet Engineering Task Force meetings, inclusive) were:

- The future of Internet addressing.
- Architectural principles of the Internet.
- Management of top-level domains in the Domain Name System.
- International character sets.
- Charging for addresses.

The IAB governs the Internet Engineering Task Force (IETF), Internet Assigned Number Authority (IANA), and the Internet Research Task Force (IRTF).

The IETF is a large, open, international community of network designers, operators, vendors, and researchers concerned with the evolution of

Internet architecture and the smooth operation of the Internet (http://www.ietf.cnri.reston.va.us/).

The IANA is a new not-for-profit organization with an international board of directors to oversee the operations of the necessary central coordinating functions of the Internet. This organization will conduct open processes to continue the critical assignment of unique parameters that allow the Internet to function (http://www.iana.org/).

The IRTF is composed of a number of focused, long-term, and small research groups. These groups work on topics related to Internet protocols, applications, architecture, and technology (http://www.irtf.org/).

REQUESTS FOR COMMENTS

You may wonder how the groups' decisions are documented. Requests for Comments (RFCs) are a series of notes, started in 1969, about the Internet (originally the ARPANET). The notes discuss many aspects of computing and computer communication, focusing on networking protocols, procedures, programs, and concepts, but also including meeting notes, opinions, and sometimes humor. TCP/IP standards are always published as RFCs.

Warning

Although TCP/IP standards are always published as RFCs, not all RFCs specify standards. Some of them have *Limited use* or even *Not recommended* status.

When a document is published, it is assigned an RFC number. The original RFC number is never updated, but when changes are required, a new RFC is issued with a new number. Therefore, when you are looking for information in RFCs, be sure that you have the most recent one. You can find the text of RFCs at www.cis.ohio-state.edu/htbin/rfc. You can also find links to RFC sites as well as a wealth of Internet information at www.internic.net.

Advantages of TCP/IP

As TCP/IP has become the industry standard protocol suite, many software vendors have included TCP/IP support in their products. Let's take a closer look at the Microsoft implementation of TCP/IP. We will make a detailed study of the advantages realized when TCP/IP is used with Windows NT.

Modern networks are large and complex. They are connected with routers and need reliable protocols to communicate. Implementing TCP/IP in a corporate network gives you a standard, routable environment. Since TCP/IP offers robust, scalable architecture, you can easily expand your network. This is why most of today's large networks rely on TCP/IP.

Imagine a large enterprise network with hundreds of computers, many of which work under different operating systems, such as Microsoft Windows NT, UNIX, and Novell NetWare. The typical problem is to connect all these computers so users can seamlessly exchange information. Obviously, this situation requires common protocols as well as connectivity utilities and tools to access and transfer data. Since TCP/IP is supported by all modern operating systems, it has become the logical choice when connecting dissimilar systems. In addition to a common network protocol, however, compatible applications are needed on both ends. Microsoft TCP/IP includes various useful utilities that provide access to foreign hosts for data transfer, monitoring, and remote control; for example: FTP, TRACERT, and Telnet.

Remember, also, that the Internet is based on TCP/IP. Adding TCP/IP to a Windows NT computer will allow it to gain Internet access (assuming, of course, that it has physical connectivity to the Internet).

Finally, Microsoft TCP/IP offers the Windows Sockets Interface, which can be used for developing client/server applications that run on Windows Sockets-compliant stacks from other vendors. By using Sockets, TCP/IP provides a robust, scalable, cross-platform client/server framework.

WHAT ARE "SOCKETS"?

The term "sockets," or Windows Sockets (also known as WINSOCK) may seem a little foreign. Sockets refer to a connection-oriented interprocess communication protocol. Interprocess communication is the way programs communicate with each other. A connection-oriented protocol is distinct from a connectionless protocol because, in connection-oriented communications, the transmitter gets a positive response from the receiver when it sends a communication. (We use a telephone call analogy for a connection-oriented protocol, and a letter analogy for a connectionless one.) In Windows Sockets, each participant in the communication agrees on a logical data location—the "socket"—at each end of the communication channel. Communications are sent to these sockets, which are kept open for the duration of the communication session.

To summarize:

- TCP/IP is an industry-standard suite of networking protocols.
- TCP/IP is a routable transport for Windows NT networks.

- TCP/IP provides the ability to share information with non-Microsoft network TCP/IP-based hosts.
- TCP/IP provides the ability to log on to remote TCP/IP-based hosts from a Windows NT workstation.
- TCP/IP adheres to Internet community standards, providing access to thousands of networks worldwide.

TCP/IP Utilities and Services

We have already seen that the Microsoft implementation of TCP/IP provides a way to access foreign hosts, tune the TCP/IP configuration, and troubleshoot connectivity problems. This is achieved through a number of tools and utilities. Knowing how to use the utilities often helps you to solve network-related problems. To get started, we'll identify the purpose of the most important Microsoft TCP/IP utilities (we will cover them in greater detail later in the book).

Microsoft TCP/IP utilities can be logically divided into several groups based on their purpose: data transfer utilities, remote execution utilities, printing utilities, and diagnostic utilities. The following tables provide an overview of the TCP/IP utilities. In Chapter 12, "Connectivity in Heterogeneous Environments," we'll look more deeply into those associated with communication between dissimilar systems.

DATA TRANSFER UTILITIES

Table 1.2 lists the tools that allow you to transfer data between two computers. The computers can be located anywhere as long as there is a TCP/IP connection between them.

Table 1.2 *TCP/IP Data Transfer Utilities*

Utility	Function
File Transfer Protocol (FTP)	Provides bi-directional file transfers between two TCP/IP hosts. One host is acting as an FTP server, while another is acting as a client.
Trivial File Transfer Protocol (TFTP)	Provides bi-directional file transfers between two TCP/IP hosts, where one is running TFTP server software.
Remote Copy Protocol (RCP)	This connectivity command copies files between a Windows NT computer and a computer running rshd, the remote shell server service or daemon. (A service is called a daemon in UNIX.)

REMOTE EXECUTION UTILITIES

These utilities (listed in Table 1.3) provide the ability to launch applications and processes on remote hosts.

Microsoft Windows NT does not provide server functionality for the UNIX REXEC command. However, the RSHSVC utility included in the Windows NT Server Resource Kit provides TCP/IP Remote Shell service for Windows NT.

PRINTING UTILITIES

TCP/IP printing utilities provide a way to submit, receive, and manage print jobs in a TCP/IP environment (see Table 1.4). TCP/IP printing utilities allow, in particular, Microsoft-based clients to submit print jobs for printers connected to UNIX computers.

DIAGNOSTIC UTILITIES

In addition to the data transfer utilities we've already discussed, Windows NT 4.0 provides tools for diagnosing TCP/IP-related problems. Table 1.5 describes the major diagnostics utilities that are included in the Microsoft TCP/IP implementation.

Table 1.3 *TCP/IP Remote Execution Utilities*

Utility	Function
Telnet	Provides terminal emulation to a TCP/IP host running Telnet server software. When you connect, your computer acts as if your keyboard is attached to the remote computer. This means that you can run programs on a computer on the other side of the world, just as if you were sitting in front of it.
Remote Shell (RSH)	Runs commands on a UNIX host.
Remote Execution (REXEC)	This connectivity command runs commands on remote hosts running the REXEC service. REXEC authenticates the user name on the remote host by using a password, before executing the specified command.

Table 1.4 *TCP/IP Printing Utilities*

Utility	Function
Line Printer Remote (LPR)	LPR lets a client application on one computer send a document to a print spooler service on another computer. The client application is usually named LPR and the service (or daemon) is usually named LPD.
Line Printer Queue (LPQ)	This diagnostic utility is used to obtain the status of a print queue on a host running the LPD server.
Line Printer Daemon (LPD)	A line printer daemon (LPD) service on the print server receives documents from line printer remote (LPR) utilities running on client systems. With LPD installed, a Windows NT server can receive print jobs from UNIX-based computers.

Table 1.5 *TCP/IP Diagnostic Utilities*

Utility	Function
Finger	Retrieves system information from a remote computer that supports the Finger service.
Address Resolution Protocol (ARP)	Displays and modifies the cache of locally resolved IP addresses to Media Access Control (MAC) addresses.
NBTSTAT	Displays protocol statistics and current TCP/IP connections using NetBIOS over TCP/IP. This utility is also used to determine the registered NetBIOS name and to view the local name cache.
Packet InterNet Groper (PING)	Verifies the availability of the remote host by sending the echo request and analyzing replies.
TRACERT	Traces the route for packets from local hosts to the specified remote host.
IPCONFIG	Displays current TCP/IP configuration, including IP address(es) and DNS and WINS addresses.
HOSTNAME	Returns the local computer's host name. You can use it in logon scripts for identification.
NSLOOKUP	Displays information from Domain Name System (DNS) name servers about a particular host or domain. You can also use this utility to check the availability of the domain name.
NETSTAT	Displays protocol statistics and current TCP/IP network connections.
ROUTE	Views and modifies the local routing table.

Installing Microsoft TCP/IP on Windows NT 4.0

Now let's install TCP/IP on your computer. Before proceeding, you need to decide on some parameters. To set up TCP/IP manually, you need to define the items listed in Table 1.6.

Be sure to keep track of assigned parameters if you are setting TCP/IP manually.

IP addresses, subnet masks, and default gateways cannot be assigned arbitrarily. The process of assigning TCP/IP parameters requires planning and the following of certain rules. For now, assume we've already calculated these parameters.

Once you have defined an IP address, subnet mask, and default gateway, you are ready to install TCP/IP.

In most cases, you will install TCP/IP during Windows NT setup (see Figure 1.1).

Manually Configuring TCP/IP

You also have the option of installing TCP/IP after Windows NT is operational. To install *Microsoft TCP/IP* on Windows NT 4.0

Table 1.6 *TCP/IP Parameters*

Parameter	Description
IP Address	An IP address is a logical 32-bit address that is used for the unique identification of a TCP/IP host. For your convenience, the 32-bit value is divided into 4 octets, 8 bits in each, and written in the decimal form. An example of an IP address is 137.200.0.10. Each computer running TCP/IP must have a unique IP address.
Subnet Mask	A subnet mask is used to determine the network ID. When TCP/IP hosts communicate, the subnet mask is used to determine whether the destination host is located on a local or remote network.
Default Gateway	If your network consists of two or more segments connected by routers, the default gateway address must be provided to access the other segment(s). TCP/IP packets, destined for remote networks, are sent to the default gateway if there is no route configured on the local host. Although this parameter is optional, communication may be limited to a local network segment if a default gateway address is omitted.

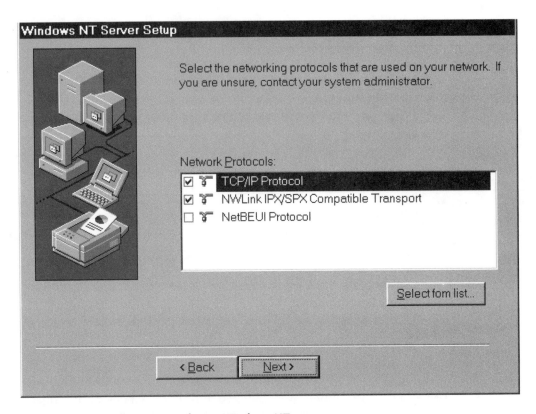

Figure 1.1   *Installing TCP/IP during Windows NT setup.*

1. From the Start menu, point to Settings, and then click Control Panel. When Control Panel appears, double-click the Network icon. The Network dialog box appears. (You can quickly launch the Network dialog box by right-clicking the Network Neighborhood icon on the desktop and choosing Properties.)
2. Click the Protocols tab.
3. Click Add. In the Select Network Protocol dialog box, choose TCP/IP Protocol and then click OK. See Figure 1.2.
4. In the TCP/IP Setup dialog box, choose No to indicate that you do not wish to use DHCP and want to configure TCP/IP parameters manually. See Figure 1.3.
5. In the Windows NT Setup dialog box, provide the full path to the in-stallation files and click Continue. After setup installs required files, click Close.

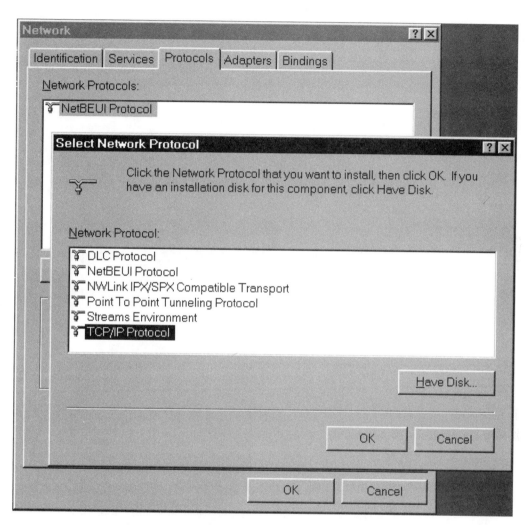

Figure 1.2   *Installing TCP-IP on Windows NT 4.0.*

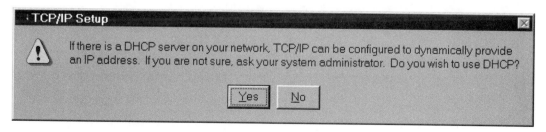

Figure 1.3   *Option to configure TCP/IP to use DHCP.*

6. The Microsoft TCP/IP Properties dialog box appears. See Figure 1.4. Type your IP address, subnet mask, and default gateway address in the corresponding boxes. (At this point, we assume you already have an IP address, subnet mask, and default gateway assigned. You will learn how to calculate them a bit later in the text.)

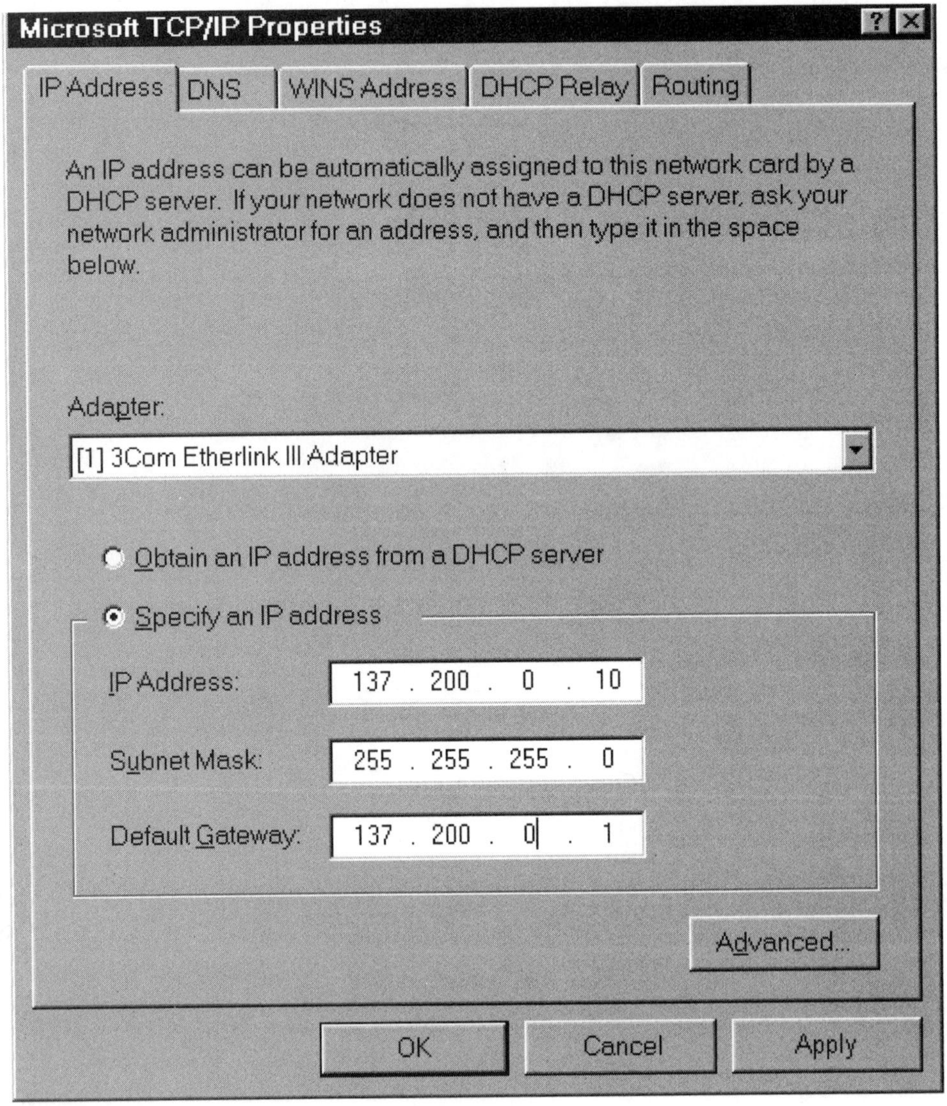

Figure 1.4 *Microsoft TCP/IP properties.*

7. Click OK.
8. After the computer recalculates the network bindings, the Network Settings Change dialog box will appear, prompting you to restart the computer. Click Yes and wait until the computer restarts.

After the computer restarts, it will have your TCP/IP settings.

Changing TCP/IP Parameters

In some cases, you will need to change existing TCP/IP parameters; for example, when you move a computer to another building. To change the TCP/IP parameters for an existing installation, perform the following steps:

1. From the Start menu, point to Settings, and then click Control Panel. Click Network icon. The Network dialog box appears.
2. Click the Protocols tab.
3. Choose the TCP/IP Protocol and click Properties.
4. The TCP/IP Properties dialog box appears
5. Make the appropriate changes to the IP address, Subnet mask, and Default gateway boxes.
6. Click OK.

The computer will configure the TCP/IP bindings and request a reboot.

Testing the TCP/IP Configuration

After you have successfully installed TCP/IP on Windows NT 4.0, it's a good idea to verify that you have set the TCP/IP parameters properly. You can perform the following steps as a basic troubleshooting procedure.

USING THE IPCONFIG UTILITY

To verify the TCP/IP configuration parameters, including the IP address, subnet mask, and default gateway, use the IPCONFIG utility. This utility is provided as a part of the *Microsoft TCP/IP* installation. IPCONFIG is useful in determining whether your parameters have been initialized, and what values these parameters have received.

IPCONFIG is a command line utility, and the simplest way to use it is to type the following at the command prompt:

```
ipconfig
```

If the TCP/IP configuration is initialized, the assigned IP address, subnet mask, and default gateway (if configured) appear. For example:

```
C:\WINNT>ipconfig
Windows NT IP Configuration
Ethernet adapter Elnk31:
        IP Address. . . . . . . . . : 137.200.0.10
        Subnet Mask . . . . . . . . : 255.255.255.0
        Default Gateway . . . . . . : 137.200.0.1
```

USING THE PING UTILITY

While the IPCONFIG utility is used to test the configuration parameters on a local computer, the PING utility will test connectivity with other computers. PING is a diagnostic tool that can report basic TCP/IP problems such as connection failures or router problems. For example, you can use the PING utility to verify that contact can be established between a client and server.

The work of the PING utility is based on the Internet Control Message Protocol (ICMP). PING sends ICMP echo packets to the host and listens for echo reply packets. PING waits up to one second for each packet sent and prints the number of packets transmitted and received. Each packet is validated against a transmitted message.

PING is also a command line utility. Its syntax is:

```
ping IP_address, where IP_address is the IP address of the
destination host
```

A successful PING returns a sequence of replies as follows:

```
C:\WINNT>ping 137.200.0.1
Pinging 137.200.0.1 with 32 bytes of data:
Reply from 137.200.0.1: bytes=32 time<10ms TTL=128
Reply from 137.200.0.1: bytes=32 time<10ms TTL=128
Reply from 137.200.0.1: bytes=32 time<10ms TTL=128
Reply from 137.200.0.1: bytes=32 time<10ms TTL=128
```

If communication problems exist, for example, if the destination node is powered down, PING output may look like this:

```
C:\WINNT>ping 137.200.0.2
Pinging 137.200.0.2 with 32 bytes of data:
Request timed out.
Request timed out.
Request timed out.
Request timed out.
```

This listing indicates that the problem is with a router:

```
C:\WINNT>ping 137.200.3.1

Pinging 137.200.3.1 with 32 bytes of data:

Destination host unreachable.

Destination host unreachable.

Destination host unreachable.

Destination host unreachable.
```

Some specific IP addresses are reserved for special purposes. For example, the IP address 127.0.0.1 is the loopback address. You can use `ping` 127.0.0.1 to check if TCP/IP is loaded correctly on your computer.

As you may have noticed, by default, the PING command sends four 32-byte packets and waits for four replies. The following syntax will cause PING to continuously send packets until interrupted with a `Control-C`:

```
ping -t IP_address
```

Note   You can use an argument of `-?` with both **PING** and **IPCONFIG** for a quick reminder of all applicable options. (e.g., `ping -?` or `ipconfig -?`)

TCP/IP Testing Sequence

Using the PING and IPCONFIG utilities, you can perform basic testing and troubleshooting tasks.

To verify a computer's configuration and check router connections, perform the following steps.

1. Use IPCONFIG to verify the TCP/IP initialization. At the command prompt, type:

   ```
   ipconfig
   ```

2. Ping the loopback address to verify that TCP/IP is installed and bound to the network adapter. (You may remember that the loopback address is simply a TCP/IP address that causes the machine to attempt communication with itself—this will test the network installation up to the point where the packet would actually go across the wire.) Type:

   ```
   ping 127.0.0.1
   ```

3. Ping the IP address of your own host to verify that it was added correctly. Type:

```
ping your_IP_address
```

If the previous steps fail, you most likely have an IP addressing problem.

4. Ping the IP address of your default gateway to ensure that it is operational. Additionally, a successful ping to the default gateway indicates that you can connect to hosts in your local subnet. (Although a successful ping of the default gateway indicates that you can connect to hosts in your local subnet, it does not guarantee you will be able to connect to *all* hosts in the local subnet.) Type:

```
ping default_gateway_IP_address
```

5. Finally, ping the IP address of the remote host to verify that you can connect through a router. Type:

```
ping remote_host_IP_address
```

If this step fails, you may have an incorrect subnet mask or an incorrect default gateway. It can also indicate the failure of a WAN link or a malfunctioning router.

If you go directly to Step 5 and successfully ping the remote host, it guarantees all previous steps would have been successful.

Microsoft Network Monitor

Sometimes network problems become too complex to solve by means of simple diagnostic tools such as IPCONFIG and PING. In this case, *Microsoft Network Monitor,* the tool that is capable of capturing network traffic, may be helpful. *Network Monitor* is able to capture and display frames (also called packets) to detect and troubleshoot problems on local area networks. *Network Monitor* is particularly useful in diagnosing hardware and software problems when two or more computers cannot communicate. If the problem is too complex, you can capture network activity and send the capture file to a technical support group or network analyst for assistance.

Microsoft Network Monitor configures the network card to capture all incoming and outgoing frames. You can define capture filters and capture triggers to capture only specific data. For security reasons, the version of *Microsoft Network Monitor* that is shipped with Windows NT Server 4.0 is limited to capturing only data originating from or destined to the computer running *Network Monitor,* as well as broadcast and multicast messages. The packets to and from other computers are invisible to the standard version of *Microsoft Network Monitor.* Microsoft Systems Management Server (SMS) includes a version of *Network Monitor* that can also capture frames sent to or from any computer on the network, edit and transmit frames on the network, and capture frames remotely. The SMS version achieves this by setting the network adapter card to the so-called promiscuous mode.

 You can use the SMS version of *Network Monitor* to capture frames remotely from network agents installed on Windows NT workstations and Windows 95 computers.

Installing Microsoft Network Monitor

You must be a member of the Administrator's group to install *Microsoft Network Monitor* on Windows NT Server 4.0.

To install *Network Monitor*

1. Log on as Administrator.
2. Launch `Control Panel`. Double-click the `Network` icon and select the `Services` tab.
3. Click `Add`. The `Select Network Services` dialog box appears. See Figure 1.5.
4. Select `Network Monitor Tools` and `Agent` from the `Network Service` list. Click `OK`.
5. You may be asked to provide the path to the Windows NT setup files. Type the full path to the Windows NT distribution point and click `Continue`.
6. Click `Close` to exit the `Network dialog` box.
7. Click `Yes` to restart the computer.

After the computer restarts, you will be able to use *Microsoft Network Monitor.*

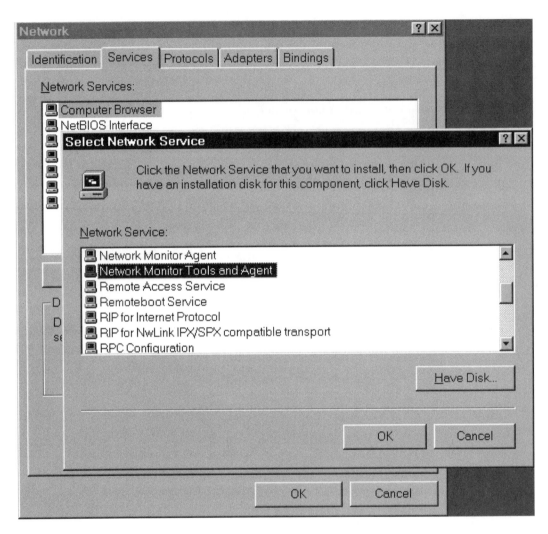

Figure 1.5   *Installing Microsoft Network Monitor on Windows NT Server 4.0.*

Using Microsoft Network Monitor to Capture and View Data

When *Microsoft Network Monitor* is installed, you can access it in the Administrative Tools (Common) folder in the Start menu. Figure 1.6 illustrates the layout of the *Microsoft Network Monitor* window.

The typical procedure for using *Network Monitor* is:

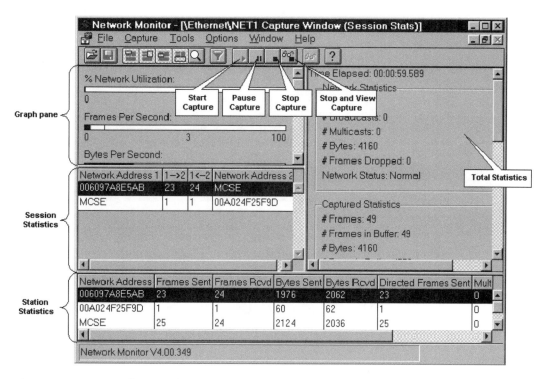

Figure 1.6 *Microsoft Network Monitor window.*

1. Start capturing.
2. Generate network traffic to capture.
3. Stop capturing.
4. View captured data.

STARTING A CAPTURE

To start capturing network traffic, use the Start Capture button on the toolbar (you can also use the Start command from the Capture menu or press F10). Captured frames are stored in the capture buffer. When the buffer overflows, new frames replace the oldest ones. You can control the buffer size with the Buffer Settings option in the Capture menu. When you are capturing, the information panes display capture statistics. The meaning of the panes is described in Table 1.7.

Table 1.7 *Microsoft Network Monitor Panes (Capture View)*

Pane	Displays
Graph	A graphical representation of the activity currently taking place on the network, including network utilization and broadcast level.
Session Statistics	Statistics about individual sessions currently taking place on the network.
Station Statistics	Statistics about the sessions in which the computer running *Network Monitor* is participating. They include bytes and frames sent and received.
Total Statistics	Summary statistics about network activity detected since the capture began.

GENERATING NETWORK TRAFFIC

To generate network traffic to analyze, use any network-based application such as *Microsoft Internet Explorer* or the PING command.

STOPPING AND VIEWING CAPTURED DATA

To stop a capture, use the `Stop Capture` button (see Figure 1.6), the `Stop` command from the `Capture` menu, or press `F11`.

To view captured data, use the `Stop and View` command from the `Capture` menu if you are currently capturing, or the `View` command from the `Capture` menu if the capture has already been stopped.

When opening a capture window, a `Frame Viewer` window appears. See Figure 1.7. The `Frame Viewer` window shows each captured frame. It contains a frame number, the time the frame was received, source and destination addresses, protocols contained in the frame, and other information. To get more detailed information about the particular frame, double-click the frame.

The `Frame Viewer` window includes the panes listed in Table 1.8.

You can save a capture to hard disk for later analysis. To do this, choose `Save As` from the `File` menu.

As we use *Microsoft Network Monitor* in the labs following this chapter, you will become familiar with its more advanced features.

Summary

In this chapter, we discussed the basics of TCP/IP. You learned that TCP/IP is not just one protocol or two protocols, but a set of protocols that have dif-

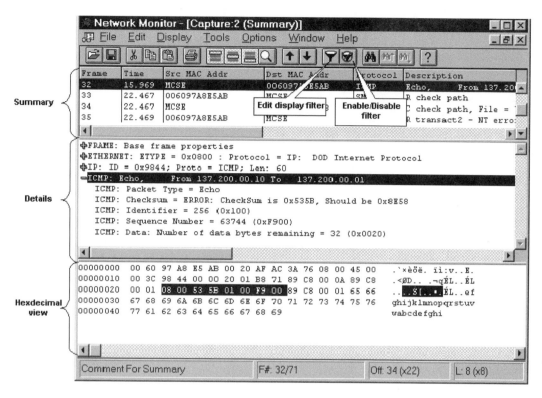

Figure 1.7 *Microsoft Network Monitor's Capture View.*

ferent purposes and properties. We covered the main advantages of using *Microsoft TCP/IP*, such as its industry-standard routable environment, its compatibility with modern operating systems, its connectivity with dissimilar systems, and its ability to provide access to the Internet. You also learned how to install *Microsoft TCP/IP* on Windows NT 4.0. Finally, we looked at a number of network analysis tools and procedures, including IPCONFIG,

Table 1.8 *Microsoft Network Monitor Panes (Frame View)*

Pane	Displays
Detail	The frame's contents, including the protocols used to send it.
Hex	A hexadecimal and ASCII representation of the captured data.
Summary	General information about captured frames in the order in which they were captured.

PING, and *Microsoft Network Monitor,* the tool that can be used to capture network traffic and analyze network-related problems.

▲ REVIEW QUESTIONS

1. *Which of the following utilities is used to capture network traffic for analysis?*
   A. IPCONFIG
   B. PING
   C. *Network Monitor*
   D. *Performance Monitor*
   E. LPD

2. *Which utility (utilities) is (are) NOT used for TCP/IP printing? (Select all that apply.)*
   A. LPR
   B. PING
   C. LPQ
   D. Telnet

3. *Which of the following choices functions as both client and server applications on Windows NT 4.0?*
   A. PING
   B. IPCONFIG
   C. FTP
   D. REXEC

4. *Which of the following is server software?*
   A. LPD
   B. LPR
   C. LPQ
   D. PING

5. *Why is it important to obtain the most recent RFC on a particular topic? (Select all that apply.)*
   A. RFC numbers are not replaced
   B. RFC numbers are reviewed and changed weekly

    C. New RFCs are created with new numbers

    D. RFC numbers correspond to their publishing date

6. *TCP/IP standards are published as* _____

    A. Manuals

    B. Requests For Comment (RFCs)

    C. Whitepapers

    D. Suggestions and rules

7. *TCP/IP is really*

    A. One protocol

    B. Two protocols: TCP and IP

    C. More than two protocols

    D. A set of rules published in RFCs

8. *Which of the following is used to connect to other hosts in TCP/IP networks? (Choose two.)*

    A. IPCONFIG

    B, FTP

    C. PING

    D. Telnet

9. *Microsoft TCP/IP has which of the following advantages?*

    A. Industry-standard routable environment

    B. Technology of connecting dissimilar systems

    C. Access to Internet

    D. All of the above

10. *RSH is used to*

    A. Copy files between computers

    B. Capture network traffic

    C. Run commands on a UNIX host

    D. Print documents on a UNIX host

11. *What parameters are used to configure Microsoft TCP/IP on Windows NT 4.0? (Choose all that apply.)*

    A. IP address

    B. Subnet mask

    C. Internal network number

    D. The maximum speed of the WAN link

12. *You want to change TCP/IP parameters. Where can you do this?*

    A. `Control Panel/Network/Protocols`

    B. `Control Panel/Network/Services`

    C. `Control Panel/Protocols`

    D. WINNT folder on drive C:

TCP/IP Architecture

In this chapter, we will take a look at the TCP/IP protocol stack to help us better understand how TCP/IP functions in the network. We'll look at the Department Of Defense (DoD) protocol layers and the Open Systems Interconnect (OSI) model to help us better understand how protocols and utilities function at various layers. We'll discuss the protocols that comprise the TCP/IP suite of protocols and look at some TCP/IP configuration and troubleshooting information.

At the end of this chapter, you will be able to:

- Discuss the protocols that support the Internet.

- List the layers in the OSI and DoD networking models.

- Describe the TCP/IP suite of protocols.

TCP/IP made early WANS possible. TCP/IP's robust set of protocols provided complete networking support to connect all hosts and sites and rapidly became the standard for such activities. Over time, the TCP/IP suite of protocols and utilities has become much more than just a standard—it has helped us usher in a new era of computing. We can now configure machines around the world and monitor events on distant computers. Although local area networking standards remained in the realm of proprietary vendor standards until the mid 1980's, they have changed so much since then that today there is nearly total interoperability in the TCP/IP world. With TCP/IP, we can connect to the world. Before we do that, however, let's look closer at what the protocol suite is capable of doing.

A strict definition of the parts of the TCP/IP protocol can be found in the Requests for Comments (RFCs) listed in Table 2.1. You may find the RFCs at www.cis.ohio-state.edu/htbin/rfc, or you can look at all the RFC search options by going to www.cis.ohio-state.edu/hypertext/information/rfc.html.

ISO/OSI and DoD Overview

TCP/IP is clearly more than just Transmission Control Protocol over Internet Protocol. When we speak of TCP/IP, we're really talking about several protocols and utilities that work together to permit interoperability of hosts on a network (local, metropolitan, or wide area). These protocols and utilities provide the means by which machines can connect to share information.

Table 2.1 *RFCs that Define TCP/IP*

Protocol/Utility	Applicable RFC
FTP	RFC 959
SMTP	RFC 821 and 822
TELNET	RFC 854
SNMP	RFC 1098, 1157, and 1212
TCP	RFC 793
UDP	RFC 768
RARP	RFC 826
ARP	RFC 903
IP	RFC 791
ICMP	RFC 792
IGMP	RFC1112
TFTP	RFC 1350
Ethernet	RFC 894
Token Ring	RFC 1042
ARCnet	RFC 1051

The Open Systems Interconnect Model

The Open Systems Interconnect (OSI) model was developed by the International Standards Organization (ISO) and helps to identify how the functions of the protocols relate to each other. By showing how the functions relate, we'll define how the parts of the protocol stack connect to permit machines to effectively communicate. As we look at the OSI model, remember it is just a concept—we don't actually see it when two hosts work together. The model, however, *is* the standard and to communicate we must adhere to the standard. If both computers trying to establish communications are configured according to the standard, communications will take place. If they're not, you may end up getting error messages, fail to initialize services, or you may get no communications at all.

The OSI model contains seven layers:

- Application Layer.
- Presentation Layer.
- Session Layer.
- Transport Layer.
- Network Layer.
- Datalink Layer.
- Physical Layer.

Figure 2.1 compares the layers of the ISO OSI model to the layers of the DoD model. These models give us a sense of how communication is expected to take place. Moving from the highest layers down to the wire, we see the application needs to be able to operate without being concerned about identifying all of the lower-level hardware and maintaining drivers for each device.

In the OSI model, the Application, Presentation and Session Layers provide services useful to applications in general. These services are separate from similar but distinct functions that take place at the lower levels. Error detection and correction, for instance, may take place at two different points in the protocol stack.

APPLICATION LAYER

The Application Layer provides support to end-user applications by providing the application programming interfaces (sets of procedure calls) that provide the engines that drive actual user applications. This layer is responsible for working with the originated data stream and communicating with

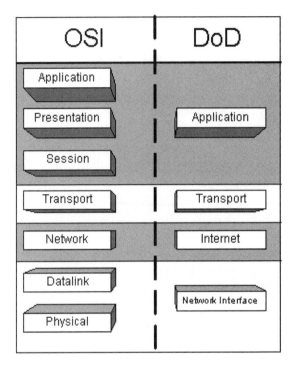

Figure 2.1 *Comparison of OSI and DoD models.*

the lower layers. Some examples of application programming interfaces (APIs) would be: Mail API (MAPI), MS FAX API (FAPI), Telephone API (TAPI), and Internet Server API (ISAPI).

PRESENTATION LAYER

The Presentation Layer provides platform-to-platform translation of syntax for the purpose of data exchange. Modification of data according to a common set of rules is done at this layer. Compression and encryption, for instance, are accomplished here.

SESSION LAYER

The Session Layer provides for the establishment, maintenance, and recovery from failures that occur between applications. When two computers establish a session to share data, control of the flow and direction, and the recovery of missing or corrupt data, are the responsibility of this layer. Depending on the type of application, you might see a simplex, half-duplex, or full-duplex data flow. Simplex is a one-way data flow. Half-duplex is the same as simplex, but implies that there is a duplex channel to permit full-duplex if so configured. Full-duplex provides two-way data flow. By providing appropriate checkpoint methods, the wire between two computers can stay full of data and only the data that does not make it properly to the distant end needs to be retransmitted.

TRANSPORT LAYER

The Transport Layer guarantees that the data is delivered in the right order and in a reliable manner. Here again, we consider error checking and correction as a means to put the information in the right order and to make certain the whole message is received.

NETWORK LAYER

The Network Layer provides routing between internetworks and shields the layers above from the details of the lower layers (the physical topology, for example). It is at this layer that we first find addressing (for example, the IP address).

DATA LINK LAYER

The Data Link Layer provides reliable transfer of data across the physical link. The Data Link Layer functions to provide formatting, error detection, link management, and data flow control. Again we find addressing—this time at the hardware layer (for example, the hardware address of the Network Interface Card).

PHYSICAL LAYER

The Physical Layer accepts data from the Data Link Layer and puts it in the right format for the physical medium. This layer specifies the requirements for the wire such as the voltage levels (electrical properties), connector types (mechanical specifications), and handshake (procedural specifications of how to connect).

DoD Four-Layer Model

More than one theory can be used to identify how the components in the TCP/IP protocol stack connect dissimilar systems. The DoD four-layer model was the original example. Let's take a look at how each Microsoft TCP/IP component or utility fits this model.

The DoD four-layer model contains:

- Network Interface Layer.
- Internet Layer.
- Transport (also known as Host-to-Host or Transmission) Layer.
- Application Layer (known earlier as the Process Layer).

Starting with the place where the signals go (the wire) and working our way up the protocol stack, we find the following layers:

NETWORK INTERFACE LAYER

The lowest layer in the model is responsible for putting frames on the wire and pulling frames off the wire. To get information to the next higher level, which is where the routing and switching take place, there must be information that permits computers to find each other on the subnetwork, or subnet. This is the hardware address of the network card. The Network Interface Card (NIC) contains a hardware address that is mapped to and used by higher-level protocols to pass information up and down the stack and back and forth across the wire.

TCP/IP can be used in a wide variety of LAN, MAN, WAN, and dial-up environments. Supported LAN types include: Ethernet, Token Ring, Fiber Distributed Data Interface (FDDI), and ARCnet. Supported WAN types include: serial lines and packet-switched networks such as X.25, Frame Relay, and ATM. Dial-up is supported by Remote Access Service (RAS) on Windows NT computers, and will be discussed later in this book. Metropolitan Area Network (MAN) types of topologies supported using TCP/IP are the same as the previously mentioned WAN types.

Each of the LAN, MAN, WAN, and dial-up types have different requirements for cables, signaling, data encoding, and so on. The Network Interface Layer specifies the requirements equivalent to the Data Link and Physical Layers of the OSI model as we noted in Figure 2.1.

INTERNET LAYER

The Internet Layer protocols provide three specific services:

- A connectionless delivery service.
- A mechanism to break the data up into individual packets or frames on the transmitting side and to put them back together on the receiving side (fragmentation and reassembly).
- The routing functions necessary to interoperate with other networks.

Five protocols are implemented at this layer:

- The Address Resolution Protocol (ARP), which determines the hardware address of the hosts.
- Reverse Address Resolution Protocol (RARP), which provides reverse address resolution at the receiving host. (Although Microsoft does not implement the RARP protocol, it is found on other vendors' systems, and is mentioned here for completeness.)
- Internet Control Message Protocol (ICMP), which sends error messages to IP when problems crop up.
- Internet Group Management Protocol (IGMP), which informs routers of the availability of members of multicast groups.
- The Internet Protocol (IP), which addresses and routes packets.

These protocols do their job by encapsulating packets into Internet datagrams and running all the necessary routing algorithms (a datagram is a connectionless or one-way communication—it is sent with no confirmation of arrival, much as when you send a letter to someone). The user data originates in one of the higher-level protocols and is passed down to the Internet Layer. The router then examines the IP address of the datagram to determine if the destination is local or remote. If both machines are on the same network (local), the datagram is forwarded directly to the destination host. If the destination host is on a different network (remote), the datagram is forwarded to the default gateway (locally attached gateway, or router) to remote networks.

When a network joins the Internet, the administrator must apply for and receive a valid IP network and host number from the Internet Information Center (InterNIC). The hosts carry out the functions mentioned here through the use of these numbers, which, when combined, are known as an IP address.

The way information is handled under the OSI or DoD models is often referred to as *encapsulation*. Encapsulation is the process of adding a header to the data accepted from a higher-level protocol. When the application *originates* the data or sends a request to `get` data, the data or request moves down through the protocol stack, and at each level, a new header is added. This increases the total size of the information until it reaches the wire. The individual zeroes and ones are sent via the wire to the remote computer, where each of the headers is opened and peeled off, much like peeling the skin and layers off an onion. The header information is stripped off at each layer, and the information is sent upwards to, finally, reach the intended application.

TRANSPORT LAYER

Transport protocols provide communications sessions between connected computers. The desired method of data delivery determines the transport protocol. The two transport protocols provided within TCP/IP are the Transmission Control Protocol (TCP) and the User Datagram Protocol (UDP). TCP provides the virtual circuit service to make end-to-end connection for user applications. Data transfer is made reliable through the use of connections and acknowledgements. UDP provides delivery, but does not use connections or acknowledgements, so it is less reliable but faster.

The terms "Host-To-Host" and "Transmission Layer," are used interchangeably with the term "Transport Layer." The Transport Layer is responsible for error detection and correction in the DoD model, and is analogous to the Transport Layer in the OSI model.

APPLICATION LAYER

Microsoft implements two program interfaces at the Application Layer to allow applications to utilize the services of the TCP/IP protocol stack: Windows Sockets (WINSOCK) and NetBIOS.

The WINSOCK interface provides a standard API under Microsoft Windows to many transport protocols such as IPX and TCP/IP. This open standard library of function calls, data structures, and programming procedures permits Windows applications to take advantage of TCP/IP. This enables Windows NT to exchange data with foreign or non-NetBIOS systems.

NetBIOS provides a standard interface to protocols that support NetBIOS naming and message services such as TCP/IP and NetBEUI. NetBIOS is used in Microsoft products to permit application communication with the lower protocol layers as well. Three TCP ports provide NetBIOS support: port 137 for NetBIOS Name Service, port 138 for Datagram Service, and port 139 for Session Service.

Several standard TCP/IP utilities and services exist at the Application Layer. For example:

- File Transfer Protocol (FTP). Used for transferring large files between remote machines.
- Simple Mail Transfer Protocol (SMTP). Used by mail servers to exchange mail.
- Simple Network Management Protocol (SNMP). Used by network monitoring machines to determine the health and status of the network.
- Telnet. Used by your machine to connect to a remote host and use its services.

The Microsoft TCP/IP Protocol Suite

Now that we've seen the theoretical models that comprise the network standards that define the use of the elements of the TCP/IP protocol suite, let's take a look at the `functionality` of the Microsoft TCP/IP protocol suite.

Address Resolution Protocol

The purpose of Address Resolution Protocol (ARP) is to permit the successful mapping of an IP address to a hardware address. The process starts where one host sends a local broadcast to obtain a hardware address and puts the resulting information into a cache for future reference.

Let's suppose you try to ping a particular IP address. The first action in this procedure is a query to the existing ARP cache. If no match for the IP address is found in the cache, an ARP broadcast is sent. The target machine answers the broadcast with its hardware address and the calling machine stores the information in its cache. Once the calling machine has the target's hardware address, it can use directed communications from that point on. (When we say "directed communications," we're talking about a communication to a particular machine versus a "broadcast" to all machines on the local network.)

RESOLVING A REMOTE IP ADDRESS

If a host tries to resolve a remote host's address to its hardware address, there is a need to traverse a router. IP routers do not permit ARP broadcasts to go from one subnet to another to minimize network and Internet traffic in general. How then does a remote IP address get resolution? This is what happens when Host 1 initiates communication with a computer for which it does not have a hardware address (Host X):

1. Host 1 initiates a command using an IP address for Host X.
2. TCP/IP determines the destination host is on a remote network.
3. Host 1 checks its internal route table for a route to the destination network via an available gateway. (If no entry is found for the remote host network, Host 1 then uses the IP address of its properly configured default gateway.)
4. Host 1 broadcasts an ARP request to resolve the gateway's IP address.
5. The gateway sends an ARP reply to Host 1's request, which updates the ARP cache on both machines.
6. Now that it knows the gateway's hardware address, Host 1 sends a request for the destination host to the gateway.

7. The gateway starts with Step 2 above and the process is repeated until a router on Host X's local network is able to resolve the hardware address.

OVERVIEW OF THE ARP CACHE

The ARP cache on each host consists of static and dynamic entries that map IP addresses to hardware addresses. Each network interface configured for TCP/IP maintains its own ARP cache. The static entries remain in the ARP cache until the computer is restarted, or until they're manually deleted. An entry will be dynamically changed if the host receives an ARP broadcast for an IP address that is already in the cache but with a different hardware address than the existing entry. An address can be added manually to the ARP cache by typing `arp -s IP_address hardware_address` (e.g., `arp -s 172.13.3.1 00-10-4B-86-76-3D`). To delete an entry, type `arp -d IP_address` (e.g., `arp -d 172.13.3.1`). To view the information in the ARP cache, type `arp -a`.

Dynamic entries are added and deleted from the ARP cache based on the exchange of information between local and destination hosts. If a dynamic entry is not used within a two-minute period, it is deleted from the cache. If it is used within two minutes, the Time to Live (TTL) is extended to ten minutes.

THE ARP UTILITY

The ARP utility can be used to display and modify the IP-to-physical address translation tables used by ARP. It uses the following syntax:

```
ARP -a [IP_Addr] [-N NIC_Addr]

ARP -s IP_Addr MAC_Addr [NIC_Addr]

ARP -d IP_Addr [NIC_Addr]
```

where:

IP_Addr	Specifies an Internet address that is or will be mapped to a hardware address in the cache.
MAC_Addr	Specifies a hardware address that is or will be mapped to an Internet address in the cache.
NIC_Addr	Specifies the Internet address of the interface that owns the cache to be viewed or modified. If this entry is not used, the first applicable interface will be used.
-a	Displays current ARP entries by interrogating the current protocol data. If IP_Addr is specified, the IP and

physical addresses for only the specified computer are displayed. If a particular interface is not specified (with the -N argument) and more than one network interface uses ARP, entries for each ARP table are displayed.

-d   Deletes the host specified by IP_Addr.

-s   Adds the host and associates the Internet address, IP_Addr, with the physical address, MAC_Addr. The physical address is given as six hexadecimal bytes separated by hyphens. This creates a static (permanent) entry.

ARP Packet Structure

The ARP packet structure is designed for IP address resolution. This structure can, however, be adapted to other types of address resolution. The actual packet structure is outlined in Table 2.2.

Internet Control Message Protocol

The Internet Control Message Protocol (ICMP) is responsible for handling the errors that occur when data packets are transmitted across a network. PING, as well as other utilities, use ICMP to operate. If a host fails to respond to a ping request, ICMP notifies the originator that the transmission was unsuccessful. ICMP messages are datagrams and are considered to be unreliable.

Table 2.2 *ARP Packet Structure*

Field	Function
Hardware Type	Indicates the type of hardware being used.
Protocol Type	Indicates the protocol that is being used for the resolution. Uses the EtherType value of 0x08-00 for IP.
Hardware Address Length	Length (in bytes) of the hardware address. For Ethernet and Token Ring, it is six bytes.
Protocol Address Length	Number of bytes of the protocol address. For IP, this is four bytes.
Operation (OPCODE) Code	Indicates the operation being performed.
Sender's Hardware Address	Source hardware address (ARP requester).
Sender's Protocol Address	Source protocol address (ARP requester).
Target Hardware Address	Destination hardware address (ARP responder).
Target Protocol Address	Destination protocol address (ARP responder).

Table 2.3 *ICMP Packet Structure*

Field	Function
Type	Uses eight bits to indicate the type of ICMP packet. Types include Echo Request and Echo Reply.
Code	Uses eight bits to indicate one of multiple functions within a specific type. If there is only one function specified, the value is set to 0.
CheckSum	Uses 16 bits to verify the ICMP portion of the packet is not corrupt.
Type-Specific Data	Additional data that can vary depending on the ICMP type.

ICMP PACKET STRUCTURE

While their length may vary, all ICMP packets use the same structure as defined in Table 2.3.

ICMP SOURCE QUENCH MESSAGES

Sometimes, during normal communications, hosts will send information faster than the routers, gateways, and links between them can handle it. Some routers can send an ICMP source quench message to request that a host transmit at a slower rate. A Windows NT TCP/IP host will accept source quench messages and comply by reducing its rate. A Windows NT computer that is being used as a router, however, will drop datagrams that cannot be buffered because it is not able to send source quench messages to the sending host.

Internet Group Management Protocol

The Internet Group Management Protocol (IGMP) is used to inform routers that a host or group of hosts, designated as members of a specific multicast group, is available on a given network. A multicast group is a set of hosts that are identified by a single destination address. Using IGMP, each router that supports multicasting is made aware of which host groups are on which networks. IGMP packets are sent as UDP datagrams, which makes IGMP packets unreliable.

IGMP PACKET STRUCTURE

The IGMP packet structure is defined in Table 2.4.

Table 2.4 *IGMP Packet Structure*

Field	Function
Version	The version of IGMP. This value is fixed at 0x1.
Type	Type of IGMP message. A type of 0x1 is called a Host Membership Query and is used by a multicast router to poll a network for members of a specified multicast group. The type 0x2 is called a Host Membership Report and is used to declare membership in a specific group or to respond to a router's Host Membership Query.
Unused	Field filled with the value of zero by the sender and ignored by the receiver.
CheckSum	Uses 16 bits to verify the IGMP portion of the packet is not corrupt.
Group Address	Used by the hosts in a Host Membership Report to store the IP multicast address. In the Host Membership Query, the group address is set to a value of all zeroes and the hardware multicast address is used to identify the host group.

Internet Protocol

The Internet Protocol (IP) provides several necessary functions such as the addressing and routing of packets to and from destination hosts. If the packets need to be fragmented and reassembled, the IP provides for this.

The IP is considered connectionless, which means that it does not expect or need to be connected to the other side to do its job. There is no session established when IP is used by itself. Because there is no positive response from the target computer when it receives a communication, there is no *guarantee* that the communication will take place, and a "best effort" is used to get information to the other side. Because of this, data can sometimes be lost or received out of sequence, and neither the sending nor receiving host know about it. In this case, acknowledgement for the receipt of packets, and the sequencing of the received packets to place them in the correct order, are the responsibility of higher-layer transport protocols, such as TCP.

IP PACKET STRUCTURE

An IP packet consists of a variable-length header that prefixes the IP data. The information contained in the header is outlined in Table 2.5.

IP ON THE ROUTER

When it traverses a router, the following happens to an IP packet:

Table 2.5 *IP Fields*

Field	Function
Version	Uses four bits to indicate the version of IP. (The current version is IP version 4.)
Header Length	Uses four bits to indicate the number of 32-bit words in the IP header. Minimum header size is 20 bytes; the smallest header length is 0x5. IP options can extend the minimum IP header size by four bytes at a time. If an IP option does not use all four bytes of the *Option* field, remaining bits are completed with zeroes so the IP header is 32 bits (four bytes).
Type of Service	Uses eight bits to indicate the quality of service desired for delivery through routers across the IP network. The eight bits contain specifics like precedence, delay, throughput, and reliability.
Total Length	Uses 16 bits to indicate the total length of the IP datagram.
Identification	Uses 16 bits to identify the specific IP packet. If the IP packet is fragmented, all of the fragments need to have the same original identification scheme so the packets can be reassembled at the destination.
Fragmentation Flags	Only two of the three potential bits for this field are used. One flags whether IP datagrams can be fragmented and the other indicates whether more fragments are to follow.
Fragment Offset	Uses 13 bits as an offset counter to indicate the position of the fragment relative to the IP payload. If no fragmentation is present, the fragment offset will be 0x0.
Time to Live	Uses eight bits to indicate the amount of time or number of hops that an IP packet can travel before being discarded.
Protocol	Uses eight bits to identify the "client" protocol—this is the protocol that provided the payload (data) for this packet and is used to break the packet down to yield the transmitted information.
Header Checksum	Provides error detection on the IP header only.
Source Address	Uses 32 bits to store the IP address of the machine that originated the message.
Destination address	Uses 32 bits to store the IP address of the target computer.
Options and Padding	Stores IP options in multiples of 32 bits. If this information does not use an even multiple of 32, the remaining bits are padded with zero to arrive at a total of 32 bits.

1. The packet's TTL is decremented for each second inside the router (a minimum decrement of one is always required; when TTL reaches zero, the packet is discarded).
2. Packets that are too large to be pushed on to the next network segment (due, for instance, to differing network standards) get broken into

smaller fragments and are numbered. A new header for each new packet, along with a packet flag to indicate its sequence, is created along with a fragment ID and fragment offset.

3. A new CheckSum is calculated and applied.

4. The hardware address of the next router is determined.

5. The packet is forwarded.

Transmission Control Protocol

Transmission Control Protocol (TCP) is *connection-oriented,* meaning the remote computer is expected to be "connected to" the remote host before data exchange takes place. TCP guarantees a more reliable method of delivery of information through the use of sequence numbers, acknowledgements, and a three-way handshake.

TCP uses byte stream communications, which is where data elements are handled as a sequence of bytes without any boundaries. Each segment of data is assigned its own sequence number so the data can be reassembled at the receiving end. To ensure that the data is received as transmitted, the receiving host must send an acknowledgement, or ACK, within a specific period of time. If the ACK is not received, the segment is retransmitted. If a segment is received in a corrupt or unusable condition, the host on the receiving end simply sends it to the bit bucket without sending an ACK. In the absence of an ACK, the sending station knows to resend the information.

TCP functions through numbered ports to provide specific delivery locations. Any port with a number of less than 256 is considered a *commonly used port.* Table 2.6 shows some of TCP's commonly used ports.

THREE-WAY HANDSHAKES

A three-way handshake is simply the way two hosts ensure they've exchanged accurate and complete data. To do so, they must make sure they're properly synchronized to send and receive portions of the data, that they each know how much data the other can receive at one time, and that

Table 2.6 *TCP Ports*

Port	Description
21	FTP
23	Telnet
53	Domain Name Server (DNS)
139	NetBIOS Session Service

they've established a virtual connection. The handshake takes place in the following three steps:

1. The machine that wishes to start the communication sends a data segment with the synchronization (SYN) flag set to *on*.
2. The target machine sends a segment with SYN on, with a sequence number to indicate the starting byte for the next segment (if any) it will send, and an acknowledgment (ACK) that includes the sequence number of the next segment it expects to receive.
3. The first machine returns a segment that contains the acknowledged sequence number and an acknowledgement number.

TCP PACKET STRUCTURE

The TCP packet consists of a TCP header with the TCP data attached. The header consists of the ten fields outlined in Table 2.7.

SLIDING WINDOWS

To ensure the most efficient communications, TCP employs a technique called *sliding windows* to keep data streams full of send and receive data. Each machine involved in data communication maintains two buffers (sliding windows), one for sending data and one for receiving data. Each of these

Table 2.7 *TCP Header Fields*

Field	Function
Source Port	TCP port of the transmitting machine.
Destination Port	TCP port of the target machine—the "delivery address" for the communication.
Sequence Number	Sequence number for the segment—used to reassemble the data and to ensure all bytes have been received.
Acknowledgement Number	The sequence number of the next byte the machine expects to receive.
Data Length	The size of the TCP segment.
Reserved	For future use.
Flags	Indicates type of information in the segment.
Window	Indicates available space in the TCP window.
CheckSum	Verifies the header is not corrupt.
Urgent Pointer	If urgent data is being transmitted, it will be indicated in the *Flags* field. This pointer points to the end of the urgent data in the segment.

windows is sized in relation to the amount of data the computer can buffer. The entire process is relatively simple:

1. When TCP receives outbound data, it places it in its outbound window and (after affixing the appropriate header information) passes it to IP for transmission.
2. The data remains in the outbound window until an acknowledgement (ACK) is received from the destination (if an ACK is not received within a specified amount of time, the data is retransmitted).
3. When the destination computer receives the packets, they are placed in the receive window and are put in the proper sequence. As the packets are properly sequenced, the receiving computer acknowledges their receipt and reports its current window size.
4. When the transmitting computer receives the acknowledgement, its send window slides to data that is waiting to be transmitted and repeats the process.

User Datagram Protocol

The *User Datagram Protocol* (UDP) is a "connectionless" protocol that does not establish a session or provide for guaranteed delivery. By connectionless, we mean that UDP packets are sent out over the network very much like a telegram—the receiving computer does not send an acknowledgement. The message is sent and we must assume it has been received. This is distinct from a telephone call, where we are able to establish two-way communication to ensure the person on the other end of the line has received and understood our message. Much like IP, UDP neither guarantees delivery nor the proper sequencing of delivered packets. If these are important to the application using UDP, the application or a higher-level protocol must supply an additional level of checking. While UDP does utilize a checksum for error checking, this is an optional field and not enforced by the protocol.

UDP is most often used in one-to-many communications of small amounts of data. Later in this book, we'll discuss broadcast "messages," especially in relation to the resolution of NetBIOS names to IP addresses. Normally when we talk of "broadcasts" in the context of TCP/IP, we're referring to UDP traffic.

UDP functions through distinct UDP ports. Although TCP and UDP may use the same port number in some instances, these numbers do not represent the same port. A UDP port is a 16-bit address that exists only to transmit datagram information to the correct location above the Transport Layer of the protocol stack—simply a location for sending messages. UDP

Table 2.8 *UDP Ports*

Port	Keyword	Description
15	NETSTAT	Network Status
53	DOMAIN	Domain Name Server
69	TFTP	Trivial File Transfer Protocol
137	NETBIOS-NS	NetBIOS Name Service
138	NETBIOS-DGM	NetBIOS Datagram Service
161	SNMP	SNMP Network Monitor

ports can receive more than one message at a time and are identified by "well-known" port numbers. Before it can use UDP, an application must supply an IP address and port number for the target of its message. Table 2.8 defines the "well-known" UDP port numbers.

UDP PACKET STRUCTURE

The UDP packet consists of an eight-byte UDP header with the UDP data appended. The header consists of the four fields outlined in Table 2.9.

Ports and Sockets

Our protocol discussion has, thus far, taken us from the wire, through the Network Interface Card, all the way up to the Transport Layer of the DoD model. The only remaining step is to see how the data flows to and from the applications that use and create it. The vehicles that accomplish this last step are *ports and sockets*. Figure 2.2 provides an overall view of where they fit into the data transmission picture.

A port provides a location for sending messages. It functions as a multiplexed message queue, which means that it can receive more than one message at a time. Ports are identified by a numerical value between 0 and 65,536. The port numbers for client-side TCP/IP applications are assigned dynamically by the operating system when a request for service is received. The port numbers for well-known server-side applications are assigned by a group called the Internet Assigned Numbers Authority (IANA) and do not change. These well-known port numbers are documented in RFCs 1060 and 1700. You can find the port numbers in the following ASCII text file:
`\winnt\system32\drivers\etc\services`

A socket is a bi-directional "pipe" for exchanging data between networked computers. The Windows Sockets API is a networking API used by

Table 2.9 *UDP Header Fields*

Field	Function
Source Port	UDP port of machine transmitting the UDP. This is an optional value, which is set to zero if not used.
Destination Port	UDP port of target machine—the "delivery address" for the UDP communication.
Message Length	The size of the UDP message. The minimum size is the header length (eight bytes).
CheckSum	Verifies that header and data are not corrupt—this is an optional field.

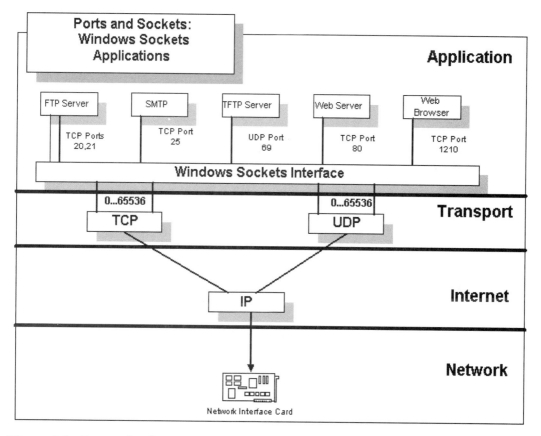

Figure 2.2 *Ports and sockets.*

Windows programmers in building Windows applications that will communicate over a network. The API consists of a set of calls which perform defined functions and pass information back and forth to the lower protocol layers. An application creates a socket when it specifies the IP address of an intended host, the type of service requested (TCP for connection-based requests, UDP for connectionless-based requests), and the port that the particular application will use. Sockets are identified within a host through the use of unique protocol port numbers.

Summary

In completing this chapter, you should have developed a good understanding of the parts and functions of TCP/IP. This will help you better understand the material we will present in subsequent chapters.

To better understand how data flows through the TCP/IP components, we reviewed the seven-layer OSI model and the four-layer DoD model and saw that data moves between layers during its journey from the application to the wire. We learned that, as data moves throughout the layers, header information is added (for transmission) or removed (for reception).

We then took a close look at the basic protocols that make up the TCP/IP suite. We found that ARP finds a computer's hardware address when the IP address is known. We learned that ICMP reports errors in the transmission of network data and that IGMP supports multicasting. The IP was found to be a connectionless protocol that operated at the layers between those concerned with physical transmission and those concerned with transport functions. We saw that IP can pass data to two transport protocols: TCP for connection-oriented communication and UDP for connectionless communication. Finally, we saw that the data handled by TCP or UDP makes its way to and from the application through ports and sockets.

▲ REVIEW QUESTIONS

> *1. What protocol handles the resolution of Media Access Control (MAC) addresses to IP addresses on your network?*
>
>   A. PING
>
>   B. ARP
>
>   C. IP
>
>   D. ICMP

2. *What protocol(s) is/are considered connectionless? (Select all that apply.)*
   A. TCP
   B. UDP
   C. IP
   D. DNS

3. *What protocol is used for NetBIOS name resolution broadcasts?*
   A. ARP
   B. IGMP
   C. TCP
   D. UDP

4. *What protocol reports errors associated with IP traffic?*
   A. IGMP
   B. ICMP
   C. ARP
   D. TCP

5. *What protocol is concerned with multicasts?*
   A. IGMP
   B. ICMP
   C. ARP
   D. TCP

IP Addressing

This chapter gives a broad overview of IP addressing. You will learn the differences between the three main address classes (class A, class B, and class C), as well as the ins and outs of network IDs and host IDs. We will discuss how to plan IP addressing and how to assign IP addresses to computers. You will be able to answer questions like "What devices need IP addresses?" We will also look carefully at subnet masks and their default values for various IP address classes.

Before implementing TCP/IP on your network, you should carefully plan your actions and develop a comprehensive working plan. To enable you to do this, we will devote a great deal of attention to planning. This chapter has many real-world examples that will help you better grasp the IP addressing picture. While you'll find some examples to be extremely easy, others will be real brainteasers.

At the end of this chapter, you will be able to:

- Identify valid and invalid IP addresses.
- Determine what devices need IP addresses.
- Discuss the classes of IP addresses.
- Identify the network ID and host ID for a particular IP address.
- Plan an IP addressing strategy.

What Is an IP Address?

In Chapter 1, "Introduction to TCP/IP," we mentioned that each system attached to an IP-based network must be assigned a unique 32-bit IP address value. As you already know, the administrator assigns the IP address to the computer. IP addresses are neither built into the operating system, nor are they part of the network adapter interface. Configured by the administrator, the IP address provides the logical identification number of a computer connected to an IP-based network.

To gain a basic understanding of what an IP address is, it is convenient to draw an analogy between an IP address and a street address. Just as a street address uniquely identifies a house on a particular street, an IP address points to a computer on a network.

Dotted Decimal Notation

We have already discussed that IP addresses are 32-bit binary numbers, but for your convenience, the 32-bit value is divided into four eight-bit fields,

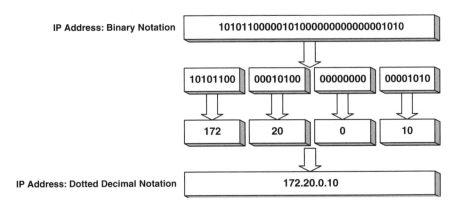

Figure 3.1 *Binary and dotted decimal notation of an IP address.*

called octets (see Figure 3.1). Octets are written in decimal form and separated with periods—this style of writing is called *dotted decimal notation*.

Although you will normally work with IP addresses written in dotted decimal form, you should be able to convert binary form to decimal. This is essential for planning and troubleshooting.

You may already know that in binary notation each bit that is set to 1 has an assigned decimal value. A bit that is set to 0 has a zero value. In an octet, the rightmost bit represents the decimal value of one, the next bit represents two, the next one four, up to the leftmost bit, which represents the decimal value of 128. To get the decimal result, you must sum all the bit values (see Figure 3.2).

Note that each octet represents a decimal number ranging from 0 (00000000 binary) to 255 (11111111 binary). Thus, the IP address 172.315.16.3 is invalid by inspection, because the second octet is greater than 255 (all bits are set to 1).

Table 3.1 illustrates some examples of how the numbers in one octet are converted from binary form into a decimal value.

You can use the Windows NT calculator to convert decimal numbers to binary, and vice versa. To do this, switch the calculator to the scientific view.

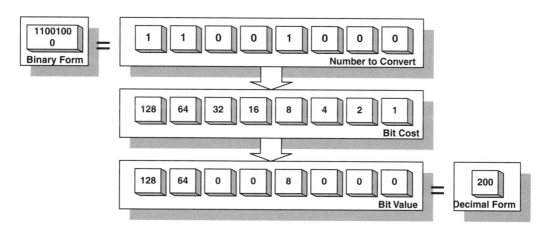

Figure 3.2 *Converting an IP address octet from binary to decimal.*

Table 3.1 *Examples of Converting One Octet from Binary to Decimal*

Binary Code	Bit values	Decimal value
00000000	0	0
00000001	1	1
00000011	2+1	3
00000111	4+2+1	7
00001111	8+4+2+1	15
00011111	16+8+4+2+1	31
00111111	32+16+8+4+2+1	63
01111111	64+32+16+8+4+2+1	127
11111111	128+64+32+16+8+4+2+1	255
11111110	128+64+32+16+8+4+2	254
11111100	128+64+32+16+8+4	252
11111000	128+64+32+16+8	248
11110000	128+64+32+16	240
11100000	128+64+32	224
11000000	128+64	192
10000000	128	128

Study Break:

Converting Binary Numbers and Decimal Values

1. Convert the following binary numbers to decimal format:

   10000001 _____

   11100000 _____

   00011111 _____

   00100000 _____

   10101010 _____

2. Convert the following decimal values to binary format:

   255 _____

   21 _____

   192 _____

   240 _____

   150 _____

Two Parts of an IP Address: Network ID and Host ID

Let's consider another example where IP addressing can be compared to the telephone numbering system. Consider the number (722) 151-1936. In this example, it is obvious that 722 is the area code, 151 the local telephone exchange, and 1936 the telephone number within the particular exchange. Things become less obvious if we omit the parentheses and hyphen and write the same telephone number as 7221511936. Now you have to take some time to distinguish the area code from the exchange and number. The same applies to IP addresses.

Just as a telephone number contains two parts—the area code and the telephone number within the area—the IP address is composed of two parts as well. The parts of an IP address are called the *network ID* and *host ID*. The border between the network ID and host ID lies somewhere in the middle. Note that there is no visual boundary between the network ID and host ID. It's like writing a telephone number with no hyphens and spaces.

> In recent years, the network ID field has often been referred to as the "network prefix".

Let's look at the IP address 172.20.0.10. The network ID and host ID are both there, but not easily distinguishable (see Figure 3.3). In this case, we may assume that the border is between the second and third octet. (Later we will learn how to determine its exact position.) In this example, the network ID is like an area code and the host ID is like a local telephone number.

The network ID identifies the systems that are located on the same physical segment, just as the area code identifies telephone subscribers lo-

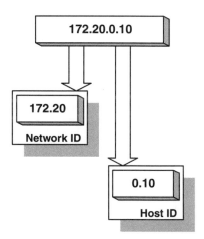

Figure 3.3 *Network ID and host ID.*

cated in a particular area. All systems on the same physical segment must have the same network ID. The host ID identifies a workstation, server, router, or other TCP/IP device within the network segment. The host ID must be unique within the given network ID, just as the local telephone number must be unique within the area code. Figure 3.4 shows three computers with different IP addresses.

Computer 2 and Computer 3 must be located in the same physical network, because the network ID of their IP addresses is the same. On the other hand, it is apparent that Computer 1 and Computer 2 are located in different network segments since their network IDs are different. Although Computer 1 and Computer 2 both have identical host IDs, there are no network problems, because these computers are located in different networks. This latter case is analogous to two people with the same telephone number but in different area codes.

Address Classes

Earlier, we said all TCP/IP hosts within a particular network segment must have the same network ID, but different host IDs. It is reasonable to ask how many host IDs are available within a specific network. To answer this question, we must determine where the border between the network and host portions of the IP address lies. Knowing this, we can determine how many bits are devoted to the network ID and host ID and thus calculate the maximum number of hosts in the network segment.

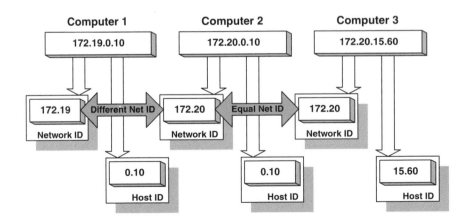

Figure 3.4 *Computers with similar but unique addresses.*

Different networks require different amounts of available host IDs. Large companies need to set up thousands of computers, while smaller companies may require only a few computers on their network segment. To provide the flexibility required to support different sized networks, the designers of the TCP/IP protocol have decided that the IP address space should be divided into several different address classes. The address classes that are available for use are *class A*, *class B*, and *class C* (two additional classes exist and are explained shortly—they are, however, not available for general use). This approach is often referred to as "*classful*" addressing.

Each class fixes the boundary between the network ID and the host ID. In other words, the class of address defines how many bits are devoted to the network ID and how many bits are used for the host ID. This indirectly defines the possible number of networks in the given class and the number of hosts per network.

Class A

Class A addresses are useful for organizations with an extremely large number of hosts. The first octet (first eight bits) is devoted to the network ID. Accordingly, the last three octets (24 bits) are host ID bits (see Figure 3.5).

One of the fundamental features of classful IP addressing is that each address contains a self-encoding key that identifies the dividing point between the network ID and host ID. Let's look at how it works.

The high-order bit of the class A address is set to zero. This serves as the self-encoding key by which class A addresses can be identified from other address classes. The next seven bits in the first octet complete the network ID. If the IP address is written in dotted decimal notation, you can distinguish a class A address by looking at the first octet. If the first octet of the IP address is between 1 (**0**0000001 binary) and 126 (**0**1111110 binary), this is a class A IP address.

Note

You may ask, what happened to 127, since it also has the leading bit set to zero. Remember, all IP addresses beginning with 127 are special case IP addresses. They represent the loopback address and thus cannot be assigned to a real host.

Another example: Your computer has been assigned the IP address 50.6.210.8. What is the network ID, host ID, and how many other computers exist in the same network? We can see that this is a class A IP address, because the first octet is 50 (between 1 and 126). Since it's a class A IP address,

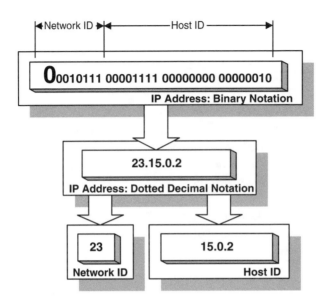

Figure 3.5 *Class A address.*

it has eight bits for the network ID (50) and 24 bits for the host ID (6.210.8). The possible number of hosts in the same network segment is about 2^{24}, or more than 16 million.

Other examples of class A IP addresses would be 30.24.5.0, 15.0.0.1, and 120.6.0.3.

How many class A networks are there? Obviously 126—exactly as many as the first octet variations allow. Each class A IP network allows more than 16 million hosts. That's why small or medium-sized organizations do not require the whole class A network.

All together, class A IP addresses cover 50% of the total IP address space.

Class B

Class B addresses are assigned to medium-sized organizations. The network ID occupies two octets. In this case, the first two bits of the IP address are fixed to be 10 binary. These two bits are the self-encoding key for class B addresses. The remaining 14 bits complete the network ID. The host ID is 16 bits in length. See Figure 3.6.

You can also identify a class B address by the decimal value of the first octet. If the first octet is between 128 (**10**000000 binary) and 191 (**10**111111

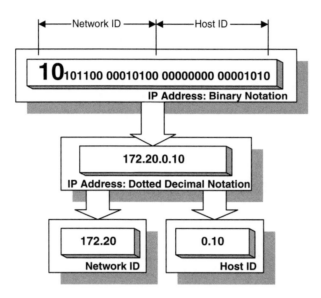

Figure 3.6 *Class B address.*

binary), you have a class B address. The total number of class B networks is 16,384—which is how much the 14 available bits in the network ID allow. The remaining two octets allow approximately 65,000 hosts per network.

For example, if your computer has been assigned an IP address of 172.20.0.10, it's in class B because the first octet of the IP address is 172, which is greater than 128 and less than 191. In this case, the network ID is 172.20 and the host ID is 0.10.

All together, class B IP addresses cover 25% of the total IP address space.

Class C

Class C addresses are used by small organizations. This standard defines three octets for the network ID and one octet for the host ID. The three high-order bits in the class C IP address are set to binary 110. The next 21 bits complete the network ID. This allows 2^{21} class C networks with 254 hosts per network (see Figure 3.7).

Written in dotted decimal notation, the first octet of the class C address ranges from 192 (**11**000000 binary) to 223 (**11**011111 binary). Some examples of class C IP addresses are 207.46.130.139 and 194.226.192.23.

All together, class C networks occupy 12.5% of the total IP address space.

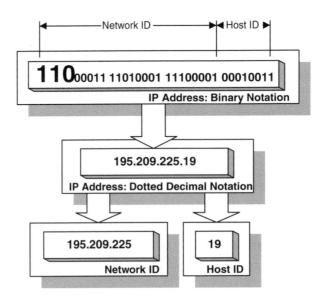

Figure 3.7 *Class C address.*

Class D

Class D is a special class of IP addresses. Class D addresses are used for multicast group usage. The multicast group may contain several hosts. The four high-order bits in class D are set to binary 1110. The remaining bits designate the specific group in which computers participate. No network and host IDs are defined in class D addresses. Class D IP addresses can be recognized by the first octet, which is between 224 (**1110**0000 binary) and 239 (**1110**1111 binary). Class D addresses are used by some applications, such as *Microsoft NetShow*™ and *WINS*.

Class E

The rest of the IP address space is reserved for class E. Class E is used for experimental addresses and it is not available for general use. The four high-order bits in the class E IP address are set to binary 1111. In decimal form, the first octet of the class E IP address is greater that 240 (**1111**0000 binary).

To summarize: IP addressing space has been divided into several address classes. Some of the classes (class A, class B, and class C) are available for assignment, while others (class D and class E) are special addresses that cannot be used to configure a computer. Figure 3.8 displays the address class summary.

Number of Networks	Number of Hosts per Network	First Octet (Binary)	Range of the First Octet (Decimal)	
126	16 777 214	0 * * * * * * *	1 - 126	Class A
16 384	65 534	1 0 * * * * * *	128 - 191	Class B
2 097 152	254	1 1 0 * * * * *	192 - 223	Class C

Figure 3.8 *Classful IP addressing summary.*

Working with Address Classes

1. Write the address class of each IP address:

   10.0.0.1   _____

   9.255.255.0   _____

   200.0.56.1   _____

   192.15.67.3   _____

   127.0.0.1 _____

   191.233.42.3 _____

2. Which of the following IP addresses pairs have the same network ID?

   10.0.0.1 and 10.45.2.6   _____

   192.56.2.6 and 192.56.1.6   _____

   131.107.2.1 and 131.107.3.1   _____

   200.0.0.1 and 200.0.0.254   _____

   191.18.3.9 and 191.18.44.3   _____

3. Your network consists of 5000 computers. Which network classes satisfy your needs?

   _____ and _____

IP-The Next Generation (IPng)

The structure of the IP packet has not been changed since the 1970's. This is, of course, a tribute to its original design. Over the past few years, however, the Internet has experienced an unprecedented growth, heralding the eventual exhaustion of available IP address space. The current version of IP, also known as IP version 4 (IPv4), defines a 32-bit host address which means that there are only 2^{32} (approximately 4 million) addresses available. Remember, not all IP addresses are available for assignment—the finite number of IP addresses will eventually be exhausted and a new version of IP needed. *IPng* is a proposed new Internet Protocol to replace IPv4. The formal name for IPng is *IPv6* (6 being the new version number). IPv6 is defined in RFCs 1883, 1884, 1885, 2147, 2373, and others (you can review these and other RFCs at www.cis.ohio-state.edu/hypertext/information/rfc.html or www.cis.ohio-state.edu/htbin/rfc).

What's new in IPv6? IPng is not just an IPv4 upgrade. You may consider IPv6 a whole new protocol. Its addresses and headers are different. It provides more options and supports auto-configuration. Some of the new features of IPv6 are:

- Extended Address Space. IPv6 addresses are 128 bits long. They can identify individual nodes and sets of nodes. IPng addresses can be unicast (single node), anycast (a group of nodes where the packet is delivered to one of the nodes—typically the nearest one), or multicast (group of nodes where the packet will be delivered to all nodes in the group) addresses. 128 bits can express over 3×10^{38} possible combinations. Unlike IPv4, IPv6 addresses are written in hexadecimal form like:

  `3A3F:BE67:F890:56CD:3412:AE52:9011:FA03`

- Simplified Header. In IPng, the header has been greatly simplified. Many of the current IPv4 fields have been omitted, while many others have been made optional. The cost of processing packets has become as low as possible. In spite of a greatly increased address size, the headers are only twice as big as those in IPv4. Anything that is not included in the IPv6 header can be added through IPv6 extension headers.

- IPng's Automatic Network Configuration. This feature is one of the key changes in IPng. It aims to ease the creation of new networks. This will allow network devices to find and claim their own network address as soon as they are installed on the network.

- Flow Control. To support applications, which require some degree of consistent throughput, delay, and jitter, a new field was added in IPv6.

Although IPv6 will make life in the TCP/IP world much easier, it's time to return to current reality. All the concepts discussed in the rest of the text correspond to IPv4 and should not be directly applied to IPng.

MCSE 3.1   Assigning IP Addresses

Up to this point, we've assumed the IP address was supplied by the administrator or Internet Service Provider. Now we are going to learn how to assign IP addresses ourselves.

Choosing a Network ID

As you remember, the network ID groups the TCP/IP hosts connected to the same network segment. The first and most basic rule of assigning IP addresses to devices is that all hosts located on the same physical network must be assigned the same network ID to communicate with each other.

If you are not connected to the Internet and never plan to be, you can technically take any valid network ID and plan your network with it. It is highly recommended, however, that you use one of the special case network IDs for private networks. The Internet Assigned Numbers Authority (IANA) has reserved three blocks of IP address space for *private networks,* as listed in Table 3.2.

The addresses described in Table 3.2 are only for hosts that do not require access to any other hosts on the Internet, any other network not under their control, or hosts that need access to only a limited set of outside services (e.g., hosts behind firewalls).

If you plan to directly connect to the Internet, you must obtain the network ID portion of the IP address from the InterNIC (http://internic.net). This guarantees the uniqueness of your IP addresses across the Internet. An enterprise that requests IP addresses for its external connectivity will never be assigned addresses from the private blocks defined above.

Table 3.2 *Private Network IP Addresses*

Network Size	From	To	
Small	10.0.0.0	10.255.255.255	1 class A network
Medium	172.16.0.0	172.31.255.255	16 class B network
Large	192.168.0.0	192.168.255.255	256 class C networks

How Many Network IDs Are Needed?

Corporate networks often consist of several network segments connected by routers. Some companies use WAN links to connect branch offices. In this case, the following rule must be applied: *Every physical network segment separated by routers requires a unique network ID.* This also applies to each wide area connection.

> Separate network segments connected by repeaters, bridges, and switches normally do not require a separate network ID. In most cases, you need a separate network ID for each network *broadcast domain.*

Let's consider the following example. The "Horns&Hoofs" corporation has the network illustrated in Figure 3.9.

Network 1 and Network 3 are connected by routers and a WAN link. Obviously Networks 1 and 3 should have dedicated network IDs. In addition, Network 2 requires a separate network ID, so that the interfaces between two routers can be assigned corresponding host IDs.

If Horns&Hoofs decides to add another network segment, but will use a bridge instead of router (see Figure 3.10), it does not require an additional network ID.

In this example, we used arbitrarily chosen network IDs. If Horns&Hoofs plans to connect its networks to the Internet, it must obtain the network ID portion of segments 1 through 3 from the InterNIC to ensure IP address uniqueness.

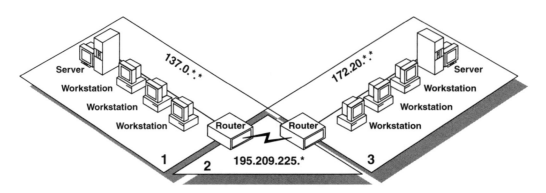

Figure 3.9   *Assigning network IDs.*

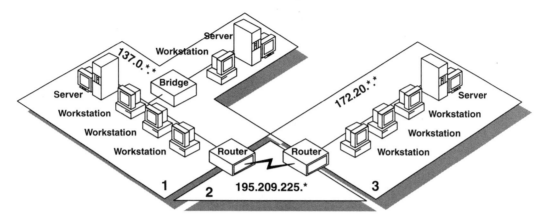

Figure 3.10 *Assigning network IDs to a network with a bridge.*

Choosing the Host ID

Once the network IDs are assigned, you should develop host IDs for your computers. In contrast to network ID assignment, host ID assignment requires no InterNIC registration. You can assign host IDs within your network as you like, but must comply with the following rule: *Within a network, all TCP/IP hosts, including computer network adapter cards and router interfaces, require unique host IDs.*

Generally speaking, the IP address is not the computer's attribute, but it's an attribute of the network adapter card to which TCP/IP is bound. If your computer has two network interfaces, you need two IP addresses, one for each card.

Let's look at how it can be implemented for Horns&Hoofs. See Figure 3.11.

Please note the following:

- Every TCP/IP host has a unique host ID within its network. (Host IDs are marked bold in Figure 3.11.)
- Routers each have two or more IP addresses assigned. Each router interface has the IP address from the corresponding network.

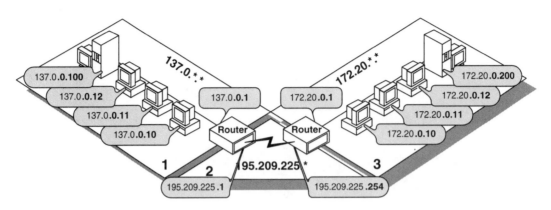

Figure 3.11 *Assigning host IDs.*

Once you have IP addresses assigned to your computers and routers, you are ready to configure the default gateway address. The IP address of the router interface is the default gateway address for every computer within its network. For example, the workstation with IP address 172.20.0.10 has a default gateway IP address of 172.20.0.1.

Valid and Invalid Host IDs and Network IDs

Some network and host IDs are reserved for special use and should not be assigned to real hosts. Follow these guidelines when assigning host and network IDs:

- The network ID cannot be 127. This ID is called the loopback address and is not for general use. For example, the IP address of 127.0.15.32 is invalid for use on the network.

- Neither the network ID nor the host ID may be all zeroes. If all bits in either are set to zero, it is interpreted as "this network only." For example, the IP addresses 0.15.6.8 (network ID is all zeroes), 10.0.0.0 (host ID is all zeroes), and 195.209.225.0 (host ID is all zeroes) are invalid.

- The network ID and host ID cannot be all ones. If all bits within the network ID or host ID are set to 1, the address is interpreted as a broadcast message. For example, the IP addresses 255.255.255.255 (network ID is all ones) 10.255.255.255 (Host ID is all ones), 172.20.255.255 (host ID is all ones), and 195.209.225.255 (host ID is all ones) are invalid.

SUGGESTIONS FOR ASSIGNING HOST IDS

Earlier, we mentioned that there are no rules for assigning valid IP addresses to hosts. You can assign IP addresses to your hosts consecutively, or number hosts by their type. For example, workstations get low host IDs and servers get high host IDs. Numbering hosts this way helps identify your computers. You can also give particular host IDs to routers so that you can easily designate them by IP address.

Configuring Microsoft TCP/IP to Support Multiple Network Adapters

We just mentioned that every TCP/IP-enabled host must have a valid IP address. What if your Windows NT computer has multiple network adapters? How would you configure TCP/IP in this case? When your Windows NT computer has multiple network adapters, you must assign each network adapter an IP address for the network segment to which it is physically attached. (Of course, we assume that network adapters are not on the same physical network segment.)

 Although Windows NT allows you to configure more than one network adapter on the same physical network, this is not a recommended configuration. In this book, we will consider that if a system has multiple network adapters, they are connected to physically different networks.

Consider, for a moment, the case when a Windows NT computer connects two networks with network IDs 137.0 and 172.20. In this situation, you must assign IP addresses to the network adapters as shown in Figure 3.12.

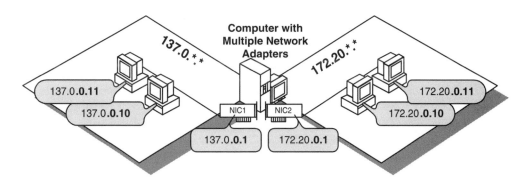

Figure 3.12 *Assigning IP addresses on a computer with multiple network adapters.*

Working with Network Adapters

If you have a computer with multiple network adapters and have access to more than one physical network segment, try the following exercise. If you have only a single network adapter and physical segment, you can still accomplish the optional portion in which you assign multiple IP addresses to the same card.

To configure TCP/IP on a Windows NT computer with multiple network adapters

1. Launch `Network` in the `Control Panel` and choose `TCP/IP Properties`.
2. From the `Adapter` list, choose a network adapter and assign a valid IP address. (See Figure 3.13.)
3. The IP address must have the network ID portion that corresponds to the network segment to which the adapter is attached.
4. Specify a subnet mask and, optionally, a default gateway address.

Perform Steps 2 through 4 for each network adapter on this computer.

You can optionally configure a single network adapter to use multiple IP addresses.

1. Click the `Advanced` button in the `TCP/IP Properties` dialog box.
2. Use the `Add` button to add additional IP addresses to a selected network adapter. (See Figure 3.14.)

This capability is useful for a system that needs to use multiple IP addresses. (A single adapter card with multiple IP addresses from different subnets can act as a router between different subnets on the same wire. While placing multiple subnets on the same physical wire may not have much practical value, it provides good training experience and may be useful when you are forced to subnet to get enough IP addresses for all the machines on a single physical network.)

You may have noticed two additional check boxes on the `Advanced` dialog. Although these aren't strictly within the scope of this course, let's provide a quick overview:

- `Enable PPTP Filtering`. This enables Point-to-Point Tunneling Protocol (PPTP) filtering. The PPTP networking technology supports multiprotocol, virtual private networks (VPNs). Selection of this option effectively disables the network adapter for all other protocols, allowing only PPTP packets.
- `Enable Security`. This sets TCP/IP security, which allows you to control TCP/IP network traffic by specific protocol type and port number. This feature is typically used on Internet servers.

In Chapter 5, "IP Routing Basics," you will see how a Windows NT computer with multiple network adapters can be configured to act as an IP router.

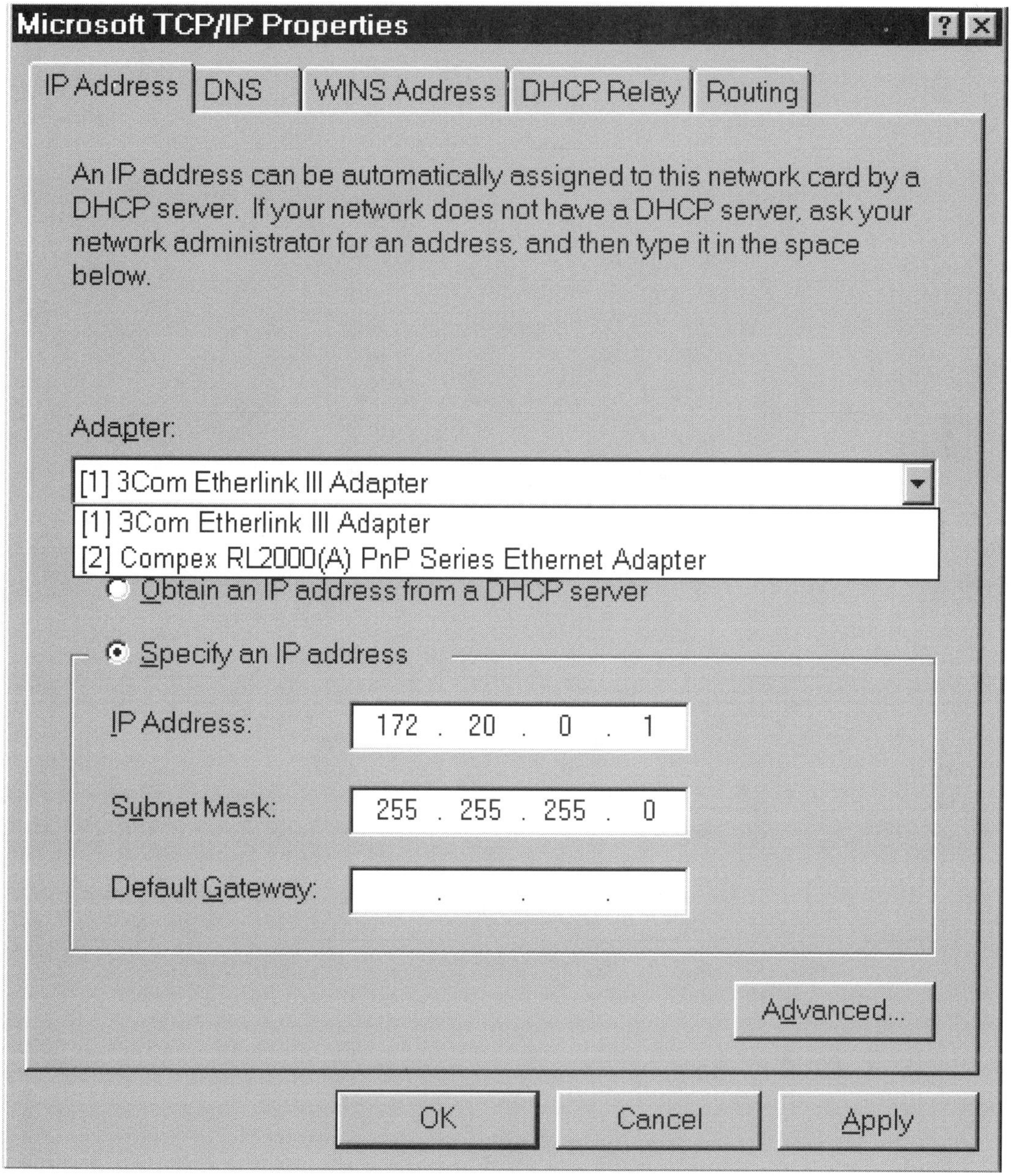

Microsoft TCP/IP Properties   ? X

IP Address | DNS | WINS Address | DHCP Relay | Routing

An IP address can be automatically assigned to this network card by a
DHCP server. If your network does not have a DHCP server, ask your
network administrator for an address, and then type it in the space
below.

Adapter:

[1] 3Com Etherlink III Adapter   ▼

[1] 3Com Etherlink III Adapter
[2] Compex RL2000(A) PnP Series Ethernet Adapter

○ Obtain an IP address from a DHCP server

● Specify an IP address

IP Address: 172 . 20 . 0 . 1

Subnet Mask: 255 . 255 . 255 . 0

Default Gateway: .   .   .

Advanced...

OK   Cancel   Apply

Figure 3.13 *Configuring TCP/IP to support multiple network adapters.*

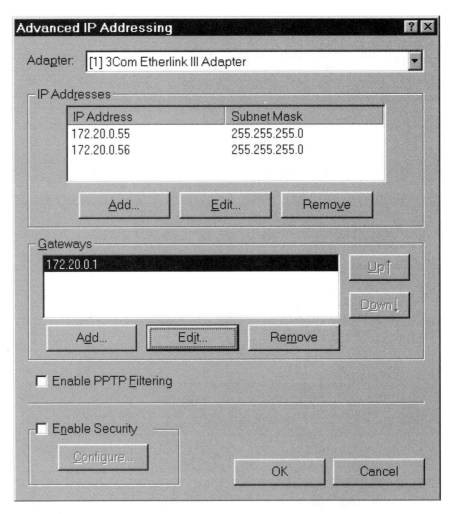

Figure 3.14: *Configuring a network adapter with multiple IP addresses.*

Study Break

Identifying an Invalid IP Address

Which of the following IP addresses are invalid for host assignment? Explain why they are invalid.

172.0.0.1 _____

200.200.200.200 _____

123.350.2.18 _____

195.209.225.255 _____

172.18.2.255   _____

255.255.255.255   _____

127.12.3.4   _____

190.56.3.0   _____

Subnet Masks

We already know how to determine the network ID and host ID with the help of the IP address class. Based on this information, we can ascertain whether two computers are located in the same or different network segments. When you set TCP/IP on your computer, however, you have no ability to explicitly specify the IP address class. Instead of the IP address class, you specify the *subnet mask*.

The subnet mask is also a 32-bit value but, unlike the IP address, the subnet mask doesn't identify any host in the network. It is used for blocking out a portion of the IP address to distinguish the network ID from the host ID. See Figure 3.15. In other words, the subnet mask specifies where the border between network ID and host ID lies.

The basic subnet mask is generated in the following way: Bits that correspond to the network ID in the IP address are set to 1 in the subnet mask, and all others are set to zero. Figure 3.16 shows how the subnet mask is applied to the network ID and host ID. Like IP addresses, subnet masks are often written in dotted decimal notation.

In this chapter, we discuss subnet masking using only 255 and 0. In the next chapter, we'll talk about subnet masks using different numbers.

Figure 3.15 *Subnet mask.*

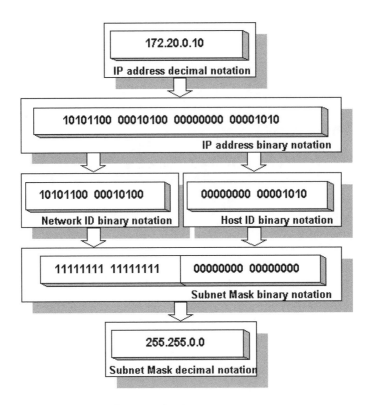

Figure 3.16 *Subnet mask.*

When you configure TCP/IP on your computer, you must specify the subnet mask, even if you have a single-segment network. The subnet mask can be either a default subnet mask, when your network is not divided into subnets, or a custom subnet mask, when your network is subnetted.

Default Subnet Masks

If you have assigned your network a network ID, and your network is not divided into segments by routers, you can use the default subnet mask. The default subnet mask depends on the address class, because different address classes have different numbers of bits dedicated for network and host IDs. Figure 3.17 shows the default subnet masks for class A, class B, and class C subnets.

Using the Subnet Mask

When a computer sends a packet to another computer, it determines if the destination host is located in the same or a remote network. If the destination computer is in the same network, a broadcast Address Resolution Pro-

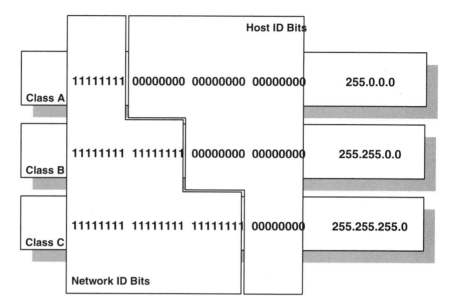

Figure 3.17 *Default subnet masks.*

tocol (ARP) request is sent to obtain the hardware (MAC) address. If the destination computer is located on a remote network, a broadcast ARP request will not work, because broadcast messages will not pass through the router to the remote network. When the destination host is not on the local network, the packet is sent to the IP address of the router, and the router takes care of delivery.

The subnet mask is used to determine whether the destination computer is local (in the same network segment) or remote (in another network segment). When TCP/IP is initialized, the computer ANDs its IP address with the configured subnet mask. Table 3.3 shows the rules of the AND operation.

ANDing extracts the network ID from the local computer IP address. See Figure 3.18.

Before the packet is sent, the IP address of the destination computer is ANDed with the same subnet mask and compared to the network ID ex-

Table 3.3 *AND Operation*

Operation	Result
1 AND 1	1
1 AND 0	0
0 AND 1	0
0 AND 0	0

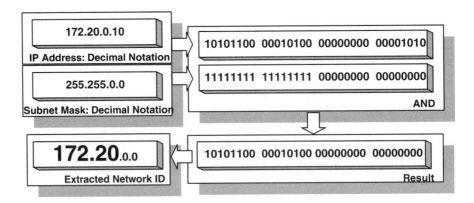

Figure 3.18. *Using the subnet mask to extract the network ID.*

tracted earlier. If both results match, the destination computer has the same network ID and thus is located in the same network segment.

Let's look at the example in Figure 3.19. Workstation 1 is configured with the IP address, subnet mask, and default gateway shown. When Workstation 1 initializes, it ANDs its IP address (137.0.0.10) with its subnet mask (255.255.0.0). The result (137.0.0.0) is the network ID of Workstation 1. When Workstation 1 sends a packet to Server 1, Workstation 1 ANDs the IP address of Server 1 (137.0.0.100) with its subnet mask (255.255.0.0). The result is 137.0.0.0. Then, Workstation 1 compares this result with its network ID and since they are the same, Workstation 1 knows that the destination host is located in the same network segment. In this case, Workstation 1 broadcasts the ARP request then sends the packet directly to Server 1.

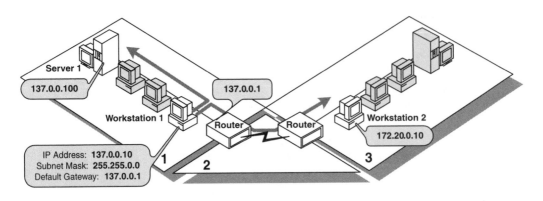

Figure 3.19. *Determining the destination of a packet.*

If Workstation 1 sends a packet to Workstation 2, the same set of actions is performed. The IP address of Workstation 2 (172.20.0.10) is ANDed with the subnet mask of Workstation 1 (255.255.0.0). The result is 172.20.0.0. This is not equal to the network ID (137.0.0.0) of Workstation 1. Because of this, Workstation 1 knows that Workstation 2 is located on a remote subnet and thus sends the packet to its default gateway (137.0.0.1). The packet reaches the router interface (137.0.0.1) and delivery of the packet becomes the responsibility of the router.

Study Break

Identifying a Default Subnet Mask

What is the default subnet mask for each of the following IP addresses?

131.107.3.4 _____

200.20.20.1 _____

191.56.2.9 _____

192.7.34.6 _____

10.6.0.0 _____

Summary

In this chapter, we looked at IP addressing. You learned what an IP address is and how to convert it from binary to dotted decimal notation. We discussed the two parts of the IP address: network ID and host ID, and saw how to define these parts depending on the IP address class. We covered three main IP address classes. We saw that class A, B, and C were available for Internet use and discovered that when moving from class A to class C we go from a few networks with many hosts each to many networks with few hosts each. We also studied how to assign network IDs depending on how many separate segments your network has. We examined a complex routed environment and considered the guidelines for assigning host IDs. Finally, we took a look at the subnet mask and how the computer uses it.

▲ REVIEW QUESTIONS

1. *What is the class of address 194.226.192.52?*

   A. Class A

   B. Class B

    C. Class C

    D. Class D

    E. Class E

2. *How many bits does the IP address occupy?*

    A. 8 bits

    B. 16 bits

    C. 32 bits

    D. 64 bits

3. *What class of network has 254 hosts per network?*

    A. Class A

    B. Class B

    C. Class C

    D. None of the above

4. *In a class C network, what octet(s) hold(s) the network ID?*

    A. First octet

    B. Third octet

    C. First three octets

    D. Last three octets

    E. Last octet

5. *Which of the following are invalid network IDs?*

    A. All 0's

    B. 127

    C. All 1's

    D. 100

    E. 195

6. *What class network is 10.0.0.0?*

    A. A

    B. Class B

    C. Class C

    D. Class D

7. *What address class is reserved for experimental use?*

    A. Class C

    B. Class D

    C. Class E

    D. None of the above

8. *How do you represent decimal 224 in binary?*

    A. 11000000

    B. 11100000

    C. 11110000

    D. 11111000

9. *How do you represent binary 01111111 in decimal?*

    A. 192

    B. 191

    C. 200

    D. 127

    E. 255

10. *What is the network ID for 200.0.0.1?*

    A. 200

    B. 200.0

    C. 200.0.0

    D. 200.0.0.1

11. *What is the host ID for 10.0.0.1?*

    A. 10.0.0.1

    B. 0.0.1

    C. 0.1

    D. 1

12. *What are the three leading bits for a class C IP address?*

    A. 110

    B. 100

    C. 001

      D. 111

      E. 010

13. *You are setting up TCP/IP on a computer in a small company. Can you assign this computer the IP address of 127.56.10.45?*

      A. Yes

      B. No, because this is a special-purpose IP address

      C. No, because the network ID is all one's

      D. No, because this is a class A IP address and is suitable for large enterprises only

14. *What is the default subnet mask for a class B network?*

      A. 255.0.0.0

      B. 255.255.0.0

      C. 0.0.255.255

      C. 0.0.0.255

      D. 255.255.255.0

15. *You set up two computers in the same network segment using the default subnet mask for the address class. You assign Computer 1 the IP address of 194.226.192.51. You assign Computer 2 the IP address 194.226.15.51. Can these two computers communicate?*

      A. Yes

      B. No, because Computer 1 and Computer 2 have the same network ID and canNOT be located in the same network segment

      C. No, because Computer 1 and Computer 2 have different network IDs and canNOT be located in the same network segment

      D. No, because Computer 1 and Computer 2 have the same host ID

16. *You are the administrator of the IT department with 200 personal computers and you plan to deploy TCP/IP. The department network consists of three segments connected with bridges. No Internet connection is planned. How many network IDs do you need?*

      A.   1

      B.   3

      C.   200

      D.   None

17. *Computer 1 has the IP address 172.20.0.10. Computer 2 has the IP address 172.20.1.11. Assume default subnetting for the address class. What statement(s) about these computers is (are) true?*

    A. Computer 1 and Computer 2 have the same network ID

    B. Computer 1 and Computer 2 have different network IDs

    C. Computer 1 and Computer 2 should be located in the same network segment

    D. Computer 1 and Computer 2 should NOT be located in the same network segment

18. *You are the administrator of a small company. The company has the network illustrated in Figure 3.20.*

19. *How many different network IDs should you allocate for this network?*

    A. 1

    B. 2

    C. 3

    D. 4

    E. 5

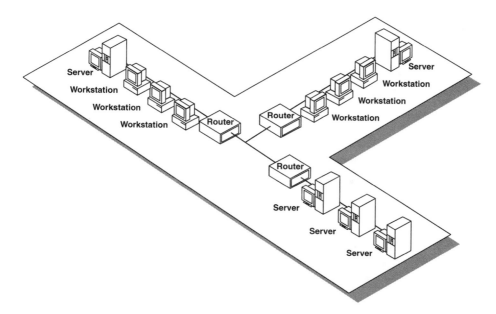

Figure 3.20 *Network example.*

Subnetting

This chapter explains fundamental subnetting concepts and procedures. After reading this chapter, you will be able to determine when subnetting is necessary and what is required to implement it. We will discuss how and when to use a default subnet mask and when to define a custom subnet mask. You will learn how to estimate the possible number of subnets and the number of hosts per subnet. At the end of this chapter, we will review a real-world example of subnetting.

At the end of this chapter, you will be able to:

- Identify whether or not a particular network needs subnetting.

- Calculate custom subnet masks.

- Designate subnets using custom subnet masks.

- Evaluate the possible number of hosts in a subnet.

- Define subnetting and supernetting schemes based on a given scenario.

77

MCSE 4.1   Discovering Subnets

Today, most modern networks consist of several network segments. In many cases, companies segment their networks to improve performance and maintainability, or to enhance network capabilities. There are several reasons why an organization might want to use more than one segment of cable. Some of them are:

- Different technologies (for example, Ethernet and FDDI) can be mixed in a consolidated network. This is not uncommon in a research environment where different topologies and network types are often combined.
- Limitations of current technologies, such as maximum segment length or maximum number of hosts per network, can be overcome.
- Smaller network segments are easier to support and troubleshoot.
- Sometimes the company's territory is split into two or more locations too far apart to connect using a particular LAN technology. In this case, high-speed point-to-point links between subnets can solve the problem.
- Redirecting traffic and localizing broadcasts within one physical network segment reduces network congestion.

Splitting networks into multiple segments has certain drawbacks when an administrator uses only methods discussed in the previous chapter. Let's look at the following example. The Horns&Hoofs Corporation network is split into three segments with routers. The company plans to connect to the Internet. (See Figure 4.1.)

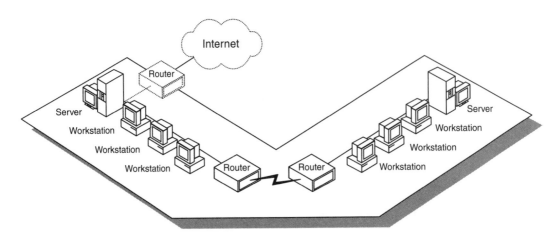

Figure 4.1   *Connecting a segmented network to the Internet.*

Earlier we said that each physical network segment must have a unique ID to communicate with other segments and the Internet. The question is, how many network IDs has Horns&Hoofs obtained from the InterNIC? With what we've learned so far, we would say the minimum number of network IDs is three (not counting the link to the Internet itself). Since each segment contains only a few computers, a class C network is clearly in order (remember, a single class C network provides 254 valid IP addresses, a class B network – 65534 IP addresses, and a class A network—more than 16 million IP addresses)—using a class A or B network would result in a considerable number of wasted host addresses. (See Figure 4.2.) Even using three class C networks, however, will consume 3×256 addresses from the global IP addressing space—far too extravagant for less than a dozen computers. If every company with a few computers in a subnet requests several class C networks, it will rapidly lead to the exhaustion of the Internet's IP address space. Someday, Horns&Hoofs may require another network segment. If the company needs to use another complete class C network for just a few computers, the local administrator will need to obtain an additional network number (ID) from the InterNIC before the new network can be installed.

The address shortage problem is aggravated by the fact that portions of the IP address space have not been efficiently allocated. The problem is not that network administrators request more IP addresses than they need, but that the traditional model of classful addressing doesn't allow the address space to be used to its maximum potential.

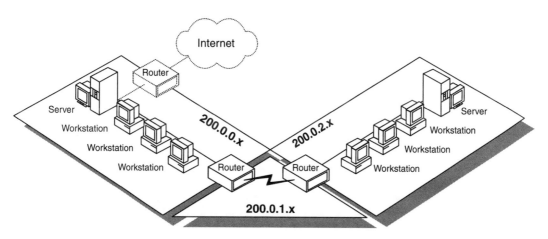

Figure 4.2 *An example of inefficient allocation of IP address space.*

Adding another level of hierarchy to the IP addressing structure will help to solve this problem. In the classful model, we have a two-level hierarchy: network ID and host ID. Using *subnetting,* we can add a third level to the hierarchy. Let's look how it works.

Typically, an organization acquires only one network ID from the InterNIC, regardless of the number of separate physical network segments the organization will use. Since each segment should have a unique ID, a unique *subnet ID* is created for each of the segments by partitioning the bits in the host ID into two parts. See Figure 4.3. One part is used to identify the segment as a unique sub-network within the company's network, and the other part is used to identify hosts.

The network ID, together with the subnet ID, is often referred to as the *extended network prefix.*

Note that it is the responsibility of the local administrator to plan and implement subnetting based on the needs of the company. Neither InterNIC nor Internet Service Providers will do this for you.

Subnetting provides the following benefits:

- The administrator has the flexibility to deploy additional subnets without obtaining additional network IDs from the InterNIC.

- Changes within the corporate network do not affect Internet routing tables because all the subnets appear to the Internet as a united network.

- The Internet IP address space can be more economically employed.

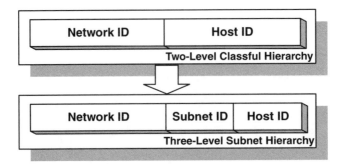

Figure 4.3 *Subnetting brings a third level to the hierarchy.*

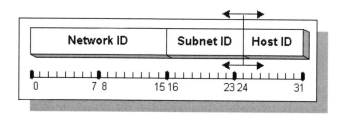

Figure 4.4 *Defining the border between the subnet ID and host ID.*

Planning Considerations

When you implement subnetting, the basic task is to define the border between the subnet ID and host ID. In other words, you need to identify how many bits are devoted to the subnet ID and how many to the host ID. (See Figure 4.4.) These values correspond to the number of segments your network has and the number of hosts per segment.

As the figure illustrates, the more bits used for the subnet ID, the more subnets are available, but fewer hosts are available per subnet. If you reserve more bits than needed for the subnet ID, it will permit you to easily add more network segments, but will limit the growth of each individual segment. On the other hand, using fewer bits than needed allows for increasing the number of hosts per subnet, but limits the number of available subnets. Figure 4.5 shows some possible divisions of a class A network.

The more subnets you have, the fewer hosts per subnet are allowed.

You can visualize the border between the subnet ID and host ID as a sliding bar. The main goal of subnet planning is to fix the bar's position to create the appropriate number of hosts and subnets.

Study Break

Subnet Brainteasers

>   1. Suppose you have a class C network 195.209.225.0. You decide to subnet it so that the length of the subnet ID is four bits. What is the length of the host ID in this case?

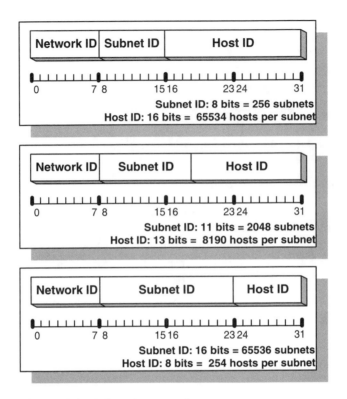

Figure 4.5 *Subnetting examples.*

2. Using the above division, you want to implement 10 hosts in each subnet. Is that possible?
3. What is the maximum number of hosts per subnet in this example?

MCSE 4.2   Subnet Design Considerations

The deployment of a TCP/IP network requires careful thought on the part of the network administrator. Before you implement subnetting, you need to determine the current needs of your organization as well as plan for future requirements. There are several key questions that must be answered:

- How many physical network segments are there in your network? (Only segments connected with routers are counted. Do not count network segments that are connected with bridges or repeaters.)

- How many subnets (network segments) will your company need in the future?

- How many hosts are there in the company's largest subnet?
- How many hosts will there be in the company's largest subnet in the future?

When determining the required number of hosts in each physical network segment, keep in mind that all computers, router interfaces, and other TCP/IP devices should be counted.

You should always estimate future network growth. After deployment, it is very time-consuming to rebuild the network when it fails to satisfy future needs. Based on the answers to the above questions, you should draft a subnetting plan that includes the following:

- Number of bits that should be allocated for the subnet ID to satisfy your needs.
- One custom subnet mask for all the physical segments in your network.
- Numerical descriptions for each network segment (subnet ID).
- A range of hosts for each network segment.

You may want to make sure that the company's address allocation provides enough bits to deploy the required number of subnets and hosts per subnet. For instance, a single class C network (256 IP addresses) does not provide the ability to deploy 16 subnets with 64 hosts in each. If a company's current network class does not permit you to fulfill your plan, you may want to acquire additional network IDs from the Inter-NIC.

Custom Subnet Mask: Changing the Default

Subnet masks were discussed in Chapter 3, "IP Addressing." As you remember, a subnet mask is essential for a host to distinguish local computers (located in the same network segment) from remote ones (located in different network segments). When we segment our network with routers, we must recalculate the default subnet mask and define a *custom subnet mask*. You may ask, why should we define a custom subnet mask? Why won't the old subnet mask work? Figure 4.6 answers this question. When the network is

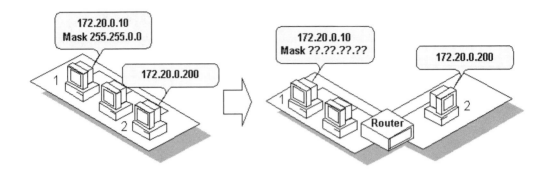

Figure 4.6 *Segmenting your network requires that you change the subnet mask.*

not subnetted, Computer 1 uses the default subnet mask to determine that Computer 2 is local. When we install a router and place Computer 2 on another network segment, we need to recalculate the old subnet mask. (Remember, in recalculating the subnet mask, we redefine what bits represent the host ID and what bits represent the subnet ID. This, in effect, defines the new subnets that contain Computer 1 and Computer 2.)

If we don't change the mask, Computer 1 will not notice the change and will still try to communicate with Computer 2 directly—the connection will be unsuccessful.

Now that we've answered the question why do we need a custom subnet mask, the next logical question is how do we calculate it?

CALCULATING THE NUMBER OF BITS FOR THE SUBNET ID

First, you must decide how many bits to allocate to the subnet ID to provide the required number of subnets. In other words, you must count the number of bits required to represent the number of network segments you need. For example, if your company needs 10 subnets, 3 bits for each subnet ID are not enough, since this provides only $2^3 = 8$ different subnet numbers. You will need to allocate 4 bits for the subnet ID. This provides $2^4 = 16$ different subnet numbers, which satisfies the company's current needs and allows some room for future growth.

One method to determine the required number of bits for the subnet ID is the following. You should convert the number of physical segments in your network to binary format and count the number of bits required to represent this number. For example, if you need six subnets, six is represented as 110 in binary format. So, you need to devote three bits for the subnet ID to deploy six subnets.

Table 4.1 *Determining the Number of Bits Required for Subnetting*

Number of Bits for the Subnet ID	Maximum Number of Subnets
1	2
2	4
3	8
4	16
5	32
6	64
7	128
8	256
9	512
10	1024
11	2048
12	4096

When the number of required subnets gets larger, Table 4.1 may be helpful.

For example, if your company needs 70 subnets, you will need to allocate a minimum of seven bits for the subnet ID, since six bits do not provide enough subnets.

CALCULATING THE SUBNET MASK

Once you've determined the number of bits for the subnet ID, you are ready to calculate the custom subnet mask. As you already know, the bits that correspond to the network ID (and now the subnet ID also) should be set to 1. The bits that match the host ID should be set to 0.

Let's look at how a class A network can be subnetted into 512 segments. According to Table 4.1, to provide 512 separate network segments, nine bits must be taken from the host ID portion. (See Figure 4.7.)

Next, you mask the network and subnet portions with ones and convert the result into dotted decimal notation. The result is your custom subnet mask. (See Figure 4.8.)

When we look at the subnet mask "255.255.128.0" we can determine that the border between the extended network prefix (network ID plus subnet ID) and the host ID lies exactly between the 16th and the 17th bits.

Since the network address can only be subnetted along binary boundaries, subnets must be created in blocks of powers of two. Thus, it is impossible to define an IP address block that contains exactly five subnets.

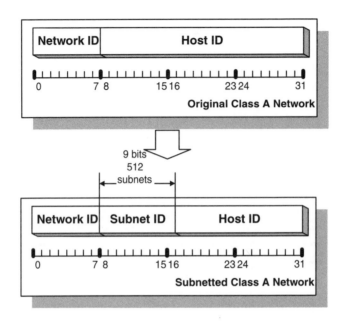

Figure 4.7 *To provide 512 subnets, you must use nine bits of the host ID.*

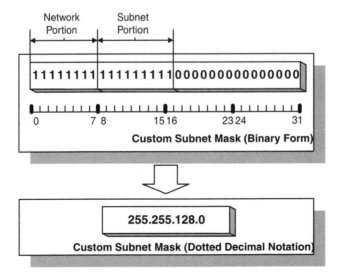

Figure 4.8 *Masking network and subnet bits.*

Selecting an Appropriate Subnet Mask

1. What subnet mask is suitable for the following situations?
   - Class A network with 6 subnets _____
   - Class B network with 13 subnets _____
   - Class B network with 120 subnets _____
   - Class C network with 19 subnets _____
2. Suppose you are an administrator of a company that has been assigned a class C network from the InterNIC. Your network consists of nine separate segments connected with routers. Two more segments will be added in the near future. Based on this information:
   - What is the minimum number of bits required for the subnet ID? _____
   - What is the number of hosts per subnet?_____
   - What is the subnet mask?_____
3. Your network has been assigned a class B network address. Currently there are 30 subnets that will grow to 60 within the next year. There will never be more than 500 hosts per subnet. What are the possible subnet masks for this scenario?
   _____ and _____
   How much growth (in terms of the maximum number of subnets and maximum number of hosts per subnet) will these subnet masks provide?
   Mask _____ will provide _____ subnets and _____ hosts per subnet.
   Mask _____ will provide _____ subnets and _____ hosts per subnet.

SUBNET MASK CONSIDERATIONS

Since the bits that identify the subnet are specified by the bitmask, there is nothing to prevent a network administrator from using low-order or non-adjacent bits for the subnet ID. When subnetting was initially defined in RFC 950, it was *recommended* that the subnet bits be contiguous and located at the most significant (high-order) bits of an IP address. Today you should use the contiguous, high-order bits for the subnet ID, since most of the modern operating systems prevent you from doing otherwise.

Defining the Subnet Numbers

Once you have calculated the custom subnet mask, the next step is to number the subnets within your network. To do this, you must go through all of the bit combinations in the subnet ID portion. All possible subnet ID bit combinations are then evaluated and converted to decimal format.

Let's look at the following example: The class C network 192.168.18.0 needs to be subnetted into eight subnets, numbered 0 through 7. We are required to describe each subnet in terms of IP addresses and subnet masks. What we already can do is calculate the length of the subnet ID portion and the subnet mask. In this example, we need to derive three bits from the original class C host portion to get eight subnets. (See Figure 4.9.)

Now we must define each subnet. In general, to define Subnet N, place the binary representation of N into the subnet field. To define Subnet #0, place binary 000 in the subnet field. To get Subnet #0 in dotted decimal notation, convert each octet to decimal form. (See Figure 4.10.)

To determine Subnet #1, place binary 001 into the subnet field. (See Figure 4.11.)

Subnets #2 through #7 are calculated in a similar way.

Table 4.2 presents the subnetting results. The bold portion of each address indicates the subnet—number field.

The whole class C network differs from Subnet #0 only by the subnet mask. If you omit the subnet mask, there is no way to tell a particular network from its Subnet #0.

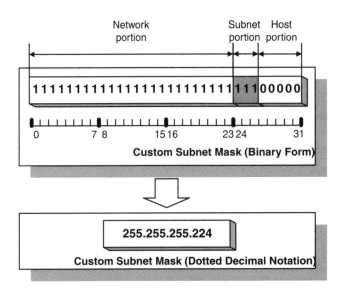

Figure 4.9 *Three bits in the subnet portion provide the necessary eight subnets.*

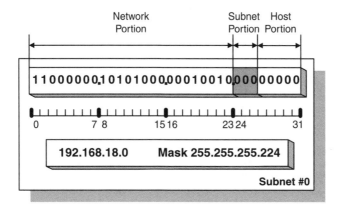

Figure 4.10 *Subnetting 192.168.18.0. Subnet #0 of 8.*

You can check if your calculations are correct by ensuring that subnets are multiples of Subnet #1. In this example, all subnets are multiples of 32. (See Table 4.3.)

When you use more than three bits for subnetting, it's more practical to define only Subnet #1 using the above procedure. Since other subnets are multiples of Subnet #1, you can calculate them simply by multiplying by the value of Subnet #1. (See Table 4.3.) For example, to calculate Subnet #4 (192.168.18.**128**), you can multiply Subnet ID #1 (192.168. 18.**32**) by 4.

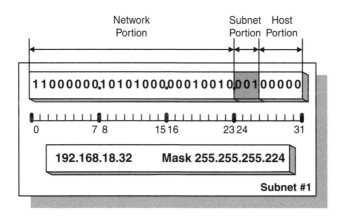

Figure 4.11 *Subnetting 192.168.18.0. Subnet #1 of 8.*

Table 4.2 *Subnetting Class C Network 192.128.18.0 into 8 Subnets*

	Binary	Decimal	Subnet Mask
Base	11000000.10101000.00010010.00000000	192.168.18.0	255.255.255.0
Subnet #0	11000000.10101000.00010010.**00000000**	192.168.18.0	255.255.255.224
Subnet #1	11000000.10101000.00010010.**00100000**	192.168.18.32	255.255.255.224
Subnet #2	11000000.10101000.00010010.**01000000**	192.168.18.64	255.255.255.224
Subnet #3	11000000.10101000.00010010.**01100000**	192.168.18.96	255.255.255.224
Subnet #4	11000000.10101000.00010010.**10000000**	192.168.18.128	255.255.255.224
Subnet #5	11000000.10101000.00010010.**10100000**	192.168.18.160	255.255.255.224
Subnet #6	11000000.10101000.00010010.**11000000**	192.168.18.192	255.255.255.224
Subnet #7	11000000.10101000.00010010.**11100000**	192.168.18.224	255.255.255.224

SPECIAL CONSIDERATIONS FOR SUBNETS WITH ALL-ONES OR ALL-ZEROS

When subnetting was first defined in RFC 950, the use of subnets with all-zeroes or all-ones was prohibited. This is because the Routing Information Protocol (RIP-1), which is used to designate networks and the paths to them, does not carry subnet masks as part of its routing table update messages. Earlier, we said that to differentiate between the entire network and its all-zeroes subnet (Subnet #0), we needed to examine the subnet mask. (Refer to Table 4.2.) If the subnet mask was not transferred in network messages, the router could not create a true picture of the network. The routing advertisements for subnet 192.168.18.0, mask 255.255.255.224, and network 192.168.18.0 mask 255.255.255.0 were therefore identical: 192.168.18.0.

Table 4.3 *Subnet #N Should Be a Multiple of Subnet #1*

	Binary	Decimal	Subnet Mask
Base	11000000.10101000.00010010.00000000	192.168.18.0	255.255.255.0
Subnet #0	11000000.10101000.00010010.00000000	192.168.18.**0**	255.255.255.224
Subnet #1	11000000.10101000.00010010.00100000	192.168.18.**32**	255.255.255.224
Subnet #2	11000000.10101000.00010010.01000000	192.168.18.**64**	255.255.255.224
Subnet #3	11000000.10101000.00010010.01100000	192.168.18.**96**	255.255.255.224
Subnet #4	11000000.10101000.00010010.10000000	192.168.18.**128**	255.255.255.224
Subnet #5	11000000.10101000.00010010.10100000	192.168.18.**160**	255.255.255.224
Subnet #6	11000000.10101000.00010010.11000000	192.168.18.**192**	255.255.255.224
Subnet #7	11000000.10101000.00010010.11100000	192.168.18.**224**	255.255.255.224

The same applies to an all-ones subnet. Routers require a subnet mask to determine if the broadcast should be sent only to the all-ones subnet or to the entire network.

You can use the all-zeroes and all-ones subnets *only* if all routers and hardware in your network support them. If you are unsure about it, it is safer not to use these subnet IDs. If you decide not to use all-zeroes and all-ones subnets, remember the following limitations:

- The number of valid subnets is decreased by two.

- Splitting your network into only two subnets is not allowed (see Figure 4.12).

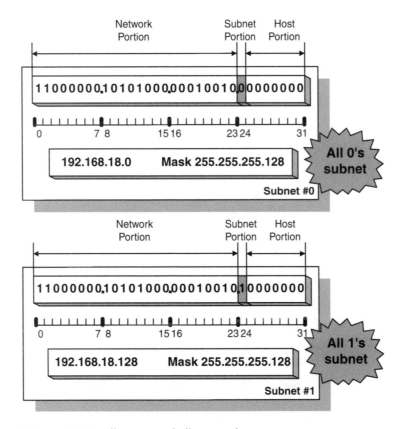

Figure 4.12 *All-zeroes and all-ones subnets.*

Study Break

Subnetting a Class C Network

Your company has been assigned a single class C network, 195.209.225.0. Currently there are only two subnets, but three more will be added in the near future. Each subnet must support the maximum possible number of hosts. You are required to implement a subnetting scheme. (Assume that routers do not support all-zeroes and all-ones subnets.)

1. How many bits would you allocate for the subnet ID? _____
2. What is the subnet mask? _____
3. Using the above calculations, fill in the following table:
   base   195.209.225.[00000000] = 195.209.225.0
   Subnet #0   195.209.225.[_____] = 195.209.225.__
   Subnet #1   195.209.225.[_____] = 195.209.225.__
   Subnet #2   195.209.225.[_____] = 195.209.225.__
   Subnet #3   195.209.225.[_____] = 195.209.225.__
   Subnet #4   195.209.225.[_____] = 195.209.225.__
   Subnet #5   195.209.225.[_____] = 195.209.225.__
   . . . . . .
4. Can you use Subnet #0 in this example? _____

Alternative Designation of Subnet Masks

We've already gotten used to the fact that subnet masks are expressed in dotted decimal notation. With the assumption that subnet IDs are contiguous and derived from high-order bits, we can simply define the number of bits that are allocated for an extended network prefix (network ID plus subnet ID) to uniquely identify the position where the host number begins. For example, there is an agreement to refer to class A networks as "/8s" (pronounced "slash eight," or just "eights") since they have the 8-bit network ID. Accordingly, class B networks are called "/16s," and class C are called "/24s".

Let's look at the subnetting example with these abbreviations. We take the same example with class C network 192.168.18.0 and eight subnets, numbered 0 through 7. Again we are required to express the subnet mask, but now we use "slashes".

The class C network has network prefix "/24". To provide eight subnets, we need three bits. The new extended network prefix should therefore be /24+3=/27. Now we have the custom subnet mask. /27 leaves $32 - 27 = 5$ bits for the host ID in each subnet, that is $2^5 = 32$ hosts per subnet. To calculate each subnet, you need to follow the same guidelines we described earlier. To define Subnet #N, you need to put the binary representation of N into the subnet ID portion and convert the result into decimal form. The /27 can be easily converted in the habitual dotted decimal notation, 255.255.255.224.

Although you might think that using slashes is easier, Windows NT has no ability to manipulate masks written in this form. You should, therefore, always convert your masks to dotted decimal notation before using them.

Defining Host Addresses for Each Subnet

Once you have calculated the subnets, you can proceed to defining host addresses for each subnet. Remember, according to Internet practice, the host-number field of an IP address cannot be all-zeroes or all-ones. In Chapter 3, we mentioned that an IP address with all-zeros in the host portion symbolizes "this network," and an address with all-ones in the host portion indicates a broadcast. Each subnet, therefore, comprises an address space block of $2^N - 2$ hosts, where N is the number of bits reserved for the host ID. For example, subnetting the class C network 192.168.18.0 with the subnet mask 255.255.255.224 provides you with 30 host addresses in each subnet. (See Figure 4.13.) Note that the all-zeroes and all-ones subnets are dimmed to indicate that you better not use them because of the limitations just discussed.

If you need to determine the valid host numbers for a particular subnet, you just need to look over all possible combinations in the host ID field, except all-zeroes and all-ones. Table 4.4 shows the possible host addresses for Subnet #5. The host portion of each IP address is displayed in bold print.

Sometimes you need to determine the broadcast address for a particular subnet. Remember, the broadcast address has all-ones in the host ID portion. For example, the broadcast address for Subnet #5 (see Table 4.4) is 192.168.18.191. Note that the broadcast address for Subnet #N is exactly one less than the base address for Subnet #(N+1).

You may have noticed that we lose IP addresses when we implement subnetting. In the previous example, a non-subnetted class C network 192.168.18.0 provided 254 valid host IDs. After subnetting, some of the host IDs became invalid. (See Table 4.5.[1]) IP addresses that became invalid after subnetting are marked bold.

You may have noticed that for every subnet, we lose exactly two IP addresses—one with all zeroes in the host ID portion, which indicates the subnet itself, and another with all-ones in the host ID portions for the broadcast

---

[1] In this example, we assumed that all equipment supports all-zeroes and all-ones subnets.

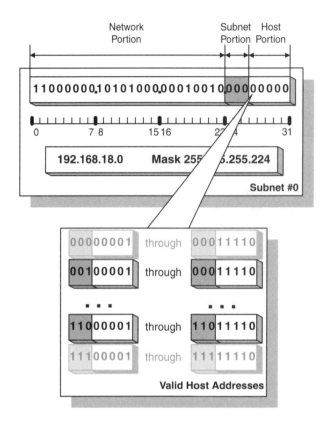

Figure 4.13 *Defining host addresses for each subnet.*

Table 4.4 *Determining Valid Host Addresses for a Given Subnet*

	Binary	Decimal	Subnet Mask
Subnet #5	11000000.10101000.00010010.10100000	192.168.18.160	255.255.255.0
Host #1	11000000.10101000.00010010.10**00001**	192.168.18.161	255.255.255.224
Host #2	11000000.10101000.00010010.10**00010**	192.168.18.162	255.255.255.224
.			
.			
.			
Host #14	11000000.10101000.00010010.10**01110**	192.168.18.174	255.255.255.224
Host #15	11000000.10101000.00010010.10**01111**	192.168.18.175	255.255.255.224
.			
.			
.			
Host #29	11000000.10101000.00010010.10**11101**	192.168.18.189	255.255.255.224
Host #30	11000000.10101000.00010010.10**11110**	192.168.18.190	255.255.255.224

Table 4.5 *IP Address Loss During Subnetting*

IP Address	Subnet Mask	Comment
192.168.18.0	255.255.255.224	**Symbolizes Subnet #0 – not valid for host ID.**
192.168.18.1	255.255.255.224	Valid host IP address. Host #1 in Subnet #0.
. . .		
192.168.18.30	255.255.255.224	Valid host IP address. Host #30 in Subnet #0.
192.168.18.31	**255.255.255.224**	**Broadcast address for Subnet #0.**
192.168.18.32	**255.255.255.224**	**Symbolizes Subnet #1—invalid host ID.**
192.168.18.33	255.255.255.224	Valid host IP address. Host #1 in Subnet #1.
. . .		
192.168.18.62	255.255.255.224	Valid host IP address. Host #30 in Subnet #1.
192.168.18.63	**255.255.255.224**	**Broadcast address for Subnet #1.**
192.168.18.64	**255.255.255.224**	**Symbolizes Subnet #2—invalid host ID.**
192.168.18.65	255.255.255.224	Valid host IP address. Host #1 in Subnet #2.
. . .		
192.168.18.254	255.255.255.224	Valid host IP address. Host #30 in Subnet #7.
192.168.18.255	255.255.255.224	**Broadcast address for Subnet #7.**

address. Remember that, depending on your hardware, IP addresses in subnets identified by all-zeroes or all-ones may be invalid for assignment.

Study Break

Subnetting a Class B Network

You have chosen a class B network address of 172.31.0.0 for your company's network and you need to subnet it into eight subnets using subnet mask 255.255.224.0. What are the valid host IP addresses for each subnet?

Subnet #0	172.31.0.0	172.31.___.___	172.31.___.___
Subnet #1	172.31.32.0	172.31.___.___	172.31.___.___
Subnet #2	172.31.64.0	172.31.___.___	172.31.___.___
Subnet #3	172.31.96.0	172.31.___.___	172.31.___.___
Subnet #4	172.31.128.0	172.31.___.___	172.31.___.___
Subnet #5	172.31.160.0	172.31.___.___	172.31.___.___
Subnet #6	172.31.192.0	172.31.___.___	172.31.___.___
Subnet #7	172.31.224.0	172.31.___.___	172.31.___.___

Supernetting

Let's consider an organization with 800 hosts. The network administrator can acquire a class B network that provides 65534 host addresses. Obviously, that is much more than needed. Rather than allocating the whole class B network, an administrator may consider obtaining several class C networks. In our example, four class C networks are enough, since they allocate more than 1024 hosts, which easily satisfies the requirement while providing future growth potential. Let's assume the organization is assigned the following class C networks:

```
210.18.8.0 mask 255.255.255.0

210.18.9.0 mask 255.255.255.0

210.18.10.0 mask 255.255.255.0

210.18.11.0 mask 255.255.255.0
```

This technique helps to conserve class A and B networks, but creates a new problem. To advertise the organization's network on the Internet, we must issue three additional entries. This can congest Internet routers and may cause delays in packet delivery.

By 1992, the exponential growth of the Internet was beginning to raise serious concerns about the ability of the Internet's routing system to scale and support future growth. These problems were related to the near-term exhaustion of the class B network address space and the rapid growth in the size of the global Internet's routing tables. To solve these problems, the concept of supernetting, or Classless Inter-Domain Routing (CIDR), was developed. It is described in RFCs 1517, 1518, 1519, and 1520.

The main idea of CIDR is that it supports route aggregation, where a single routing table entry can represent the address space of perhaps thousands of traditional classful routes. In contrast to subnetting, supernetting borrows bits from the network ID and masks them as the host ID.

Let's return to our example with the four class C networks. Note, in Figure 4.14, that all four networks have identical parts in the network ID portion up to the grayed area. When we consolidate the IP address range allocated by each of these class C networks, we get the range 210.18.9.1–210.18.11.254. On the other hand, the same block of IP addresses can be expressed with the single designation 210.18.9.0, mask 255.255.252.0. As you can see in Figure 4.14, the blocks of IP addresses described with both methods are identical, but supernetting helps control the amount of routing information in the Internet's backbone routers, reduces route flapping (rapid

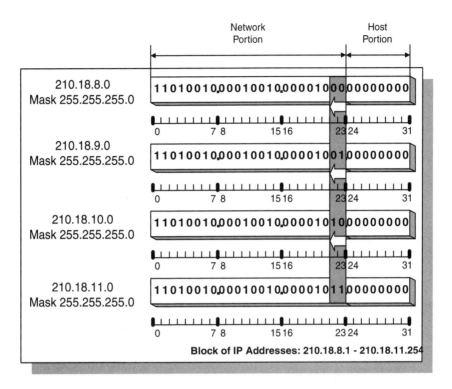

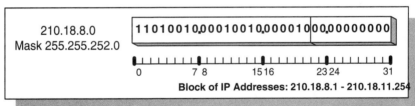

Figure 4.14 *Concept of supernetting.*

changes in route availability), and eases the local administrative burden of updating external routing information.

Another example of supernetting is found on backbone routers. In this case, we express the multitude of class C networks from 195.0.0.0, mask 255.255.255.0 through 195.255.255.0, mask 255.255.255.0 with a single designation: 195.0.0.0, mask 255.0.0.0.

Study Break

Supernetting a Class C Network

You have chosen several class C networks for your company's intranet. These class C networks range from 200.0.0.0 though 200.0.31.0.

How can you supernet these class C networks to advertise them to Internet routers with a single routing table entry? _____ , mask _____

Subnetting Example

Now we are ready to perform a typical planning task. Suppose you are the administrator of the organization whose network plan is illustrated in Figure 4.15. Currently there are only five network segments, but six more will be required during the coming year. The number of computers in each segment is different, but no segment has more that 2000 hosts. Routers separate each segment. You are required to plan a subnetting scheme that will meet today's needs while allowing for future growth.

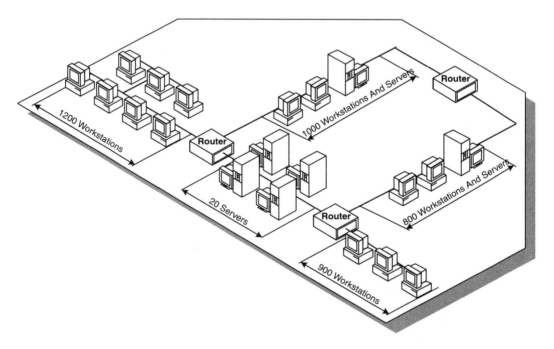

Figure 4.15   *Subnetting example.*

Since your company has no plans to connect to the Internet[2], you choose an IP address block from the private address space, 172.16.0.0.

To complete this task, you must:

- Decide the number of required subnets.
- Calculate the number of bits required to support these subnets.
- Verify that the chosen network ID is enough for deployment of the desired number of subnets with the given number of hosts per subnet.
- Determine a custom subnet mask.
- Assign each host an IP address from the corresponding subnet.

The number of required subnets corresponds to the number of physical network segments. In our current example, we have five network segments and expect six in the coming year. We need to plan, therefore, for a minimum of 11 subnets.

The next step is to determine the number of bits that provide the required number of subnets. According to Table 4.2, three bits for the subnet ID portion will give us $2^3 = 8$ subnets, but since we don't know whether all our hardware supports all-zeroes or all-ones subnets, we need to subtract two. So, with three bits allocated for the subnet portion, we have only six valid subnets, which is not enough. The next step is to try allocating four bits for the subnet ID portion. Four bits provide $2^4 = 16$ subnets, but again, we need to subtract two to avoid problems with all-zeroes and all-ones subnets. Since we have chosen a class B network ID, we have 16 bits in the host portion. Borrowing four bits for the subnet ID leaves 12 bits for hosts in each subnet. Twelve bits in the host ID field are enough for $2^{12} - 2 = 4094$ valid host IDs. We subtracted two to account for all-ones (broadcast address) and all-zeroes (this subnet) in the host portion. The capability to support more than 4000 hosts per subnet satisfies the current requirement and allows for future growth. You could also try allocating five or six bits to the subnet ID. Subnetting options are illustrated in Table 4.6. Bold typeface indicates configurations that satisfy current requirements.

Let's choose four bits for the subnet ID and 12 bits for the host ID.

---

[2] In the *real world*, one should carefully consider the idea that they will never connect to the Internet. Are there really any successful organizations with an IT base that will *never* connect to the Internet? Unless the company will access the Internet through a proxy or firewall which will mask its actual IP addresses, it is wise to plan your IP addressing with ultimate Internet connectivity in mind.

Table 4.6   *Different Variants of Subnetting*

Bits for Subnet ID	Bits for Host ID	Number of Subnets	Hosts per Subnet
3	13	8(6)	8190
4	**12**	**16(14)**	**4094**
5	11	32(30)	2046
6	10	64(62)	1022

Now we should calculate the custom subnet mask. Recall that we can get the custom subnet mask by setting all network ID and subnet ID bits to binary 1 and converting to dotted decimal form. (See Figure 4.16.)

The custom subnet mask becomes 255.255.240.0. Note that this subnet mask is used for every subnet within the network. With this subnet mask, the network is divided into 16 subnets. Each subnet may have the same number of hosts: $2^{16} - 2 = 4094$.

Let's number subnets as shown in Figure 4.17, and then calculate the range of host IDs for each subnet. Note that we started numbering subnets beginning with 1 because we decided not to use Subnet #0 (all-zeroes) in this network.

The next step is to express each subnet in dotted decimal notation. To do this, we must put the binary representation of the subnet number into the subnet portion and convert to decimal notation. Table 4.7 shows these

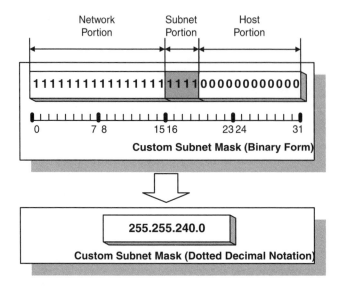

Figure 4.16   *Calculating the custom subnet mask.*

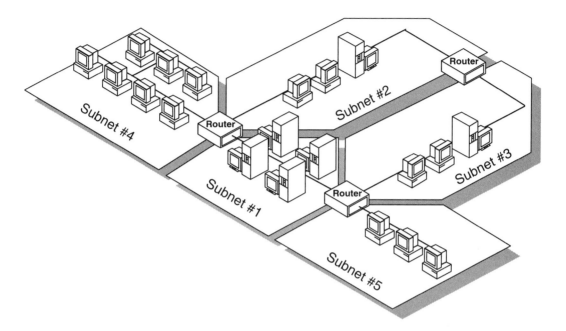

Figure 4.17 *Subnetting example showing number of subnets.*

steps. Binary values are written in square brackets. Values in bold typeface correspond to subnet IDs.

Table 4.7 shows only five subnets. Subnets 6 through 15 are not needed now, but we can calculate them using the shortcut method—multiplying by Subnet #1.

The next step is to determine the host IP addresses for each subnet. Remember, to define the IP address for Host #N within a particular subnet, you must place the binary representation of N in the host ID portion and then convert the result into dotted decimal form. In this example, however, for all subnets except Subnet #1, we will calculate the range of IP addresses

Table 4.7 *Calculating the Subnet Numbers*

	Third Octet in Binary Form	Decimal	Subnet Mask
Base	172.16.0.0	172.16.0.0	255.255.255.0
Subnet #1	172.16.[**0001**][0000].0	172.16.16.0	255.255.240.0
Subnet #2	172.16.[**0010**][0000].0	172.16.32.0	255.255.240.0
Subnet #3	172.16.[**0011**][0000].0	172.16.48.0	255.255.240.0
Subnet #4	172.16.[**0100**][0000].0	172.16.64.0	255.255.240.0
Subnet #5	172.16.[**0101**][0000].0	172.16.80.0	255.255.240.0

Table 4.8 *Calculating Host IP Addresses for Subnet #1*

	Third Octet in Binary Form	**Decimal**	**Subnet Mask**
Subnet #1	172.16.[0001][**0000**].[**00000000**]	172.16.16.0	255.255.240.0
Host #1	172.16.[0001][**0000**].[**00000001**]	172.16.16.1	255.255.240.0
Host #2	172.16.[0001][**0000**].[**00000010**]	172.16.16.2	255.255.240.0
.			
.			
.			
Host # 4094	172.16.[0001][**1111**].[**11111110**]	172.16.31.254	255.255.240.0
Broadcast	172.16.[0001][**1111**].[**11111111**]	172.16.31.255	255.255.240.0

instead of specifying them individually. Table 4.8 shows the calculations for Subnet #1. Again, binary values are written in square brackets. Symbols in bold typeface indicate the host portion.

Note that the first valid host IP address is one greater than the base address for Subnet #1. The last valid IP address is two less than the base address for the next subnet. Table 4.9 shows the host IP address ranges for other subnets.

Next we should assign hosts and routers the IP addresses from the corresponding range. (See Figure 4.18.) The last step is to provide these values during TCP/IP setup.

Summary

In this chapter, we looked at the ins and outs of subnetting. You learned the benefits of subnetting, as well as its drawbacks. We introduced a third level of hierarchy—the subnet ID—and discussed how to calculate it. You are now familiar with the process of determining custom subnet masks and evaluating the number of hosts they provide. Finally, we spent quite a bit of time with a subnetting example, which prepared you to effectively plan a real TCP/IP network.

Table 4.9 *Host IP Address Ranges*

	Subnet	**Start IP Address**	**End IP Address**	**Subnet Mask**
Subnet #1	172.16.16.0	172.16.16.1	172.16.31.254	255.255.240.0
Subnet #2	172.16.32.0	172.16.32.1	172.16.47.254	255.255.240.0
Subnet #3	172.16.48.0	172.16.48.1	172.16.63.254	255.255.240.0
Subnet #4	172.16.64.0	172.16.64.1	172.16.79.254	255.255.240.0
Subnet #5	172.16.80.0	172.16.80.1	172.16.95.254	255.255.240.0

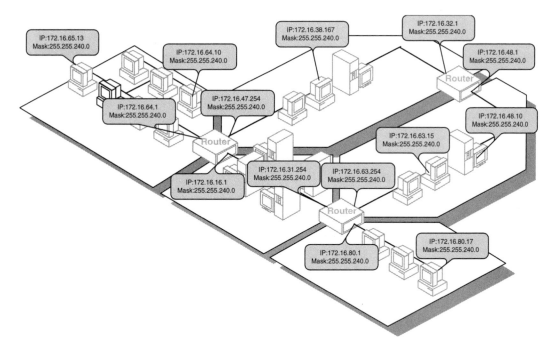

Figure 4.18 *Assignment of IP addresses.*

▲ REVIEW QUESTIONS

1. *How many bits in the subnet ID portion provide five subnets?*
   A. 1
   B. 2
   C. 3
   D. 255

2. *You acquired a class B network ID. Your network has six subnets and seven more are expected in the next year. What is (are) the subnet mask(s) that satisfy(ies) these requirements?*
   A. 255.255.192.0
   B. 255.255.224.0
   C. 255.255.240.0
   D. 255.255.248.0

3. *Your class C network is divided into eight subnets. What is the maximum number of hosts in each subnet?*

    A. 8

    B. 16

    C. 30

    D. 32

    E. 62

4. *You are given an address of 220.56.45.0. You need to provide five subnets with at least 12 hosts in each. What subnet masks could be used to accomplish this?*

    A. 255.255.255.192

    B. 255.255.255.224

    C. 255.255.255.240

    D. 255.255.255.248

5. *Assuming that all hardware supports all-ones and all-zeroes subnets, which subnet mask will provide exactly 64 subnets for a class A network?*

    A. 255.255.0.0

    B. 255.0.0.0

    C. 255.224.0.0

    D. 255.248.0.0

    E. 255.252.0.0

6. *You have subnetted your network 137.0.0.0 into 256 subnets. What is the maximum number of hosts in each subnet?*

    A. 254

    B. 137

    C. 65534

    D. 8

    E. 224

7. *You have subnetted your class C network 195.209.225.0 into eight subnets. Which of the following are valid host IP addresses for subnet 195.209.225.32, mask 255.255.255.224?*

    A. 195.209.225.31

    B. 195.209.225.39

    C. 195.209.225.46

    D. 195.209.225.63

    E. 195.209.225.76

8. *What is the broadcast address for subnet 195.209.225.64, mask 255.255.255.224?*

    A. 195.209.225.0

    B. 195.209.225.95

    C. 195.209.225.96

    D. 195.209.225.255

    E. 195.209.225.254

9. *Your host has an IP address of 172.18.31.0, mask 255.255.240.0. Is it a valid host IP address?*

    A. Yes

    B. No

10. *Your host has an IP address of 195.209.225.15, mask 255.255.255.240. Is it a valid host IP address?*

    A. Yes

    B. No

11. *Your host has an IP address of 172.25.15.76, mask 255.255.240.0. Which hosts should be located in the same network segment?*

    A. 172.25.13.255

    B. 172.25.15.89

    C. 172.25.15.254

    D. 172.25.15.255

    E. 172.25.16.1

12. *Your host has an IP address of 195.209.225.69, mask 255.255.255.248. Which hosts should be located in the remote network segment?*

    A. 195.209.225.65

    B. 195.209.225.61

    C. 195.209.225.80

    D. 195.209.225.71

    E. 195.209.225.70

13. *You are going to supernet four class C networks. What subnet mask must you use?*

   A. 255.255.255.192

   B. 255.255.252.0

   C. 255.255.255.0

   D. 255.255.248.0

   E. 255.255.192.0

14. *Your organization has received eight class C IDs from the InterNIC. They range from 200.20.64.0 through 200.20.71.0. How can you advertise them to the Internet using supernetting?*

   A. 200.20.64.0, mask 255.255.0.0

   B. 200.20.64.0, mask 255.255.255.0

   C. 200.20.64.0, mask 255.255.248.0

   D. 200.20.64.0, mask 255.255.240.0

   E. 200.20.64.0, mask 255.255.224.0

IP Routing

You might be wondering how all the packets get through the internetwork to the destination computer? Read on and you'll see how IP routing works and how IP packets find their paths through routers. We'll discuss the differences between direct and indirect routing and learn how to build a router on a Windows NT computer. We'll also look at the concepts of dynamic routing and develop some guidelines on how to combine static and dynamic routers in one network. Finally, we will learn to use the TRACERT utility to trace and troubleshoot IP networks.

At the end of this chapter, you will be able to:

- Explain how IP routing works.

- Explain the differences between *static* and *dynamic* routing.

- Configure a Windows NT computer to function as an IP router.

107

- Build a static routing table.
- Use the TRACERT utility to isolate route problems.

Routing Basics

While introducing subnetting in Chapter 4, "Subnetting and Supernetting," we simply assumed that when a packet is destined for a remote network, it is forwarded to the host's default gateway and then delivered to the destination node. We said that it was the responsibility of the router to deliver the packet to the recipient computer. The process of transferring data across an internetwork from a source host to a destination host is called *routing*. Routing also implies choosing the best path over which to send packets. Routing can be understood in terms of two processes: *host routing* and *router routing*.

Host Routing

The simplest case of routing—*host routing*—occurs when a computer sends an IP packet and decides whether the destination is local or remote. You might remember that the computer does this by comparing the network ID of the destination host with its own network ID. If these two values match, the host can send the packet directly to the destination computer by querying the destination MAC address. When a host can deliver a packet directly, this is referred to as *direct delivery*. Direct routing does not require any additional devices to participate in packet delivery. (See Figure 5.1.)

If the destination host is located on a remote subnet, the computer forwards the packet to its configured default gateway. This is referred to as *indirect delivery*. If you intend to connect to remote subnets, you must configure your computer with the default gateway address. The default gateway IP

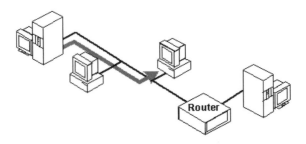

Figure 5.1 *Direct delivery.*

address corresponds to the IP address of the router's interface to which your computer must send packets destined for other networks. Since routers are not transparent devices (in other words, computers do not automatically become aware of routers), you must manually configure each TCP/IP host with a router IP address (default gateway address).

To configure a Windows NT computer with a default gateway address, follow these steps:

1. Launch `Control Panel`.
2. Double-click `Network`.
3. Go to the `Protocol` tab, choose `TCP/IP` protocol properties, and type the IP address of the default gateway in the `Default Gateway` box. (See Figure 5.2.)

You can configure your Windows NT computer with multiple default gateways. To do this, click `Advanced` in the `TCP/IP Properties` dialog box and input additional default gateways in the `Gateways` box. You can add up to five default gateways in this dialog box.

It's easy to say that if a computer cannot deliver a packet directly, it forwards the packet to its default gateway. But what if there are several possible paths? In other words, what if there are several alternative routers to which an IP packet can be forwarded? (See Figure 5.3.) In this case, the computer must decide in what direction a particular packet must go.

To make these decisions, the IP module of the host computer sending the packet consults its routing table, which stores the preferable paths to remote subnets.

Routing Table

In TCP/IP networks, routing tables do not only exist on routers—every TCP/IP host has a routing table. The routing table consists of several entries, each of which symbolizes a path to a particular network or host. Figure 5.4 presents the structure of a routing table entry.

NETWORK ID

The network ID field is the key point of the routing table entry. When a host consults its routing table for a path to the destination network, it compares

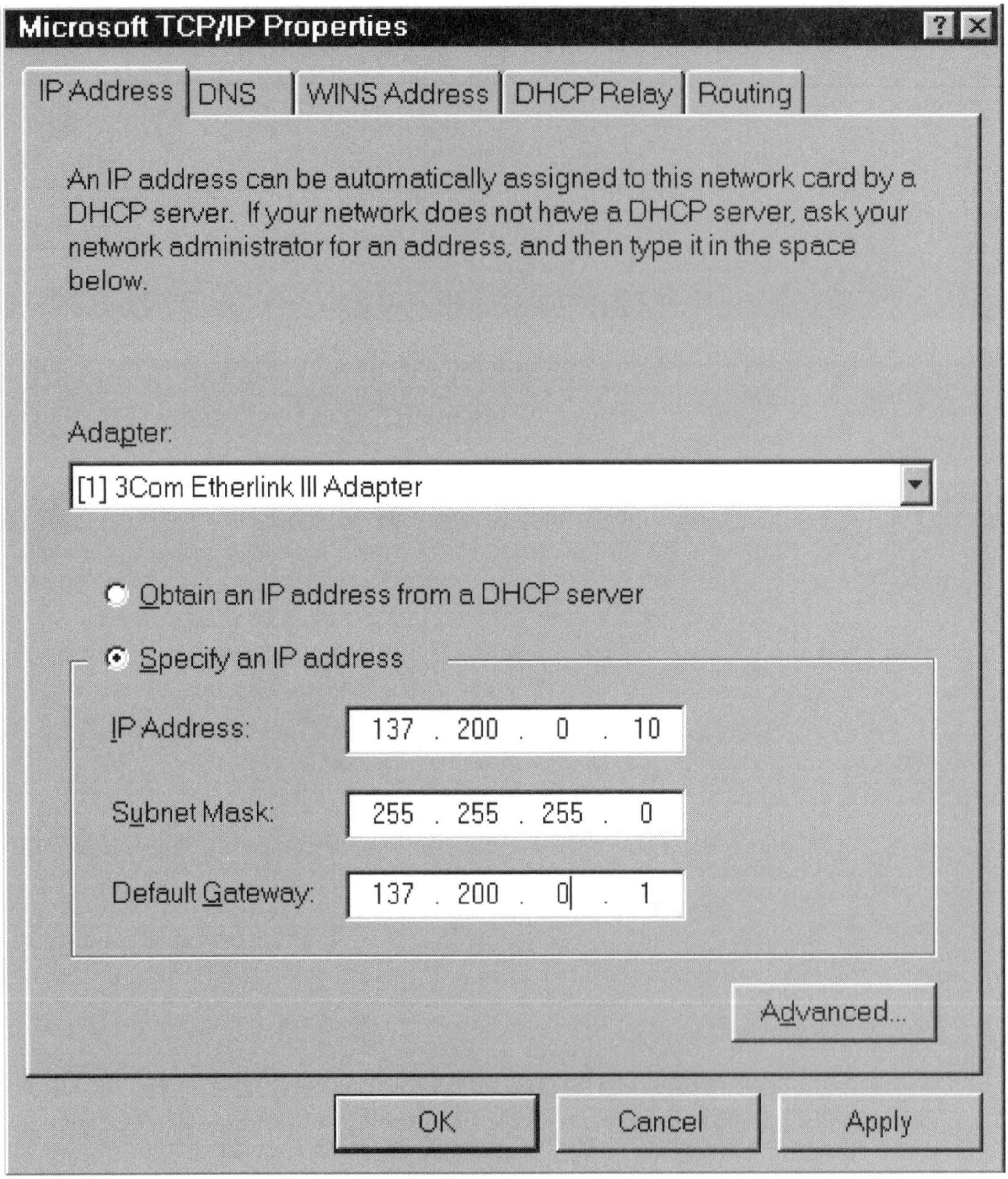

Microsoft TCP/IP Properties   [?] [X]

IP Address | DNS | WINS Address | DHCP Relay | Routing |

An IP address can be automatically assigned to this network card by a
DHCP server. If your network does not have a DHCP server, ask your
network administrator for an address, and then type it in the space
below.

Adapter:

[1] 3Com Etherlink III Adapter   [▼]

  ◯ Obtain an IP address from a DHCP server

  ◉ Specify an IP address

    IP Address: 137 . 200 . 0 . 10

    Subnet Mask: 255 . 255 . 255 . 0

    Default Gateway: 137 . 200 . 0 . 1

                                              [Advanced...]

            [OK]   [Cancel]   [Apply]

Figure 5.2   *Default gateway address configuration.*

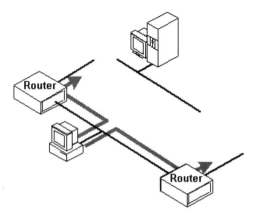

Figure 5.3 *The computer might have several ways to send a packet.*

the network ID with the destination IP address of the arrived packet header. The network ID field is often represented by the IP address and subnet mask pair. For example, the network ID of 172.20.0 will be represented by 172.20.0.0, mask 255.255.255.0.

GATEWAY ADDRESS

The gateway address field contains the address to which the packet destined to the given network is to be forwarded.

INTERFACE

The interface field represents the IP address of the host's interface (network adapter card) through which the packet will be forwarded. An important thing to check when ensuring that a routing table entry is correct is that the gateway address and interface address have the same network ID.

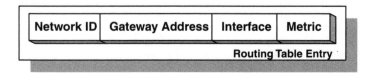

Figure 5.4 *Routing table entry.*

METRIC

The metric field indicates the route cost. This field is useful when there are multiple routes to a given network. When several routes exist in the routing table, the route with the lowest metric will be chosen.

Metrics can be calculated using different preferences. For example, a common metric type indicates the *hop count* or, in other words, the number of routers or networks that must be passed to reach the target network. (See Figure 5.5.)

The metric field can also express a delay, or a measure of time that is required for the packet to reach the destination network. In this case, slow WAN links or congested networks will result in higher metrics and therefore will be less likely chosen by routers. Another good criterion for a metric value is the route's throughput.

The routing table entry also has a lifetime field to indicate the amount of time the route is considered valid. When the route entry's lifetime expires, the route is removed from the routing table. This provides a way for routers to conform to network changes.

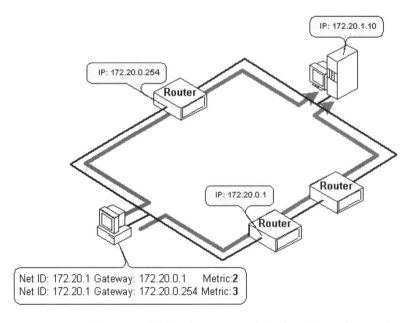

Figure 5.5 *The metric field in the routing table can indicate the number of hops to the given network.*

Here is an example of a routing table:

Network Address	Netmask	Gateway Address	Interface	Metric
127.0.0.0	255.0.0.0	127.0.0.1	127.0.0.1	1
172.20.0.0	255.255.255.0	172.20.0.10	172.20.0.10	1
172.20.0.10	255.255.255.255	127.0.0.1	127.0.0.1	1
172.20.1.0	255.255.255.0	172.20.0.1	172.20.0.10	2
172.20.1.0	255.255.255.0	172.20.0.254	172.20.0.10	3
224.0.0.0	224.0.0.0	172.20.0.10	172.20.0.10	1
255.255.255.255	255.255.255.255	172.20.0.10	172.20.0.10	1

The routing table lifetime field is typically not shown in routing table listings.

When you configure a Windows NT computer with a default gateway IP address, the new routing table entry for network ID 0.0.0.0 is added automatically. This is referred to as a *default route*. An example of a default route is:

```
0.0.0.0      0.0.0.0      172.20.0.1   172.20.0.10  1
```

To see your host routing table, type `route print` at the command prompt. Does your routing table have default routes? Does the gateway address of the default route correspond with your computer's default gateway?

When a host wants to send an IP packet, it examines its routing table for the destination network ID. If a match is found, the host picks up the gateway's IP address and the IP address of the interface, and sends the packet along the detected path. If no explicit route has been found, the host uses the default route to deliver the packet.

Let's trace the host's activity when it wants to send an IP packet to a remote host. (See Figure 5.6.)

Let's assume that the routing table of the host contains the following entries:

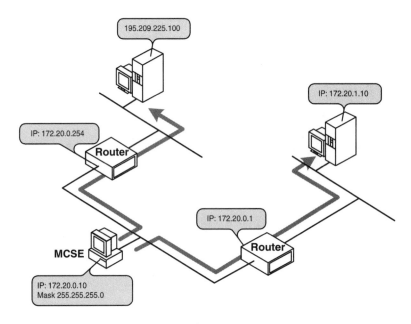

Figure 5.6 *Host routing example.*

```
Network Address    Netmask          Gateway Address   Interface        Metric
0.0.0.0            0.0.0.0          172.20.0.1        172.20.0.10        1
195.209.225.0      255.255.255.0    172.20.0.254      172.20.0.10        2
```

When computer MCSE wants to send an IP packet to the computer with IP address 195.209.225.100, MCSE checks its routing table. The second line of the routing table gives the path to the appropriate subnet. (Although route 0.0.0.0 is listed first, it will be used *only* if no explicit route for the target network is found.) The packet is forwarded to router 172.20.0.254 through interface 172.20.0.10. Later we will discuss how routers handle incoming packets.

When computer MCSE wants to send an IP packet to 172.20.1.10, there is no explicit route in the routing table. In this case, the default route is used and the IP packet is forwarded to router 172.20.0.1.

TCP/IP Dead Gateway Detection

A Windows NT computer can be configured with multiple default gateways. In this case, the TCP module can detect a failure of the first default gateway and make the necessary adjustments to the routing table to use another default gateway. This is referred to as *dead gateway detection*.

Let's discuss how this works in Windows NT. Suppose the TCP connection attempts to send a TCP packet through the first configured default gateway, but receives no response because of router failure. After the TCP timeout value, subsequent connections will be attempted until the total number of attempts reaches one-half of the Registry value for TCPMax-DataRetransmissions. (This value is a REG_DWORD entry and is found in HKEY_LOCAL_MACHINE\SYSTEM\CurrentControlSet\Services\Tcpip\Parameters\.) If no response is received, the dead gateway detection algorithm switches to the next gateway in the list. If the original gateway comes up again, the algorithm does not use it. There are some implementations of dead gateway detection algorithms that are more cautious about advising IP to switch gateways. With these algorithms, only the IP address that detects the unresponsive gateway is switched to the new gateway. Once 25 percent of the TCP connections have been moved to the next default gateway, the algorithm advises IP to change the default gateway for the whole computer.

For example, let's say a machine has eight existing TCP connections to different IP addresses routed through the default gateway. If the first connection is unable to communicate through the gateway, it will be moved to a new gateway. When the second connection experiences problems, it too will be transferred. When the third connection experiences difficulty, more than 25 percent of the existing connections will have been detected as bad and all remaining connections will transfer to the new gateway. The new gateway will become the computer's new default gateway as long as it continues to function properly.

Default gateway detection is enabled by default on computers that have multiple default gateways configured. The Registry parameter that enables dead gateway detection can be found in HKEY_LOCAL_MACHINE\SYSTEM\CurrentControlSet\Services\Tcpip\Parameters\EnableDeadG-WDetect.

Router's Decisions

When an IP packet arrives at the router's interface, the router first checks whether the packet is destined to the router itself. It does this by examining the destination IP address in the packet's header. If the destination IP address matches the router's IP address, the packet is passed to the next layer up, TCP, for further processing.

In most cases, the packet is not destined for the router since routers do not normally provide high-level services. In this case, the router must either deliver it to the destination host or forward the packet to another router.

If the destination network matches the network to which the router is attached, this is considered a direct delivery. (When we say the router is attached to the network, we suggest that the router has at least one interface with an IP address from the network.) The router obtains the hardware address of the destination host with an ARP request, and forwards the IP packet to the destination host's physical address. (See Figure 5.7.)

If the destination network is not directly attached, the router forwards the IP packet to the next intermediate router. To do this, the MAC address of the intermediate router is obtained and the packet is sent to the intermediate router's physical address—this is referred to as an indirect delivery of the IP packet. (Before forwarding the packet to the intermediate router, the routing table is consulted to find the best path to the target network—see Figure 5.8.)

Types of Routing

Before forwarding an IP packet, each TCP/IP device consults its routing table. Note that all routing decisions are made based on the information in a local routing table that physically resides on the system making the routing decision. That means there is no single integral view of the internetwork gathered by a central server. Each router and end host makes its *own* routing decisions. This can cause the path taken from the source to the destination to differ from the path taken from the destination back to the source.

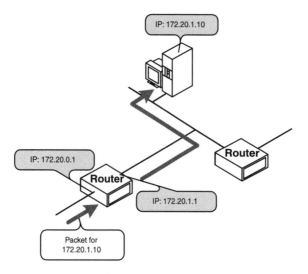

Figure 5.7 *Router's direct delivery.*

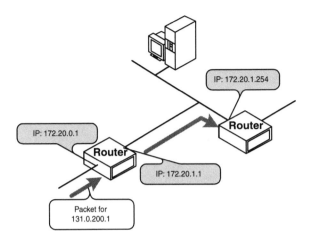

Figure 5.8 *Router's indirect delivery.*

For routing between networks to work correctly, routers and hosts must have knowledge of other network IDs and preferred paths to those IDs, or they must be configured with a default route. On large enterprise networks, the routing tables must be configured such that network traffic travels along optimal paths. If a new network is added, it must be reflected in all routing tables, so every computer can reach it. There must therefore be a mechanism to permit routers and hosts to exchange routing information. Without such a mechanism, network administrators would have to modify the routing tables manually to reflect network topology changes such as the addition of a new network segment.

MCSE 5.1   Static Routing

A router that does not exchange routing table information with other routers is known as a *static* router. The routing table of a static router is constructed manually. A network administrator, based on his/her knowledge of the internetwork topology, manually builds and updates the routing table by explicitly defining all routes or by using default route entries.

By default, a static router can communicate only with networks to which it has a configured interface. For example, in Figure 5.9, Static Router A can send IP packets only to its adjoining networks. Shaded areas are unreachable for Router A and thus Computer 1 cannot communicate with Computer 2 with the current network configuration.

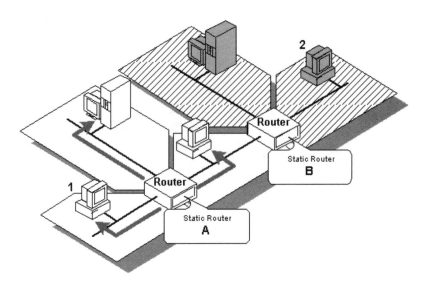

Figure 5.9 *Static router behavior.*

To route packets to other networks, each static router must be manually configured with a route for each network in the internetwork. Manual configuration of every routing table entry can be very time-consuming. You can alternatively configure a static router with a default route. This can be illustrated by the following example. We'll configure static routes in one direction and default routes in the other direction (either solution will, of course, work for either direction).

To route IP packets to network 172.20.5.0 (see Figure 5.10), the following static routing table entry must be created on Router A:

```
Network Address      Netmask       Gateway Address   Interface       Metric
172.20.5.0        255.255.255.0      172.20.3.254    172.20.3.12
```

This routing table entry specifies that to reach network 127.20.5.0, mask 255.255.255.0, the packet must be sent to 172.20.3.254 through interface 172.20.3.1. When Router B receives packets destined to network 172.20.5.0, it can deliver them directly since it has a configured interface in that network.

To reach network 172.20.4.0 (see Figure 5.11), the following second static routing table entry must be added on Router A:

```
Network Address      Netmask       Gateway Address   Interface       Metric
172.20.4.0        255.255.255.0      172.20.3.254    172.20.3.12
```

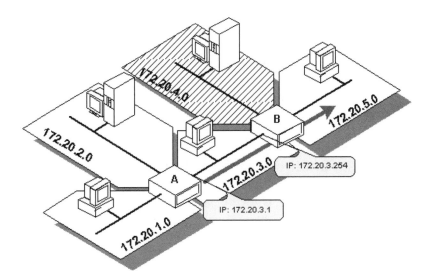

Figure 5.10 *To reach the remote network, a static route must be created (1).*

The next step is to configure Router B so that it can route packets to networks 172.20.1.0 and 172.20.2.0. To demonstrate another approach, let's configure a default route on Router B. (Of course we could have created two static routes to networks 172.20.1.0 and 172.20.2.0 instead of specifying the default route.)

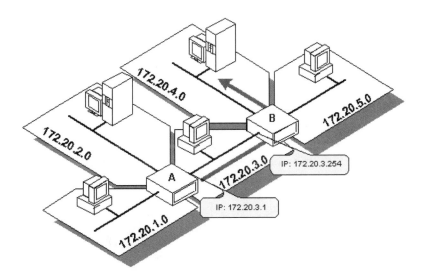

Figure 5.11 *To reach the remote network, a static route must be created (2).*

Network Address	Netmask	Gateway Address	Interface	Metric
0.0.0.0	0.0.0.0	172.20.3.1	172.20.3.254	1

In this example, for hosts to communicate with other hosts on the internetwork, their default gateway address must be configured to match the IP address of the nearest router interface.

MCSE 5.2   Configuring a Windows NT Server Computer to Function as a Static IP Router

Windows NT has the built-in ability to function as a static IP router. The static IP router can be enabled by creating a multihomed system and checking the `Enable IP forwarding` check box.

Study Break

Static Router Setup

To configure a Windows NT computer to function as a static router you must:

1. Install multiple network adapter cards and appropriate drivers, or configure multiple IP addresses on a single card. (You can configure multiple IP addresses using the `Advanced` button on the `IP Address` tab of the `TCP/IP` dialog.).
2. Configure each adapter with a valid IP address and subnet mask in the `TCP/IP Properties` dialog box.
3. Check the `Enable IP forwarding` check box on the `Routing` tab. (See Figure 5.12.)

After doing this, you will need to add static routes or a default route to remote networks using the `ROUTE add` command (which we will cover shortly) to communicate with remote networks. One method of configuring a static route without manually adding routes to a routing table is to configure a multihomed computer's default gateway address as the local interface of the next router. (See Figure 5.13.)

Note There are several kinds of multihoming: multiple NICs and multiple IP addresses per NIC. Each NIC can be configured to use multiple addresses through the use of the control panel. Also, more addresses can be added in the Registry under `HKEY_LOCAL_MACHINE\SYSTEM\CurrentControlSet\Services\<adapter_name>\Parameters\Tcpip\IPAddress`.

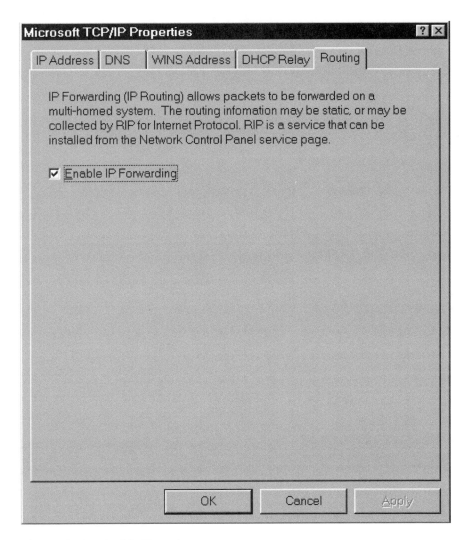

Figure 5.12 *Enable IP routing.*

Note that in the TCP/IP configuration, you can add a default route for each network card. This will create a 0.0.0.0 route for each. Only one default route, however, will actually be used.

Modifying the Routing Table

So far, we've discussed how the routing table should look, but haven't discussed how to create or change one. In Windows NT, the ROUTE command

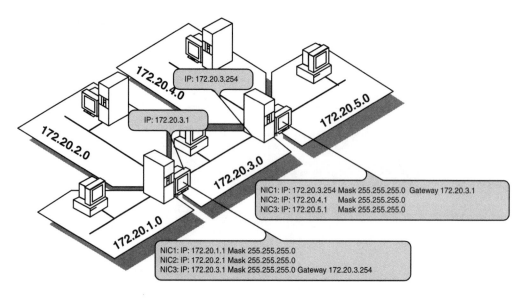

Figure 5.13 *Configuring Windows NT static routers.*

is used (from the command prompt) to add, delete, and modify static entries in the routing table. Table 5.1 shows the ROUTE command's syntax. For example, to configure Static Routers A and B from our recent discussion (refer to Figures 5.10 and 5.11.), use the following sequence of commands:

```
Router A:
route add 172.20.5.0 MASK 255.255.255.0 172.20.3.254
route add 172.20.4.0 MASK 255.255.255.0 172.20.3.254

Router B:
route add 0.0.0.0 MASK 0.0.0.0 172.20.3.1
```

Table 5.1 *ROUTE Command*

Syntax	Description
ROUTE add [network] MASK [netmask] [gateway]	Adds a route to the routing table.
ROUTE -p add [network] MASK [netmask] [gateway]	Adds a persistent route.
ROUTE delete [network] [gateway]	Deletes a route from the routing table.
ROUTE change [network] [gateway]	Modifies a route.
ROUTE print	Displays the routing table.
ROUTE -f	Clears all routes.

Note

Static routes are stored in memory and are deleted when the computer is restarted. To preserve routes, use the –p parameter. Persistent routes are stored in the Windows NT Registry.

Study Break

Viewing Routing Tables

1. To view your computer's routing table, launch the command prompt and type `route print`. Do you have default routes? If yes, record the default gateway address.

_____

2. Type `route add 10.0.0.0 MASK 255.255.0.0` _your_default_gateway_
3. Type `route print` Do you have a route to network 10.0?
4. To change a route, type `route change 10.0.0.0` _another_host_from_your_network_
5. Type `route print` to view the routing table. Which gateway does the route to 10.0 have?
6. To delete an unneeded route, type `route delete 10.0.0.0`
7. Type `route print` and verify that the route has been deleted.

Dynamic Routing

Although static routers can work well on small networks, static networks are not suited to large, dynamic environments. Static routers are not fault-tolerant—if a network link goes down, a static router cannot automatically update its routing table and provide an alternative path for IP packets. It's time to look at *dynamic routers*.

A router with dynamically configured routing tables is known as a dynamic router. Dynamic routers have their routing tables built and maintained automatically by communicating with other dynamic routers. Dynamic routers automatically exchange update messages with routes to known networks. If Routers A and B in Figure 5.11 were dynamic routers, no additional configuration would be needed for all subnets to communicate.

Dynamic routers are fault-tolerant. The dynamic routing table entries learned from other routers have a finite lifetime and must be constantly updated to be valid. If a network link goes down, update messages stop coming and the associated routing table entries expire. When a routing table entry expires, the router does not send IP packets along the failed path. These changes are propagated to other dynamic routers. Using these procedures, dynamic routers sense the internetwork topology through the discovery and expiration of learned routes.

Dynamic routing relies on special routing protocols such as Routing Information Protocol (RIP) and Open Shortest Path First (OSPF).

Routing Information Protocol

Routing Information Protocol (RIP) for IP is used by dynamic routers to exchange routing information on an IP internetwork. RIP relies on the User Datagram Protocol (UDP) to forward route announcements. All RIP messages are sent over UDP port 520. A RIP-enabled router sends broadcast messages containing the network IDs of the networks it—the router—can reach and the distance (hop count) to these networks. Each time a RIP router receives a network ID announcement, it increases the hop count value, updates its routing table, and advertises the learned router to any intermediate routers. The maximum hop count for RIP is 15—networks requiring a greater number of hops are considered unreachable.

Not all RIP-enabled routers send out RIP packets. A RIP router that receives RIP broadcasts but does not propagate any RIP messages is known as a `silent RIP` router.

Figure 5.14 shows the *Network Monitor* capture of RIP packets. Note that each RIP packet can carry several network ID announcements.

Although RIP can work well in small and medium-sized networks with a small number of routers, it is not suitable for large enterprises. The following features of RIP make it a less desirable solution for large networks:

- The maximum RIP packet size is 512 bytes—large routing tables must be sent as multiple RIP packets.

- A RIP-enabled router sends RIP packets every 30 seconds through all attached interfaces. Since RIP uses MAC-level broadcasts, large routing tables can create a significant impact on network throughput. This is especially problematic on slow WAN links (for example, dial-up connections), where RIP packets can take large portions of bandwidth.

- Each routing table entry learned through RIP is given a three-minute timeout. If no update message is received, the entry is removed from the

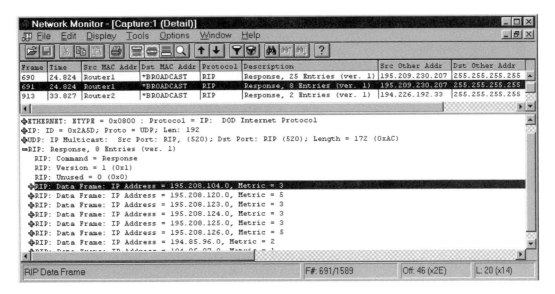

Figure 5.14 *RIP broadcasts.*

routing table after that period has elapsed. When a link problem occurs, it can take several minutes before the router discovers the problem and even longer before the topology change is propagated to the rest of the network. This feature is often referred to as *slow convergence*.

- Networks cannot be farther than 15 hops from each other. Since RIP packets have 15 as the maximum hop count, networks that require a greater number of hops are considered unreachable.

To overcome these limitations, other routing protocols can be used; for example, routing protocol OSPF (Open Shortest Path First). Open Shortest Path First is an Internet Engineering Task Force (IETF) standard, link-state routing protocol used for routing IP. OSPF is a more sophisticated routing protocol than RIP. Developed in response to the inability of RIP to serve large, heterogeneous internetworks, OSPF is a link-state protocol based on the Shortest Path First (SPF) algorithm. This algorithm computes the shortest path between one source node and the other nodes in the network.

 Windows NT does not include built-in support for the OSPF routing protocol. To use OSPF with Windows NT, you must install the Routing and Remote Access Service (RRAS).

Windows NT Computer as a Dynamic Router

A computer running Windows NT 4.0 can be configured as a dynamic router by installing *RIP for Internet Protocol* service. To install *RIP for IP,* use the `Services` tab on the `Network` dialog box. (See Figure 5.15.)

When *RIP for IP* is installed on a computer with only one network adapter, it will only receive RIP routing announcements and update its routing table—it will not send any routing announcements. This is known as *silent RIP.* To change this behavior, you can set the Registry parameter of `HKEY_LOCAL_MACHINE\System\CurrentControlSet\Services\IpRip-\Parameters\SilentRIP` to 0.

For more information about Windows NT Registry parameters for RIP, see Knowledge Base article Q169161, Registry Parameters for *RIP for IP* Version 1.

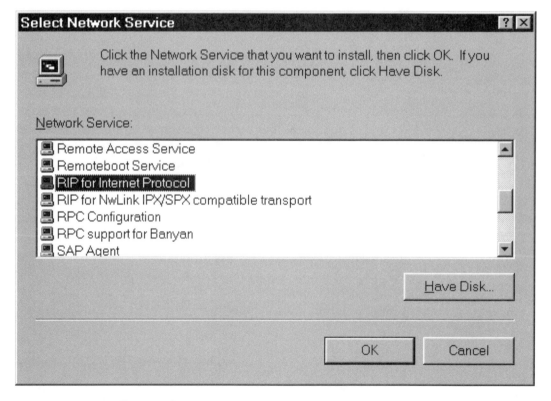

Figure 5.15 *Installing RIP for IP.*

Static and Dynamic Routers in the Same Network

A static router does not exchange routing information with dynamic routers. This can cause potential problems in environments where static and dynamic routers are used together. To solve the problem, you must add static routes to the routing tables of both static and dynamic routers. (See Figure 5.16.) The procedure for configuring static routes on a RIP router will vary with each type of RIP router. Figure 5.16 assumes the RIP router is Windows NT-based and can be configured using the ROUTE command.

> Some RIP implementations do not propagate static routes. For the network in Figure 5.16 to be visible from the Internet, you may need to configure static routes on remote routers as well.

Using the TRACERT Utility to Verify IP Routes

The TRACERT command is a route-tracing utility used to determine the path that an IP packet has taken to reach a destination. The TRACERT utility is useful for determining route problems such as routing table errors, slow routers, and router malfunctions. TRACERT has the functionality of

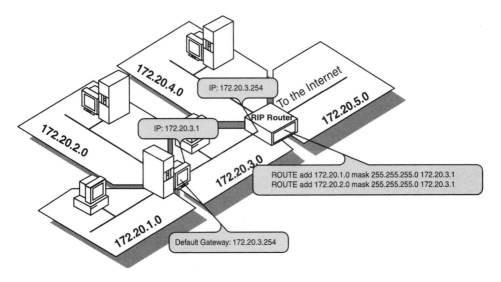

Figure 5.16   *Integrating static and dynamic routers.*

the PING utility, but goes further to display the path taken by a packet to the destination computer. The TRACERT command can be used to determine where a packet stopped on the network. Following is an example of TRACERT output:

```
C:\WINNT>tracert www.ru

Tracing route to www.ru [194.87.12.23]
over a maximum of 30 hops:

1    40 ms    80 ms    <10 ms    gw.csa.ru [194.226.192.33]
2    <10 ms   10 ms    10 ms     2048K.RUN.NET [194.85.165.169]
3    10 ms    <10 ms   10 ms     bbn-spb-gw.runnet.ru [194.85.36.30]
4    10 ms    10 ms    20 ms     Moscow-M9-IX-T0.RUN.NET [193.232.80.246]
5    41 ms    20 ms    20 ms     M9-IX-100M.demos.NET [193.232.244.35]
6    194.87.0.1 reports: Destination net unreachable.
Trace complete.
```

The output's first column is the Time To Live (TTL) value set by TRACERT (as we'll soon see, this is actually a hop count). The next three columns show round-trip times in milliseconds for three attempts to reach the destination with the set TTL. An asterisk (*) means that the attempt timed out. The fourth column is the host name (if it was resolved) and IP address of the resource that replied to the TRACERT packet.

TRACERT is a standard TCP/IP utility for route checking. In some operating systems, it is known as TRACEROUTE.

The TRACERT utility determines the route taken to the destination host by sending ICMP messages with varying Time-to-Live (TTL) values. As you may remember, each router must decrease the value in the TTL field by at least one, and when the new TTL reaches zero, the router discards the packet and sends the ICMP "Time Exceeded" message. In practice, the TTL is the hop count a packet can go before it is discarded. The TRACERT command utilizes this feature and starts by sending an ICMP packet with TTL=1. The first router to receive this packet decreases the TTL value (since the new TTL now equals zero), discards the packet, and returns an ICMP "Time Exceeded" message. The TRACERT utility receives the ICMP "Time Exceeded" message and displays the first router in the trace list. TRACERT

Table 5.2 *Tracert Options*

Option	Function
`-d`	Do not resolve addresses to host names.
`-h maximum_hops`	Maximum number of hops to search for target.
`-j host-list`	Lose source route along host list.
`-w timeout`	Wait timeout milliseconds for each reply.

then increments the TTL by one on each subsequent transmission until the target responds or the maximum TTL (hop count) is reached.

> **Some routers do not send ICMP "Time Exceeded" messages, but drop IP packets with zero TTLs silently. Such routers are invisible to the TRACERT utility.**

TRACERT can also be used with the following syntax using the options described in Table 5.2:

```
tracert [-d] [-h maximum_hops] [-j host-list] [-w timeout]
target_name
```

Study Break

Check the Route

To check the route to your default gateway, type:

```
tracert your_default_gateway
```

How many hops are there between your computer and your default gateway? To check the route to www.yahoo.com, type:

```
tracert www.yahoo.com
```

How far is www.yahoo.com?

Summary

This chapter introduced some important routing concepts. You learned that routing functions are not only performed by routers, but also by host computers. When a host makes routing decisions, we refer to it as host routing.

We saw that direct delivery occurs when a TCP/IP host or router can deliver a packet itself. We compared direct delivery to indirect delivery, which occurs when a packet must be forwarded to an intermediate router. Hosts and routers make forwarding decisions based on their local routing tables. We studied routing table entries and you learned the purpose of the network ID, gateway, and metric fields. We discussed the concept of the default gateway and how it is used by the routing table. You may remember that configuring a computer with a default gateway address adds the special default route (0.0.0.0) to the host's routing table. When multiple default gateways have been configured on a particular Windows NT computer, the host can take advantage of the TCP dead gateway detection algorithm and automatically switch to the next gateway when the primary is unavailable.

We mentioned that a computer running Windows NT could be configured as a static router by installing multiple network adapter cards and enabling IP forwarding. It was pointed out that static routes must be added to communicate with remote networks. We also saw that a Windows NT computer can act as a dynamic router. To implement dynamic routing on a Windows NT machine, RIP for Internet Protocol Service must be installed. We reviewed the primary features of the Routing Information Protocol (RIP) and saw that RIP wasn't a desirable solution in large dynamic networks because of its broadcast nature and nontrivial impact on network performance. Finally, we learned how to modify a Windows NT routing table and demonstrated the use of the TRACERT utility.

▲ REVIEW QUESTIONS

1. *What is routing?*
   A. The process of tracing the route from one host to another
   B. The process of counting the number of hops between hosts
   C. The process of transferring data across an internetwork from a source host to a destination host
   D. The process of modifying the routing table

2. *(True or False) Only routers can make routing decisions.*

3. *When a particular computer can send an IP packet without using a router, this is referred to as _____ delivery*
   A. Direct
   B. Host

    C. Straightforward

    D. Smart

4. *Which utility is used to modify the routing table?*

    A. TRACERT

    B. ROUTE

    C. IPCONFIG

    D. IFCONFIG

5. *What's the purpose of the metric field in the routing table?*

6. *A routing table defines paths to other* _____

    A. Routers

    B. Gateways

    C. Networks

    D. Users

7. *Suppose a host with an IP address of 172.20.1.10 has the following routing table fragment:*

Network Address	Netmask	Gateway Address	Interface	Metric
0.0.0.0	0.0.0.0	172.20.1.1	172.20.1.10	1
195.209.225.0	255.255.255.0	172.20.1.2	172.20.1.10	3
195.209.225.0	255.255.255.0	172.20.1.3	172.20.1.10	2

The host wants to send an IP packet to 195.209.225.100. To which gateway will this IP packet be forwarded?

    A. 172.20.1.1

    B. 172.20.1.2

    C. 172.20.1.3

    D. The IP packet will be discarded since there is no route to the destination network

8. *Suppose a host with the IP address of 172.20.1.10 has the following routing table fragment:*

Network Address	Netmask	Gateway Address	Interface	Metric
0.0.0.0	0.0.0.0	172.20.1.1	172.20.1.10	1
195.209.225.0	255.255.255.0	172.20.1.2	172.20.1.10	3
195.209.225.0	255.255.255.0	172.20.1.3	172.20.1.10	2

The host wants to send an IP packet to 131.0.200.100. To which gateway will this IP packet be forwarded?

   A. 172.20.1.1

   B. 172.20.1.2

   C. 172.20.1.3

   D. The IP packet will be discarded since there is no route to the destination network

9. *Which of the following is true about static routing?*

   A. Static routers do NOT exchange routing information with other routers

   B. Static routers can be implemented only on a multihomed Windows NT computer

   C. By default, static routers can route packets ONLY to networks to which they have a configured interface

   D. Static routers cannot have default gateways

10. *You want to add a new static route to network ID 172.25.0.0 on a multihomed Windows NT computer. You type the* ROUTE add *command. The route you just added works correctly, but when the computer is restarted, there is no route to 172.25.0.0. What's wrong?*

   A. Static routers cannot preserve routes after reboot

   B. The new route has timed out

   C. The ROUTE command was used without the –p switch

   D. The computer received a RIP announcement with a better path to the given network

11. *You want to implement a static IP router on a Windows NT computer. What must you do? (Select all that apply.)*

   A. Install multiple NICs or bind multiple IP addresses to a single NIC

   B. Install TCP/IP

   C. Enable IP forwarding

   D. Install *RIP for IP*

12. *You want to add a route to a remote network using the ROUTE utility. Which information must you supply to do this? (Select all that apply.)*

   A. IP address of the remote network

   B. Subnet mask

    C. Gateway IP address

    D. Local IP address

13. *Routing is a function of* _____

    A. IP

    B. TCP

    C. NT Server

    D. ARP

    E. NetBIOS

14. *A multihomed computer is a computer configured with multiple*

    A. Protocols

    B. IP addresses

    C. Network interfaces

    D. Operating systems

    E. User profiles

15. *Which is better for small, frequently changing networks with a small number of routers?*

    A. RIP

    B. Static routers

    C. NetBEUI

    D. Static routing

16. *How can you clear all routes in the Windows NT routing table?*

    A. `ROUTE delete`

    B. `ROUTE -f`

    C. `ROUTE -d`

    D. `ROUTE -s`

17. *How can you enable routing in Windows NT?*

    A. Using the IPCONFIG utility

    B. Using the PING utility

    C. Using the TRACERT utility

    D. Using the `TCP/IP Properties` dialog box

18. *How can you configure a default route on a Windows NT computer?*

    A. Using the IPCONFIG utility

    B. Using the ROUTE utility

    C. Using the TRACERT utility

    D. Using the `TCP/IP Properties` dialog box

19. *Refer to the network diagram in Figure 5.17. How must you configure Routers A and B so that the two workstations will be able to communicate? (Select all required steps.)*

    A. Configure a default gateway for Router A to 192.168.2.254

    B. Configure a default gateway for Router A to 192.168.3.1

    C. Configure a default gateway for Router B to 192.168.2.1

    D. Configure a default gateway for Router B to 192.168.1.1

20. *You have implemented a static router on a Windows NT Server computer (see Figure 5.18). What must you do to permit the two workstations to communicate? (Select all required steps.)*

    A. Set the default gateway on Workstation A to 192.168.1.1

    B. Set the default gateway on Workstation B to 192.168.2.1

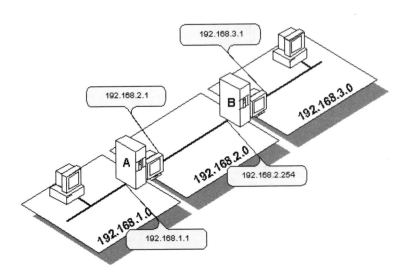

Figure 5.17 *Illustration for Review Question 19.*

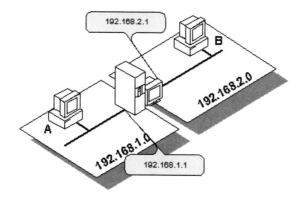

Figure 5.18 *Illustration for Review Question 20.*

C. Add static routes to subnets 192.168.1.1 and 192.168.2.1 on the multihomed computer

D. No additional configuration is needed

Dynamic Host Configuration Protocol

While configuring a few machines with IP addresses can be a moderately tedious task, the management of the IP configuration of a large number of client and server computers can quickly become a nightmare. Even minor errors in IP addresses and subnet masks can cause a machine to become unavailable to the network. Duplicate IP addresses can bring down every machine with the duplicate address, or possibly the entire network. In addition to duplicate IP address problems, the physical movement of computers can cause other inconsistencies. Simply connecting a computer to a new wire can place it on a subnet it's not configured for—once again causing its network functions to cease.

Microsoft TCP/IP mitigates the duplicate address problem by sending an *Address Resolution Protocol* (ARP) broadcast prior to initializing the TCP/IP stack. If another machine responds (indicating the address is already in use), the address is not initial-

137

ized on the new machine. Additionally, each machine receives a duplicate IP address warning.

When configuring a computer to use TCP/IP, we also need to configure a number of other features. Incorrect settings for the *Windows Internet Naming Service* (WINS), *Domain Name System* (DNS), and *default gateway* can occur through machine movement or reconfiguration, and can result in disastrous network consequences. Keeping track of all these factors on a large number of computers could quickly take all the time of the network administrator. Even a relatively minor network change (such as the introduction of a new WINS server) could require the reconfiguration of a large number of workstations with the attendant possibility of mis-configuration and network paralysis.

Before you head for the Internet to find another line of work, take heart! *The Dynamic Host Configuration Protocol* (DHCP) can be installed on one or more machines in your network to permit the automatic and centralized administration and configuration of a number of critical TCP/IP factors (including all those mentioned above). DHCP was developed as a cooperative effort between vendors and the *Internet Engineering Task Force*. It is covered under the following RFCs: 1533, 1534, 1541, and 1542 (these RFCs may be found at http://info.internet.isi.edu/7c/in-notes/rfc). DHCP works by "leasing" an IP address to a client for a specified period of time. When the client "signs" the lease, the DHCP server can throw in a number of options, such as WINS, DNS addresses, and default gateways, at no additional charge!

At the conclusion of this chapter, you'll be able to:

- Define DHCP.
- Explain the advantages of using DHCP.
- Explain the steps of the DHCP process.
- Describe the DHCP lease duration and renewal process.
- Install a DHCP server on a Windows NT computer.
- Configure a DHCP scope.
- Configure DHCP options.
- Install and configure a DHCP Relay Agent.
- Explain DHCP planning considerations.
- Test the DHCP implementation.
- Manage the DHCP database.
- Analyze DHCP network traffic.

The DHCP Process

The choreography between a DHCP client and DHCP server is a four-step process that permits the allocation and confirmation of important TCP/IP configuration information:

1. During the start-up process, the client computer initializes with a NULL IP address, broadcasts a DHCPDISCOVER message containing its hardware address and computer name, and requests an IP address from any DHCP server. (At this point, the machine knows no valid TCP/IP parameters, so it uses 0.0.0.0 as the source address and 255.255.255.255 as the destination address of the DHCPDISCOVER message.)

2. Any DHCP server that receives the DHCPDISCOVER broadcast and that has available valid configuration information for the client will respond with a DHCPOFFER message. Since the client still doesn't have an IP address at this point, the DHCPOFFER is sent via broadcast. The message contains the client's hardware address, an IP address offer, an appropriate subnet mask, the IP address of the server making the offer, and the lease duration. When the offer is made, the DHCP server marks the offered IP address as unavailable to prevent it from being offered to another client pending the original client's decision to take the lease. If a DHCP client does not hear from a DHCP server at startup, it retries four times every five minutes. Retries are made at 2, 4, 8, and 16-second intervals (plus a random amount between 0 and 1000 milliseconds). If no offer is received after the four attempts, the client will continue to seek a lease every five minutes until one is obtained.

3. The client selects one of the DHCP offers (normally the first one it receives) and responds with a DHCPREQUEST message. This message contains the IP address of the selected DHCP server, as well as a request for additional configuration information (e.g., WINS server address, DNS server address, etc.). Because the client's TCP/IP protocol is still not fully initialized, this message is also sent via broadcast. Since the DHCPREQUEST broadcast is received by all the DHCP servers who originally responded to the DHCPDISCOVER broadcast, the unselected servers are able to determine that their offers were rejected (by examining the message for the IP address of the *selected* server). Rejected servers then mark the IP addresses they offered as available.

4. The selected DHCP server responds with a DHCPACK (acknowledgment) message, containing a lease for the accepted IP address and any

other configuration parameters that might be available. This message is also sent via broadcast but, once it is received, the TCP/IP initialization is completed on the client. With initialization complete, the client machine is considered a *bound DHCP client,* which will be able to use TCP/IP for network communications.

> **Although the steps outlined here may seem fairly complex, they can be reduced to a simple acronym: DORA, for** `Discover, Offer, Request, Acknowledge.`

DHCP Lease Duration

DHCP leases may be assigned for a duration as short as one minute, as long as 999 days, 23 hours, and 59 minutes, or they may be assigned for an unlimited duration. When half of the client's lease period has elapsed, the client will attempt to renew the lease with the original DHCP server. If the server responds with a DHCPACK message, the lease is renewed and the client continues to use the originally assigned parameters. If the server responds with a DHCPNACK[1] (negative acknowledgment) message, the client is forced to send a DHCPDISCOVER broadcast and seek a new lease. If the original server doesn't respond, the client will continue to attempt to contact that machine until its lease is 7/8 (87.5%) complete. Once past the 7/8 point, the client will broadcast to any DHCP server in an attempt to renew its current lease. Any server can respond with a DHCPACK to renew, or a DHCP-NACK to force negotiation of a new lease. If the client fails to renew or renegotiate a lease prior to the expiration time of its current lease, it will lose its capability to use TCP/IP until it can obtain a new lease. When a lease expires, the server granting the lease actually keeps the lease marked as leased and unavailable for an additional 24 hours from the expiration time. This delay protects the lease if the client is in a time zone different from the DHCP server and the two computers' clocks are not synchronized. It also allows for the situation where the lease expired when the client was off the network.

---

[1] A DHCPNACK message is typically sent when a client's configuration information is incorrect. This may occur because the client has physically moved to a different subnet, or because the network configuration has changed since the lease was granted.

When a DHCP client is shut down, it retains its lease. (The lease information is retained in the Registry for Windows NT/Windows9x, and in DHCP.BIN for Windows for Workgroups or DOS clients.) When the machine is restarted, it attempts to renew the lease. If it receives a DHCPACK, the lease is renewed. A DHCPNACK will force the negotiation of a new lease. If the client gets neither a DHCPACK nor a DHCPNACK, it will continue to use the lease until it expires.

Installing DHCP on a Windows NT 4.0 Server

All this discussion of DHCP won't do anyone any good unless a DHCP server is actually installed, configured, and available on the network! To that end, let's take some time and install one. Any Windows NT Server version 3.5 or later can be configured as a DHCP server. The machine MUST have a static IP address and subnet mask. In other words, a DHCP server CANNOT also be a DHCP client. In addition to a static IP address and subnet mask, all other configuration information (WINS, DNS, default gateway, etc.) must also be statically configured. Additionally, if DHCP is running on a network with no DHCP Relay Agents and with routers that do not support RFC 1542, a DHCP server is required on each subnet (RFC 1542 and DHCP Relay Agents will be discussed later in this chapter). The installation of a DHCP server is done through the Services tab of the Network dialog box (see Figure 6.1). Since Windows NT will need to copy several files from the installation CD-ROM, ensure you have one available prior to the installation.

1. Select Add and Microsoft DHCP Server (see Figure 6.2).
2. Click OK and the system asks you to ensure that the Windows NT distribution files are available.
3. Make sure the appropriate directory is entered in the Windows NT Setup dialog box (see Figure 6.3) and click Continue.
4. Shortly after installation begins, you are shown a dialog box reminding you that the DHCP server can't also be a DHCP client (see Figure 6.4).
5. Reconfigure your adapter(s) for static IP addresses (if required) and click OK to continue.
6. Once the installation is complete, you are returned to the Network dialog box. Click Close and the system updates the network bindings.
7. At the conclusion of this step, you are given the option to restart the computer—click OK to restart the machine and complete the installation.

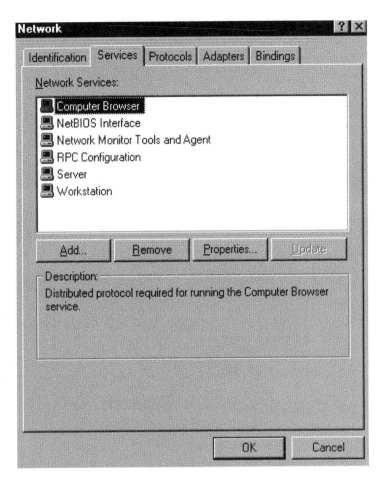

Figure 6.1 *Services tab of the* Network *dialog.*

Configuring DHCP Scopes and Options

Once we have installed DHCP, we still need to configure a *scope* and options for it to do us any good! DHCP server configuration is accomplished through the *DHCP Manager* program, accessible through `Administrative Tools (Common)` in the `Start` menu.

Adding a Scope

A scope is simply a range (or pool) of IP addresses and a subnet mask the DHCP server can lease to its clients. The scope also includes the lease dura-

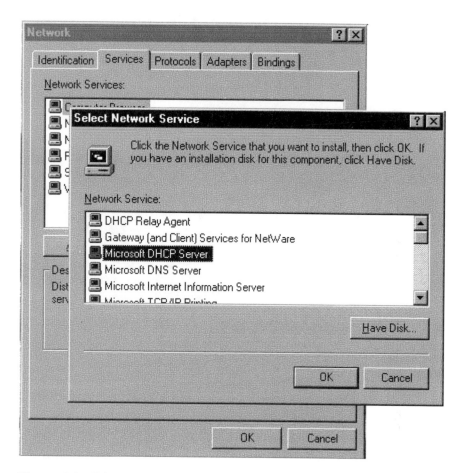

Figure 6.2 *Select Microsoft DHCP Server.*

tion and an optional name and comment. Each DHCP server must have at least one scope. Each scope on the server can represent a pool of IP addresses for one and only one subnet (although the server may be configured with scopes for several different subnets).

1. To add a scope, open the *DHCP Manager* through the Administrative Tools (Common) menu option.
2. If this is the first time you've run the application, it won't be aligned with any server. To correct this, double-click on *Local Machine* under DHCP Servers. This will cause the title bar to read DHCP Manager - (Local) and will align the *DHCP Manager* with your local server (see Figure 6.5).

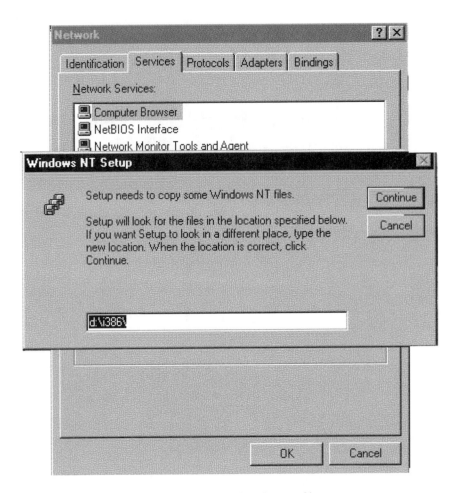

Figure 6.3 *Directory for Windows NT distribution files.*

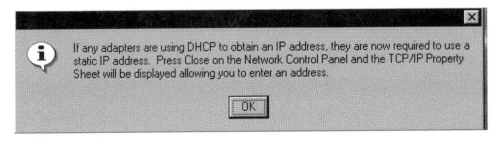

Figure 6.4 *Static IP address required.*

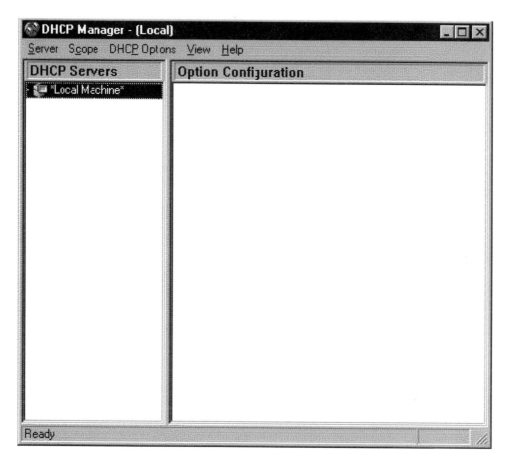

Figure 6.5 *DHCP Manager.*

3. Next, click on the Scope menu and select Create to reveal the Create Scope dialog box (see Figure 6.6).
4. Under IP Address Pool, enter the starting and ending IP addresses you wish to place in your scope, as well as the appropriate subnet mask for the scope's subnet.
5. If you have some IP addresses within the scope that are not to be given out to DHCP clients (this may be because the scope contains IP addresses that have already been assigned to non-DHCP clients as static addresses), enter the starting and ending addresses of the excluded range under Exclusion Range and click Add → to enter the range in the Excluded Addresses window.

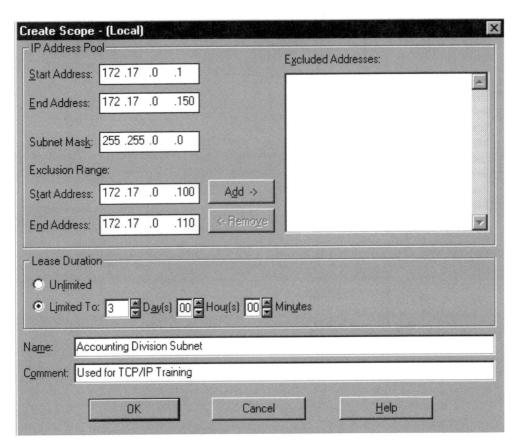

Figure 6.6 `Create Scope` *dialog box.*

6. You may enter several ranges of excluded addresses if required (this is not a mandatory entry). Under `Lease Duration`, select either `Unlimited` to permit leases that never expire or select `Limited To` and enter the desired values for `Day(s)`, `Hour(s)`, and `Minute(s)` before the lease must be renewed. You may also give your scope a name (which will be displayed after the IP address in the *DHCP Manager*) and include an additional comment. Neither the `Name` nor `Comment` fields require an entry.

7. Once you have filled the appropriate fields, click `OK`.

8. If you have done everything correctly, you are shown a dialog box that indicates the scope has been successfully created and asks if you wish to activate the scope. Only activated scopes are available to clients. You may either click `Yes` to activate the scope now or click `No` and activate it later through `Scope|Activate`.

The new scope is now visible in the *DHCP Manager* window as shown in Figure 6.7. As currently configured, the server will be available to provide IP addresses and subnet masks to any DHCP client that asks for an IP address on the subnet covered by the scope we just created. Although DHCP servers would be quite useful if they provided only IP addresses, their capability to provide additional TCP/IP information further reduces the burden of TCP/IP administration. To configure this additional information, we must set DHCP options.

Configuring DHCP Options

You can configure options through the *DHCP Manager's* DHCP Options menu. Two types of options can be set: *scope* and *global* options. Scope options apply only to the scope currently selected in the DHCP Servers window. When entered, scope options are depicted by a series of computer icons preceding them in the Option Configuration window. Scope options are appropriate when a particular value applies only to that scope. The address of a default gateway, for instance, would be valid only on a single

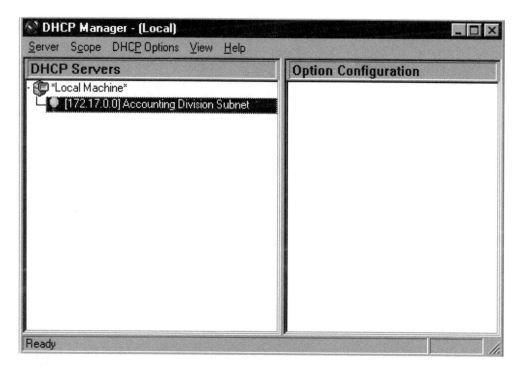

Figure 6.7 *New scope created and activated.*

subnet, making it a great candidate for a scope option. Global options, on the other hand, apply to every scope defined on the server. They are represented by a globe icon in the `Option Configuration` window. The address of a DNS server, for instance, could be valid for machines on several subnets and would likely be best used as a global option. Since we have configured only one scope for our server, the distinction between scope options and global options may seem a little fuzzy. Still, it's important to understand the difference and to make the appropriate choice to permit proper operation when and if additional scopes are added. Although the number of DHCP options that can be set is limited only by your ability to create them (*DHCP Manager* comes with a set of pre-defined options and you can create options of your own using `DHCP Options|Defaults`), we will set options only for a default gateway and WINS and DNS servers.

DEFAULT GATEWAY

A *default gateway* is simply a router that will permit the client to seek contact with machines not on its subnet. Since the address of a default gateway is subnet-specific, we will add the default gateway (or *router*) as a scope option.

1. In *DHCP Manager,* select `DHCP Options|Scope`, highlight `003 Router`, and click `Add` → to add this option to the `Active Options` window (see Figure 6.8).
2. But wait! The job isn't done yet. For the newly installed router to do us any good, we must also enter the router's IP address. To do this, click the `Value>>>` button. The `DHCP Options: Scope` dialog box expands to reveal an `Edit Array` button (see Figure 6.9).
3. Click on this button and enter the IP address of the default gateway in the `New IP Address` edit box (as shown in Figure 6.10).
4. Click `Add` → to add the IP address to the `IP Addresses` window.
5. Click `OK` to exit the `Array Editor` and then click `OK` again to exit the `DHCP Options: Scope` dialog box. The default gateway (router) option is complete.

DNS SERVER

Installation of the DNS server option is very similar to adding a default gateway. Since the address of our DNS server will be applicable to all subnets, however, we will install it as a global option.

1. While still in the *DHCP Manager,* select `DHCP Options|Global` and add option `006 DNS Servers`, just as we did when adding the router.

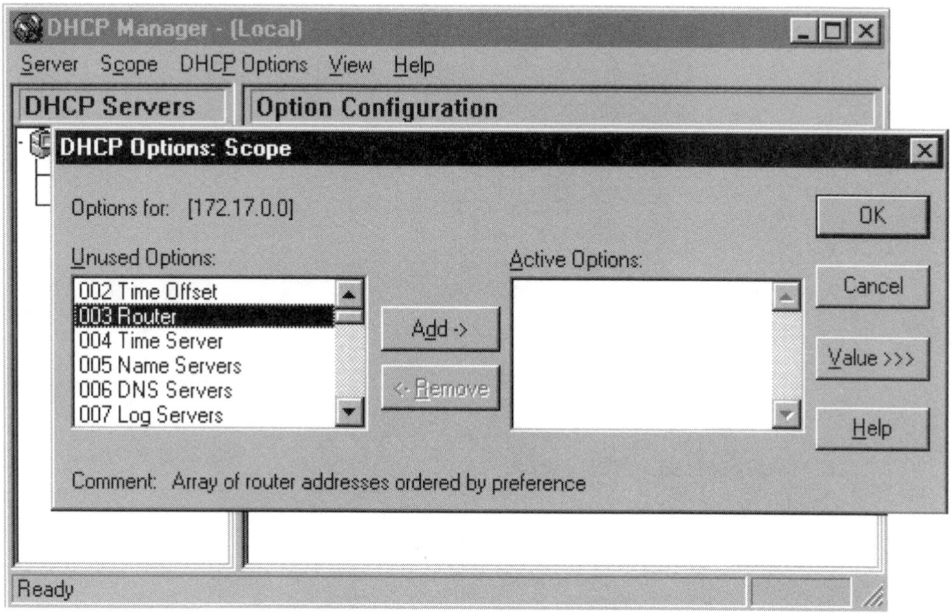

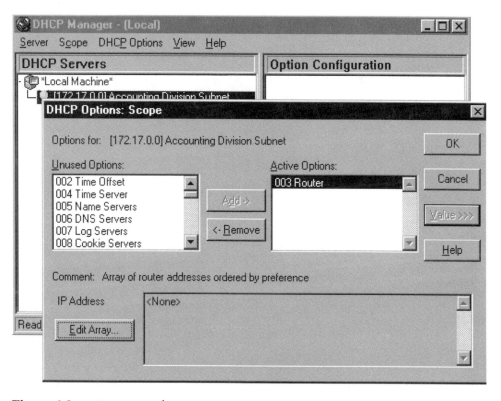

Figure 6.8 *Add a router.*

Figure 6.9 `Edit array` *button.*

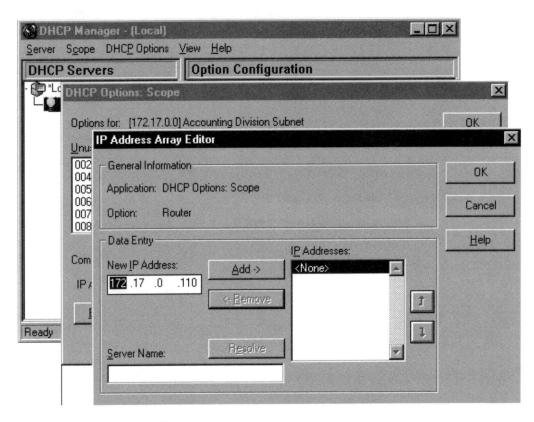

Figure 6.10 *Router IP address.*

2. Click on Value>>>, then Edit Array, and enter the IP address of the DNS server. Next, click OK twice and the DNS server appears as a global option in the Option Configuration window.

If a DNS server IP address is set in DNS Service Search Order on the DNS tab of the TCP/IP Properties dialog of the Network dialog box on the client, this local information will supersede that received from DHCP for the client. This is a two-edged sword! To change the DNS information for a single DHCP client, you can do so simply by entering information at the local machine. Remember, though, that the machine will no longer use the DNS server information provided by DHCP. When converting a computer to a DHCP client, be sure to check the DNS tab to determine if any information was previously set.

WINS SERVER

Setting options for a WINS server is a bit more involved than adding a DNS server or default gateway. We will need to set both the IP address of the WINS server and the method for NetBIOS name resolution. Since these items are not specific to a particular subnet, we will add our WINS server as a global option.

1. Using *DHCP Manager,* select DHCP Options|Global and choose option 044 WINS/NBNS servers.

2. Notice that as soon as you click Add →, you are shown a dialog box reminding you that you must also add option 046 WINS/NBT Node Type. Make a mental note of this and click OK.

3. Enter the IP address of the WINS server in the same manner we used for the default gateway and DNS server. Click OK to close the IP Address Array Editor and return to the DHCP Options|Global dialog.

4. Select option 046 WINS/NBT Node Type and click the Value>>> button (if required) to reveal the Node Type Edit window (see Figure 6.11). This screen allows you to select the default method (s) for name resolution. By default, no node type is selected (0×0). This screen gives you the option to select either a *B-node (0×1), P-node (0×2), M-node (0×4),* or *H-node (0×8).* All of which appears very interesting, but somewhat meaningless without a brief explanation! A *B-node* is a *broadcast* node. If configured to use a B-node, the client will attempt NetBIOS name resolution through broadcast only and will never call on the WINS server! A *P-node* is a *point-to-point* node. When using a P-node, the client will attempt name resolution through the WINS server only (computers configured to use P-node will neither use a broadcast message for name resolution nor respond to a name resolution broadcast made by another machine on the network). An *M-node* is a *mixed* node. Using this scheme, broadcast resolution is attempted first. If that method fails, the client will contact the WINS server. Finally, an *H-node* is a *hybrid* node. With a hybrid node, the client first contacts the WINS server. If the WINS server cannot provide resolution, the client resorts to a broadcast. Since the H-node provides primary use of WINS with a broadcast backup, select this node type by entering 0×8 in the edit box. Click OK to close the DHCP Options|Global dialog box and complete the DHCP configuration. (We will delve a bit more deeply into name resolution modes in the next chapter.)

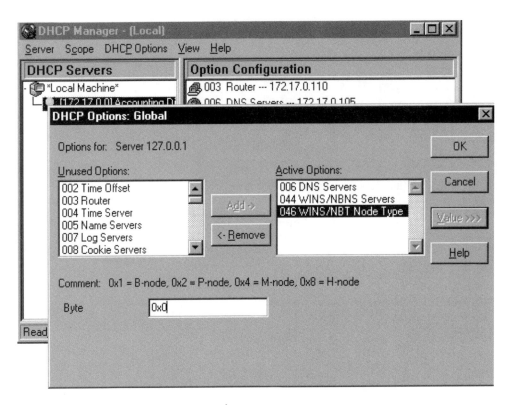

Figure 6.11 `Node Type Edit` *window.*

Warning

If a WINS server IP address is set in the `Primary WINS Server` or `Secondary WINS Server` field on the `WINS Address` tab of the `TCP/IP Properties` dialog of the `Network` dialog box on the client, this local information will supersede that received from DHCP for the client. As with DNS configuration information, to change the WINS information for a single DHCP client, you can do so simply by entering information at the local machine. Remember, though, that the machine will no longer use the WINS server information provided by DHCP. When converting a computer to a DHCP client, be sure to check the `WINS` tab to determine if any information was previously set.

As shown in Figure 6.12, your DHCP server is now capable of providing clients with an IP address and subnet mask, as well as a default gateway and the addresses for WINS and DNS servers. This has sharply reduced the client TCP/IP configuration load. Furthermore, to change the address of one of the servers or the node type, the administrator needs only to alter those

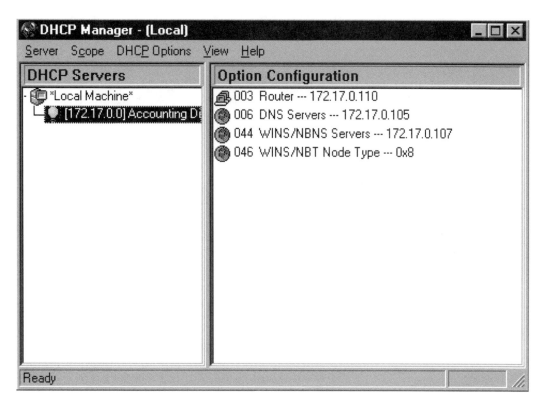

Figure 6.12 *DHCP local and global options.*

values at the DHCP server rather than visiting every workstation in the network! If, for instance, you've added an additional DNS server and wish to configure all your DHCP clients to use it, simply perform the following steps:

1. In *DHCP Manager,* select DHCP Options|Global. (We installed DNS as a global option. If we had installed it as a scope option, we would have used DHCP Options|Scope.)
2. In the Active Options window, select 006 DNS Servers and click the Value>>> button.
3. Click the Edit Array button, enter the IP address for the new server, and click Add.

Adding a DHCP Server

If you are operating on a production network that uses DHCP, you may need to disconnect your machine from the network since your computer will begin to provide IP addresses to network DHCP clients as soon as you configure a scope—make sure you consult your network administrator prior to performing this exercise. If, on the other hand, you're sitting at a lone machine with no network connection, you'll have to use your own machine as the server, default gateway, DNS server, and WINS server. This makes the exercise substantially less exciting, but will permit you to accomplish all the configuration steps!

1. Install DHCP. The first step is to actually install the server. Refer to the section titled *"Installing DHCP on a Windows NT 4.0 Server"* and perform the listed steps to install the DHCP server.
2. Add a Scope. With your server running, you must now create a scope. If you are connected to a production network, consult with your network administrator for IP addresses to use in the scope. Otherwise, you can add IP addresses from the Ten Net (e.g., 10.0.0.2– 10.0.0.100). Refer to the section titled *"Adding a Scope"* and follow the steps to add a scope.
3. Configure a Default Gateway. Now it's time to add the default gateway. If there is a default gateway available to you in your network, use its IP address. (You can either check the `TCP/IP Properties` dialog's `IP Address` tab of your own machine or consult your network administrator for the information.) If you are at a stand-alone machine, you may use your own IP address here. (This chapter shows how to accomplish this as a scope option. Since you have only one scope, you may add this as a scope or global option, but would typically use a scope option here in case you were to later add additional scopes.) Refer to the section titled *"Default Gateway"* and complete the listed steps.
4. Add a DNS server. We can now add a DNS server as a global option. As with the default gateway, use an existing DNS server (if one is available), otherwise use your own IP address. (Contact your network administrator to see if you have any DNS servers available.) Refer to the section titled *"DNS Server"* and follow the steps to install this option.
5. Add a WINS server. Finally, let's add a WINS server and name resolution node. Again, check with your network administrator and use an existing WINS server address if one is available; otherwise, use your own IP address. When installing the name resolution node, select the hybrid node (we'll talk more about these in the next chapter). Refer to the *"WINS Server"* section and follow the listed steps.
   Now refer to Figure 6.12. Does your *DHCP Manager* display show a scope and scope and global options similar to those in the diagram?

MCSE 6.2   DHCP Relay Agent

Now that your DHCP server is up and running with a single scope, what if you wanted to add another scope? You could give out IP addresses for machines on other subnets, but since they must use non-routable broadcast traffic to reach your DHCP server, how will they communicate with the DHCP server? The answer is the *DHCP Relay Agent!* A router that conforms to RFC 1542 will perform as a DHCP Relay Agent. When an IP request packet reaches a DHCP Relay Agent, the Relay Agent will forward the request to the next network, but will tag the packet with the requestor's home network to ensure the DHCP server will return an address for the appropriate subnet.

DHCP is partially based on an earlier RFC called the Bootstrap Protocol. Because of this, DHCP Relay Agents are sometimes referred to as *BOOTP Relay Agents.*

Configuring a Windows NT Server as a DHCP Relay Agent

A multihomed Windows NT server configured as a router (with multiple IP addresses and with *IP forwarding* enabled) can be additionally configured as a DHCP Relay Agent, making it an RFC 1542-compliant router. A *multihomed* server is one equipped with more than one network interface card and which can operate on more than one subnet.

You may also install the DHCP Relay Agent on a Windows NT server that is NOT configured as a router. A non-router DHCP Relay Agent will accept the IP lease request and forward it through the appropriate router to a DHCP server on a remote network.

1. Install the DHCP Relay Agent service through the `Services` tab of the `Network` dialog box, just as we did to install the DHCP server.
2. At the conclusion of the installation, you may be asked if you wish to add an IP address for a DHCP server. If you respond `Yes`, you will be taken to the `DHCP` tab of the `TCP/IP Properties` dialog of the `Network` dialog (see Figure 6.13). If you answer `No` or if you are not given the opportunity to add a DHCP server address, select the `Network` dialog, select the `Protocols` tab, select `TCP/IP,` and click on the `Properties` button.
3. Select the `DHCP Relay` tab (Figure 6.13).

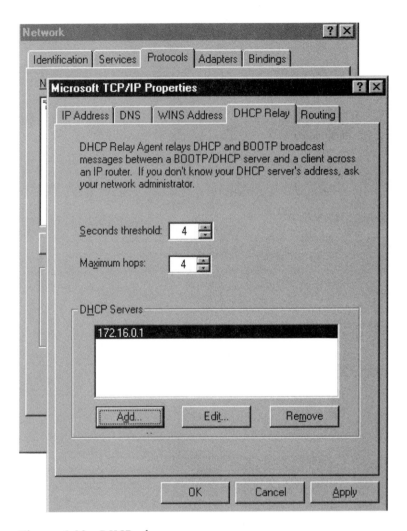

Figure 6.13 *DHCP relay.*

4. Click the Add button and enter the IP addresses of all the DHCP servers to which you want your Relay Agent to forward IP request packets.

Seconds Threshold and Maximum Hops may be left at their default values. Seconds Threshold represents the amount of time the IP request packet will be limited to the local subnet before the Relay Agent will forward it. Maximum Hops sets the maximum number of times the IP request packet will be routed before it is discarded. With the DHCP Relay Agent functioning, your DHCP server can provide IP addresses to DHCP clients on subnets beyond its home network (provided it possesses valid IP address information for them). This will permit you, for instance, to maintain DHCP servers on a single subnet that can provide DHCP information to clients on neighboring subnets. It also allows you to give each DHCP server addresses for neighboring subnets. Each DHCP server can then give out appropriate addresses (through the Relay Agent) in the event the DHCP server that usually services the subnet goes down.

Study Break
_____

Adding the DHCP Relay Agent Service

In an earlier exercise, you installed the DHCP server service. You would not typically install the Relay Agent on the same machine running DHCP server (this would be superfluous because any DHCP client that could reach the Relay Agent on your machine should also be able to obtain a lease from the DHCP server on your machine). This exercise will, however, allow you to try your hand at configuring a DHCP Relay Agent. Check with your network administrator (if applicable) to see if there is a DHCP server on another network segment that is qualified to provide information for your network. If so, configure your computer as a Relay Agent for that server (use the DHCP server's IP address). If there are no servers available, you can use your own IP address, but you should understand that configuring a machine as a Relay Agent to a DHCP server operating on the same computer has no practical application and is used here as a training opportunity only. Refer to the steps listed in this section and install a DHCP Relay Agent. What does a functioning Relay Agent permit DHCP clients on your network to do?

DHCP Planning and Operational Considerations

Now that we have seen how to set up and configure a DHCP server, DHCP-Relay Agents, and DHCP-capable routers (which can simply be a multi-homed Windows NT computer with the DHCP Relay Agent installed), let's spend a little time looking at how to plan and optimize DHCP services on the network.

Clients

Will all your machines become DHCP clients? If not, you'll need to ensure that the non-DHCP clients have static addresses that don't conflict with any of your DHCP address pools. Does a DHCP client require a specific IP address? If so, you'll need to reserve the address using _DHCP Manager_.

1. Select `Scope|Add Reservations` to reveal the `Add Reserved Clients` dialog box (see Figure 6.14).
2. Enter the IP address you wish to reserve and the machine's MAC address (`Unique Identifier`). Note that the MAC address is entered here without the hyphens we normally see when looking at it using IPCONFIG (discussed in the next section) and other utilities.
3. You may also enter a `Client Name` and `Client Comment` for better identification.

DHCP clients can be configured on computers running Windows NT (Workstation or Server), Windows 95/98, Windows for Workgroups 3.11 (running TCP/IP-32), Microsoft Network Client 3.0 for Microsoft-DOS (with the real-mode TCP/IP driver), or LAN Manager 2.2c (LAN Manager 2.2c for OS/2 is not supported).

Subnets

Will your server provide IP addresses for multiple subnets? If so, ensure you've installed DHCP Relay Agents unless all your routers are RFC 1542-compliant. You will also need to make sure you've installed scopes on the DHCP servers that support the additional subnets.

Servers

Remember that DHCP servers must operate on a Windows NT server using a static IP address. How many servers are required? If your network has multiple subnets and you don't have RFC 1542-compliant routers or DHCP

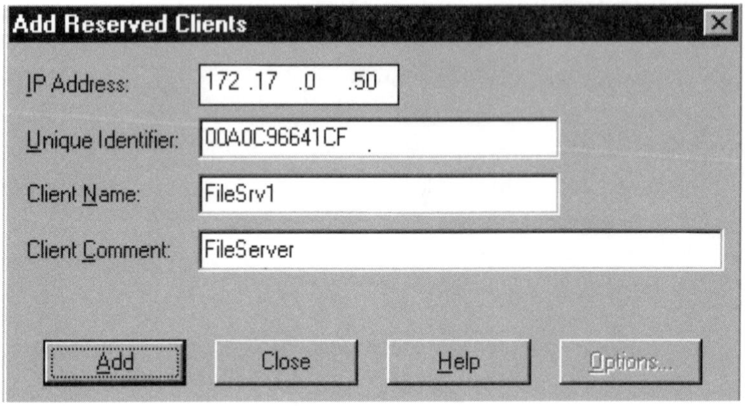

Figure 6.14 *Add* `Reserved Clients` *window.*

Relay Agents, you'll need a DHCP server on each subnet. There should always be at least two DHCP servers available to DHCP clients to ensure clients can get addresses when a server goes down. When servers are used across multiple subnets, Microsoft recommends that each server should have scopes that comprise 70-75 percent of the available IP addresses on its local subnet and 25-30 percent of the available addresses on a remote subnet. Remember that DHCP servers don't talk to each other; it is critical, therefore, to ensure each server has a pool of IP addresses that aren't contained in any other server's address list.

Options

Determine what options your DHCP server will use. Will you configure your server to supply a router address (for a default gateway), a DNS server address, a WINS server address, or any additional options?

Client Configuration

All this excitement about DHCP won't do us much good unless we configure some machines to act as DHCP clients. DHCP cannot force its information on any machine. The machine must first be configured to ask for the information! To configure a Windows NT computer to act as a DHCP client, simply go to the Network dialog and select Protocols|TCP/IP/Protocol|Properties. Click on the IP Address tab and click the Obtain an IP address from a DHCP server radio button (see Figure 6.15). If the system previously had static *IP Address, Subnet Mask,* and *Default Gateway* values, they will be lost when you click OK or Apply.

IPCONFIG and IP Parameters

The IPCONFIG utility permits the viewing of client configuration information, as well as the release and renewal of IP address leases. (A similar utility, WINIPCFG, provides comparable capabilities for Windows 95/98 computers through a graphical user interface.) IPCONFIG is executed from the Windows NT command prompt with the following syntax:

```
Ipconfig [/? | /all | /release [adapter] | /renew
[adapter]]
```

By typing IPCONFIG, you can view the machine's IP address, subnet mask, and default gateway. If the IP address is shown as 0.0.0.0, you can conclude that the client was unable to obtain an IP address from the DHCP server (if, of course, the machine is a DHCP client). You can type IPCONFIG

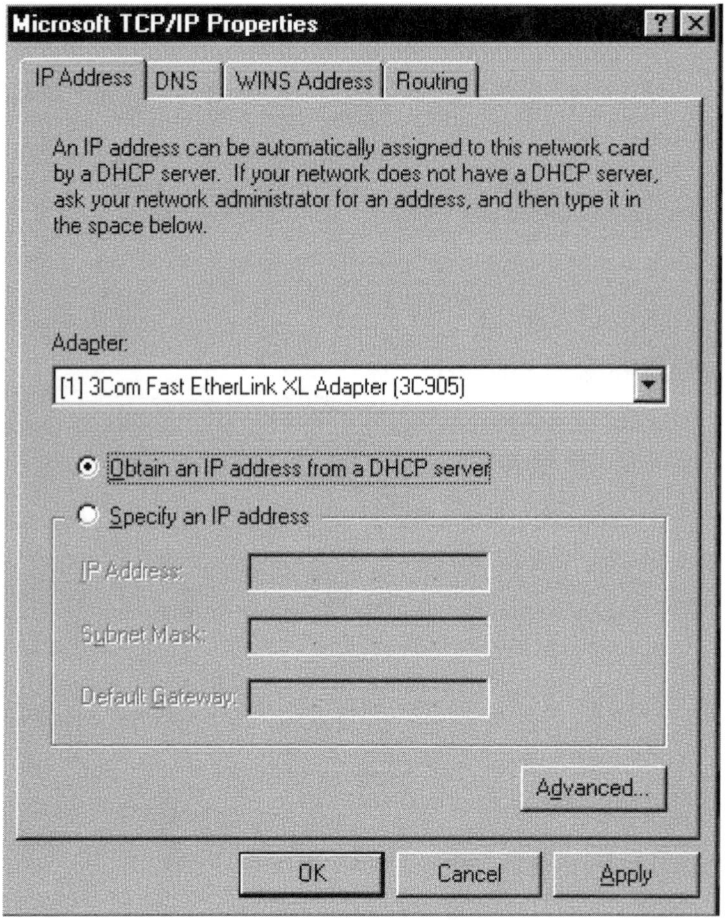

Figure 6.15 *DHCP client configuration.*

/RENEW to force an IP address renewal for the adapter specified, or IPCON-
FIG /RELEASE to force the release of a DHCP-supplied address for a particular adapter. If no adapter names are supplied, the release or renew will be
for all adapters bound to TCP/IP on the machine. By typing IPCONFIG
/ALL, you can view the detailed parameter list displayed in Figure 6.16. In
addition to the basic information provided by IPCONFIG, the /ALL option
provides other important information such as WINS and DNS server addresses, the default gateway address, and the computer's MAC address
(physical address). If any DHCP-supplied data is shown as zeroes or is not
available, suspect a problem with the DHCP lease.

```
C:\>ipconfig /all

Windows NT IP Configuration

        Host Name . . . . . . . . . : FilSvr3
        DNS Servers . . . . . . . . : 172.17.0.105
        Node Type . . . . . . . . . : Hybrid
        NetBIOS Scope ID. . . . . . :
        IP Routing Enabled. . . . . : No
        WINS Proxy Enabled. . . . . : No
        NetBIOS Resolution Uses DNS : No

Ethernet adapter E190x1:

        Description . . . . . . . . : 3Com 3C90x Ethernet Adapter
        Physical Address. . . . . . : 00-60-08-20-A2-86
        DHCP Enabled. . . . . . . . : Yes
        IP Address. . . . . . . . . : 172.16.0.20
        Subnet Mask . . . . . . . . : 255.255.0.0
        Default Gateway . . . . . . : 172.16.0.9
        DHCP Server . . . . . . . . : 172.16.0.10
        Primary WINS Server . . . . : 172.16.0.1
        Secondary WINS Server . . . : 172.16.0.10
        Lease Obtained. . . . . . . : Monday, November 23, 1998 3:48:01 PM
        Lease Expires . . . . . . . : Thursday, November 26, 1998 3:48:01 PM
```

Figure 6.16 *Results of* IPCONFIG/ALL.

Managing the DHCP Database

As you might have guessed, since DHCP must handle a large amount of data (IP addresses, subnet masks, lease durations, WINS/DNS addresses, etc.), it must maintain a database. Fortunately, DHCP uses the Microsoft Jet database engine (the same engine that runs *Microsoft Access*), which has proven to be a robust and reliable product, requiring very little user intervention.

DATABASE BACKUP AND RESTORATION

The database is automatically backed up every hour and written to the \systemroot\SYSTEM32\DHCP\BACKUP\JET directory. The default backup interval is set at 60 minutes in HKEY_LOCAL_MACHINE\SYSTEM\Current-ControlSet\Services\DHCPServer\Parameters\BackupInterval (a copy of the Registry key is also stored as \systemroot\SYSTEM32\DHCP\BACKUP\DHCPCFG. In the event of corruption, the database is automatically restored when the DHCP server service is started (or restarted), but manual restoration may be accomplished using two methods:

1. Copy the contents of the \systemroot\SYSTEM32\DHCP\BACKUP\JET directory to the \systemroot\SYSTEM32\DHCP directory and restart the DHCP server service.
2. Set the HKEY_LOCAL_MACHINE\SYSTEM\CurrentControlSet\Services\DHCPServer \Parameters\RestoreFlag value to 1 and restart the service. This will force the server to accomplish an automatic restore. Once the restore is complete, the RestoreFlag value will be automatically reset to zero.

COMPACTING THE DATABASE

Windows NT Server 4.0 will automatically compact the DHCP database. Earlier Windows NT versions did not, however, offer this convenience. Whenever the database approaches 30 MB on a Windows NT 3.51, or earlier system, you should take action to compact the database. To compact the database:

1. Stop the DHCP Server service (use the Control Panel|Services option or type net stop dhcpserver at the command line prompt).
2. Go to the \systemroot\SYSTEM32\DHCP directory and run the *JET-PACK* utility. To run JETPACK, type jetpack dhcp.mdb temp.mdb (you may actually use any filename for "temp.mdb" as long as it has an .mdb extension). This action causes dhcp.mdb to be compacted into temp.mdb.
3. When the compact is complete, temp.mdb is copied back to dhcp.mdb and temp.mdb is deleted.
4. Once you have compacted the database, restart the DHCP server service (use the Control Panel|Services option or type net start dhcpserver at the command line).

FILES USED BY THE DHCP DATABASE

The files listed in Table 6.1 are used by the DHCP database. They are located in \systemroot\SYSTEM32\DHCP and should be neither deleted nor modified.

Table 6.1 *DHCP Database Files*

Filename	Description
DHCP.MDB	DHCP database
DHCP.TMP	DHCP.TMP
J50.LOG	Database transaction log—used by DHCP for automatic data recovery
SYSTEM.MDB	Database file that DHCP uses to store database structure information

Analyzing the Impact of DHCP Traffic on the Network

DHCP is designed to place minimal impact on the network. While you won't typically need to spend a lot of time trying to optimize DHCP network traffic, a good working knowledge of the DHCP network signature will permit you to isolate difficulties arising from DHCP configuration problems such as short lease durations or the forwarding of DHCP messages from subnets for which the server has no scope. There are two main types of DHCP network communications: *IP address lease acquisition and IP address lease renewal.* We will look at these activities using the Network Monitor that we installed in Chapter 1, "Introduction to TCP/IP."

IP ADDRESS LEASE ACQUISITION

As we mentioned at the start of this chapter, the IP address lease acquisition process consists of four steps: *Discover, Offer, Request,* and *Acknowledgement.* Each step uses a frame of 342–590 bytes, depending on the client and selected configuration options. The total process is depicted in Figure 6.17, which shows *Network Monitor's* high-level representation of the four steps—we'll drill down through one of them in a moment.

The four steps are typically accomplished in a quarter second and place 1,368 bytes on the network. You'll remember that we said that all the initial lease acquisition traffic is accomplished through broadcast—this is verified by the *Network Monitor* depiction.

All four frames have essentially the same structure, so we'll look at the features of the Discover frame to help us understand what is going on in the process. Looking first at the frame's Ethernet header (shown in Figure 6.18), we can see a destination address of all Fs, indicating a media access control broadcast. We can also verify a 342-byte frame length.

A look at the IP header (shown in Figure 6.19) shows a source address of 0.0.0.0 and a destination address of 255.255.255.255. The zeroes are because this client is still in want of an IP address. The 255s signify a network broadcast—if the network has BOOTP-compliant routers, this addressing will permit forwarding these packets to other subnets.

Frame	Time	Src MAC Addr	Dst MAC Addr	Protocol	Description
7	92.676	Client1	*BROADCAST	DHCP	Discover
8	92.702	DHCPSVR	*BROADCAST	DHCP	Offer
9	92.703	Client1	*BROADCAST	DHCP	Request
10	92.764	DHCPSVR	*BROADCAST	DHCP	ACK

Figure 6.17 *Lease acquisition steps as shown in Network Monitor.*

```
⊟ETHERNET: ETYPE = 0x0800 : Protocol = IP:  DOD Internet Protocol
 ⊕ETHERNET: Destination address : FFFFFFFFFFFF
 ⊕ETHERNET: Source address : 00600820A286
  ETHERNET: Frame Length : 342 (0x0156)
  ETHERNET: Ethernet Type : 0x0800 (IP:  DOD Internet Protocol)
  ETHERNET: Ethernet Data: Number of data bytes remaining = 328 (0x0148)
```

Figure 6.18 *Ethernet header.*

The *User Datagram Protocol* (UDP) header shows a source port (BOOTP client) of 68 and a destination port (BOOTP server) of 67 (see Figure 6.20). If your routers support these ports, they are BOOTP-(RFC 1542) compliant and will be able to forward your IP requests to other subnets. If your router does not support ports 67 and 68, it is not BOOTP-compliant. In this case, you'll need to ensure that DHCP Relay Agents are installed on any networks which contain DHCP clients that will use this router to contact a DHCP server. As you might expect, all of the DHCP work is done under the DHCP header.

Looking at the request header, we can see all the IP addresses are set to zero in the Discover message (see Figure 6.21). This, obviously, is because no DHCP lease has been consummated at this point. The only identification here is the client's MAC address. By the time we get to the Acknowledgement message (see Figure 6.22), the client can find its leased IP address in the Your IP Address field and the other provided network options under the Option field.(The discerning student will notice the lease length is set

```
⊟IP: ID = 0x0; Proto = UDP; Len: 328
  IP: Version = 4 (0x4)
  IP: Header Length = 20 (0x14)
 ⊕IP: Service Type = 0 (0x0)
  IP: Total Length = 328 (0x148)
  IP: Identification = 0 (0x0)
 ⊕IP: Flags Summary = 0 (0x0)
  IP: Fragment Offset = 0 (0x0) bytes
  IP: Time to Live = 128 (0x80)
  IP: Protocol = UDP - User Datagram
  IP: Checksum = 0x39A6
  IP: Source Address = 0.0.0.0
  IP: Destination Address = 255.255.255.255
  IP: Data: Number of data bytes remaining = 308 (0x0134)
```

Figure 6.19 *IP header.*

```
⇒UDP: IP Multicast:   Src Port: BOOTP Client, (68); Dst Port: BOOTP Server (67)
 UDP: Source Port = BOOTP Client
 UDP: Destination Port = BOOTP Server
 UDP: Total length = 308 (0x134) bytes
 UDP: UDP Checksum = 0xE14F
 UDP: Data: Number of data bytes remaining = 300 (0x012C)
```

Figure 6.20 *UDP header.*

to four minutes. Although such a short lease duration is hardly recommended, it did facilitate a quick lease renewal for the purpose of generating renewal frames to depict in this book!)

ADDRESS LEASE RENEWAL

The lease renewal process is quite similar to the acquisition process, except that we can go directly to the *Request* phase and, since the DHCP client has a valid IP address when making the renewal request, communications need not be carried out at the broadcast level. Were you to examine the frames shown in Figure 6.23, you would find their contents very similar to those of the IP address acquisition process. As with acquisition frames, these are typically 342 bytes in length and the entire renewal process takes about 100 milliseconds.

```
⇒DHCP: Discover                (xid=4D4621AF)
  DHCP: Op Code            (op)     = 1 (0x1)
  DHCP: Hardware Type      (htype)  = 1 (0x1) 10Mb Ethernet
  DHCP: Hardware Address Length (hlen) = 6 (0x6)
  DHCP: Hops               (hops)   = 0 (0x0)
  DHCP: Transaction ID     (xid)    = 1296441775 (0x4D4621AF)
  DHCP: Seconds            (secs)   = 0 (0x0)
 ⊕DHCP: Flags              (flags)  = 0 (0x0)
  DHCP: Client IP Address (ciaddr) = 0.0.0.0
  DHCP: Your   IP Address (yiaddr) = 0.0.0.0
  DHCP: Server IP Address (siaddr) = 0.0.0.0
  DHCP: Relay  IP Address (giaddr) = 0.0.0.0
  DHCP: Client Ethernet Address (chaddr) = 00600820A286
  DHCP: Server Host Name   (sname)  = <Blank>
  DHCP: Boot File Name     (file)   = <Blank>
  DHCP: Magic Cookie = [OK]
 ⊕DHCP: Option Field       (options)
```

Figure 6.21 *DHCP Discover header.*

```
⊟DHCP: ACK                     (xid=5F84263B)
   DHCP: Op Code               (op)     = 2 (0x2)
   DHCP: Hardware Type         (htype)  = 1 (0x1) 10Mb Ethernet
   DHCP: Hardware Address Length (hlen) = 6 (0x6)
   DHCP: Hops                  (hops)   = 0 (0x0)
   DHCP: Transaction ID        (xid)    = 1602496059 (0x5F84263B)
   DHCP: Seconds               (secs)   = 0 (0x0)
  ⊕DHCP: Flags                 (flags)  = 0 (0x0)
   DHCP: Client IP Address (ciaddr) = 0.0.0.0
   DHCP: Your   IP Address (yiaddr) = 172.16.0.1
   DHCP: Server IP Address (siaddr) = 0.0.0.0
   DHCP: Relay  IP Address (giaddr) = 0.0.0.0
   DHCP: Client Ethernet Address (chaddr) = 00600820A286
   DHCP: Server Host Name   (sname)  = <Blank>
   DHCP: Boot File Name     (file)   = <Blank>
   DHCP: Magic Cookie = [OK]
  ⊟DHCP: Option Field       (options)
     DHCP: DHCP Message Type       = DHCP ACK
     DHCP: Renewal Time Value (T1) =  0:02:00
     DHCP: Rebinding Time Value (T2) =  0:03:30
     DHCP: IP Address Lease Time   =  0:04:00
     DHCP: Server Identifier       = 172.16.0.10
     DHCP: Subnet Mask             = 255.255.0.0
     DHCP: Router                  = 172.16.0.9
     DHCP: NetBIOS Name Service    = 172.17.0.107
     DHCP: NetBIOS Node Type       = (Length: 1) 08
     DHCP: Domain Name Server      = 172.17.0.105
     DHCP: End of this option field
```

Figure 6.22   *DHCP Acknowledgement header.*

DHCP TRAFFIC OPTIMIZATION

As we've already stated, DHCP has only a minor impact on the network. There are, in fact, only two areas where optimization can prove fruitful: lease duration and DHCP threshold.

LEASE DURATION • Obviously, the longer the lease duration, the less DHCP renewal traffic will be required on the network. Why, then, don't we simply

Frame	Time	Src MAC Addr	Dst MAC Addr	Protocol	Description
1183	212.858	Client1	DHCPSVR	DHCP	Request
1184	212.889	DHCPSVR	Client1	DHCP	ACK

Figure 6.23   *IP address renewal.*

make all our leases good forever? If you have a very large address pool and a static environment, this would be a great idea. Most of us need to make changes from time to time, however. If, for instance, your DHCP clients never need to ask to renew their leases, they run the risk of missing changes and additions you make to WINS servers, DNS servers, and other DHCP-supplied information. If this were the case, your only choice would be to cancel each DHCP lease and force all your clients to renegotiate their leases. Additionally, if your address pool is close to the number of DHCP clients in your environment, you run the risk of running out of addresses when machines go down or are moved to different subnets.

To optimize the lease duration, take a look at address pool size and the stability of your network. As the pool size and stability grow, you can consider increasing the lease duration three days beyond the default. Conversely, if you have a particularly small pool or dynamic environment, you may need to shorten the lease duration. RFC 1541 does not allow a lease duration of less than one hour. The Microsoft implementation of DHCP, however, permits assigning a lease duration as short as one minute for testing. Microsoft emphasizes that durations of less than one hour should not be used in a production environment, warning that the DHCP server may function irregularly.

DHCP THRESHOLD · If you're using DHCP Relay Agents to accomplish DHCP leases across multiple networks, you may be forwarding DHCP packets when you don't need to, contributing to unnecessary cross-network traffic. This occurs when the local DHCP server is slow to respond to DHCP requests and the Relay Agents forward the requests to other servers. This may occur if the local server is tasked with other operations in addition to DHCP, or if it is busy handling DHCP requests. If you discover that too many of your DHCP requests are going to other networks, you may want to lighten the load of the DHCP server or create another local DHCP server and split your address pool between the two local servers. If you can't make either of those modifications, you may be able to configure the Relay Agent to wait longer before forwarding the DHCP request. If you are using the Windows NT server DHCP Relay Agent, this property can be configured using the DHCP `Relay` tab of the `TCP/IP Properties` dialog (see Figure 6.13).

The `Seconds Threshold` value determines how long the Relay Agent will wait for a client to get a DHCP offer before forwarding the request to another network. The default value is 4. If your DHCP requests consistently forward to other networks, try increasing this value to ten. This should permit two complete local DHCP requests before they are forwarded across the network. (You'll remember, from our discussion of the *DHCP process,* that clients do not wait forever for a DHCP response. Be careful when adjusting the `Seconds Threshold` value that you don't make it longer than the client is willing to wait.)

Summary

In this chapter, we discovered that the Dynamic Host Configuration Protocol permits us to dynamically assign IP addresses and other pertinent TCP/IP parameters. By performing these functions for us, DHCP lowers the administrator's workload by eliminating the need to configure and reconfigure TCP/IP properties at each workstation. This also reduces the likelihood of incorrectly entered or duplicate IP addresses and makes the reassignment of an IP address and other TCP/IP properties a snap when a computer moves from one network segment to another. We saw the DHCP process was a simple four-step process consisting of *lease request, lease offer, lease selection,* and *lease acknowledgement.* We saw that DHCP clients obtain a lease for a specified duration and attempt renewal prior to the lease's expiration. We installed a DHCP server, configured a scope, and set scope and global options for a default gateway, a WINS server, and a DNS server. We found that a DHCP Relay Agent is required to forward DHCP requests to other networks, and saw how to install and configure one. We saw how to test the DHCP implementation by typing IPCONFIG /ALL, and looked at some ways to maintain the DHCP database itself. Finally, we spent some time with *Network Monitor* to see how DHCP packet traffic actually looks on the network.

▲ REVIEW QUESTIONS

1. *Your DHCP scope includes IP addresses from 130.110.5.1 through 130.110.5.120. You have non-Windows machines that use IP addresses in the 130.110.5.70 through 130.110.5.82 range. What can you do to ensure that the non-Windows IP addresses aren't given out by the DHCP server?*

2. *You physically move a DHCP client computer to a new subnet, but it fails to function on the network. What might account for this?*

3. *Your network has 700 computers on five subnets. You use a single DHCP server to provide addressing information. You have just added two DNS servers to the network and plan to add them to the DHCP server. How would you configure the DHCP option to provide this same information to all clients?*

4. *When installing the DHCP WINS server option, what must you also install and configure?*

5. *What can you use to determine the current DHCP client configuration?*

6. *DHCP will assign IP addresses to all machines on your network. You want all your servers to boot with the same IP address each time. How can you configure DHCP to make this work?*

7. *What information must you supply when making a client address reservation?*

8. *You plan to use DHCP in your network. You have three subnets. Two subnets host only Windows NT desktop computers and the third subnet hosts only Windows 98 laptop computers. You want Windows NT computers that haven't logged onto the network within 60 days to release their IP address reservations. You want the laptops to release their IP address reservations if they don't log onto the network within five days. How would you set DHCP up to ensure this happens?*

9. *Your network has three subnets called A, B, and C. You have a DHCP server on the A network and want clients on all subnets to be able to use it. Where would you place DHCP Relay Agents?*

10. *Your DHCP server provides clients with the IP address of the WINS server. You want to ensure your clients use WINS before resorting to broadcast name resolution. How do you configure DHCP?*

11. *What information do you need when setting up a DHCP Relay Agent?*

12. *You have two subnets each with their own DHCP server. How can you configure your network to provide DHCP server redundancy?*

NetBIOS over TCP/IP

So far we've discussed many operations accomplished by, through, and for TCP/IP. All of these operations have at least one thing in common: they involve communication between computers. Do computers actually speak TCP/IP? Well ... not exactly. The native language of computers (or, more accurately, applications running on computers) is the *Network Basic Input/Output System,* or *NetBIOS.* In the TCP/IP arena, NetBIOS is transmitted over the network by TCP/IP as a protocol within a protocol.

At the conclusion of this chapter, you will be able to:

- Define NetBIOS and identify the services it provides.

- Define NetBIOS names.

- Explain the NetBIOS name registration, discovery, and release processes.

- Explain the advantage of using NetBIOS name scopes.

- Explain why NetBIOS name resolution is important.
- Identify and explain NetBIOS name resolution methods.
- Create and properly employ an LMHOSTS file.
- Use NBTSTAT to monitor NetBIOS over TCP/IP connections.
- List the priority order of Microsoft NetBIOS name resolution methods.

Sytek Corporation developed NetBIOS in the early 1980's for IBM to permit applications to communicate over a network. NetBIOS is essentially a session-level *interface* and a session management and data transport *protocol*.

NetBIOS operates at the Application Level and the Session/Transport Level. At the Application Level, NetBIOS is a standard *application programming interface* (API) that permits user applications to communicate with network protocol software. Any protocol (such as TCP/IP) that supports the NetBIOS interface will support programs using the NetBIOS API. At the Session/Transport Level, NetBIOS functions through underlying protocol software such as the *NetBIOS Frames Protocol* (NBFP), *NetBIOS Extended User Interface* (NetBEUI), or *NetBIOS Over TCP/IP (NetBT)* to accomplish the network I/O required for the NetBIOS API to function on the network.

NetBIOS supports the following network services:

- Network name registration and verification.
- Session establishment and termination.
- Connection-oriented session data transfer.
- Connectionless datagram data transfer.
- Support protocol (driver) and adapter monitoring and management.

Of all the services provided by NetBIOS, the one we have most control over is its network naming feature. Because of this, we'll spend the rest of the chapter learning about NetBIOS names and how we can find a particular computer (host) through the use of those names and the NetBIOS services.

NetBIOS Names

What, you may ask, is a NetBIOS name? NetBIOS names are simply the names we give computers and other NetBIOS resources within a network. A NetBIOS name is given to a Windows NT computer during installation. This is the name you see when you look at the Identification tab of the Network dialog. These names make it easy for us to identify a resource (it is far easier to remember the name *Server1*, for instance, than to try to remember an IP or MAC address). NetBIOS names allow us to identify particular resources (such as an Exchange Server or SQL Server) without regard to a particular transport protocol. An Exchange Server could, for instance, function on multiple protocols using the NetBIOS name as long as there was a way to associate that name with a particular address (more on this later).

A NetBIOS name is a unique 16-byte address. NetBIOS names may be unique (to identify a single resource) or grouped (to communicate with several computers simultaneously). As we'll see, unique names are used not merely to communicate with a single computer, but with a single process running on a computer. NetBIOS names consist of a 15-character computer name plus a sixteenth character that identifies a particular process. Table 7.1 shows the sixteenth character associated with some common processes. Every Windows NT network service registers a NetBIOS name, and each Windows NT network command uses these services through their NetBIOS names.

NetBIOS Name Registration, Discovery, and Release

NetBIOS names are only useful if they are recognized by the machines on the network. To make this happen, the names must be registered, the machines must be able to determine what name corresponds to a particular machine, and when the machine owning the name leaves the network, the name should be removed from the list of valid names.

Table 7.1 *Common NetBIOS Names*

Registered Name	Description
\\computer_name[00h]	Name registered for Workstation Service.
\\computer_name[03h]	Name registered for Messenger Service.
\\computer_name[20h]	Name registered for Server Service.
\\username[03h]	Name of current user. This name is registered by the Messenger Service. This permits the user to receive messages sent through NET SEND. If the user is logged on to several computers, the first computer the user logs on to receive the message.
\\domain_name[1Bh]	The domain name registered by the primary domain controller that is also the domain master browser. (If a WINS server is queried for this name, it resolves it to the IP address of the computer that registered the name.)

NAME REGISTRATION

When a computer boots up and initializes its services, it registers its NetBIOS name with a NetBIOS *name registration request.* The request is made either through a direct message to a NetBIOS name server or through a broadcast. If the name was previously registered by another host, a *negative name registration response* is returned. If registration was attempted through broadcast, the negative response comes from the computer that previously registered the name. If a message to a name server was used, the response comes from the name server. If a negative name registration response is received, the computer suffers an initialization error; otherwise, the machine continues its initialization with the knowledge that it has successfully registered its name with the network.

NAME DISCOVERY

When a machine on a local network wishes to find a machine by its NetBIOS name, it either uses a broadcast or queries the local NetBIOS name server. If the designated name is found on the network, a *positive name query response* is sent by the name server or (if a broadcast was used) by the host possessing the name.

NAME RELEASE

When a NetBIOS application or service stops (this can be either when the individual service is stopped or when the computer is shut down), the host sends a *name release* message to the name server (if a name server was used), or simply stops sending negative name resolution responses when another machine attempts to register the same name (if a broadcast was used). This releases the NetBIOS name and makes it available to other hosts.

NetBIOS Name Scopes

The NetBIOS namespace can be segmented by appending a scope ID to the NetBIOS name. In Figure 7.1, WORKSTN1.ENG and WORKSTN2.ENG can communicate with SERVER1.ENG, but not SERVER1.ACTG, and WORKSTN1.ACTG and WORKSTN2.ACTG can communicate with SERVER1.ACTG, but not SERVER1.ENG.

When scope IDs are not used, NetBIOS names must be unique throughout the entire network; with scope IDs, names must be unique only within a scope. NetBIOS resources within a scope, however, are not able to communicate with resources outside their own scope using NetBIOS over

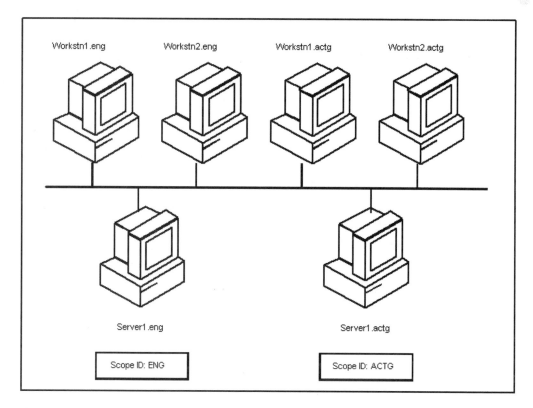

Figure 7.1 *NetBIOS scopes.*

TCP/IP. The NetBIOS scope becomes part of the NetBIOS name, resulting in a unique NetBIOS name. In Figure 7.1, even though the two servers have the same NetBIOS name, the different scope IDs make them unique. You configure the scope ID from the WINS Address tab of the TCP/IP Properties dialog box as shown in Figure 7.2.

In practice, NetBIOS name scopes are rarely used. Aside from being able to create a greater number of unique NetBIOS names in the local network, the chief advantage of name scopes is the ability to make one group of machines invisible to other machine groups. This is similar to having machines on different physical networks except that there is no vehicle to permit machines in different scopes to communicate using NetBIOS names. If you plan to communicate with machines across the network and over the Internet, you should not use NetBIOS name scopes.

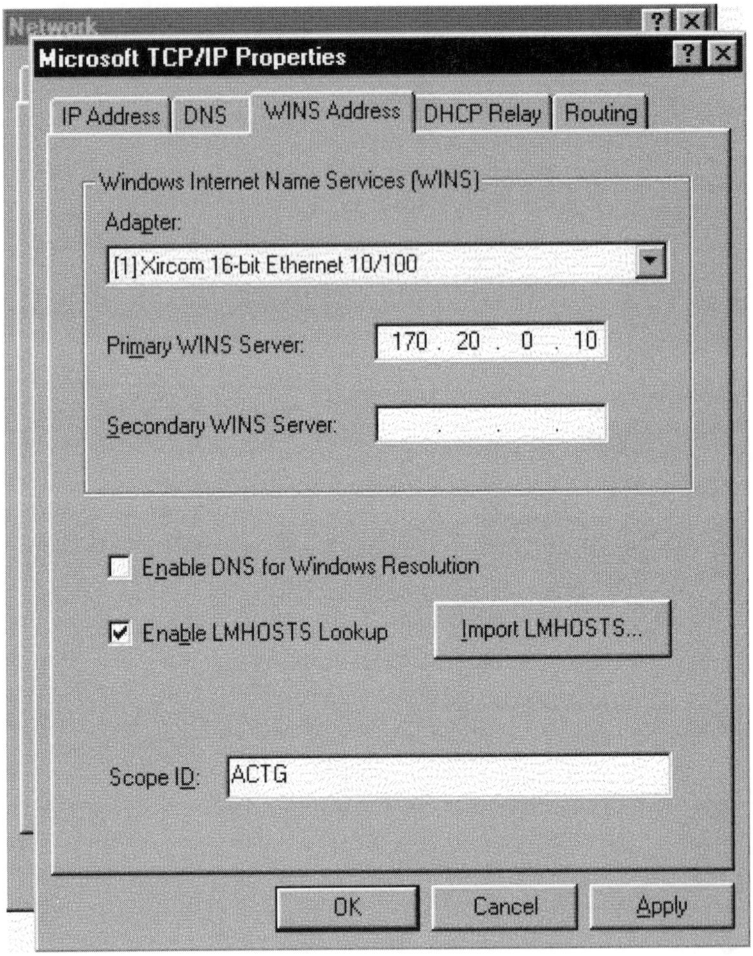

Figure 7.2 *Setting the Scope ID.*

NetBIOS Name Resolution

TCP/IP does NOT use NetBIOS names! Why, then, are we even discussing NetBIOS names in a TCP/IP book? As we said before, NetBIOS names permit us to identify resources in a protocol-independent fashion. They also make it easier for humans to remember and identify resources. How then do we resolve the issue of using NetBIOS names with TCP/IP? The key to this question is *name resolution*. For TCP/IP to function when presented with a NetBIOS name, it must have a way to determine the IP address that goes with the name. This determination is called mapping, or resolution. There are several methods to accomplish this name resolution.

Standard Name Resolution Methods

The following methods are standard throughout TCP/IP networks:

- NetBIOS Name Cache. Every time a machine resolves a name, it places it into its local name cache. When it needs to find the IP address for a NetBIOS resource, it checks its own cache first.
- NetBIOS Name Server (NBNS). An NBNS is any server implemented under RFC 1001/1002 to provide NetBIOS name resolution. A computer trying to locate a NetBIOS resource can query the NBNS for a name/IP address mapping. Microsoft's implementation is called the *Windows Internet Name Service.* It is the subject of the next chapter.
- Local Broadcast. If a computer can't find a mapping in its cache or from a name server, it can send a broadcast over the local network. If the target computer receives the broadcast, it will respond with its IP address to permit full TCP/IP communication.

You can review all the RFCs discussed in this book at www.cis.ohio-state.edu/htbin/rfc

Name Resolution Methods Supported by Microsoft

In addition to the standard resolution methods, Microsoft has developed some additional ways to map NetBIOS names and IP addresses:

- LMHOSTS File. An LMHOSTS file is a text file on the local computer that contains both the NetBIOS name and IP address of Windows networking computers on remote networks. As we will see later in this chapter, an LMHOSTS file requires manual entry and maintenance.
- HOSTS File: Like the LMHOSTS file, the HOSTS file is a text file on the local computer that requires manual entry and maintenance. Unlike the LMHOSTS file, the HOSTS file maps IP addresses to fully-qualified domain names (e.g., SERVER1.MYNET.COM) rather than Net-BIOS names (HOSTS files use the same format as the 4.3 Berkeley Software Distribution UNIX\etc\hosts file). For this reason,

HOSTS files may be used to resolve IP addresses for both Windows and non-Windows networks. This file is frequently used in name resolution for TCP/IP utilities. (HOSTS files are fully covered in Chapter 10 of this text.)

- Domain Name System (DNS): The Domain Name System is a server that maintains a database of IP addresses and fully-qualified domain names. Like the HOSTS file, DNS requires manual entry and maintenance and can be used for resolution in Windows and non-Windows networks. When a client needs an IP address mapping, it can query the DNS server in much the same way as it would query a NetBIOS name server. (DNS is fully covered in Chapter 11 of this text.)

Broadcast Name Resolution

Broadcast resolution is the most basic form of name resolution. When a computer (*source computer*) needs to establish a TCP/IP session with another machine (*target computer*), it first checks its NetBIOS name cache. If the target computer's name was resolved recently by the source computer, the IP address mapping will be found in the source computer's cache and no further action will be required. If, on the other hand, the cache does not contain a mapping for the target computer, the source computer will broadcast a *name query request* on the local network. The request contains the *target computer's* NetBIOS name and the *source computer's* IP address.

> Don't be confused by the terms! Remember, the *NetBIOS name cache* is a list of NetBIOS names the computer has recently resolved, while the *NetBIOS name table* contains a list of NetBIOS machine, group, and user names that apply to the local machine.

Every computer on the network, upon receiving a broadcast, checks its NetBIOS name table to determine if it owns the name being sought. The computer that owns the name uses the *Address Resolution Protocol* and source computer's IP address to determine the source computer's MAC address. Using the MAC address, the target computer sends the IP address resolution message (*name query response*) to the source computer and a network session is established.

The problem with broadcast name resolution is that it usually works only on the local network. This is because most routers are incapable of forwarding broadcast traffic. Routers that can forward broadcasts typically have the capability turned off to prevent excessive network traffic (to forward broadcasts, the router must have UDP ports 137 and 138 enabled). To reliably obtain name resolution across multiple networks, we will need to find additional name resolution capabilities.

Using a NetBIOS Name Server to Resolve Names

Using a NetBIOS name server (NBNS) will reduce broadcast traffic on the local network and can permit the resolution of NetBIOS names for hosts on other networks. The typical NetBIOS name server collects IP address mappings from its client computers when they initialize on the network (the NetBIOS name server used in Windows environments is WINS, which will be fully explored in the next chapter). When an NBNS client needs to contact another computer and can't find the appropriate IP address mapping in its cache, it contacts the NBNS for the information. If the NBNS cannot be found or doesn't have the required mapping information either, the client may resort to a broadcast or other methods, depending on how it's configured.

NBNS clients typically find the name server by using the server's IP address. This means they can route to a designated server on another network if required. It also means they can obtain name resolution without adding to the local network's broadcast traffic.

Name Resolution Nodes

Are you wondering how a computer knows when to broadcast and when to query a NetBIOS name server? If you're not, perhaps you should be. Well, the answer is through use of NetBIOS over TCP/IP resolution nodes. These nodes are simply Windows NT Registry values that tell the computer how to go about name resolution (name resolution nodes are defined in RFCs 1001 and 1002). You'll remember, in the last chapter, we saw how DHCP can automatically set the node for you. If you're not using DHCP, you can change the node type manually by entering the appropriate hexadecimal value in `HKEY_LOCAL_MACHINE\SYSTEM\CurrentControlSet\Services\Netbt\Parameters`.

Let's take a look at the nodes we can use:

B-NODE

The B-node is represented by a value of 0×1. This is a *broadcast* node, and it tells the system to use broadcast (actually a UDP datagram) resolution. If broadcast resolution fails, the computer will not attempt to find a NetBIOS name server.

Microsoft systems use the *Microsoft enhanced B-node* (also designated by 0×1). With the enhanced B-node, computers search the LMHOSTS file (more thoroughly covered later in this chapter) at TCP/IP initialization for entries designated by #PRE. Those entries are loaded into the machine's NetBIOS name cache, which, as we've seen, is the first name resolution method used by a computer.

Microsoft systems default to the enhanced B-node unless they are configured to use a WINS server.

Remember that broadcast name resolution typically works only within the local network and can increase the network load because of the attendant increase in broadcast message traffic.

P-NODE

Designated by 0x2, the P-node is called a *point-to-point* node. Computers using the P-node will accomplish name resolution through use of a NetBIOS name server. If the name server is down, or if the name server cannot provide the appropriate mapping, the P-node computer will NOT resort to broadcast name resolution. While this can curtail local broadcast traffic, when the name server goes down, it will bring communications, even on the local network, to a halt.

M-NODE

The M-node is a *mixed* node and is represented by 0×4. M-node systems use B-node resolution first and resort to P-node resolution if the B-node attempt fails. While this is the most complete resolution plan we've seen so far, it does little to limit network broadcast traffic.

H-NODE

A value of 0×8 indicates an H-node, or *hybrid* node. Under an H-node, a system first attempts P-node resolution. Should that fail, the system seeks resolution through B-node broadcasts. The H-node not only provides a comprehensive resolution plan, it limits network traffic by ensuring broadcasts are used only as a last resort. Microsoft systems configured to use at least one WINS server are configured to use the H-node by default.

DNS Name Resolution

When broadcast and NetBIOS name server resolution fail, the system still has a few tricks up its sleeve. One of these tricks is the Domain Name System (DNS) server, which is thoroughly discussed in Chapter 11. If the computer is configured to obtain information from a DNS server, it can use the server much like it would use a NetBIOS name server. The DNS server doesn't resolve a NetBIOS name; however, it resolves a fully-qualified domain name (e.g., SERVER1.MYNET.COM). If the fully-qualified domain name exists and represents the NetBIOS name being sought, an IP address mapping will be returned. DNS can provide name resolution for both Windows and non-Windows clients.

MCSE 7.1   The LMHOSTS File

Another name resolution method is the LMHOSTS file. This is a static text file that is stored on the local machine. The LMHOSTS file is named *LMHOSTS* (with no extension), and it resides in \systemroot\system 32\drivers\etc (in this context, \systemroot refers to the directory containing the Windows NT system files; this directory is \WINNT by default in Windows NT 4.0). The file contains NetBIOS names and IP address mappings for computers on the remote network. You can create an LMHOSTS file with any text editor, or you can use the sample LMHOSTS file (LMHOSTS.SAM) found in \systemroot\system32\drivers\etc as a template. Figure 7.3 shows a simple LMHOSTS file.

You should use the following guidelines when creating an LMHOSTS file:

- Entries are not case-sensitive.
- Place each entry on a separate line.
- Enter the IP address in the first column, and type its corresponding computer name immediately after it.

```
205.10.12.10    Wkstn1
205.10.12.11    Wkstn2
200.18.22.10    Server1    #PRE       # SQL Server
200.18.22.12    Server2    #PRE       # Print Server
210.22.18.10    Server3    #PRE       # Exchange Server
```

Figure 7.3 *Sample LMHOSTS file.*

- Separate the address and computer name by at least one space or tab.
- The # character usually marks the start of a comment. It is also used to designate special keywords.

LMHOSTS Keywords

LMHOSTS files use a number of predefined keywords to make the list more useful and easier to create and maintain. Some of the more useful keywords are detailed in Table 7.2, while Figure 7.4 provides an example of how to employ them.

 Keywords listed in this section can be used in LMHOSTS files using Microsoft TCP/IP. LAN Manager 2.*x*, however, will treat these keywords as comments.

Table 7.2 *LMHOSTS Keywords*

Keyword	Meaning
#PRE	Causes an entry to be preloaded into the NetBIOS name cache. #PRE entries in LMHOSTS are looked up and cached prior to WINS lookup.
#DOM:domain_name	Associates an entry with the domain specified by domain. This affects how the Browser and Logon Services behave in routed TCP/IP environments. It ensures datagram requests are forwarded to remote subnets and will permit machines to obtain logon validation by browsing domain controllers (for their domains) located in other subnets.
#INCLUDE filename	Causes the system to seek the LMHOSTS formatted file called filename and parse it as if it were local. If you use a universal naming convention (UNC) *filename,* you can use a centralized LMHOSTS file on a server. You must place an IP address mapping in your LMHOSTS file for the server and identify it with the #PRE keyword before the #INCLUDE section (otherwise, #INCLUDE will be ignored).
#BEGIN_ALTERNATE	Groups multiple #INCLUDE statements. The success of any #INCLUDE statement causes the group to succeed.
#END_ALTERNATE	Marks the end of an #INCLUDE grouping.
#NOFNR	Prevents the use of NetBIOS-directed name queries on LAN Manager UNIX systems.
#MH	Permits multiple entries for multihomed computers.
\0 × nn	Allows the entry of nonprinting characters in NetBIOS names. Enclose the NetBIOS name in quotation marks and use \0 × nn hexadecimal notation to specify a hexadecimal value for the character.

```
205.10.12.10 Wkstn1
205.10.12.11 Wkstn2
200.18.22.20 "sfile        \0x14"                          # Special file server
210.22.18.12 Server4        #PRE
210.22.18.14 Server5        #PRE    #DOM:Resource1    # Resource group's PDC
200.18.22.10 Server1        #PRE                      # SQL Server
200.18.22.12 Server2        #PRE                      # Print Server
210.22.18.10 Server3        #PRE                      # Exchange Server
#BEGIN_ALTERNATE
#INCLUDE \\Server4\public\lmhosts                     # adds LMHOSTS from server4
#INCLUDE \\Server5\public\lmhosts                     # adds LMHOSTS from server5
#END_ALTERNATE
```

- The server named **"sfile   \0x14"** contains a special character after the 15 characters in its name (including blanks), so its name is enclosed in quotation marks.
- Server4 and Server5 are preloaded so they can be used later in an #INCLUDE statement as centrally maintained LMHOSTS files.
- Server1, Server2 and Server3 are preloaded, based on the #PRE keyword.

Figure 7.4 *LMHOSTS file showing keyword use.*

Of all the LMHOSTS keywords, the one used most frequently is #PRE. When using this entry, it's important to remember that the NetBIOS name cache and LMHOSTS file are read sequentially. To increase efficiency, it is best to put the computers you access most frequently at the top of the list and entries tagged with #PRE at the bottom. Since #PRE tagged entries are cached at TCP/IP initialization, they'll be read from the list only once (at initialization).

> LMHOSTS files are static and must be maintained on each computer (except for those portions that are #INCLUDEd from another server). Make sure you update all **LMHOSTS** files each time a computer is added, removed, or renamed in your networking environment.

Enabling LMHOSTS Lookup and Importing LMHOSTS Files

LMHOSTS lookup is enabled on the WINS Address tab of the TCP/IP Properties dialog box as shown in Figure 7.5. By default, the LMHOSTS name resolution method is enabled when TCP/IP is installed on a computer.

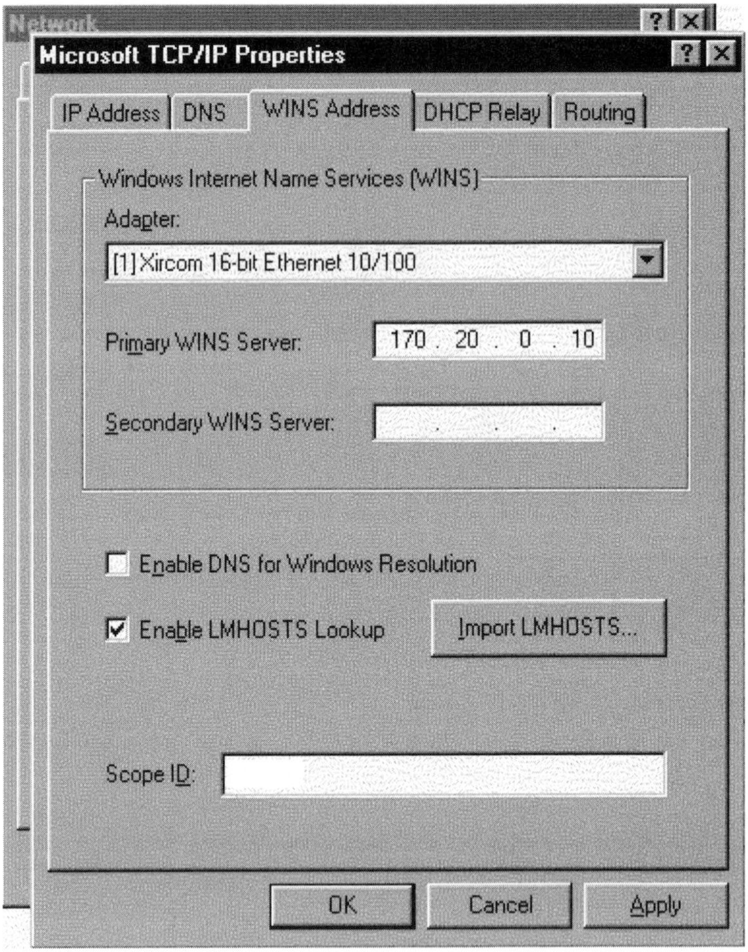

Figure 7.5 *Enable LMHOSTS lookup.*

Figure 7.5 also reveals the `Import LMHOSTS` button. Clicking this button permits you to import LMHOSTS from another text file. (The file can be in another directory, a network share, or on a floppy disk. As long as the text in the file meets the LMHOSTS format, the file can have any valid filename.) When the file is selected through this option, the contents are imported into the `\systemroot\system32\drivers\etc` directory and given the name LMHOSTS. The new file will replace any existing LMHOSTS file currently in the directory.

LMHOSTS Name Resolution Problems

LMHOSTS name resolution is a simple and reliable process. Unfortunately, as with any manual system, we frequently induce our own problems. Here are the most common LMHOSTS name resolution problems:

- *An entry for a remote host doesn't exist in the LMHOSTS file.* It is likely a machine was added or renamed within your networking environment and a corresponding LMHOSTS entry wasn't made. This could be a problem in the local LMHOSTS file or an oversight in a file that is #INCLUDEd in the local LMHOSTS file.

- *The NetBIOS name in the LMHOSTS file is misspelled.* A misspelled entry is as good as no entry at all. We frequently look at the file, see the name, and decide the problem must lie somewhere else. Attention to detail in LMHOSTS files is of critical importance.

- *The IP address is invalid for the NetBIOS name.* Getting the numbers right is as important as good spelling. Other possible problems here could be that the machine was given a new IP address, became a DHCP client, or had a conflicting mapping on a DNS server.

- *There are multiple entries for the same NetBIOS name.* Carefully check your LMHOSTS file to ensure each entry is unique. (If you are using a text editor such as *Microsoft Word* or *Wordpad,* you can use the search features to ensure you don't have duplicate entries.) When duplicate names are listed in the file, only the first name is used. If the first entry is incorrect, the mapping will not work. You may be looking at a good entry in the file while your problems are being caused by a bogus entry above.

> **Try to use each entry in the LMHOSTS file after creation to verify that it is correct. You can use an entry by using the** net **command or by pinging the resource using its NetBIOS name.**

Study Break

LMHOSTS Refresher

This would be a good time to find your LMHOSTS file and make sure it makes sense to you. You should also make sure your machine can use LMHOSTS resolution.

1. Find LMHOSTS. In this exercise we'll find the LMHOSTS file and make an entry for a computer. If you can obtain a name/IP address mapping for another computer in your network, enter that information when told to do so. If you are at a computer that is not on a network, or if you don't have IP address information for other computers, you can enter a line for your own computer. Remember, however, that there is no practical reason to place an IP address mapping for a local computer in its own LMHOSTS file unless the file will be imported by other machines or will be imported to a WINS server (importing to a WINS server is discussed in the next chapter).

   Look in your `WINNT\System32\Drivers\etc` directory. If there is an existing LMHOSTS file, use *Notepad* to open it and view its contents. If there is no current entry for the computer you selected, add a line for it using the other entries as a guide. If no LMHOSTS file is found, open the sample file, `LMHOSTS.SAM` (located in the same directory). Using the sample entries as a guide, make an entry for the selected computer. If there was no LMHOSTS file in the directory, you may save this sample file as LMHOSTS (without the .SAM extension).

2. Enable LMHOSTS lookup. Using Figure 7.5 as a reference, view the `WINS Address` tab of the `TCP/IP Properties` dialog. Is the `Enable LMHOSTS Lookup` check box checked? Remember that it is checked by default when TCP/IP is installed. If it is not checked, check it and close the dialog.

   By performing the previous actions, you have ensured your computer is able to use the static entry you entered for the machine you selected at the start of this exercise. In the final section of this chapter, you'll discover that LMHOSTS is the final NetBIOS name resolution your computer will try (prior to resorting to the HOSTS file and DNS server).

Using NBTSTAT

The NBTSTAT command line utility enables us to check the state of current NetBIOS over TCP/IP connections. It will also allow you to determine your registered name and scope ID and permits you to update the LMHOSTS cache. NBTSTAT is particularly useful for troubleshooting the NetBIOS name cache. NBTSTAT features are described in Table 7.3 and its syntax is as follows:

```
nbtstat [-a RemoteName] [-A IP_address] [-c] [-n] [-R]
[-r] [-S] [-s] [interval]
```

Examples

Two of the most useful NBTSTAT queries involve the NetBIOS cache and NetBIOS name table. The following example depicts a name cache query:

```
C:\>nbtstat -c
Node IpAddress: [200.22.18.36] Scope Id: []
```

Table 7.3 *NBTSTAT Parameters*

Parameter	Description
-a	Returns the remote computer's name table given its host name.
-A	Lists the remote computer's name table given its IP address.
-c	Displays the NetBIOS name cache.
-n	Lists the NetBIOS names registered by the client, either by b-node broadcast or by a WINS server.
-R	Manually purges and reloads the NetBIOS name cache using LMHOSTS entries tagged with #PRE. Ensure you use this after changing entries tagged by #PRE to update their new values in the current cache.
-r	Lists name resolution statistics for Windows networking.
-S	Displays workstation and server sessions, listing the remote hosts by IP address only.
-s	Displays workstation and server sessions. It attempts to convert the remote host IP address to a name using the HOSTS file.
Interval	Redisplays selected statistics, pausing interval seconds between each display. Press CTRL+C to stop redisplaying statistics. If this parameter is omitted, nbtstat prints the current configuration information once.

```
        NetBIOS Remote Cache Name Table

Name          Type        Host Address    Life [sec]
-------------------------------------------------------

WKSTN2     <20> UNIQUE    200.22.18.34      660
```

Here we see that the computer WKSTN1 has obtained a name/IP address mapping for WKSTN2. The returned information shows the mapping and indicates the entry will remain in the cache for 660 seconds from the time NBTSTAT was executed.

The next example shows a query to return the local machine's NetBIOS name table:

```
Z:\>nbtstat -n

Node IpAddress: [200.22.18.36] Scope Id: []

        NetBIOS Local Name Table

Name          Type        Status
----------------------------------------

WKSTN1     <00> UNIQUE     Registered
WKSTN1     <03> UNIQUE     Registered
DAVE       <03> UNIQUE     Registered
WKSTN1     <20> UNIQUE     Registered
DOMAIN1    <1E> GROUP      Registered
```

The output shows the registered names for the computer's workstation (`<00>`), Messenger (`<03>`), and Server (`<20>`) Services, as well as the current user (`DAVE`) and the machine's parent domain (`DOMAIN1`).

Microsoft Methods of Resolving NetBIOS Names

Windows NT 4.0 and later systems have a wide repertoire of techniques for NetBIOS name resolution, as shown in Figure 7.6 and described here.

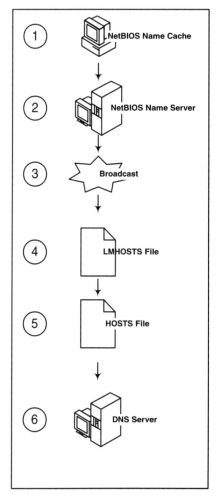

Figure 7.6 *Microsoft NetBIOS name resolution steps.*

- Name Cache. The first step in name resolution is always to check the local name cache.
- NetBIOS Name Server. If the cache does not yield the appropriate information, three attempts are made to contact a NetBIOS name server. For this to happen, the machine must be configured to go to a name server. This step is normally accomplished before resorting to broadcast, but may be attempted after broadcast, depending on the setting of the *name resolution node.*
- Broadcast. If the NetBIOS name server doesn't resolve the name, the computer will generate three broadcasts on the local network.
- LMHOSTS. If broadcast doesn't yield the necessary information, the local LMHOSTS file is parsed.
- HOSTS. At this point, NetBIOS resolution has failed and the system attempts host name resolution. This is resolution through a fully-qualified domain name, which corresponds to a NetBIOS name. To proceed to this step, the computer must be configured to use a DNS server and the `Enable DNS for Windows Resolution` check box must be checked on the `WINS Address Property` page of the `TCP/IP Properties` dialog (see Figure 7.7). The first step in host name resolution is to check the HOSTS file on the local computer for an IP address mapping. (We will thoroughly discuss the HOSTS file in Chapter 10.)
- DNS. If a mapping was not found in the HOSTS file, the computer sends a resolution request to its configured DNS server. If the DNS server doesn't initially respond, the computer will make additional attempts at 5, 10, 20, and 40 seconds.

If none of the aforementioned name resolution techniques is successful, the Windows NT command that prompted the resolution attempt fails and returns an error.

Summary

In this chapter we saw that NetBIOS was the native language of network application communication and that NetBIOS could be carried by a transport protocol over the network. NetBIOS over TCP/IP is, therefore, really a protocol within a protocol.

We saw that NetBIOS provided a number of important networking functions, including session establishment and connection-oriented and connectionless data transfer. The function we spent most of our time with, however, was NetBIOS name registration and resolution. We saw that before

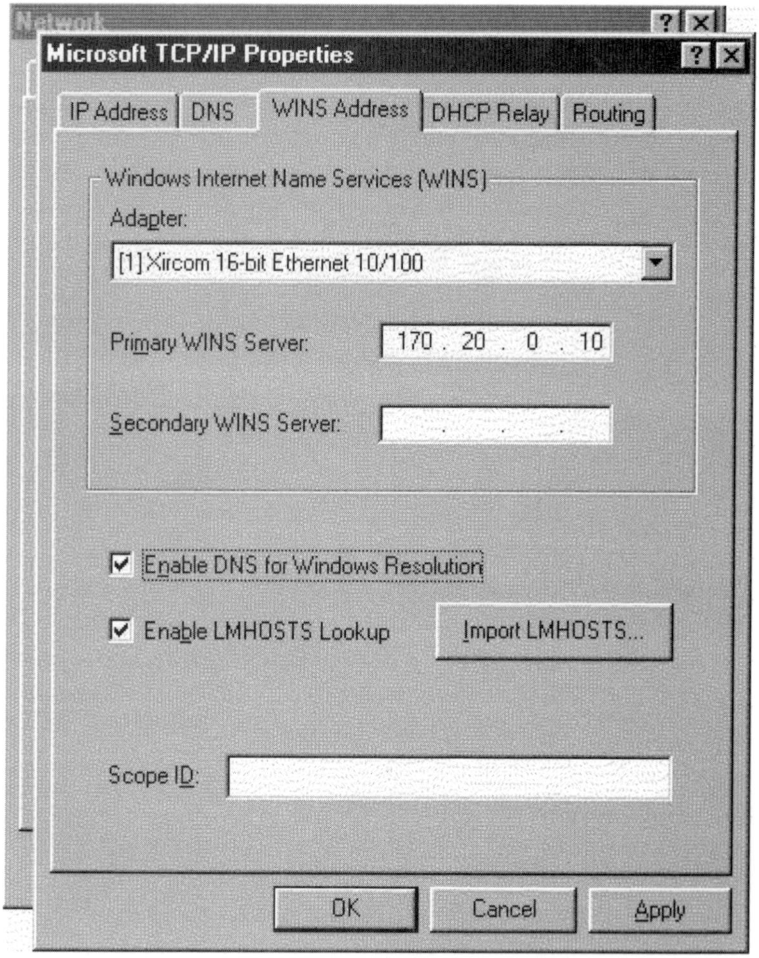

Figure 7.7   *Enable DNS for Windows resolution.*

a TCP/IP connection can be established, NetBIOS names must be resolved to an IP address (and then to a MAC address) and learned a number of ways name resolution could be accomplished.

When a computer first initializes under TCP/IP, it attempts to register its NetBIOS name with a name server or (by broadcast) with the machines on the local network. If the name hasn't already been registered by another machine, the name is registered on the network and becomes that machine's identity.

When a computer needs to establish a session with another computer, it first checks its own NetBIOS name cache to resolve the target computer's name to an IP address. If the cache doesn't yield an IP address mapping, the computer queries a NetBIOS name server, then tries a name resolution broadcast, checks the LMHOSTS file, then the HOSTS file, and finally queries its DNS server. If none of these methods yields an IP address mapping, the TCP/IP session will not be established. We discovered that we can set a *name resolution node* to control the order in which the computer uses name server and broadcast resolution and saw that the NBTSTAT utility provides a way to monitor and control a number of NetBIOS over TCP/IP functions.

We also learned how to create an LMHOSTS file and saw that it was simply a text file containing IP addresses and NetBIOS names. We reviewed a number of keywords that permitted us to preload selected LMHOSTS entries into the NetBIOS name cache and include other LMHOSTS entries into the local machine's LMHOSTS file. We found that, although the LMHOSTS file is a simple text file, it requires constant manual maintenance to ensure it contains the NetBIOS names and IP addresses of network resources with which the local computer needs to communicate.

▲ REVIEW QUESTIONS

1. *Vicky has a Windows NT Workstation computer that is configured to use an LMHOSTS file and an H-node. If her machine is a WINS client, in what order will it perform name resolution?*

     A. WINS server, local cache, LMHOSTS file, broadcasting

     B. WINS server, local cache, broadcasting, LMHOSTS file

     C. Local cache, WINS server, broadcasting, LMHOSTS file

     D. Local cache, broadcasting, WINS server, LMHOSTS file

2. *Linda wants to view the NetBIOS name cache on her computer. What should she type on the command line?*

     A. `arp -a`

     B. `nbtstat -c`

     C. `ping`

     D. `netstat -c`

     E. `nbtstat -r`

3. *You plan to install a Windows NT computer on a subnet of your domain. All domain controllers are located on other subnets. Your TCP/IP network does not use WINS. How can you make sure that logon attempts from the machine you'll install are validated by a domain controller?*

    A. Add a `#PRE` entry and a `#DOM` entry for each domain controller in your domain to the machine's LMHOSTS file

    B. Add a `#DOM` entry for each domain controller in your domain to the machine's HOSTS file

    C. Change the machine's subnet mask to match that of one of the domain controllers

    D. Install DHCP Relay Agents and WINS Proxy Agents

4. *Tim's Windows-based network doesn't use a WINS server, relying instead on LMHOSTS files. He discovers that one of his workstations cannot connect to a server because of an incorrect IP address in the workstation's LMHOSTS file. After correcting the entry, what should Tim do?*

    A. Delete the current LMHOSTS file

    B. Run `netstat -r`

    C. Run `nbtstat -R`

    D. Run `netstat -R`

    E. Run `nbtstat -r`

5. *Sandy manages a Windows NT domain, which resides on three subnets. The PDC is located on Subnet 2, while Subnets 1 and 3 contain BDCs. Sandy's network does not employ WINS; how can she ensure that the BDCs can communicate with the PDC?*

    A. Configure the PDC for IP forwarding

    B. Configure each BDC to use an H-node

    C. Create an LMHOSTS file on each BDC with a `#DOM` tagged entry for the PDC

    D. Create a HOSTS file on the PDC with `#PRE` tagged entries for the BDCs

6. *Bob needs to create an LMHOSTS entry for the PDC on a newly installed workstation. The workstation is named RECEPTION with an IP address of 200.10.0.12. The domain controller's name is SALESPDC and its IP address is 200.10.0.2. Both machines are in the SALES domain. How should Bob construct the PDC entry?*

A. 200.10.0.12 salespdc #pre #dom:sales

B. 200.10.0.2 salespdc #pre #dom:sales

C. 200.10.0.2 #salespdc #dom #pre:sales

D. 200.10.0.2 reception #pre:salespdc #dom:sales

E. 200.10.0.2 reception #pre:sales #dom:salespdc

7. *Lynn manages a large network that relies on LMHOSTS files for name resolution. One of her users complains that the time required to connect to remote hosts has become excessive. Lynn examines the user's LMHOSTS file and discovers a large number of* #PRE *and* #DOM *tagged entries in the file. What can Lynn do to increase the speed with which the LMHOSTS file is read?*

   A. Move all the #PRE and #DOM tagged entries to the top of the file

   B. Delete the #PRE tag from every #DOM tagged entry

   C. Move the #PRE and #DOM tagged entries to the bottom of the file

   D. Delete all the #PRE and #DOM entries

8. *Your network uses a DHCP server to assign IP addresses and WINS information. You want to ensure that your computers use WINS before resorting to broadcast name resolution. What node should you specify in the DHCP options?*

   A. P-node

   B. B-node

   C. H-node

   D. M-node

9. *You want to simplify your LMHOSTS maintenance by using an* #INCLUDE *statement in the LMHOSTS file of your workstations to load LMHOSTS information from a central server. What should you do to ensure that the* #INCLUDE *information is properly loaded into the cache? (Select two.)*

   A. Use a #PRE tag after the #INCLUDE statement

   B. Enclose #BEGIN_ALTERNATE and #END_ALTERNATE   after the #INCLUDE

   C. Use the Universal Naming Convention (UNC) to specify the remote server

   D. Use a #DOM tag before the #INCLUDE statement

   E. Use a #PRE tag before the #INCLUDE statement

10. *Mike changed the NetBIOS scope value on the* `WINS Address` *tab for several of his computers. What effect did this have on those machines?*

A. Forced them to use the WINS database

B. Permitted their names to preload into the group's NetBIOS cache

C. Preloaded their names into the corresponding HOSTS file

D. Isolated them on the network

Implementing Windows Internet Name Service

By now, you should have determined that NetBIOS name resolution is critical to the operation of your network. You should have also decided that NetBIOS name resolution broadcasts don't enhance network operation and that maintaining an LMHOSTS file is a real pain. Before you start looking for another protocol to meet your needs, read on. The *Windows Internet Name Service* (WINS) will automatically track NetBIOS names for your network and make sure all your machines can match names and IP addresses with ease. This chapter will tell you how to put a WINS server on the job, how to tell other machines in the network about it, how to get it to work with other WINS servers, and how to maintain and monitor it. (A WINS server is one of a class of servers known as NetBIOS Name Servers (NBNS). Because it is a fully automated server, it is considered an *enhanced* NBNS.)

At the conclusion of this chapter, you will be able to:

195

- Describe the use and benefits of the Windows Internet Naming Service (WINS).
- List and explain the steps of the WINS process.
- Outline the basic WINS planning considerations.
- Install and configure a WINS server.
- Describe the benefits of using WINS Proxy Agents.
- Install and configure a WINS Proxy Agent.
- Configure WINS push and pull replication partners.
- Display, manage, and maintain the WINS database.

The WINS Process

For WINS to operate, each machine that will use it for name resolution must know the WINS server's IP address. This includes machines that register their names with WINS, as well as machines that interrogate WINS for a name/IP address match. (Actually, we'll be introduced to WINS Proxy Agents in a few paragraphs. WINS Proxy Agents can permit machines that don't know the WINS IP address to indirectly get a name resolution from a WINS server.) Machines configured with the WINS server's IP address are known as *WINS clients*. (WINS clients may also be given the address of a secondary WINS server.) Since WINS clients must always know where to find the WINS server, WINS servers *must* have static IP addresses.

The basic WINS process consists of three simple steps:

- When a WINS client starts up, it registers with the designated WINS server, providing its NetBIOS name and IP address.
- When a WINS client wishes to contact another machine, it queries the designated WINS server for an IP address to match the NetBIOS name of the computer it's looking for.
- If the WINS server finds a NetBIOS name/IP address mapping for the desired machine in its database, it returns the information to the client.

As you can see, the WINS database is dynamically updated each time a client starts up. Because of this, the WINS database is always up-to-date.

Now that we know the basic WINS process, let's dig a bit deeper. WINS concerns itself with four basic processes: *name registration, name renewal, name release,* and *name query and response*. WINS is based on RFC 1001 and 1002 and uses standard methods for name registration, discovery, and release. The WINS name renewal procedures are peculiar to NetBIOS name servers.

You can review all the RFCs mentioned in this book at www.cis.ohio-state.edu/htbin/rfc

Name Registration

When a WINS client starts, it sends a name registration request directly to the designated WINS server. The name registration actually occurs when the client's services (such as Workstation and Server) start. When it receives the registration request, the WINS server checks its database to determine if this name is already registered by another machine. If the client's NetBIOS name is unique, the server returns a message indicating successful registration and the amount of time the registration will be valid (the registration duration is known as *Time to Live,* or TTL). If the WINS server finds a duplicate Net-BIOS name in its database, it sends a name query request to the currently registered owner. The request is sent three times at half-second intervals. (If the computer has more than one network interface card, three requests are sent to each card). If the currently registered computer answers one of the queries, the new client receives a negative registration response from the WINS server. If the currently registered machine fails to respond, a successful registration message is returned to the new client. If the WINS client isn't able to contact the designated WINS server at startup, it makes two additional attempts (the additional attempts are made by default at 15-second intervals). If, after the three attempts, it still can't find the designated WINS server, it will attempt to contact a secondary WINS server (provided it has been configured with the IP address of an additional server). If the client is unable to reach any WINS server, it may broadcast its NetBIOS name to the network to ensure another machine isn't currently using that name.

Name Renewal

As we have seen, a successful name registration is good only for a specified duration. After one-eighth of the initial duration or *Time to Live* (TTL) has elapsed, the client will attempt to refresh its name registration. If the WINS server doesn't respond, the client continues to seek a refresh every two minutes until it gets a response, or until half of its TTL has expired. With 50% of its TTL remaining and with no contact from the primary WINS server, the client attempts contact with the secondary WINS server (if it is configured with one). The client makes refresh attempts with the secondary server every one-eighth of the remaining TTL until it makes contact, or until 50% of the remaining TTL has expired, at which time it returns to attempting contact with the primary WINS server. The WINS server's name refresh response contains a new TTL, effectively extending the client's name registration. After the client successfully refreshes its initial name registration, future refresh requests are sent when 50% of the new TTL has elapsed.

Name Release

Since we don't wish to fill the WINS database with unnecessary data, a well-behaved WINS client will release its name at shutdown. When a WINS client undergoes a normal shutdown, it sends a name release request to the server for each of its registered names. The request contains the NetBIOS names to be removed and their associated IP addresses. When the server receives the request, it checks its name database. If its database shows the NetBIOS name associated with a different IP address, or if it discovers a database error, it will send a negative response to the client. Otherwise, the WINS server marks the client's name as inactive and sends a positive response containing the released name with a TTL of zero.

Name Query and Response

The default configuration for a WINS client uses the hybrid node (also known as H-node) for NetBIOS over TCP/IP. Under the H-node, a client first queries a WINS server and, if unable to find a NetBIOS name/IP address mapping, resorts to a broadcast. The entire process consists of only three basic steps:

- When the client executes a Windows NT network command, it first checks its own NetBIOS name cache to see if it has an IP address/NetBIOS name mapping for the machine it's trying to reach.
- If the desired information isn't found in cache, the client queries its primary WINS server. If the primary server fails to respond, the client makes two additional attempts before trying the secondary WINS server (if one is designated). If either WINS server responds, the client uses the information to contact the desired host.
- If WINS servers are available, but they cannot resolve the name request, the WINS client receives a "Requested name does not exist" message. If the client receives such a message or if it receives no WINS server response at all, it will resort to a broadcast. (Lack of WINS response may be because all WINS servers are down, the client has a bad WINS server IP address, network problems, or other factors preventing proper WINS contact.) If the client still cannot find a NetBIOS

name/IP address match, it may still be able to obtain name resolution through the LMHOSTS or HOSTS files or by querying a DNS server.

If the primary WINS server responds with a "Requested name does not exist" message, the client accepts this answer and does not pursue contact with a secondary WINS server.

WINS Planning and Implementation

Let's look at some planning considerations prior to actually installing and configuring a WINS server.

Planning

What are the requirements for a WINS server? A WINS server must be a Windows NT server (does not need to be a domain controller) with a static IP address, subnet mask, default gateway, and other TCP/IP parameters as required. (Although the IP address can be assigned by a DHCP server using an IP address reservation, this will make your WINS server DHCP-dependent and is not recommended.)

How many WINS servers do I need to install? Since name resolution requests are directed datagrams that route between subnets, one WINS server can service an entire internetwork. The addition of a second WINS server is, however, a good idea since it provides a measure of fault tolerance.

How many clients can a WINS server handle? The average WINS server can handle 1,500 registered NetBIOS names and will respond to around 4,500 queries per minute. A single pimary/backup WINS server pair can easily handle 10,000 clients. Additionally, since a WINS thread will run on each processor of a multiprocessor computer, a performance gain of 25% is realized for each added processor. (You may also improve performance by disabling WINS logging in *WINS Manager*. If, however, your WINS server crashes, you will likely lose your most recent WINS updates.)

What are the requirements to be a WINS client? Any computer running Windows NT Server or Workstation 3.5× or newer, Windows 95, Windows 98, Windows for Workgroups 3.11(must be running Microsoft TCP/IP-32), Microsoft Network Client 3.0 for MS-DOS, or LAN Manager 2.2c for MS-DOS can become a WINS client. To become a WINS client, the computer must be provided with the IP address of a primary WINS server and (optionally) the IP address of a secondary WINS server.

Implementation

To implement WINS on our network, we'll first install WINS on a Windows NT server. Once the server is installed, we'll need to configure static mappings for non-WINS clients and will configure a WINS Proxy Agent to extend WINS name resolution to non-WINS clients. Finally, we'll configure our client machines to participate in WINS. We've already seen how to use DHCP to configure a WINS client; here we'll use a static configuration to accomplish the same thing.

MCSE 8.1   WINS Installation

The installation of a WINS server is done through the `Services` tab of the `Network` dialog box. (See Figure 8.1.)

1. Select `Add` and `Windows Internet Name Service` (see Figure 8.2).
2. Click `OK` and the system asks you to ensure that the Windows NT distribution files are available. Make sure the appropriate directory is entered in the `Windows NT Setup` dialog box and click `Continue`.
3. Once the installation is complete, you are returned to the `Network` dialog box. Click `Close` and the system updates the network bindings.
4. At the conclusion of this step, you are given the option to restart the computer—click `OK` to restart the machine and complete the installation.

If WINS is installed on a multihomed server (one with more than one network adapter card), it will accept name registrations and queries on each of its IP addresses.

Study Break

Confirming WINS

1. Refer to the steps at the beginning of this section and install a WINS server on your computer.
2. Select `Control Panel|Services` and verify that *Windows Internet Name Service* is running.

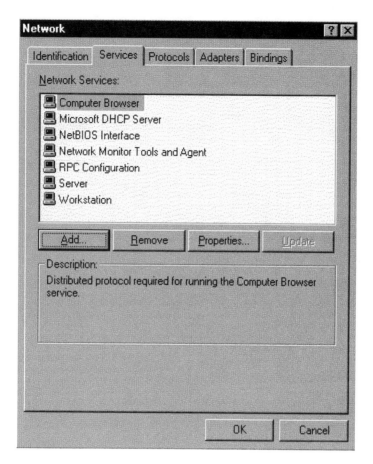

Figure 8.1 *Services tab of Network dialog.*

Configuring Static Entries and Proxy Agents

Although your newly installed WINS server is now fully functional and ready to handle the requests of any WINS client, a bit of configuration will enable it to service some non-WINS clients too.

Static Entries

By adding static IP address/NetBIOS name mappings for non-WINS clients, we can use the WINS server to provide this information to our WINS clients.

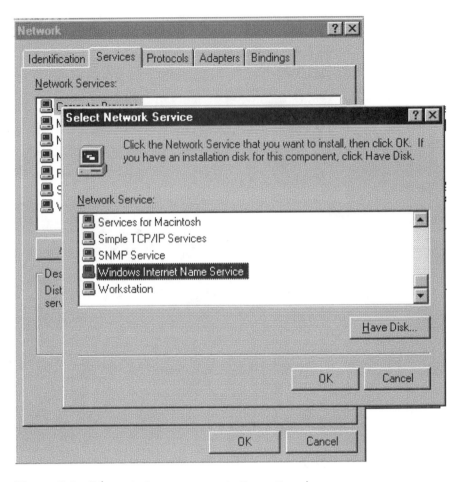

Figure 8.2 *Select* Windows Internet Name Service.

1. To configure a static mapping, go to Start, select Administrative Tools (Common), and launch the *WINS Manager,* which was installed on your system when you installed the WINS server (see Figure 8.3).
2. Click on the Mappings menu and select Static Mappings. When the Static Mappings dialog box opens, click Add Mappings.
3. You now see the Add Static Mappings dialog box. Type the name and IP address of the non-WINS client in the appropriate fields and select the appropriate type in the Type box (Table 8.1 details the meaning of each type).
4. Next, click on Add and the mapping is added to the database.
5. To add more static mappings, repeat the above process for each and click close when you're done. If you have an LMHOSTS file that already

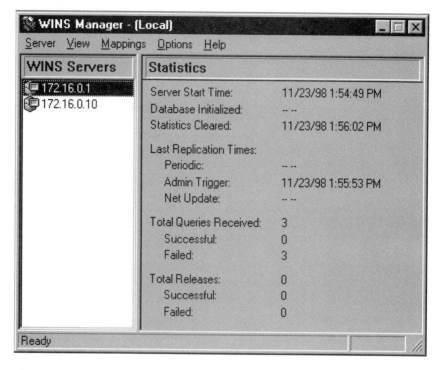

Figure 8.3 *WINS Manager.*

contains static mappings, you may import the mappings from the file by clicking on the `Import Mappings` button and providing the path to the LMHOSTS file you wish to import.

Remember that static mappings are *static*. This means that any time such a mapping changes, you'll need to manually change it in the *WINS Manager* (either by actually making the change or by importing an updated LMHOSTS file).

Figure 8.4 shows the `Add Static Mappings` dialog box.

Static mappings are added to the database when you click `Add`. Because of this, the `Static Entry` dialog boxes have no cancel feature. If you add an entry in error, you will need to return to the `Static Mappings` dialog box and delete the mapping there.

Table 8.1 *Static Mapping Types*

Option	Description
Unique	Allows you to specify a unique name in the database, with one address per name.
Group	Allows you to specify a normal group, where addresses of individual members are not stored in the WINS database and there is no limit to the number of members that can be added to the group. The client broadcasts name packets to communicate with normal groups.
Domain Name	Allows you to specify a group with NetBIOS names that have 0x1C as their sixteenth byte. A domain name group stores up to 25 addresses for members. For registrations after the twenty-fifth address, WINS overwrites a replica address or, if none is present, it overwrites the oldest registration. If you choose this option, additional controls appear so that you can add multiple addresses to the list. Click an address in the list, and then click Up or Down to change its order in the list.
Internet Group	Internet groups are user-defined, special groups that store up to 25 addresses for members. Click this option to specify your own group of NetBIOS names and IP addresses. (By default, a space character (0x20) is appended to the name as the sixteenth byte. You can override this by placing a new character in brackets at the end of the Internet group name. WINS will pad the name with spaces up to the fifteenth character and use the new character (the one in brackets) as the sixteenth character.) The Internet Group option will permit you to group resources, such as printers, RAS servers, and *Network Monitor* agents for easy browsing. If you choose this option, additional controls appear so that you can add multiple addresses to the list. Click an address in the list, and then click Up or Down to change its order in the list.
Multihomed	Allows you to specify a unique name that can have more than one address (multihomed computers). The maximum number of addresses is 25. For registrations after the twenty-fifth address, WINS overwrites a replica address or, if none is present, it overwrites the oldest registration. If you choose this option, additional controls appear so that you can add multiple addresses to the list. Click an address in the list, and then click Up or Down to change its order in the list.

Study Break

Adding a Static Mapping

Let's try adding a static mapping for a non-WINS client on your network. Check with your network administrator for the name and IP address of a non-WINS client you can add. If you have no non-WINS clients in your network or if you are at a stand-alone machine, you may enter a mapping for

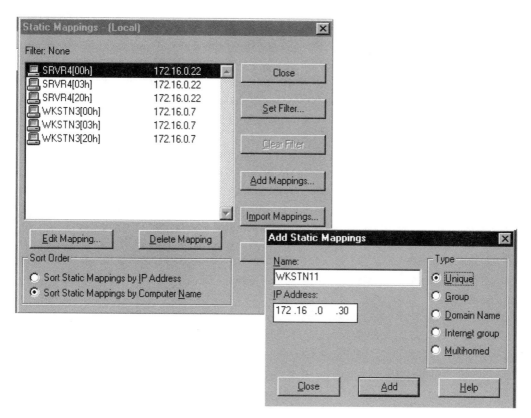

Figure 8.4 *WINS Static Mappings dialogs.*

your own machine. (Since a WINS server communicates only with those machines that are configured to communicate with it, you can do no harm to the network by entering erroneous data here. Remember, however, except for a training exercise, a WINS server would not typically be given a static mapping for itself since it should be configured as its own client.)

1. Refer to the steps listed at the beginning of this section to enter a static mapping for your WINS server.
2. Do you get a result similar to that shown in Figure 8.4?
3. If you created an LMHOSTS file in Chapter 7, use the `Import Mappings` button to import the file.

WINS Proxy Agents

Now that our WINS clients can get addresses of non-WINS clients through static mappings, it is only fair that we provide non-WINS clients an opportunity to obtain name resolution from our WINS server too. To do this, we can employ WINS Proxy Agents, which facilitate both name registration and name resolution for non-WINS clients. A WINS Proxy Agent simply listens for a NetBIOS name resolution broadcast and forwards it as a request to a designated WINS server.

NAME REGISTRATION

When a non-WINS client broadcasts a *name registration message,* the Proxy Agent forwards the request to the WINS server to ensure that a duplicate name isn't already registered. This is strictly a name validity check. If a duplicate name is found, a negative registration message is returned, otherwise the WINS server makes no response. Regardless of name validity, the non-WINS client's NetBIOS name will not be registered in the WINS server's database (automatic WINS name registration is for WINS clients only, others must be registered by static mapping as explained above).

NAME RESOLUTION

When a non-WINS client makes a *name resolution request,* the Proxy Agent comes to its aid. First the Proxy Agent checks its own NetBIOS name cache. If it can make the name resolution from its cache, it returns the information to the client and the WINS server is never bothered. If the Proxy Agent can't provide the requested information, it forwards the request to the WINS server. When the WINS server responds with the address match, the Proxy Agent adds the information to its cache and passes it on to the client.

It is a good idea to place a WINS Proxy Agent on each subnet that has non-WINS clients. Even if the subnet has routers configured to forward broadcasts (UDP ports 137 and 138 enabled), placing a WINS Proxy Agent on each subnet will reduce broadcast traffic and is encouraged. No more than two WINS Proxy Agents may be placed on any subnet and each Proxy Agent must be a WINS client (Proxy Agents cannot be WINS servers). Any computer running Windows NT Server or Workstation 3.5× or newer, Windows 95, Windows 98, or Windows for Workgroups 3.11(must be running Microsoft TCP/IP-32) can be configured as a WINS Proxy Agent.

Warning

Placing more than two WINS Proxy Agents on a subnet results in multiple resolution messages to the WINS server for the same client.

CONFIGURING A WINDOWS NT COMPUTER AS A WINS PROXY AGENT

Creating a Proxy Agent requires only a simple Registry edit. Launch the *Registry Editor* (*Regedit* or `Regedt32`) and `open HKEY_LOCAL_MACHINE\System\CurrentControlSet\Services\ NetBT\Parameters` and set `EnableProxy` to 1. Once this value is changed, simply restart the machine and you have a WINS Proxy Agent (ensure this machine is configured as a WINS client).

WINS Client Configuration

The WINS server and Proxy Agents are now functioning, but we still need to configure some computers to be WINS clients. This step turns out to be the easiest of all. Go to the `Network` dialog, select the `Protocols` tab, select `TCP/IP` and click on the `Properties` button. Click on the `WINS Address` tab and enter a `Primary WINS Server` and `Secondary WINS Server` IP address in the appropriate fields (shown in Figure 8.5). (If your network has only one WINS server, enter its IP address into the `Primary WINS Server` edit box.)

Database Replication between WINS Servers

So far, we've had fun configuring WINS servers and WINS Proxy Agents, but what if we want to operate a WINS service on multiple subnets or between subnets? What if we want to ensure a client can get a WINS name resolution on another subnet quickly and efficiently, and what if we want to minimize the amount of traffic routed between subnets? The solution to all of this is as simple as configuring our WINS server to replicate its database with a WINS server on another subnet (see Figure 8.6). Properly configured, WINS servers can get the name resolution information for another subnet directly from that subnet's WINS server. This permits the server to fully service all of its clients and eliminates the requirement for individual clients to route requests to a WINS server on the other subnet. Since replication between servers is accomplished only when a particular entry changes (WINS entry added or released), inter-network WINS communication is sharply reduced.

WINS servers configured to replicate their databases are known as *push partners, pull partners,* or *push-pull partners.*

- A push partner sends a message to its pull partners, notifying them its database has changed. The pull partners then respond with a replica-

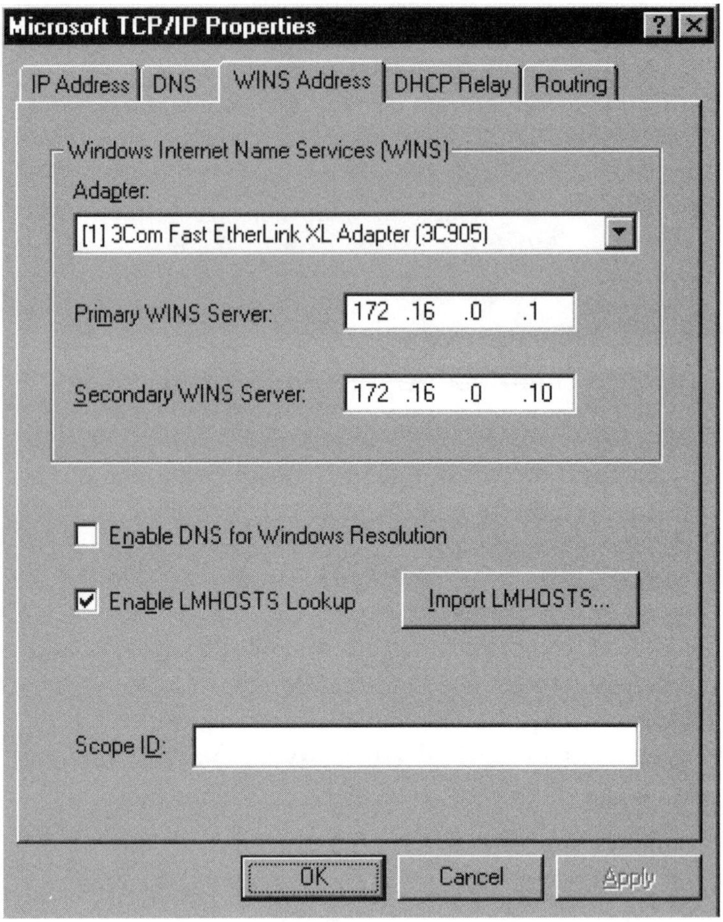

Microsoft TCP/IP Properties
IP Address
DNS
WINS Address
DHCP Relay
Routing
Windows Internet Name Services (WINS)
Adapter:
[1] 3Com Fast EtherLink XL Adapter (3C905)
Primary WINS Server:
172 .16 .0 .1
Secondary WINS Server:
172 .16 .0 .10
Enable DNS for Windows Resolution
Enable LMHOSTS Lookup
Import LMHOSTS...
Scope ID:
OK
Cancel
Apply

Figure 8.5 *WINS server addresses.*

Router
WINS
Push-Pull Partner
WINS
Push-Pull Partner

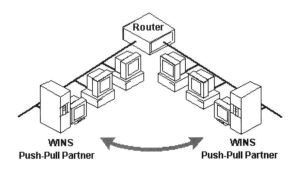

Figure 8.6 *Push-Pull partners on multiple subnets.*

tion request, which causes the push partner to send a copy of the new entries. Change messages are transmitted based on an arbitrary number of WINS updates, as configured by the WINS administrator (this number is known as the *update count*), or immediately, initiated by the WINS administrator using *WINS Manager*. A push partner may also be configured to send a push message at system startup.

- A pull partner requests WINS entries having a higher version number than that received during its last replication. The version number comparison ensures the pull partner always receives the most up-to-date information without requiring the transmission of redundant information. Pull partners request changes at system startup, based on a message from their push partner, an arbitrary time interval, as configured by the WINS administrator, or immediate replication, initiated by the WINS administrator using the *WINS Manager*.

Typically, WINS servers are configured as both push and pull partners to ensure complete database replication. Primary and backup WINS server pairs *must* be push-pull partners to ensure complete database replication. You may want to configure a machine as just a pull partner if it will replicate between sites and over a slow link since you can configure replication to occur at specific intervals. When a fast network link is available, push partners (or push-pull partners) provide the best response since replication will occur after a predetermined number of changes have occurred to the database.

MCSE 8.3 Configuring WINS Database Replication

Configuring your own push and pull partners is an easy process:

1. First, launch the *WINS Manager* from the `Administrative Tools (Common)` program group. Select the `Server` menu and click on `Replication Partners` to reveal the `Replication Partners` dialog box (see Figure 8.7).
2. Click `Add` and enter the IP address of the WINS server you want to partner with. Under `Replication Options`, check both `Push Partner` and `Pull Partner`. (Actually, you could configure the server only as a `Push Partner` or a `Pull Partner` if you wanted only those features. Your server must be entered in the other server's `Replication Partners` dialog box before replication can take place. You may access the other server by double-clicking its icon under `WINS Servers` on the *WINS Manager* main screen. When connected to another server, the

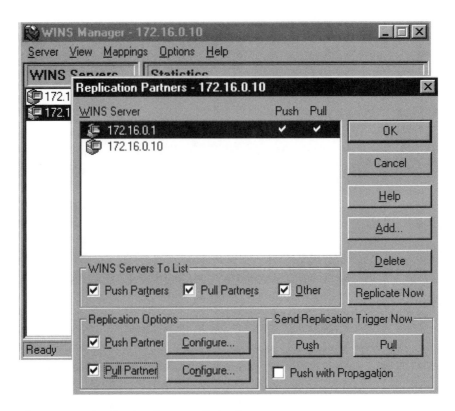

Figure 8.7 *Replication Partners dialog box.*

WINS Manager title bar changes from `WINS Manager - (Local)` to show the IP address of the remote server.)

3. Click on the `Push Partner Configure` button, enter the `Update Count` to indicate how many new database entries the server must have before sending a push message, and click `OK`. The minimum value allowed is 20; the actual value should be based on the number of name registrations the server typically handles and the desired replication frequency.

4. Click on the `Pull Partner Configuration` button, enter a `Start Time` and `Replication Interval,` and click `OK`. If you want replication to begin immediately, click the `Replicate Now` button on the `Replication Partners` dialog box (see Figure 8.7).

5. To initiate push or pull replication with a particular WINS server, highlight the desired server in the `WINS Server` box of the `Replication Partners` dialog and click the desired button under `Send Replication`

`Trigger Now`. Selecting the `Push with Propagation` check box will cause the selected servers to propagate a push message to their pull partners if any new entries are received (multiple servers may be selected by holding down the `Control` key while clicking).

When configuring WINS servers running on multihomed computers for replication, all of their IP addresses must be entered as replication partners.

Automatic Replication Partners

Replication may be configured to occur automatically on your network. If your network is capable of multicasting, the WINS server will automatically find other WINS servers. This is done by multicasting to 224.0.1.24 every 40 minutes (this is the default value, but it may be altered by changing the value of `McastIntvl` (`REG_DWORD`) found in `HKEY_LOCAL_MACHINE\SYSTEM\ CurrentControlSet\Services\Wins\Parameters`—the value is entered in seconds). If it finds a WINS server, it automatically configures it as a push and pull partner with pull replication set for every two hours. Automatically created partnership data is also maintained automatically. When a WINS server is discovered through multicast, it is automatically removed as a replication partner at shutdown. To set up automatic replication, enter `UseSelfFndPnrs` (`REG_DWORD`) under `HKEY_LOCAL_MACHINE \SYSTEM\ CurrentControlSet\Services\Wins\Parameters` and set its value to 1.

If the network doesn't support multicasting, automatic replication will occur only for WINS servers found on the local subnet.

Implementing Automatic Replication

You will be able to perform this exercise ONLY if there is another WINS server in your environment. Check with your network administrator for the address of another accessible WINS server (and for permission to replicate with it). As an alternative to the following procedure, you can use the same steps but configure your computer as a pull partner and the other server as a push partner.

1. In *WINS Manager,* select `Server|Add WINS Server` and enter the name or IP address of the other server. You can now administer both servers.
2. Refer to the steps at the beginning of this section to configure `both` servers as push-pull partners (of each other).
3. Click on the `Replicate Now` button.
4. Wait a few minutes for the replication to take place.
5. Double-click on your server in the *WINS Manager* main screen.
6. `Select Mappings|Show Database` and highlight the other server in the `Select Owner` window.
7. Did your server receive mappings from its push-pull partner?

WINS Server Configuration

Although WINS servers generally take care of themselves quite well, we can take a few configuration steps to make our network more efficient. The most important WINS configuration consideration is to ensure the WINS database is periodically purged of entries that are no longer valid. These may be entries that were previously released or those registered by another WINS server but never removed. This can be done in *WINS Manager.* You can do it manually by using the `Initiate Scavenging` option from the `Mappings` menu (see Figure 8.8), or it can be accomplished by setting the appropriate options in the `Server Configuration` dialog. To set configuration options, select the `Server` menu and click `Configuration`. This will reveal the `Configuration` dialog shown in Figure 8.9. The options in this dialog will drive the server to perform cleanup activities at specified intervals.

- `Renewal Interval` sets the time interval at which a client must renew its name on the server.
- `Extinction Interval` is the interval between the time a database entry is marked as `released` and the time it's marked *extinct*.
- `Extinction Timeout` is the length of time before an extinct entry is scavenged from the WINS database. The default time for each of these entries (`Renewal Interval`, `Extinction Interval`, `Extinction Timeout`) is 144 hours (six days). As you can see, by default, a released entry will remain in the database for 12 days (six to become extinct and six more to be removed). An entry from a machine that

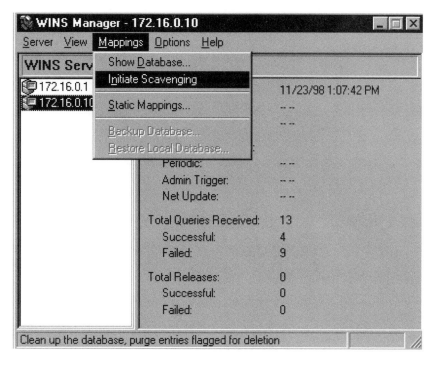

Figure 8.8 *Initiate Scavenging.*

leaves the network without releasing its information can remain in the database for 18 days. `Extinction Interval` and `Extinction Timeout` cannot be less than the `Renewal Interval`, except that `Extinction Timeout` can't be less than 24 hours and will remain at 24 if `Renewal Interval` is set lower.

- `Verify Interval` specifies the time after which the WINS server checks to ensure names it received from other servers are still active. This option is set to 576 hours (24 days), which is the minimum allowable value.

- `Pull Parameters: Initial Replication` determines if replication will be pulled at system startup. The `Retry Count` option sets the number of times the system will attempt to connect to a partner (if the partner fails to respond the first time). When the `Retry Count` is used up, pull replication will be attempted again once the `Replication Interval` has elapsed.

- `Push Parameters: Initial Replication` forces a push notification at system startup (note that this is off by default). `Replicate on`

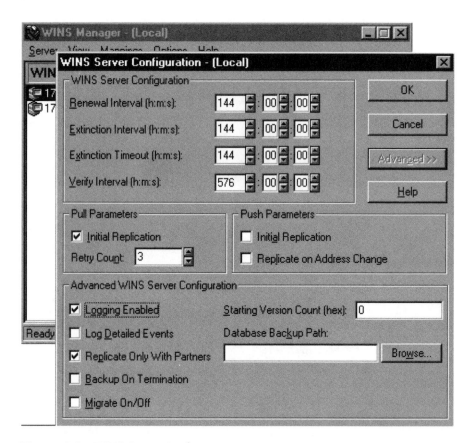

Figure 8.9 *WINS Server Configuration options.*

`Address Change` forces a push notification when an address changes in a mapping record.

Clicking the `Advanced` button will reveal several "advanced options:"

- `Logging Enabled` controls the logging of database changes.
- `Log Detailed Events` permits verbose event logging (leave off to enhance performance).
- `Replicate Only With Partners` permits replication only with those servers entered in this server's `Replication Parameters` dialog box.
- `Backup on Termination` forces a database backup whenever the WINS service is stopped (except during normal system shutdown).

- `Migrate On/Off` causes static unique and multihomed records in the database to be considered dynamic when they conflict with a new registration or replica. If the records are no longer valid, they will be overwritten by the new registration or replica. You should use this option if you are upgrading non-Windows NT systems to Windows NT.

- `Starting Version Count` sets the highest version ID number for the database. Use this to specify a new version when the database becomes corrupt and requires a fresh start.

- `Database Backup Path` sets the directory in which to store the WINS database backup. It is this directory that is used for an automated WINS restore. Don't specify a network directory.

> **Tip** Ensure your server is selected in *WINS Manager* (`WINS Manager - (Local)` showing in the title bar) and select `Server|Configuration`. Change the `Renewal Interval` to 7 days.

The WINS Database

You're probably tired of reading about the WINS database without actually getting to see it. We can fix that right now! Select the *WINS Manager*'s `Mappings` menu and click `Show Database`. This will reveal the dialog depicted in Figure 8.10 and show the contents of the WINS database. Note that you may show all the mappings in the database or only those originating from a selected owner. You may also display the database sorted by `IP Address`, `Computer Name`, `Expiration Date`, `Version ID`, or `Type` (sorts based on normal group, multihomed, domain name, and Internet group types). To view entries from a particular machine or range of IP addresses, the `Set Filter` button permits narrowing your display. To view a range of IP addresses, you may use the '*' wildcard character (e.g., 131.107.*.*).

The `Mappings` window shows the actual database entries. Entries in this window begin with a single or multiple computer icon. A single computer denotes a unique name entry, while a multiple computer icon designates a *group, domain name, Internet group,* or *multihomed* computer. The next entries are the registered NetBIOS name and IP address (NetBIOS name is always listed first, except when the list is sorted by IP address). A check mark in the `A` column shows that the entry is active, while a cross in

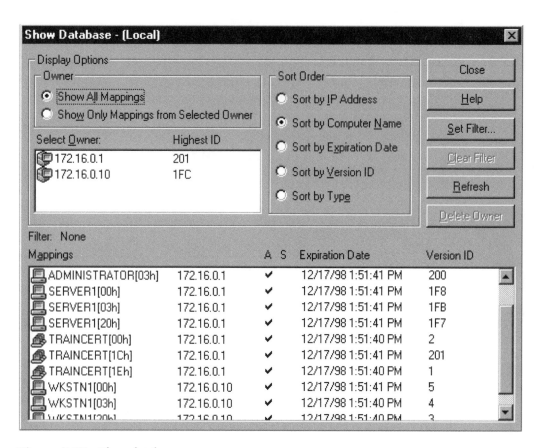

Figure 8.10   *Show database.*

this column indicates the name is no longer active and will soon be removed
from the database. A check in the S column indicates the entry is for a static
mapping. The Expiration Date shows the date and time when the entry
will need to be renewed. Finally, the Version ID is a unique hexadecimal
number used by the server's pull-partner to determine if this is a new record.
The Delete Owner button permits you to delete a WINS server and all its
entries from the current database. Ensure the desired WINS server is selected
in the Select Owner window and click on the Delete Owner button.

WINS Database Maintenance

Like DHCP, WINS uses the Microsoft Jet database engine, a reliable database product that requires very little user intervention.

DATABASE BACKUP AND RESTORATION

The database is automatically backed up every three hours after you specify the backup directory in *WINS Manager*. Additionally, individual changes are tracked in a log file between backups so restoration can be accomplished right up to the point where the WINS database crashed. You may force an immediate backup using the `Backup` option on the `Mappings` menu. In the event of corruption, you can restore the database using one of the two following methods:

1. Stop and restart the WINS server service. The WINS server service will automatically restore the database if it detects corruption.
2. Go to the *WINS Manager* `Mappings` menu and click `Restore Database`. You will get the opportunity to specify the directory containing the backup copy and the restore will be initiated.

COMPACTING THE DATABASE

Windows NT Server 4.0 will automatically compact the WINS database. Earlier Windows NT versions did not, however, offer this convenience. To manually compact the database, use the following procedure: First stop the WINS server service (use the `Control Panel|Services` option or type `net stop wins` at the command line prompt). Next, go to the `\systemroot\SYSTEM32\WINS` directory and run the *JETPACK* utility. To run JETPACK, type `jetpack wins.mdb temp.mdb` (you may actually use any filename for `temp.mdb` as long as it has an .mdb extension). This action causes the `wins.mdb` to be compacted into `temp.mdb`. When the compact is complete, `temp.mdb` is copied back to `wins.mdb` and `temp.mdb` is deleted. Once you have compacted the database, restart the WINS server service (use the `Control Panel|Services` option or type `net start wins` at the command line).

FILES USED BY THE WINS DATABASE

The files listed in Table 8.2 are used by the WINS database. They are located in `\systemroot\SYSTEM32\WINS` and should be neither deleted nor modified.

Summary

This chapter has shown us that the use of the Windows Internet Naming Service (WINS) permits the quick resolution of a NetBIOS name with its IP address. Because WINS maintains a database of NetBIOS name and IP ad-

Table 8.2 *WINS Database Files*

File Name	Description
WINS.MDB	WINS database
WINSTMP.MDB	Temporary database file
J50.LOG	Database transaction logs—used by WINS for automatic data recovery
J50.CHK	A WINS checkpoint file

dress mappings, the resolution can be done quickly, efficiently, and without broadcast traffic. The WINS process is automatic and covers both database construction and employment. When a WINS client starts, it provides the WINS server with its NetBIOS name and IP address. When a WINS client requires NetBIOS name resolution, it queries the WINS server, which replies with the mapping, if it is available. If a client can't obtain a mapping from the WINS server, it may resort to a broadcast.

Any Windows NT server can become a WINS server. Although only one server is required per subnet, adding a second server provides a backup capability. Most Microsoft operating systems can be configured as a WINS client. WINS clients may be configured statically or through DHCP. In addition to the automatically created WINS database entries, we may configure static mappings in the database to cover computers that cannot be configured as WINS clients. WINS Proxy Agents can be installed to permit non-WINS clients to receive WINS name resolution information.

WINS servers can be configured to replicate database information as pull, push, or push-pull partners. WINS database replication allows WINS servers on different subnets to provide WINS resolution while minimizing internetwork traffic. Replication also permits primary and backup WINS servers to maintain identical databases. A WINS server can be configured to properly clean up expired entries at optimal time intervals. Database entries can be viewed through the *WINS Manager*. Although the WINS database is based on the relatively self-maintaining Jet database engine, capabilities exist to manually back up, restore, and compact the data.

▲ REVIEW QUESTIONS

1. Sandy has two subnets (A and B) connected by a router. She's installed a WINS server on Subnet A. What can she do to permit UNIX computers on Subnet B to obtain name resolution from the WINS server on Subnet A?

      A. Create static mappings for the UNIX computers

      B. Install a BOOTP Relay Agent on either subnet

      C. Install a WINS Proxy Agent on Subnet A

      D. Install a WINS Proxy Agent on Subnet B

2. *Mike has two LANs in different cities connected by a T1 line. He installs WINS servers at each location and wants to ensure each server replicates its database entries to the other. What is the best way to do this?*

3. *You have two subnets connected through a router. Each subnet uses its own WINS server and you find that machines on one subnet can't communicate with machines on the other subnet. How can you correct this?*

      A. Install WINS Proxy Agents on each subnet

      B. Configure each client to use the WINS server on the other subnet as a secondary WINS server

      C. Configure the WINS servers as replication partners

      D. Once both machines are running, use *WINS Manager* to initiate database scavenging

4. *How can you ensure a computer registers its name with a particular WINS server?*

5. *Kim wants her WINS server to provide her WINS clients with name resolution information for five UNIX computers on her network. What must she do?*

      A. Provide the UNIX machines with the WINS server's IP address

      B. Add a static mapping on the WINS server for each UNIX machine

      C. Make the UNIX computers push partners of the WINS server

      D. A WINS server cannot provide UNIX name resolution

6. *Kim decides to use static mappings for the scenario in the previous question. What type of entry should she add?*

      A. Domain name

      B. Group

      C. Internet group

      D. Multihomed

      E. Unique

7. *Kim also needs to add a static mapping for a computer with three network cards. What type of entry should she add in this case?*

   A. Domain name

   B. Group

   C. Internet group

   D. Multihomed

   E. Unique

IP Internetwork Browsing and Domain Functions

It's time now to put your knowledge of NetBIOS name resolution and the Windows Internet Name Service (WINS) to use. Remember how often you open *Network Neighborhood* and see an incorrect or incomplete list of servers and workstations. You may remember situations where a computer has been shut down, but the *Network Neighborhood* application still shows it active. Sometimes you are surprised that you can connect to a server but cannot see it in the browse list. Now it's time to shed some light on issues such as these. This chapter explains how browsing for NetBIOS resources and domain functions works in a TCP/IP environment. You will be presented with the ins and outs of the browser service. You will learn how to configure and use the LMHOSTS file to support domain activity. We will also discuss how implementing WINS can solve internetwork browsing problems.

At the end of this chapter, you will be able to:

- Explain how the Windows NT browsing service works.

221

- Describe the mechanisms of IP browsing.
- Identify common browsing problems in TCP/IP environments.
- Describe how a domain logon works in an IP internetwork.
- Explain how browsing occurs in a WINS environment.
- Explain what entries in the LMHOSTS file are essential for browsing and domain functions.

Browsing Overview

In large organizations, it may be very tedious to locate a desired resource, such as a shared folder or a network printer. To share resources efficiently, users must be able to view what servers and workstations are available in the network and what shared resources they have access to. Users on a Windows NT network often need to know what computers are accessible from their workstations. For example, when you double-click the *Network Neighborhood* icon or launch *NT Explorer,* it's convenient to see the graphical representation of all available network resources in your workgroup or domain (and perhaps in other domains as well). (See Figure 9.1.) The list of network resources is often referred to as the *browse list*.

The browse list of network resources is maintained by a special Windows NT service, called the *computer browser service*. Viewing the list of available network resources is called *browsing*.

The computer browser service was first introduced in Microsoft Windows for Workgroups. The main purpose of the browser service is to collect and distribute the list of network computers that are sharing file, print, and other resources. The browser service was initially designed for computers located on a single network segment and, originally, did not support WAN environments. Since then, browser features have been significantly enhanced. The current browser service has WAN capabilities that permit Windows NT computers to browse resources located on both local and remote network segments.

Note

The ability to browse should not be confused with the ability to `connect` to a computer (e.g., through the *net use* command). In many cases, you may be able to successfully connect to a remote computer even if you can't see it in the browse list.

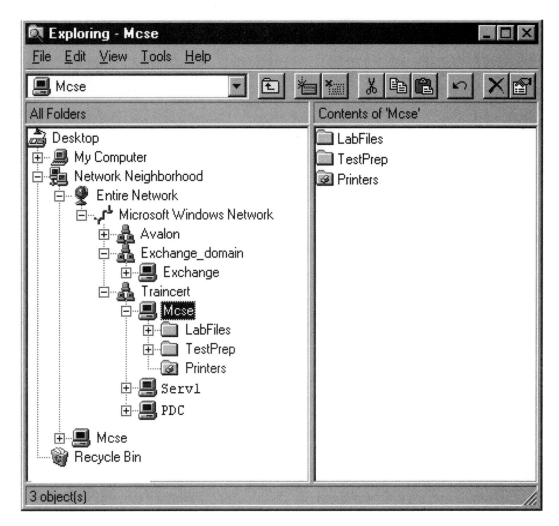

Figure 9.1 *Browsing network resources with Windows NT Explorer.*

Browser Roles

Technically, the computer browser service is simply a series of lists of available network resources. These lists are distributed to specifically assigned computers that perform browser services on behalf of other computers. Windows NT assigns browser tasks to specific computers. Computers work together to provide a centralized list of shared resources. Thanks to the browser service, not every computer on the network has to maintain its own browser list. This fact reduces the amount of network traffic required to build and support a list of available network resources, which saves CPU time and memory resources.

There are several browser types: *domain master browser, master browser, backup browser, potential browser,* and *browser client* (non-browser). Table 9.1 briefly presents the main functions of each browser type. We will cover each of them in greater detail a bit later.

A single computer can play multiple browser roles. For example, the master browser computer may also be a backup browser. You can identify the computer's current browse role using the BROWMAN and BROWSTAT utilities from the Microsoft Windows NT Resource Kit.

MCSE 9.1   Browsing in One IP Subnet

Browsing within one subnet is a little bit different from browsing across a WAN. We'll start our discussion with common browsing concepts, using local browsing as an example. We will then discuss how browsing works across routes. We will also look at potential browsing problems and discuss some recommended solutions.

Table 9.1 *Browser Roles*

Role	Description
Browser Client	Browser client (often referred to as non-browser) does not maintain a browse list. When a list of network resources is needed, the browser client queries backup browsers for one.
Master Browser	Master browser (MBR) is responsible for collecting browse information to create and maintain a browse list. If a domain spans more than one subnetwork, the master browser maintains the browse list for the portion of the domain on its subnetwork. The master browser then distributes the browse list to the backup browsers.
Backup browser	Backup browser (BBR) receives a copy of the network resource browse list from the master browser and distributes the list upon request to computers in the domain or workgroup.
Potential browser	Potential browser (PBR) is not a browser server. It is, however, capable of maintaining a network resource browse list and can be elected as a master browser. A potential browser can also act as a backup browser, if instructed to do so by the existing master browser.
Domain master browser	Domain master browser (DMBR) is responsible for collecting announcements for the entire domain, including remote subnets. The domain master browser then provides the synchronized list of all domain resources to master browsers in other subnets. The domain master browser is always the primary domain controller of the domain.

How Does a Computer get into the Browse List?

Computers that have server components installed (such as Windows 95 computers with File and Print Services for Microsoft Networks, or Windows NT Server or Workstation computers) should be presented in the browse list to permit users to easily locate them. When a computer with a server component starts, it announces itself to the network to advertise its ability to service client requests.

The browser host announcement packet in TCP/IP networks is a broadcast frame destined for the NetBIOS name `domain <1Dh>`, where domain is the domain name to which the announcing computer belongs. (See Figure 9.2.)

Figure 9.2 depicts the host announcement for computer MCSE, which is a member of TRAINCERT domain.

Once a computer not currently tasked with a browser role has started, it announces itself every 12 minutes.

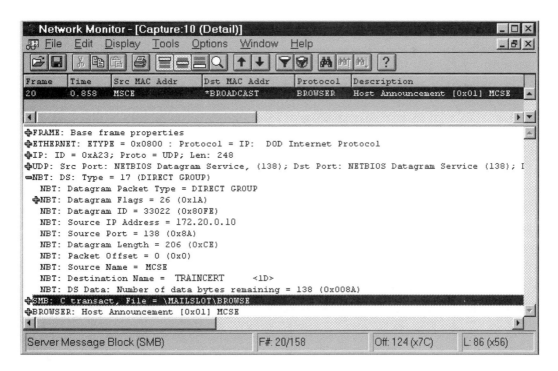

Figure 9.2 *Host announcement.*

You can change the browser announcement time in the Registry. To do this, go to `HKEY_LOCAL_MACHINE\System\CurrentControlSet\-Services\LanmanServer\parameters` and add an `Announce` key with a type of `REG_DWORD`. Set its value to the number of seconds that the browser should wait between announcements.

Master Browser

Now we know that computers announce their presence to the network with a special broadcast packet, but who catches these announcement packets? The answer is *the master browser*. The master browser is responsible for creating the primary copy of the browse list. The master browser picks up the computer announcements destined to the *domain <1Dh>* NetBIOS name (the NetBIOS name *domain <1Dh>* is registered by the master browser). When the master browser receives such an announcement from a computer, it adds that computer to its browse list. This is often referred to as a *collection process*. This process is illustrated in Figure 9.3. Initially, the network has only one computer online—the one named PDC. Computers MCSE and Serv1 are powered down (shown as dimmed). The powered down machines do not appear in the browse list. At boot time, each computer sends a broadcast announcement, which causes it to appear in the browse list.

If your domain consists of several subnets separated by routers, each subnet has its own master browser.

Being a mater browser, the computer has one more function. It broadcasts a *DomainAnnouncement* datagram once every 15 minutes. A *Do-*

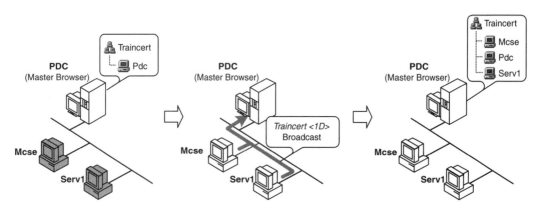

Figure 9.3 *Browsing collection process.*

mainAnnouncement datagram contains the name of the domain, the name of the master browser for that domain, and other additional information. When another master browser receives such a datagram, it adds the new domain to its browse list.

Backup Browser

The backup browser receives a copy of the browse list from the master browser. Later in this chapter, we'll see that the backup browser also services client requests by sending them a copy of the browse list. Backup browsers contact the master browser every 15 minutes to get the updated copy of the browse list. (See Figure 9.4.) The process of pulling the browse list from the master browser to the backup browser is referred to as the *distribution process.*

If a backup browser cannot contact the master browser, a new master browser is elected. This is called a *browser election* and will be discussed in detail later in this chapter.

All Windows NT domain controllers are automatically configured to become backup browsers if needed. Normally there is one backup browser for every 32 computers.

What Happens when a Computer Needs to Browse?

When a non-browser computer (one that does not maintain its own copy of a browse list) needs to browse (for example, when a user launches *Network Neighborhood*), it obtains the current browse list from a backup browser. But

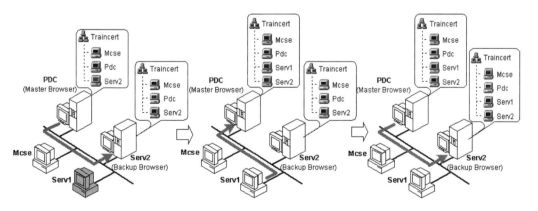

Figure 9.4 *Browsing distribution process.*

before this, the browser client needs to determine the IP addresses of the backup browsers. To get the addresses of the backup browsers, the computer sends a so-called *GetBackupListReq* request to the NetBIOS name *domain<1Dh>* (in TCP/IP networks, the *GetBackupListReq* request for *domain <1Dh>* is encapsulated in a broadcast IP datagram). Additionally, if the browser client is configured with a WINS server address, the request for the domain master browser (*domain <1Bh>*) is sent to the WINS server.

When the master browser gets the *GetBackupListReq,* it responds with a list of backup browsers for the given subnet. This is accomplished with a *GetBackupListResponse* packet. The response includes a list of all the backup browsers for the domain/workgroup on the local subnet. (See Figure 9.5.)

Once the client has received a list of backup browsers from the master browser, it selects three servers from this list and caches them. Using backup browsers for future client requests reduces load on the master browser. Later when a computer needs to browse, it selects one of the three cached names, and performs the following actions in the sequence listed:

1. Establishes a TCP session with the chosen backup browser.
2. Establishes a NetBIOS session with the chosen backup browser.
3. Establishes a null session to IPC$.

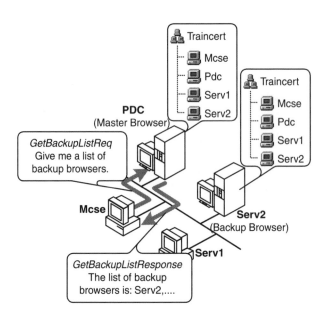

Figure 9.5 *Browser client retrieves a list of backup browsers.*

The client then issues an RPC (Remote Procedure Call) to the backup browser requesting a browse list, which the backup browser returns. (See Figure 9.6.)

> Only Windows NT clients talk with backup browsers using RPCs. Windows 9× and Windows for Workgroups clients use the *NetServerEnum* API call.

WHAT'S A NULL SESSION TO IPC$?

What exactly *is* a null session to IPC$? IPC stands for interprocess communication—the way programs (such as the browser service) communicate with each other. IPC$ is a share created on each Windows NT computer through which interprocess communication can take place. Here, by establishing an IPC$ session, the browser service on the client is opening a communications channel with the browser service on the backup browser. A null session (as opposed to a validated session) is used because browsing can occur without a valid trust relationship. The null session is analogous to an anonymous login, permitting the computer to obtain a browse list without regard to resource permissions.

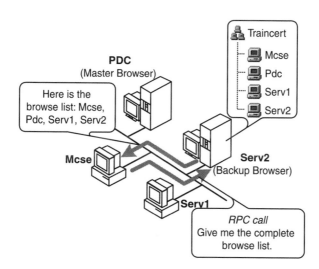

Figure 9.6 *Browser client retrieves the browse list from a backup browser.*

The full conversation of the browser client with master and backup browsers is illustrated in Figure 9.7. Once the browser client gets the browse list, it can display it in *Network Neighborhood* or *Windows NT Explorer*. If the user double-clicks a particular server in the browse list, the client contacts this server and acquires a list of the server's available shared resources.

 In Windows NT versions prior to 4.0, as well as in Windows 95 and Windows for Workgroups, the data limit for the list of servers is set to 64K. Because of this, the browse list for a single workgroup or domain is limited to approximately 3000 computers under these operating systems.

When Does a Computer Disappear from the Browse List?

Have you noticed that a computer can be turned off but it will still remain in the browse list for a while? Under what conditions does the computer disappear from the browse list? Unfortunately, the computer browser service does not have a special announcement to indicate when a computer is about to be turned off. Instead, computers are deleted from the browse list silently. If the master browser has not heard from a non-browser for three consecutive an-

Frame	Time	Src MAC Addr	Dst MAC Addr	Protocol	Description
176	3.061	MCSE	*BROADCAST	BROWSER	Get Backup List Request [0x09]
178	3.064	MasterBrowser	MCSE	BROWSER	Get Backup List Response [0x0a] 2 Servers
179	3.068	MCSE	BackupBrowser	TCP	....S., len: 4, seq: 26061519-2606152
180	3.068	BackupBrowser	MCSE	TCP	.A..S., len: 4, seq:1668120632-1668120
181	3.068	MCSE	BackupBrowser	TCP	.A...., len: 0, seq: 26061520-2606152
182	3.068	MCSE	BackupBrowser	NBT	SS: Session Request, Dest: BackupBrowser
183	3.068	BackupBrowser	MCSE	NBT	SS: Positive Session Response, Len: 0
184	3.070	MCSE	BackupBrowser	SMB	C negotiate, Dialect = NT LM 0.12
185	3.071	BackupBrowser	MCSE	SMB	R negotiate, Dialect # = 7
186	3.079	BackupBrowser	MCSE	SMB	R session setup & X, and R tree connect &
187	3.079	MCSE	BackupBrowser	SMB	C session setup & X, Username = , and C t
194	3.092	MCSE	BackupBrowser	SMB	C transact, Remote API
195	3.095	BackupBrowser	MCSE	SMB	R transact, Remote API (response to frame
196	3.096	BackupBrowser	MCSE	NBT	SS: Session Message Cont., 173 Bytes
197	3.096	MCSE	BackupBrowser	TCP	.A...., len: 0, seq: 26062077-2606207

Figure 9.7 *Browser client requesting the browse list.*

nouncement periods, the master browser will remove the non-browser from its browse list. Thus, a non-browser computer will be in the master browser's browse list for three 12-minute announcement cycles after it—the non-browser—has been shut down. Because it can take up to 15 minutes for a backup browser to receive an updated browse list, it is possible that a computer will appear in the browse list as long as 51 minutes after it is no longer available to the network. This behavior is by design.

Browser Elections

You may ask what happens if the master browser goes down unexpectedly? Who will maintain the browse list then? Fortunately, the computer browser service is designed to handle such situations. For example, when a computer fails to locate the master browser, it forces the designation of a new master browser by sending an *ElectionForce* datagram. This process of determining the new master browser is called *browser election*.

When an election is being forced, one of the master browser candidates initiates the election by sending a special datagram called the *election* datagram. When other master browser candidates receive this election datagram, they examine the *election criteria* inside it. If a particular browser has better election criteria than the computer that sent the election datagram, it will issue its own election datagram. The election criterion for the browser is based on the operating system type, browser's current role, and its current state. For example, a Windows NT Server will win a browser election over a Windows NT Workstation. (Machines are elected in the following order: Windows NT Server, Windows NT Workstation, Windows for Workgroups/Windows 9×.)

The election process ensures there will always be only one master browser in a given subnet.

CONFIGURING BROWSERS

You may ask, how can I control whether a computer becomes a browser or not? Unfortunately Windows NT does not provide a convenient way to configure the browser service. You must edit the Registry.

Using the Registry editor, you can configure your Windows NT computer:

- To be a browser (that means the computer will become a browser).
- Never to be a browser (that means that the computer will not participate in browser elections and will never become a browser, neither master nor backup).

- To be a potential browser (that means that the computer will become a browser depending on the number of currently active browsers).

To set up the browser configuration, use the Registry path:

```
HKEY_LOCAL_MACHINE\System\CurrentControlSet\Services\
Browser\Parameters\MaintainServerList
```

The allowable values for the `MaintainServerList` parameter are:

No   The computer will never participate as a browser

Yes   The computer will become a browser. Upon startup, the computer attempts to locate the master browser and if it fails to do so, will force an election. This computer will always become a browser, either master or backup. (This is the default value for domain controllers.)

Auto   This computer will possibly become a browser, depending on the number of currently active browsers. It is referred to as a potential browser. (This is the default value for Windows NT Workstations and Windows NT member servers.)

Another parameter in the Registry helps to determine which servers become master browsers and backup browsers. The Registry path for it is:
```
HKEY_LOCAL_MACHINE\System\CurrentControlSet\Services\
Browser\Parameters\IsDomainMaster
```
Setting this parameter to `True` or `Yes` makes a computer a preferred master browser. When a preferred master browser starts, it forces an election. A preferred master browser has priority in browser elections. That means, if nothing prevents it, the preferred master browser will always win an election. (In the event of a tie, the system resorts to using criteria such as the way the computers' names alpha-sort and the amount of time the computers have been running.)

Unless the computer is configured as a preferred master browser, this parameter will always be `False` or `No`.

MCSE 9.2   Browsing across Subnets

Browsing is usually no problem in a single network segment. When your domain spans more that one subnetwork, however, each subnetwork acts as an independent browsing entity. Every subnet has its own master browser and backup browsers. Browser information transmission relies on broadcast traffic, and since browser packets do not cross routers, browsing across IP networks can create certain problems. Because of this, computers on your network segment are often unable to browse remote members of the domain. (See Figure 9.8.)

To browse across subnets, either routers must be configured to forward broadcasts or there must be a special computer able to gather information from all network segments. Let's discuss these two solutions.

The IP Router Solution

When computers in different subnets cannot see each other's browse lists, IP routers can be configured to forward broadcast packets between the subnets. All NetBIOS over TCP/IP (NetBT) broadcasts are sent to UDP port 137, which is defined as a NetBT Name Service. (For more information about NetBIOS over TCP/IP, read RFCs 1001 and 1002.) If the router is configured to forward NetBIOS broadcasts, browsing works just as if all computers were on the same network segment. While the IP router solution solves the incomplete browse list problem, it has the following drawbacks:

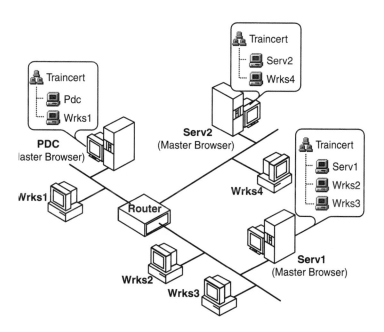

Figure 9.8 *In a subnetted network, each segment acts as an independent browsing entity.*

- Propagates all NetBIOS over TCP/IP broadcast traffic across an internetwork.
- Requires additional router configuration.
- Can lead to browser election conflicts and error reports in the event log.

As you can see, router reconfiguration is, perhaps, not the best solution. To make browsing work across routers, you can configure a computer to gather information from all network segments. This is a job for the domain master browser and is the next area we'll examine.

Domain Master Browser

Let's now discuss how WAN browsing can be implemented with the domain master browser. As seen in Table 9.1, the domain master browser is always the Primary Domain Controller (PDC). The domain master browser is responsible for collecting computer name information for the entire domain, including remote network segments. Based on this information, the domain master browser builds the domain browse list.

Let's see how it works in greater detail. The master browsers on each network segment announce themselves to the domain master browser by using a directed datagram (a *directed* datagram, you'll recall, resolves to an IP address and, therefore, *will* travel across a router) called a *MasterBrowserAnnouncement datagram*. (See Figure 9.9.) Later in this chapter, we will see how the subnet master browser finds the domain master browser.

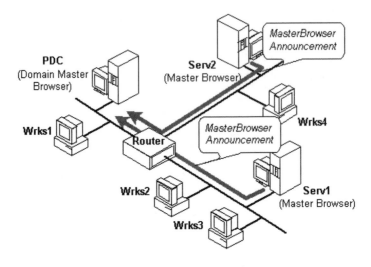

Figure 9.9 *MasterBrowserAnnouncement datagram.*

Once it receives the *MasterBrowserAnnouncement* datagram, the domain master browser knows that there are master browsers in the same domain. The domain master browser then sends the *NetServerEnum* call to the master browser of the particular network segment to obtain a copy of that master browser's browse list. (See Figure 9.10.)

The domain master browser next *merges* its own browse list with the browse list from the master browser. Now the domain master browser has an updated browse list with computers from other subnets. (See Figure 9.11.)

The described process repeats every 15 minutes and guarantees that the domain master browser has a complete browse list of all the computers in the domain.

 Note Since a workgroup does not have a PDC, neither does it have a domain master browser. This imposes some limitations to workgroup browsing, particularly if the network spans more that one subnet. A workgroup can't actually span subnets. If a workgroup is found on two subnets, it actually functions as two workgroups with identical names. Since there is no domain master browser to unite the two workgroups, browsing between them cannot occur!

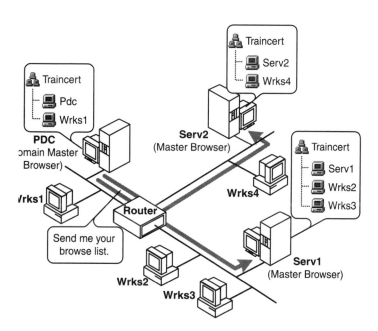

Figure 9.10 *The domain master browser requests the master browser's browse list.*

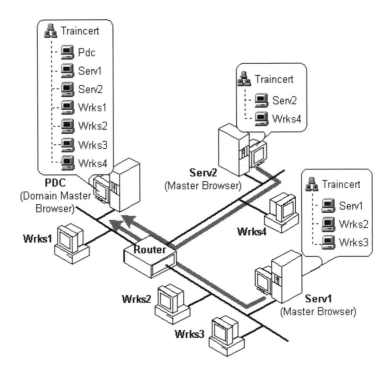

Figure 9.11   *The domain master browser updates its browse list.*

So we seem to have found a solution. If your domain spans several subnets, the PDC, acting as a domain master browser, takes care of synchronizing your subnet browser lists. But stop! There is one question that is still unanswered. We mentioned that subnet master browsers contact the domain master browser with a directed datagram. But how do the master browsers know where their domain master browser is? Fortunately, there are two methods to solve this problem:

- LMHOSTS file.
- WINS.

LMHOSTS File Solution

To implement direct communication between master browsers from remote subnets and the domain master browser, NetBIOS name resolution must function correctly. You might remember that configuring an LMHOSTS file can permit your system to resolve NetBIOS names for machines on remote subnets.

To ensure that each master browser can communicate directly with the domain master browser, a special LMHOSTS file entry must be added. This entry must include the IP address of the domain master browser (the IP address of the PDC), as well as the #DOM and #PRE options. For example:

```
172.20.0.100   PDC   #PRE   #DOM:TRAINCERT
```

You must include this entry in every master browser's LMHOSTS file. Additionally, the domain master browser must have an LMHOSTS file with mappings for every master browser for each network segment.

An example of an LMHOSTS file implementation is illustrated on Figure 9.12.

Optionally you can use the #PRE and #DOM switches for master browser entries in the LMHOSTS file of every master. When multiple entries exist for the same domain, the master browser will try them all, but only the domain master browser will respond.

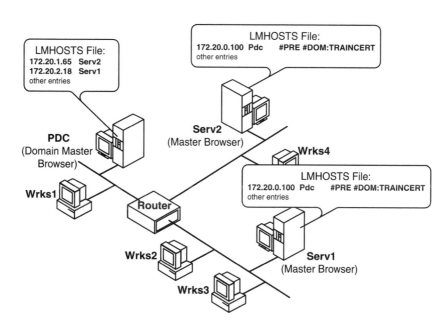

Figure 9.12 *LMHOSTS file solution for WAN browsing.*

When dealing with multiple domains and multiple subnets, the most reliable way to ensure all machines can browse all other machines is to include LMHOSTS entries for each domain controller in the local domain and at least an entry for each PDC in each remote domain.

WINS Solution

WINS also solves NetBIOS broadcast problems. As discussed earlier, WINS does this by dynamically registering a computer's NetBIOS name, and IP address. The domain master browser registers a special NetBIOS name, *domain<1Bh>*. Master browsers periodically query the WINS server and thus know the domain master browser's IP address. Additionally, the domain master browser will periodically request the list of *other* domains that are registered in the WINS database. The domain master browser does this by issuing a wildcard query ending with *<1Bh>*. The WINS server responds with a list of all domains that have their domain master browsers registered in the WINS database. The domain master browser then does a reverse query for each individual *domain<1Bh>* name to learn the location of domain master browsers for that domain.

WINS is the recommended method for domain browsing. WINS has certain enhancements that make it superior to the LMHOSTS file. For example, WINS is far more flexible with remote domain browsing, it is easily monitored, and WINS problems can be quickly diagnosed.

Domain Functions in the TCP/IP Environment

Browsing is not the only domain function that relies on broadcasts. Activities such as logging on to a domain, changing passwords, and replication among domain controllers also prompt broadcasts. Since, as we've already seen, IP routers do not normally forward broadcasts, a form of directed traffic must be used to accomplish such tasks across subnets. Once again, we can rely on the LMHOSTS file and WINS server to help us to do this.

LMHOSTS Solution

To log on to the domain, the client broadcasts the message directly to the domain and also looks for any `#DOM:domain` entries in the LMHOSTS file. If such an entry exists, the client sends the message directly to the computer listed in this entry. You should ensure that each domain controller in the client's LMHOSTS file is identified with the #DOM tag. If the domain controller on the local subnet is off-line, the client will be able to find a domain controller on a remote subnet and log on to the domain. (While the domain controller may be on a remote subnet, it must obviously still be a member of the client's domain to effect a logon.)

> If there are no domain controllers in the client's subnet, a #DOM entry is required if the user wants to log on.

To permit domain user account database synchronization, the primary domain controller must have #DOM entries for all backup domain controllers, and vice versa. Additionally, each backup domain controller should have a #DOM entry for the domain's other backup domain controllers. This will allow domain controller promotions and demotions to occur seamlessly.

WINS Solution

If WINS is implemented, the client will contact the WINS server and ask for a list of domain controllers within the particular domain. The query is issued for the *domain <1Ch>* group entry, where *domain* is the name of the domain the client wishes to log on to. The WINS server replies with a list of up to 25 domain controllers. The client can then send messages directly to the domain controller.

Summary

This chapter provided a detailed description of the Windows NT computer browser service. We discovered the browser service is used to build a list of available network servers and their shared resources. We learned that not every computer has to maintain a browse list, but that browse lists are distributed to specifically assigned computers that perform browser services on behalf of other computers. We saw that browsers have specific roles, such as master browser, backup browser, and non-browser. It is important to remember also that the Primary Domain Controller is assigned a specific role as domain master browser.

We have seen that browsing in a single network segment is usually a straightforward process with no attendant difficulty. WAN browsing, however, was shown to be a bit more complex, since routers do not typically forward broadcasts. We described the two methods that make WAN browsing possible: LMHOSTS files and WINS. Finally, we extended the browser discussion to other domain functions that rely on broadcasts and saw that they also require an LMHOSTS file or WINS server to be able to function across subnetworks.

▲ REVIEW QUESTIONS

1. *If you can successfully ping Server RED and you can connect to Server RED with the* `net use` *command, then you can see Server RED in the browse list.*

   A. True

   B. False

2. *Which of the following are browser roles? (Choose all that apply.)*

   A. Master browser

   B. Backup browser

   C. Potential master browser

   D. Default browser

3. *If a computer is the domain master browser, it cannot be a master browser or a backup browser.*

   A. True

   B. False

4. *How does a non-browser computer get to the browse list?*

   A. The computer issues the directed datagram to the Primary Domain Controller

   B. The computer registers itself on the WINS server and thus gets into the browse list

   C. The computer sends the special host announcement broadcast frame

   D. The computer registers itself on the DHCP server to get into the browse list

5. *Whose function is described here? It is responsible for creating the primary copy of the browse list by receiving the host announcements destined to the domain <1Dh> name.*

   A. Master browser

   B. Primary domain controller

   C. Backup browser

   D. Domain master browser

6. *Kim powers down her computer, but it is still displayed in the* Network Neighborhood *application on other computers. What's wrong?*

   A. Kim's computer is not WINS-enabled

   B. Kim's computer is a DHCP server

   C. Kim's computer has a static entry in the WINS database

   D. This is expected behavior; Kim's computer can remain in the browse list up to an hour or more

7. *What guarantees that there is one and only one master browser in the subnet?*

   A. The Primary Domain Controller regulates this

   B. The WINS server regulates this

   C. Browser elections regulate this

   D. There can be an unlimited number of master browsers in the subnet

8. *Why are there problems with browsing in an IP internetwork?*

   A. Browser service is not WAN-aware

   B. Browser elections do not work over long distances

   C. IP routers do not, by default, typically propagate browser announcements

   D. IP routers do not propagate NetBT packets

9. *How can you make WAN browsing work for a particular domain? (Select all that apply.)*

   A. Configure the IP routers to propagate the NetBT broadcast traffic

   B. Implement WINS and make the domain master browser and all master browsers WINS clients

   C. Implement an LMHOSTS file and identify appropriate entries
      with the #DOM tag

   D. Implement DHCP and make all computers DHCP clients

10. *How does WINS aid in the collection of domains that should appear in the
    browse list?*

   A. The primary domain controller of each domain registers the *domain <1Dh>* name in the WINS database

   B. Domain master browsers query WINS for a list of *domain <1Dh>*
      names to complete their browse lists

   C. The WINS server builds the list of all registered names and
      passes it to domain master browsers

   D. WINS does not aid in the collection of domains

11. *How can you ensure that John will be able to log on to the domain if there
    is no domain controller available in his subnet?*

   A. Make John's computer a WINS client

   B. Ensure that the primary and backup domain controllers are
      WINS clients

   C. Make John's computer a master browser

   D. Make John's computer a preferred master browser

   E. Answers A & B

   F. Answers B & C

   G. There is no way to do it

12. *How can you ensure that John will be able to log on to the domain if there
    is no domain controller available in his subnet and his computer cannot be
    configured as a WINS client?*

   A. Configure the LMHOSTS file on John's computer; put the entries for available domain controllers in the LMHOSTS file

   B. Configure the LMHOSTS file on every domain controller; put
      the entry for John's computer in the LMHOSTS file

   C. Make John's computer a master browser

   D. Make John's computer a preferred master browser

   E. There is no way to do it

13. *Your domain spans several subnets. How can you ensure that domain user
    database synchronization works? (Choose all that apply.)*

A. Make every domain controller a WINS client

B. Create an LMHOSTS file and insert entries with #PRE and #DOM tags for every domain controller; distribute this LMHOSTS file to every domain controller

C. Make every domain controller a master browser

D. Make the primary domain controller a domain master browser

14. *You have 50 Windows NT Workstation computers configured as members of the workgroup named PRODUCTION. Your workgroup spans three subnets. When users open the* Network Neighborhood *application, they see computers only from their local subnet. What steps must you take to permit users to see remote computers in their browse list?*

A. Implement an LMHOSTS file on every computer in the workgroup

B. Make all workstations WINS clients

C. Configure one workstation from each subnet to become a master browser

D. There is no way to do it

15. *Your TCP/IP network contains multiple domains and functions across four subnets. You do not use WINS. What entries must you include in the LMHOSTS file of each computer to ensure every machine in your network can browse every machine in every domain?*

A. One entry for a backup domain controller in each domain (local and remote)

B. An entry for each domain controller in the local domain

C. One entry for the PDC in each remote domain, and one entry for each domain controller in the local domain

D. An entry for each DNS server in the network

Host Name Resolution

So far we've looked chiefly at TCP/IP and its interaction with Windows-based machines. Most of our study has centered on how to communicate with computers possessing NetBIOS names and much of our concern has been on how to resolve a NetBIOS name to an IP address and, ultimately, to a MAC address. We will now broaden our horizon a bit and discuss a computer naming system that can be used with any computer running TCP/IP. While we will still concentrate on how to network with Windows NT computers, we will see that in the TCP/IP world, you can communicate if you know only the IP address. (You ultimately need a MAC address for communication, but TCP/IP will help you get that as long as you have an IP address.) As we've seen, using just an IP address can get tiresome. Unfortunately, NetBIOS names are available only in the Windows environment (or on other systems that have third-party NetBIOS helper programs). The good news is: Computers not fortunate enough to be members of the Windows fold can use a *host*

245

name that can be related to an IP address just like a NetBIOS name. The better news is that Windows computers can also have and work with host names, making this a robust method of computer naming!

At the conclusion of this chapter, you will be able to:

- Explain TCP/IP naming schemes.
- Define a host name and explain the difference between a *host name* and a *NetBIOS name*.
- Describe the methods of host name resolution.
- Outline the Microsoft host name resolution process.
- Create, edit, and maintain a HOSTS file.

TCP/IP Naming Schemes

Network communication ultimately requires a MAC address. On TCP/IP networks, an IP address is a necessary piece of information to acquire a MAC address. Using IP addresses for everything in large environments can be tedious for humans, and applications rarely use IP addresses. Because of this, friendly computer names are used almost exclusively. We must, therefore, have some method or methods to resolve friendly names to IP addresses, and vice versa.

In the Windows world, we use NetBIOS names. NetBIOS names permit us to identify IP addresses in a format that is easier to work with and remember. NetBIOS names have the added advantage of providing some degree of protocol independence within Windows networks. In other words, if I identify a machine with a NetBIOS name (e.g., "MyComputer") that corresponds to a particular IP address, the IP address will have no meaning if I access the machine using the IPX/SPX protocol, but the machine will *still* be known as "MyComputer." While most network communications in a Windows environment can be accomplished by using a NetBIOS name *or* an IP address, some applications are written specifically for named communication (e.g., connecting to a SQL Server or Exchange Server). Connectivity in these cases *must* be accomplished through use of a NetBIOS name.

In the UNIX environment, all network communication can be accomplished through the use of an IP address (which, of course, is translated to a MAC address). To relieve the tedium of always using IP addresses, however, you may also use a *host name* or *fully-qualified domain name*. (A fully-qualified domain name (FQDN) is a combination of the host and domain name. FQDNs are fully explored in the next chapter.) Windows systems can also communicate through host names and FQDNs. (Originally, Windows computers using Microsoft network commands, such as `net use`, could use only NetBIOS names in those commands. Current Windows operating systems permit the use of IP addresses, host names, and FQDNs in most network commands.)

What Is a Host Name?

A *host name* is any alias that can be assigned to a computer to identify a TCP/IP host. By default, in a Windows environment, the host name is the NetBIOS name. This, however, is not required—a host name can be *any* 256-character string. A single computer can even have multiple host names.

 Although the host name does not have to correspond to the NetBIOS name, if the names are not the same, only standard host name resolution methods will work. If the system has to resort to Microsoft host name resolution methods, resolution will fail if these names differ.

Like the NetBIOS name, a host name can be used in place of an IP address in TCP/IP utilities. The host name will always correspond to an IP address stored in the machine's HOSTS file or in a DNS database. If the host name is the same as the NetBIOS name, it will also correspond to an IP address stored on a NetBIOS name server or LMHOSTS file.

Unlike NetBIOS names, host names are created when they are placed in a HOSTS file or loaded on a DNS server. To assign a host name to a Windows NT 4.0 computer, select the DNS tab of the `TCP/IP Properties` dialog (in the `Network` dialog) and set the name as shown in Figure 10.1. In the figure, the computer's host name is `MyComputer` and the FQDN is `MyComputer.mydomain.com`. Typing `HOSTNAME` at the command prompt will reveal the host name of the local computer.

Host Name Resolution

Just as with NetBIOS names, a host name doesn't do much good if we can't resolve it to an IP address. The methods of name resolution listed below should look familiar since they're essentially the same methods we discussed

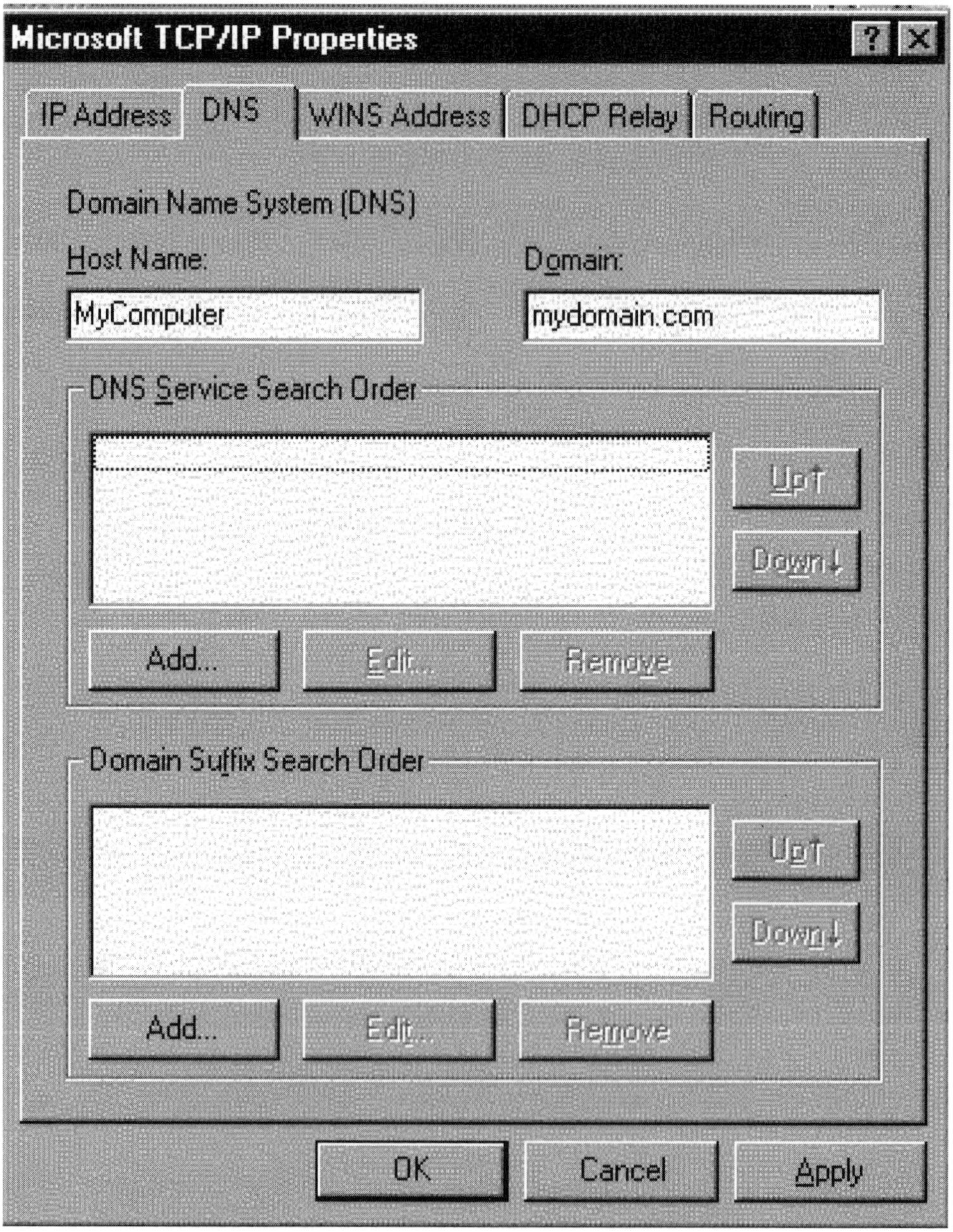

Figure 10.1 *Setting the host name of a Windows NT 4.0 computer.*

for NetBIOS name resolution. The perceptive student will, however, notice that they're listed in a different order.

Standard Name Resolution Methods

The following methods are standard throughout TCP/IP networks:

- Local Host Name. The first step in host name resolution occurs when the local machine checks its own host name. If it discovers the destination host name is the same as its configured host name, it doesn't need to perform any further resolution.
- HOSTS File. The HOSTS file is a text file on the local computer that requires manual entry and maintenance. Checking this file is always the second host name resolution step (after checking the local host name). The HOSTS file maps IP addresses to host names or FQDNs. (HOSTS files use the same format as the 4.3 Berkeley Software Distribution UNIX\etc\hosts file.) We will look at HOSTS files in some detail later in this chapter.
- Domain Name System (DNS). The DNS is a server that maintains a database of IP addresses and FQDNs. Like the HOSTS file, DNS requires manual entry and maintenance. (DNS is fully covered in the next chapter.)

Microsoft Name Resolution Methods

In addition to standard resolution methods, if the host name and NetBIOS name are the same, some Microsoft methods can be used to map host names to IP addresses on Windows systems.

- NetBIOS Name Server (NBNS). An NBNS is any server implemented under RFC 1001/1002 to provide NetBIOS name resolution. A computer trying to contact a machine with a particular host name can query the NBNS for a name/IP address mapping. If the host name is equivalent to a NetBIOS name found in the NBNS database, the NBNS will return the IP address mapped to the NetBIOS name. (As we've seen, the Microsoft implementation of an NBNS is WINS.)
- Local Broadcast. If a computer can't find a mapping from a name server, it can send a broadcast over the local network. If the target computer receives the broadcast and recognizes the host name as its NetBIOS name, it will respond with its IP address to permit full TCP/IP communication.

- LMHOSTS File. An LMHOSTS file is a text file on the local computer that contains both the NetBIOS name and IP address of Windows networking computers on remote networks. If the host name is equivalent to a NetBIOS name found in the LMHOSTS file, the computer will use the IP address mapped to the NetBIOS name.

Name Resolution Using a HOSTS File

If you remember what you learned about name resolution using the LMHOSTS file, you already have a good idea about the function of the HOSTS file. Like the LMHOSTS file, the HOSTS file resides on the local machine and requires manual update and maintenance. Unlike the LMHOSTS file, which is used to find only remote machines, the HOSTS file contains mappings for both local and remote hosts.

When a computer needs to resolve a host name, it first checks to see if the host name is the same as the local host name (in other words, it checks to see if the name it's looking for is its own). If the host name being sought is not the local host name, the computer checks its HOSTS file for an appropriate mapping. If the HOSTS file doesn't contain the required information, the computer will attempt name resolution using the alternate methods described in the previous section (DNS, NBNS, etc.). If none of the host name resolution methods yields an IP address mapping, the network communication fails and the user receives an error message.

Once an IP address mapping is obtained (through the HOSTS file or other name resolution method), the computer will use the Address Resolution Protocol (ARP) to resolve the host name to a hardware address. If the host is on the local network, ARP will return the host's hardware address. (ARP first checks its cache to see if it has already obtained a mapping; if none is found, it uses a broadcast to resolve the IP address to a MAC address.) If the host is on a remote network, ARP returns the hardware address of a router that can lead to the destination host and the communication is *routed* to it. (In Windows NT, this address is typically that of the default gateway.)

Name Resolution Using a DNS Server

Like the HOSTS file, a *Domain Name System* (DNS) server maintains IP address mappings in a manually maintained and updated list (DNS is fully explored in the next chapter). As you might expect, however, the DNS does not need to reside on the local computer. Another distinction between the HOSTS file and a DNS server is, while a HOSTS file can contain host names and FQDNs, the DNS server contains only FQDNs (host name resolution using FQDNs is no problem since the host name is found within the FQDN).

DNS name resolution is very similar to resolution using the HOSTS file. Assuming the calling computer is configured to use DNS name resolution, when it is unable to locate a mapping in its HOSTS file, it queries the configured DNS server. If the DNS server has a mapping, it returns the information and the computer uses ARP to resolve the host name to a hardware address. If the host is on the local network, ARP returns the host's hardware address. If the host is on a remote network, ARP returns the hardware address of a router that can lead to the destination host and the communication is routed to it.

If the server does not respond, the client makes several additional attempts at varying intervals. If the sever fails to respond after the additional attempts, or if it responds but has no mapping for the desired target host, the client tries other methods. If the client isn't configured to use additional resolution methods, or if they fail, communication cannot be established with the target host and an error message is returned.

The Microsoft Host Name Resolution Process

Windows NT computers can be configured to use several host name resolution methods. The name resolution sequence is depicted in Figure 10.2. If one of the methods fails, the Windows NT computer continues to the next method until it obtains a mapping or until all methods have failed. For all methods to function properly, the Windows NT computer must be configured to use them. For NetBIOS-based methods to operate properly, the host name being sought must be equivalent to the target computer's NetBIOS name.

As shown in Figure 10.2, Windows NT employs the following host name resolution steps in the order listed:

- Local Host Name. The first step in host name resolution is to check to see if the host name being sought is the same as the local host name. If they are the same, the name is resolved and the communication accomplished without actual network activity.

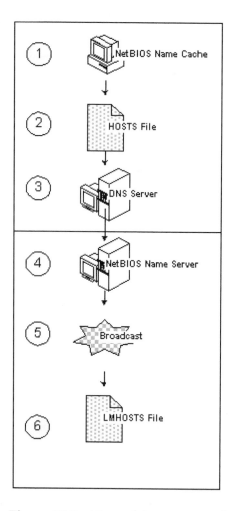

Figure 10.2 *Microsoft host name resolution process.*

- HOSTS. If the host name being sought is different from the local host name, the computer checks its HOSTS file. If a mapping is found, the host name is resolved.
- DNS. If a mapping was not found in the HOSTS file, the computer sends a resolution request to its configured DNS server. If the DNS server doesn't initially respond, the computer will make additional attempts at 5, 10, 20, and 40 seconds.
- NetBIOS Name Server. If DNS cannot resolve the host name, the client computer makes an assumption that the host name it seeks is on

a computer whose NetBIOS name is the same as its host name. (If this is a bad assumption, this and the remaining steps will yield an incorrect—or no—result.) The client first checks its NetBIOS name cache to see if it has recently resolved a NetBIOS name that is the same as the host name. If the cache does not yield the appropriate information, three attempts are made to contact a NetBIOS name server. For this to happen, the machine must be configured to go to a name server. This step is normally accomplished before resorting to broadcast, but may be attempted after broadcast depending on the setting of the *name resolution node* (name resolution nodes were fully explained in Chapter 7).

- Broadcast. If the NetBIOS name server doesn't resolve the name, the computer will generate three broadcasts on the local network.
- LMHOSTS. If broadcast doesn't yield the necessary information, the local LMHOSTS file is parsed.

If none of these methods yields an IP address mapping, the client computer will be able to communicate with the host it is seeking only through use of the IP address.

MCSE 10.1   Configuring the HOSTS File

As already discussed, a HOSTS file is simply a text file found on the local machine with IP address mappings that correspond to host names (or FQDNs) for machines with which the local computer is likely to want to communicate. If you fully understand the construction of the LMHOSTS file, discussed in Chapter 7, you already know a great deal about the HOSTS file. HOSTS files contain only IP addresses, host or fully-qualified domain names, and comments, making them a bit easier to construct than LMHOSTS files. An example HOSTS file is depicted in Figure 10.3.

In constructing a HOSTS file, simply enter the IP address followed by at least one space or Tab. Next, type the host name or FQDN. Finally, to include a comment, type a pound sign (#) followed by your comment. Each line is limited to 255 characters. The *localhost* entry is found in HOSTS files by default.

Host name resolution by Windows computers is *not* case-sensitive. That is to say, HOSTS files residing on Windows computers aren't case-sensitive. UNIX computers are, however, *very concerned* about the proper case when referring to host names. An easy way to ensure your HOSTS file will work regardless of the system in question is to use both an upper-case

```
127.0.0.1        Localhost               #loopback
205.10.12.10     Wkstn1
205.10.12.11     Wkstn2

205.10.12.24     gateway                 #Default Gateway2

200.18.22.10     Server1                 # SQL Server
200.18.22.12     Server2                 # Print Server
210.22.18.10     Server3                 # Exchange Server

102.54.94.97     rhino.microsoft.com

131.107.2.100    unixhost
131.107.2.100    UNIXHOST

131.107.3.1      unixhost2.udomain.com
131.107.3.1      UNIXHOST2.UDOMAIN.COM
```

Figure 10.3 *Sample HOSTS file.*

and lower-case entry for the same host name (as shown in Figure 10.3 for
`unixhost` and `unixhost2`).

Just as with the LMHOSTS file, the HOSTS file resides in the `\system-`
`root\system32\drivers\etc` directory. The HOSTS file is simply named
`hosts`, with no file extension. All TCP/IP-configured Windows NT computers have a default HOSTS file. The default file contains a few example mappings (commented out), as well as a mapping for the loopback address.

Study Break

Making a Host File Entry

Check your `\systemroot\system32\drivers\etc` directory (remember, in this
context, `\systemroot` refers to the directory containing the Windows NT system files — this
directory is `\WINNT` by default in Windows NT 4.0) for a HOSTS file. If one is there, use
Notepad to open it. Is there an entry for your computer? If not, enter a line in the file for your machine.

If there was no HOSTS file in the directory, use *Notepad* to create your own HOSTS file with
an entry for your computer. Save the file in `\systemroot\system32\dri-`
`vers\etc`.

Now, let's prove that the HOSTS file really works. Open the HOSTS file on your machine and create an entry for one of the computers in your network (if you don't have information on the other machines, or if you're at a stand-alone machine, you can make another entry for your computer). Use the correct IP address, but use `TSTSRVR` as the computer's host name. Now, go to a command prompt and ping `TSTSRVR` (by name). Did you get a response? Ping the computer with its correct name. Did it respond to that too? You have, essentially, told your computer to use `TSTSRVR` as a host name for the computer in addition to any other host name it may have. You could ping using both identities because both entries correspond to the same machine. If there was no HOSTS file entry for the computer's real name, resolution of that name would likely be carried out by NetBIOS.

Summary

In this chapter we looked at *host names* and how they're resolved to IP addresses and, ultimately, to MAC addresses. We saw that a host name is simply a way of referring to a computer without actually using the machine's IP address. We learned the host name could be the same as or different from the NetBIOS name (although the default in Windows systems is for both names to be the same). We saw that a host name is, essentially, any name that can be mapped to a machine's IP address.

We discovered that host name resolution begins when the computer checks to see if the host name it's seeking is its own. If the host name differs from the local computer's name, we saw that the calling host checks its local HOSTS file and then a DNS server (if so configured). We also saw that Microsoft computers can resort to the NetBIOS methods of using a NetBIOS name server, broadcast, or LMHOSTS file when standard host name resolution methods fail. We learned that the NetBIOS methods work only in the case where the host name and NetBIOS name is the same (this is usually the case).

Finally, we learned how to construct a HOSTS file. We discovered that HOSTS files contain IP addresses and host names, or fully-qualified domain names. We also learned that, although Windows systems are not concerned about capitalization when using the HOSTS file, other systems (such as UNIX) are. We should, therefore, make our entries case-accurate or use both upper- and lower-case entries when creating HOSTS files that will be used by non-Windows systems.

▲ REVIEW QUESTIONS

1. *The following HOSTS file entries are from a Windows NT server. Which entries will fail to connect to the UNIX server, USrvr? (Select all that apply.)*

```
A. 200.18.22.2      #USrvr       UNIX Server
B. 200.18.22.2      USRVR        #UNIX Server
C. 200.18.222       USrvr        #UNIX Server
D. 200.18.22.2      UNIX Server  #Usrvr
```

2. *The following HOSTS file entries are from a UNIX server. Which entries will successfully connect to the computer using the host name* `MyClient`*? (Select all that apply.)*

```
A. 200.18.22.20     myclient     #client computer
B. 200.18.22.20     MYCLIENT     #client computer
C. 200.18.20.22     MyClient
D. 200.18.22.20     #MyClient    client computer
```

3. *Sandy will use FTP to retrieve files from a UNIX server. Her computer is not a DNS client. What can she use to connect to the UNIX machine? (Select all that apply.)*

   A. WINS

   B. LMHOSTS

   C. DHCP

   D. HOSTS

4. *Tim is trying to troubleshoot a connectivity problem between his Windows NT computer and a UNIX server. His HOSTS file contains the following entries:*

```
A. 200.18.22.10     server1.mycorp.com
B. 200.18.22.11     server2.mycorp.com
```

   When Tim types `ping server1.sales.mycorp.com,` *he receives a "Bad IP Address" message, but when he types* `ping 200.18.22.10,` *he gets a good response. What is the most likely cause of the problem?*

   A. The host name in the HOSTS file uses the wrong case

   B. PING cannot be used with host names

   C. Tim is using the wrong fully-qualified domain name

   D. The LMHOSTS file has the wrong entries

5. *Your Windows NT computer cannot connect to other computers on your network using host names. Your HOSTS file looks like the following:*

```
A. 127.0.0.1 #Localhost #Loop Back
B. 200.18.200.20 #Sales #Sales Server
```

C. `200.18.200.36 #Marketing #$Marketing Server`

D. `200.18.200.11 #printer #laser $printer`

E. `200.18.200.50 #Gateway #%Default%gateway`

How can you correct the file?

A. Remove all the embedded spaces in the file

B. Remove the first pound sign (#) character from each line

C. Remove the first dollar sign ($) character from each line

D. Remove all the percent sign (%) characters from the file

6. *Vicky's computer uses a HOSTS file to connect to remote servers. Her HOSTS file contains the following entries:*

A. `122.12.10.25 SalesSrv #Sales Department Server`

B. `112.36.5.22 FileSrv #FTP File Server`

C. `122.22.5.24 MktSrv #Marketing Server`

D. `122.36.10.12 DevSrv #Development Server`

When Vicky uses the command `ftp FileSrv`*, she connects to a UNIX server on a remote network. When she types* `ftp 122.36.5.22`*, however, the operation fails. What is the likely cause of the problem?*

A. The UNIX server's LMHOSTS file has entries that conflict with Vicky's HOSTS file

B. Vicky does not have IP permissions on the UNIX server

C. `122.36.5.22` is not the IP address of an FTP server

D. FTP will not work with IP addresses

Domain Name System

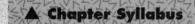
Are you tired of name resolution yet? As we've seen, name resolution is, arguably, the most critical piece in the network communication puzzle. We've become proficient in a number of name resolution methods but, so far, they've all been useful only within our local network or in networks close to it. To date, our name resolution methods have been able to handle only a relatively small list of NetBIOS or host names. In this chapter, we'll learn how to resolve names for the entire Internet...and beyond!

This chapter starts with a general overview of the *Domain Name Space* and *Domain Name System* (DNS) and proceeds to a more specific treatment of the DNS package that comes with Windows NT 4.0.

At the conclusion of this chapter, you will be able to:

- Explain why a *Domain Name System* was required.

259

- Describe a *Domain Name Space.*
- Explain zones of authority.
- List and define the roles played by name servers.
- Describe the DNS name resolution process.
- Describe the files and records used by DNS.
- Outline the concerns required by DNS implementation planning.
- Install and configure a DNS server on a computer running Windows NT 4.0 Server.
- Integrate a DNS server with other name servers.
- Configure a DNS server to operate in any of its roles.
- Configure a client computer to use DNS.
- Use the NSLOOKUP utility to troubleshoot a DNS server.

Domain Name System Basics

Before we actually make DNS work, we will spend some time looking at the genesis of the system and studying its characteristics.

The Need for a Domain Name System

In its infancy, the ARPANET (the forerunner of today's Internet) consisted of only a few hundred machines. As you might imagine, name resolution could have been accomplished with a simple HOSTS file. In fact, the ARPANET originally did use such a file. It was located on a server at the Stanford Research Institute's Network Information Center (SRI-NIC) and was called `Hosts.txt`. The ARPANET naming system was a flat name structure, or *flat name space*. This rather impressive-sounding term simply meant that the system consisted of a list of unique names. Names did not fit into any kind of hierarchy. In other words, in a flat name space, hosts were like people with only first names. We could have only one each of Bill, Bob, Mary, and Lisa, but since we could think of more first names than we had computers, this wasn't a problem.

In those early days, we rarely changed or added computer names, so the `Hosts.txt` file needed to be updated only a couple of times a week. With a small number of hosts, there was little difficulty in getting to the file even though it was maintained on only a single server at one location.

If the ARPANET had remained a network of a few hundred computers, there is little chance you'd be reading this book. We all know the Internet has grown exponentially since those good old days. Can you imagine trying to come up with a first name for your computer that is unique across the entire Internet? How long do you think it would take to access the `Hosts.txt` file today? How large a hard drive would be required for the `Hosts.txt` file and how long would it take to search through it? How would you like to add or subtract entries in `Hosts.txt` every time a machine joined or left the Internet?

Clearly some changes were required. The first step was to go from the flat name space to a *hierarchical name space*. Now Bill, Bob, Mary, and Lisa can have last names to differentiate them from other Bills, Bobs, Marys, and Lisas. Bill might become *Bill Microsoft,* while Mary might be *Mary Senate.* With the new name space came a new system of servers to maintain it. Now, instead of a single text file on a single machine, we have *Domain Name System* (DNS) servers scattered throughout the Internet (as well as on countless private networks). Each server can maintain its own list of names and can contact other DNS servers if it needs to find names it doesn't maintain.

The Domain Name System

The Domain Name System (DNS) is simply a client/server-based distributed database management system that maintains records for computers in a Domain Name Space. Described in RFCs 1034 and 1035, DNS operates at the Application Layer and uses the User Datagram Protocol (UDP) and the Transmission Control Protocol (TCP). (The client will always attempt to use UDP for increased performance. If the returned information is too long for a UDP broadcast message, it will return in a truncated form. In this case, the client will resort to TCP.) You can think of DNS as an automated telephone book. If you wanted to call *Mary Senate,* you would look for *Mary* by checking all the *Senates* in the book's *S* section. When you found *Mary's* entry, you would write down her telephone number and give her a call. Using DNS, we work our way through the hierarchy of the Domain Name Space until we find the appropriate host and determine its IP address.

RESOLVERS

The client side of the DNS process is called the *resolver.* The resolver can refer to the computer that is attempting to obtain a name resolution or to the piece of software running on that computer that will make the actual name request. (Here, when we talk of "client side," we're referring to any machine that wishes to obtain an address mapping.)

Resolvers can be built into applications, or they can be library routines designed for just this purpose.

NAME SERVERS

As you may have deduced, the *name server* is the server side of the DNS process. Just as with the *resolver*, this term may be used to refer to a machine or a piece of software. The name server attempts to provide a computer or domain name to IP address mapping. If it cannot, it may forward a request to another name server that can. Name servers are grouped into levels known as *domains*.

DOMAIN NAME SPACE

A Domain Name Space provides a hierarchical way of naming hosts. It is analogous to the layout of a phone book, where we first located the book for the appropriate locale, then found the *S* section, looked for the *Senates*, and finally found *Mary Senate*. The Domain Name Space is divided into a number of domains at different levels, as shown in Figure 11.1.

ROOT-LEVEL DOMAIN • The top Domain Name Space level is called the *root* domain. This is simply the starting reference from which all lower domains are located. The root domain has no label or, more accurately, has a null label. It is depicted by a single dot (.) in a domain name.

The root-level domain is simply "understood" in domain names. Using a final dot is strictly optional.

TOP-LEVEL DOMAINS • *Top-level* domains represent the major divisions of a Domain Name Space. These domains contain *second-level* domains and hosts. Table 11.1 shows the current top-level domains.

SECOND-LEVEL DOMAINS • *Second-level* domains are directly subordinate to the top-level domains. These domains contain host names as well as lower-level domains (*subdomains*). Typically, second-level domains represent major organizations such as a company, college, governmental branch, or military service. The `Senate` domain, for instance, could contain computers such as `ftp.senate.gov`, and subdomains like `finance.senate.gov`. The finance subdomain might contain a computer called `chmn.finance.senate.gov`.

HOST NAMES • Host names represent individual computers within domains or subdomains. When the host name is appended to the domain name, we call

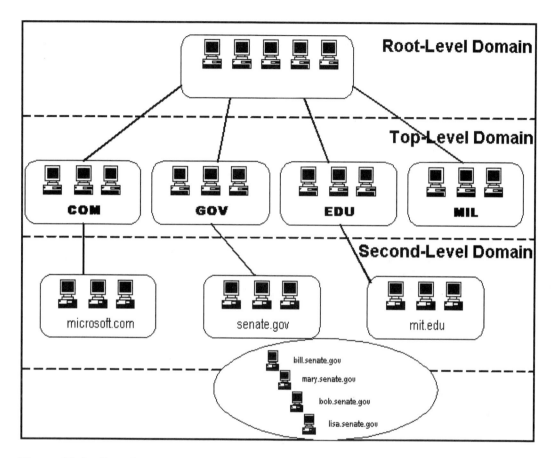

Figure 11.1 *Domain name space.*

Table 11.1 *Current Top-Level Domains*

Domain Name	Definition
com	Commercial organizations
edu	Educational institutions
org	Not-for-profit organizations
net	Internet-related networks
gov	Non-military government organizations
mil	Military government organizations
num	Phone numbers
arpa	Reverse DNS
xx	Two-letter country code

the resulting concatenation a *fully-qualified domain name* (FQDN). The FQDN for the host `Mary`, shown in Figure 11.1, would be `mary.senate.gov`.

Zones of Authority

A zone of authority delineates the portion of the Domain Name Space that belongs to a particular name server. The name server is responsible for storing address mappings for everything within its zone of authority. A zone of authority contains at least one domain (or subdomain), and may contain some or all of the subdomains in the zone's root domain.

> The zone's root domain shouldn't be confused with the root-level domain. A zone's root domain is simply the highest level domain contained in the zone. The zone's root domain may or may not contain subdomains.

In Figure 11.2, Zone 1 encompasses the senate domain (`senate.gov`), as well as the subdomain for the rules committee (`rules.senate.gov`). Zone 2 contains `finance.senate.gov`, while Zone 3 controls `ethics.senate.gov`. The advantage found in separating a domain into different zones may be found in better workload distribution for the name servers or in more efficient data replication. While a single domain can be split into multiple zones of authority, a single name server can be assigned more than one zone.

Roles for Name Servers

DNS servers can be configured to operate in a variety of roles. Beyond simply maintaining their zone databases, servers can function as a team to manage zone data across the entire network. Not mutually exclusive, DNS server roles are listed in Table 11.2 and explained below.

PRIMARY NAME SERVERS

The primary name server is what you have likely envisioned during the discussion thus far. A primary server maintains zone data in local files. When you make changes to zone data (add, delete, or alter domains or hosts), you do it at the primary server level.

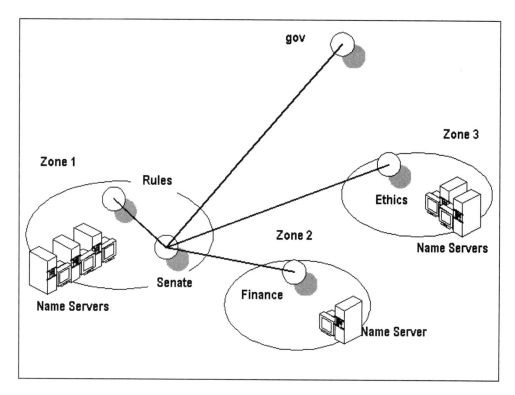

Figure 11.2   *Zones of authority.*

SECONDARY NAME SERVERS

In its *secondary server* role, the DNS server obtains zone information from another server in the network—one with authority for the particular zone. When a secondary server acquires such information, the operation is known as a *zone transfer*.

Table 11.2   *DNS Server Roles*

Role	Function
Primary Name Server	Maintains zone data locally
Secondary Name Server	Obtains zone data from master name server
Master Name Server	Provides zone data to secondary server
Caching-Only Server	Maintains no zone data
Forwarder	Designated to forward requests to remote networks
Slave	Permitted to work only through forwarders

Using secondary servers provides a number of enhancements to the DNS environment. A secondary name server provides a backup for the primary. Once it has completed a zone transfer, it will be capable of supporting clients while the primary is off-line. A secondary server can provide faster data access. If your network is separated by a WAN link, maintaining a primary server on one side of the link and a secondary server on the other side will permit clients to access DNS zone information without the attendant delay in crossing the slow link. In a busy DNS environment, a secondary server can also reduce the load on the primary name server.

Since information for each zone is stored in a separate file, a secondary server for one zone can be a primary server for another zone. This "dual role" capability permits a more efficient way of managing DNS servers.

MASTER NAME SERVERS

A *master name server* is a primary or secondary name server from which a secondary server obtains zone information in a zone transfer. When you define a secondary zone on a name server, you must also designate a *master name server* for that zone (this designation is known to the server upon which you've defined the secondary zone only). When the secondary server starts up, it conducts a zone transfer with the designated master server. A secondary server cares only that it can get the zone information and pays no attention to the master server's status as primary or secondary for that zone.

CACHING-ONLY SERVERS

As we'll soon see, all DNS servers cache name queries they have resolved. A *caching-only server*, however, does nothing else. These machines are not authoritative for any zones and conduct no zone transfers. They keep no zone data in their local databases. Every time a caching-only server takes part in a name resolution, it stores the information in its cache.

Caching-only servers can help in reducing the load on a primary or secondary server where the same names are frequently resolved. They can relieve traffic across a slow link much as a secondary server can. When employing a caching-only server, remember that it will have no information at all when it starts, but must "learn" everything it knows in the course of its business. (If you're wondering how it can do this, keep reading—we'll start to cover that information in the next section.) This can actually increase efficiency across a slow link since the caching-only server can give out frequently requested information on its side of the link without effecting a zone transfer that would increase overall link traffic.

FORWARDERS

When a DNS name server must communicate with other DNS name servers on the public Internet to resolve a name request, it does so through a *forwarder*. Servers designated as forwarders are the only computers allowed to carry out wide-area communications across the Internet. Any other DNS name server within the local network would be configured to use a forwarder and supplied with IP addresses for the DNS name servers designated as forwarders. A server configured to use forwarders receives a DNS request that it can't resolve through its own files and passes the request to a forwarder. The forwarder takes action to resolve the request and returns the result to the requesting server, which provides the information to the original requester. If the forwarder is unable to satisfy the request, the original name server will take other action to attempt to locate the desired information. (Actually, any server not configured to *use* a forwarder *is* a forwarder by the above definition. DNS servers are, therefore, forwarders by default. We'll see exactly how to configure a server to use forwarders a little later in this chapter.)

SLAVES

DNS servers that have been configured to use forwarders exclusively are known as *slaves*. These machines are configured to return a failure message if the forwarder is unable to resolve the request and do not attempt to contact other name servers if the forwarder fails to satisfy the request.

DNS Name Resolution

Now that we understand some of the basics of DNS, let's take a look at the query process. When looking for information, the resolver (client) can make three different kinds of queries: a *recursive*, *iterative*, or *inverse* query.

RECURSIVE QUERY

If a resolver sends a *recursive query* to a name server, that name server must return the requested information. It cannot simply return a message referring the resolver to a different name server. If the name server receiving the recursive query is unable to locate the requested information, it may query other name servers, but it *must* respond to the resolver with either the information request or an error message stating that the name or domain does not exist. This is the type of request typically made by a resolver to a name server or by a name server to a forwarder.

ITERATIVE QUERY

An *iterative query* is typically made by a DNS server to other DNS servers in response to a recursive query from a resolver which it—the original server—cannot answer. Under an iterative query, the queried server responds with the best answer it currently has.

Figure 11.3 illustrates an iterative query that begins as a recursive query. The local client (resolver) needs to contact the machine known as `mary.senate.gov`. The resolution process is as follows:

1. The resolver, using a recursive query, asks the local name server for a mapping to `mary.senate.gov`.
2. Unable to find the requested domain name (`senate.gov`) in its local zone files, but required to provide an answer to the resolver, the local

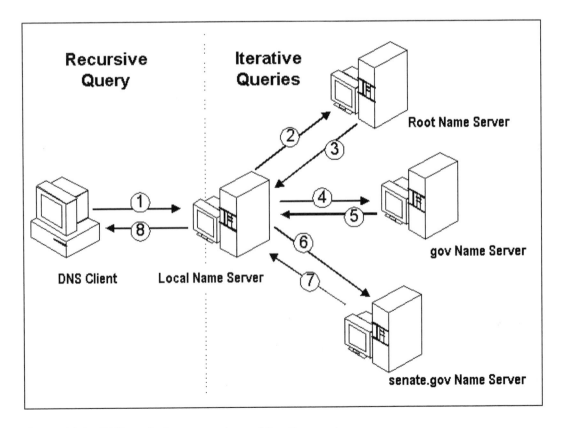

Figure 11.3 *DNS resolution—recursive and iterative queries.*

server sends an iterative query to a `root name server` to obtain a mapping for `mary.senate.gov`.

3. The root name server responds with the IP address of a name server for the `gov` top-level domain.

4. The local name server sends an iterative query for `mary.senate.gov` to the `gov` server.

5. The `gov` server responds with the IP address of a name server for the `senate.gov` domain.

6. The local server then sends an iterative query to the `senate.gov` server.

7. The `senate.gov` server returns the IP address mapping for `mary.senate.gov`.

8. The local name server returns the mapping to the resolver.

INVERSE QUERY

Sometimes we know an IP address, but need to know the host name. Unfortunately, the DNS name space is constructed to provide IP addresses when host names are known and not the other way around. Originally, the only way to find this information was by performing an exhaustive search of every domain in existence!

Since the number of hosts and domains in the world is increasing at a rapid rate, searching the entire Internet each time a host name is required would result in a lot of network traffic, consume many resources and much time, and wouldn't be any fun. Fortunately, a special domain, called `in-addr.arpa`, contains reverse look-up information in nodes named after the dotted decimal numbers that make up IP addresses.

As you've noticed, IP addresses get more specific from left to right, while domain names get more specific from right to left. To resolve this discontinuity, the octets are reversed in the `in-addr.arpa` domain. When organizations are assigned their class A, B, or C IP addresses, they are also assigned administration of the appropriate lower limbs of the `in-addr.arpa` domain.

The `in-addr.arpa` domain contains special resource records known as *pointer* (PTR) records, which associate the IP address with the appropriate host name. To find the host name associated with `200.22.18.36`, for instance, you'd query the DNS server for the PTR for `36.18.22.200.in-addr.arpa`. The PTR would contain both the host name and its associated IP address. Ensuring the creation of pointer records is an extremely important part of DNS administration.

CACHING AND TIME TO LIVE (TTL)

Each time a name server receives information, it caches it for later use. As you might imagine, in the process of servicing a recursive query, a name server will likely accumulate a great deal of information. Retaining this information for an extended period of time creates two problems. Since DNS data can change over time, the data can become inaccurate. Even if data accuracy could be assured, retaining every bit of data received by a name server for every one-time request it serviced over the course of its lifetime would require a great deal of storage space.

The *Time to Live* (TTL) value alleviates both problems by limiting the time the name server will cache a particular piece of data. When entering information into the name server, the administrator sets a TTL for each record. A small TTL guards against inaccurate and inconsistent data, while a larger TTL reduces the load on name servers by permitting more cached data. When selecting a TTL, it is important to balance these two factors.

As soon as a name server caches a piece of data, it begins to decrement the TTL. When the TTL reaches zero, the data is flushed from the cache. If a name server receives a request that can be filled from its cache, it will forward the information with the *decremented* TTL. This is analogous to buying a bottle of milk at the supermarket. Let's say you buy a bottle with a freshness date that expires in seven days. You bring it home, put it in your refrigerator for three days, and then give it to your neighbor. Your neighbor will be able to safely use the milk for only four (not seven) days. When the resolver receives DNS data, it will also cache it for further use. The TTL is honored on resolvers just as it is on name servers.

DNS Files

Typically, Domain Name Systems are configured by editing text files. Windows NT 4.0, however, provides a more user-friendly interface, which makes administration of local and remote Microsoft DNS servers much more pleasant. With the understanding that your administrative tasks can be carried out easily under a Windows graphical user interface (GUI), we will turn to the actual text files to help us build a better understanding of what really goes on inside a DNS server.

Under RFCs 1034 and 1035, several text files define the DNS system configuration and database. These files include the *database, reverse lookup, 127 reverse lookup,* and *cache* files, and can include a *boot* file. Even though we rarely look at raw files when using the Windows NT DNS GUI, they are critical to the operation of the DNS server and are explained in detail in this section.

DATABASE FILE

The DNS database file is a text file that represents most of the name server's knowledge base for a particular zone. By default, the database file uses the zone name with .dns appended to it. For example, if your zone were senate.gov, the database file would be called senate.gov.dns. Windows NT 4.0 provides a sample DNS database file called place.dns (look for the file in the WNNT\System32\DNS\Samples directory). You can rename this file using the aforementioned naming convention and add records to it for your DNS zone (assuming you don't want to use the GUI provided by Windows).

The database file is the file that is, ultimately, replicated between DNS *master name servers* and *secondary name servers*. The information contained in the database file is found in a series of line entries called resource records. The SOA, A, NS, PTR, CNAME, MX, and HINFO record types are defined in RFC 1034 (we'll discuss the PTR record in the next section). Additionally, Microsoft has created the Microsoft-specific record types WINS and WINS-R. Even if you never plan to create a record outside the GUI, understanding how the records are put together will help you when configuring your DNS server.

START OF AUTHORITY RECORD · The first record in a DNS database file must be the Start of Authority (SOA) record. This record contains the general parameters that control the DNS zone using the format:

```
IN SOA <source host> <contact e-mail> <serial number>
<refresh time> <retry time> <expiration time> <Time to Live>
```

- source host. Host name of computer on which the DNS server is running.
- contact e-mail. Internet e-mail address of the DNS server's administrator.
- serial number. This is the "version number" of the database file. Expect this number to increase each time the database file changes.
- refresh time. The interval (in seconds) a secondary server uses to check with its master server to determine if the database file has changed and to request a zone transfer.
- retry time. The amount of time (in seconds) that a secondary server will wait before re-attempting a zone transfer after a communications failure with the master server.

- `expiration time`. The amount of time (in seconds) that a secondary server will keep trying to download a zone. If the secondary server is unable to obtain the new zone information after this period, it will discard the old zone information.
- `time to live`. The amount of time (in seconds) another DNS server is allowed to cache resource records from this database file. If an individual resource record does not contain an overriding TTL value, it is this parameter that determines the record's TTL.

Figure 11.4 shows a sample SOA record. Note that the at sign (@) indicates "this computer" and `IN` identifies this as an Internet record. The `senate.gov` host name is terminated by a period. This is because any host name not so terminated will automatically have the root domain appended to it. The normal at sign (@) found in the administrator's e-mail address has been replaced with a period (that is, `administrator@senate.gov` has become `administrator.senate.gov`). Note the use of semicolons to indicate comments and the use of parentheses to enclose line breaks that span more than one line.

NAME SERVER RECORD • The Name Server (NS) record contains a reference to each name server that can be used to look up hosts in the domain. A zone may have several NS records if several name servers are applicable to that zone. The record uses the format:

```
<domain> IN NS <nameserver host >
```

Look at the following NS record:

```
@ IN NS lisa.senate.gov
```

In this case, the at sign means "this domain," `IN` identifies this as an Internet record (as before), and `lisa.senate.gov` is identified as an additional name server that can service the domain.

```
@  IN SOA  mary.senate.gov. administrator.senate.gov. (
   1          ; serial number
   10800      ; refresh [3 hours]
   3600       ; retry [1hour]
   604800     ; expire [7 days]
   86400 )    ; time to live [1 day]
```

Figure 11.4 *SOA record.*

HOST RECORD · The Host record (**A** record) maps a host name to an IP address. Host records make up the bulk of the database file and use the following format:

```
<host name> IN A  <IP address>
```

Actual Host records would look like the following:

```
mary             IN A  202.22.18.32
lisa             IN A  202.22.18.34
localhost        IN A  127.0.0.1
```

CNAME RECORD · The CNAME record is a canonical name record. This entry permits you to associate more than one host name with the same IP address. Also referred to as aliasing, this record permits you to identify a single machine with several functions. This is particularly useful when configuring a specific machine for Internet roles. CNAME records use the format:

```
<alias>      CNAME <host name>
```

The following records identify the machine `lisa.senate.gov` as a generic file server called `SenateFiles,` as well as the Internet-related `www` and `ftp` server:

```
SenateFiles         CNAME lisa
www                 CNAME lisa
ftp                 CNAME lisa
```

Communication for `SenateFiles.senate.gov, www.senate.gov,` and `ftp.senate.gov` will all be referred to the machine called `lisa.`

MAIL EXCHANGE RECORD · The Mail Exchange (MX) record identifies the host that processes mail for this domain. If there is more than one MX record, the resolver will attempt contact with mail servers starting with the lowest preference value (which indicates the highest priority). The MX record format is:

```
<domain> IN MX <preference> <mailserver host >
```

The following records would ensure that mail addressed to `sensmith@senate.gov` would be delivered first to `sensmith@bill.senate.gov` if the `bill` server were available, and then to `sensmith@bob.senate.gov` if the `bill` server were unavailable:

```
@  IN MX 1 Bill
@  IN MX 2 Bob
```

Proper entry of the MX record is one of the most critical steps to setting up any e-mail service and cannot be overemphasized.

Warning A mail server identified with an MX record also requires an A record. Failure to employ both records is one of the most common causes of e-mail failure!

HOST INFORMATION RECORD • The Host Information (HINFO) record contains information about a host's hardware type and operating system. Originally, this record was intended to permit services like FTP sites to determine how to work with the host. Machine and system types used in the record should come from those listed in RFC 1340. In practice, however, this record is rarely implemented and most people use it only to track hardware information within their network. Entries from the RFC are usually replaced by information meaningful to the local administrator, but completely meaningless to the Internet. If you choose to use the HINFO record, consider that you are, essentially, telegraphing your machine types and operating systems to the world—easing, considerably, the job of any would-be hacker. The proper format for the HINFO record is:

```
<host name> IN HINFO <machine_type> <operating_system>
```

The following example would identify the machine lisa as an Intel 80386-based machine running a 32-bit Windows operating system:

```
Lisa IN HINFO INTEL-386 Win32
```

WINS RECORD • The WINS record is defined as part of the zone database file. Specific to Windows NT, it may be attached only to the zone root domain. The record provides the DNS server the IP address of an appropriate WINS server. This permits the DNS server to use WINS lookup for any requests for hosts in the zone root which are not found in its database. The WINS record uses the following format:

```
<domain> IN WINS <IP address of WINS server>
```

WINS-R RECORD • The WINS-R record provides reverse lookup capability for hosts identified through a DNS/WINS tie. The WINS-R permits the DNS server to use a NetBIOS name lookup for any reverse lookup requests for IP addresses in the zone root which are not statically defined with PTR records. The WINS-R record uses the following format:

```
<domain> IN WINS-R <domain to append to returned NetBIOS
names>
```

For example:

```
@ IN WINS-R senate.gov.
```

REVERSE LOOKUP FILE

The reverse lookup file contains the Pointer (PTR) records to permit a resolver to find a host name when an IP address is known. The reverse lookup file is named like a zone file according to the `in-addr.arpa` zone for which it contains PTR records.

The format for the zone file name is `z.y.x.w.in-addr.arpa`, where `w, x, y`, and `z` represent the octets of the IP address. In the case of the Class B network `152.60.22.0`, the file name would become `60.152.in-addr.arpa`. In addition to PTR records, the reverse lookup file contains SOA and NS records.

A number of applications implement security based on the names of connecting hosts. If a client attempts to access a particular resource under this security method, the server controlling the resource would contact the DNS server to determine the client's host name. If the host name didn't match the list of approved hosts on the resource server, or if the DNS were unable to find the host name, access to the resource would be denied.

THE POINTER RECORD · Central to the reverse lookup file is the Pointer record (PTR). The Pointer record contains a static mapping of IP addresses to host names within a reverse lookup zone. IP numbers are entered with their octets in reverse order and `in-addr.arpa.` is appended to the end to create a record. The address `200.22.18.30` for instance, would be represented by `30.18.22.200.in-addr.arpa.` The Pointer record uses the following format:

```
<ip reverse domain name> IN PTR <host name>
```

For example:

```
10.18.22.200.in-addr.arpa. IN PTR filsvr.senate.gov.
```

127-REVERSE LOOKUP FILE

Known as the `Arpa-127.rev` file, this is the database for the `127.in-addr.arpa.` domain. It is used for reverse lookups of IP numbers in the 127 network, such as `localhost`. The file is, otherwise, identical to the reverse lookup file in form and function.

CACHE FILE

Known as `cache.dns`, the cache file contains host information needed to resolve names beyond the DNS server's authoritative domains. It contains names and addresses of Internet root name servers. Microsoft provides a default file (see Figure 11.5) for users on the Internet that provides the DNS server with A and NS records for DNS servers authoritative for the root domains. If you will NOT connect to the Internet, replace the default cache file with a file that contains the name servers authoritative for the root of your private network. You can find a current Internet cache file at:

`FTP://rs.internic.net/domain/named.cache`

Are you confused by the "3600000" entries in the `cache.dns` record fields? When the cache file was originally constructed, the field was used for a cache Time to Live for the file entries (1000 hours in this case). Current name servers do not, in fact, discard root server data, so this field is actually DNS folklore, and has no actual function.

```
.                        3600000   IN   NS   A.ROOT-SERVERS.NET.
A.ROOT-SERVERS.NET.      3600000        A    198.41.0.4
;
; formerly NS1.ISI.EDU
;
.                        3600000        NS   B.ROOT-SERVERS.NET.
B.ROOT-SERVERS.NET.      3600000        A    128.9.0.107
;
; formerly C.PSI.NET
.
.
.
H.ROOT-SERVERS.NET.      3600000        A    128.63.2.53
;
; formerly NIC.NORDU.NET
;
.                        3600000        NS   I.ROOT-SERVERS.NET.
I.ROOT-SERVERS.NET.      3600000        A    192.36.148.17
```

Figure 11.5 *Excerpt from Microsoft default cache.dns file.*

BOOT FILE

The boot file is not actually defined in any RFC, but it is part of the Berkeley Internet Name Domain (BIND) implementation of DNS. If you are going to administer your DNS through changes to the text files instead of using the GUI, you should configure your server to use a boot file. (To configure to use a boot file, change the `HKEY_LOCAL_MACHINE\CurrentControlSet\Services\DNS\Parameters\EnableRegistryBoot` from 1 to 0. This will direct the server to retrieve initialization information from your boot file instead of the Windows NT Registry.) The boot file is a simple ASCII text file named `boot`, which controls the startup behavior of the DNS server. Boot file commands must start at the beginning of a line. The following commands are used in the boot file:

DIRECTORY COMMAND · This specifies the directory which contains the other files referred to in the boot file. It uses the format `directory <directory>` as follows:

```
directory c:\winntsvr\system32\dns
```

CACHE COMMAND · The cache command identifies the cache file. This command is a mandatory entry and the cache file it refers to MUST be present on the disk. The command uses the following format: `cache <filename>`

For example: `cache . cache`

PRIMARY COMMAND · Identifies this name server as authoritative for a particular domain and specifies a zone file which contains the resource records for the domain. The boot file can contain more than one primary command record. The command uses the following format: `primary <domain> <filename>`

For example: `primary senate.gov senate.dns`
         `primary ethics.senate.gov ethics.dns`

SECONDARY COMMAND · Specifies a domain for which this name server is authoritative in a secondary role. Includes a list of master server IP addresses from which the zone information may be downloaded. It also specifies a local file for caching the zone. As with the primary command, the boot file can contain more than one secondary command record. The command uses the following format: `secondary <domain> <hostlist> <local filename>`

  For example: `secondary rules.senate.gov 200.22.18.32 rules.dns`

FORWARDERS COMMAND • Identifies a DNS server designated as a forwarder. The command uses the following format: `forwarders <hostlist>`

For example: `forwarders 200.22.18.38 202.20.200.99`

SLAVE COMMAND • Indicates that the use of the forwarders command is the only way to resolve queries. This command can only follow a forwarders command.

For example: `forwarders 200.22.18.38 202.20.200.99 slave`

DNS Implementation Planning

With your newfound DNS knowledge, I'm sure you're eager to begin setting DNS servers right away. Before we get down to actually installing the software, however, let's spend a little time looking at some planning factors. The overall configuration of your DNS environment depends on a number of considerations, not the least of which are the size of your organization and its operating locations and the degree of fault tolerance you need in your network.

If your organization (or at least its network) is small, it may be more efficient to have your DNS clients work with DNS servers maintained by your Internet Service Provider (ISP). Your ISP will likely charge for the service, but will be able to maintain entries for all the hosts you designate. Regardless of who actually maintains the DNS servers, any organization that plans to connect to the Internet must provide the InterNIC with its domain name and the IP address of at least two DNS servers that service that domain. (Depending on the arrangement with your ISP, all of these tasks may be accomplished by the ISP. If you aren't going to use the Internet, you will, of course, not need to coordinate with the InterNIC, but will need to create your own DNS servers.)

If you're setting up your own DNS servers, it's a good idea to configure at least two per domain—a primary and a secondary. This will provide sufficient redundancy to allow your network to continue to function if one goes down. When using two or more DNS servers, another consideration is the replication schedule (you'll recall that replication is governed by information entered in the SOA record). If your host name information is very dynamic, you'll need a relatively short replication interval. This will ensure your secondary server remains up-to-date, but will increase the degree of network traffic. A good balance in this area is very important, as you might imagine.

Once your DNS servers are installed and running, you'll need to register with the DNS server that is immediately above you in the Domain Name

Space (see Figure 11.6). If your DNS servers are on the second level, you'll need to contact the InterNIC and provide information such as the names and addresses of your DNS servers, contact information for your domain administrator(s), and the date that the domain will actually become available on the network. If your domain is below the second level, you must contact the domain administrator for the domain immediately above you. You'll need to provide your DNS information, as well as anything else the administrator requires.

If you need to register with the InterNIC, you can find online registration services at `http://internic.net,` **or you can call their help line at (703) 742–4777.**

MCSE 11.1   DNS Installation and Configuration

Now that you understand how DNS works and have a good idea of the overarching planning considerations for DNS implementation, it's time to actually install a DNS server on a Windows NT 4.0 server. But wait! There's one

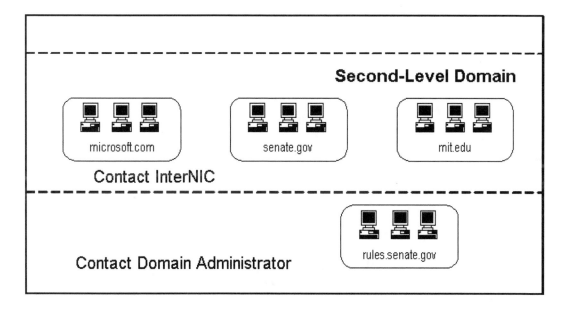

Figure 11.6 *Domain registration.*

more important consideration. It is critical that TCP/IP be properly configured on the machine that will run the DNS server. Obviously, the machine MUST have a static IP address. This means it shouldn't be a DHCP client or, if it is, it should have a client address reservation as defined in Chapter 6, "Dynamic Host Configuration Protocol." Additionally, you should check the DNS tab of the TCP/IP Properties dialog (see Figure 11.7) to ensure host and domain names are properly specified. If these entries are present, SOA, A, and NS records for the server will be automatically created during the installation. If they're not present, only the SOA record will be created.

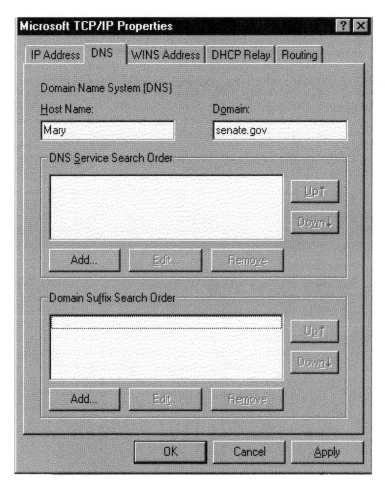

Figure 11.7 *Host and domain names.*

Installing the Service

Once we're sure our TCP/IP data is correctly configured, we can proceed to the actual server installation. As you might have guessed, DNS installation is very similar to that of all the other TCP/IP services we've installed thus far. The first step is a visit to the (Control Panel) Network dialog's Services tab. Select Add and highlight Microsoft DNS Server as shown in Figure 11.8. (Remember to have the installation CD-ROM handy—the system will need to copy files from it.) Once the appropriate files are copied, close the Network dialog and you'll be prompted to restart the computer. Accept the restart and the DNS service will start automatically.

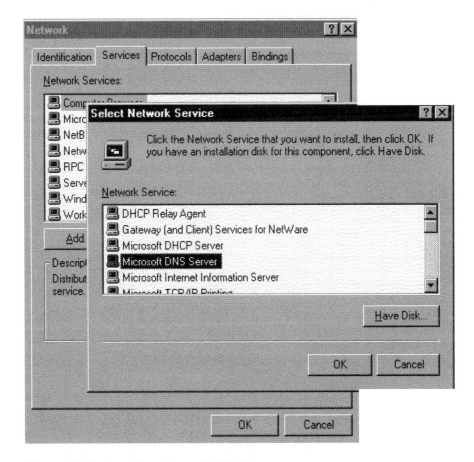

Figure 11.8 *Installing Microsoft DNS Server.*

Configuring the DNS Server

Now that your DNS server is installed and running, it needs to be configured to do some work! Right now it is running as a caching-only Internet name server because it has only the Internet root information it has found in the default cache file and knows nothing about the network on which it operates. (Actually, even if the DNS server were completely configured, it wouldn't do a lot of good unless we configured some clients to use it. We'll see how to do that a bit later.) Although we'll look at a myriad of configuration options, configuring a DNS server boils down to a few relatively simple steps:

- Add your server to the *DNS Manager.*
- Configure the server to use forwarders and/or to be a slave server (as required).
- Create primary and/or add secondary zones.
- Create reverse lookup zones (as required)
- Add resource records (as required).

The first step in DNS configuration is to add your server to the *DNS Manager.* You can launch the *DNS Manager* from the Administrative Tools (Common) program group. Once you have the *DNS Manager* running, select DNS from the menu bar and click on New Server as shown in Figure 11.9.

This will bring up the Add DNS Server dialog box, in which you should enter the host name, the NetBIOS name, or the IP address of the computer on which you just installed the DNS service (as shown in Figure 11.10).

Once you have created your server, note that the system adds the cache and some basic reverse lookup zones (see Figure 11.11). The cache contains information loaded from the cache file, while the reverse lookup zones contain information to permit reverse lookups of your server's NS and SOA records for its loopback and broadcast addresses.

Select *DNS* from the *DNS Manager* menu bar and click on Properties. This reveals a dialog with three tabs, as shown in Figure 11.12. The Interfaces tab permits you to identify which network interface cards will participate in DNS on a multihomed computer. The default is to use all interfaces. The Forwarders tab permits you to configure your server to use a forwarder and also enables you to make it a slave to the forwarder. The Boot Method tab displays the boot method currently being used (from the Registry or from the boot file). Note that the Boot Method tab is for display only. The actual boot method must be changed in the Registry as previously discussed.

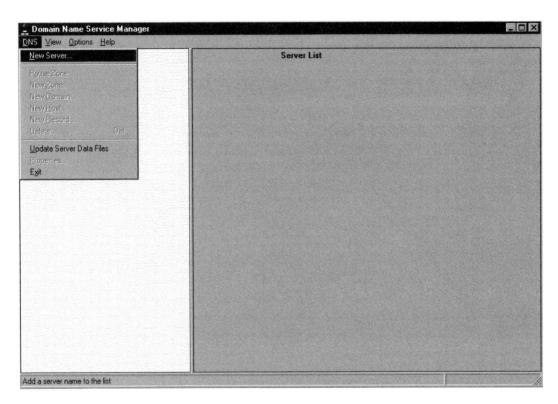

Figure 11.9 *Add new DNS server.*

ADDING ZONES AND SUBDOMAINS

For your server to service your network, you'll need to determine the hierarchy for your DNS domains and zones and ensure they're properly identified in the server. You can add a primary zone to the server by highlighting the server name and selecting New Zone from the DNS menu. This starts the *Zone Wizard*—select New Zone as shown in Figure 11.13.

Click Next and enter the name of the zone you wish to create. If you press the Tab key, the *DNS Manager* will fill in the name of the database file (see Figure 11.14).

Microsoft DNS uses the default database filename zonename.dns. This is distinct from other DNS servers that use the naming convention Db.zone.

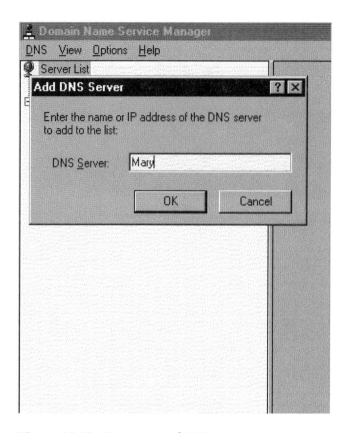

Figure 11.10   *Enter name of DNS server.*

Figure 11.11   *Initial DNS server information.*

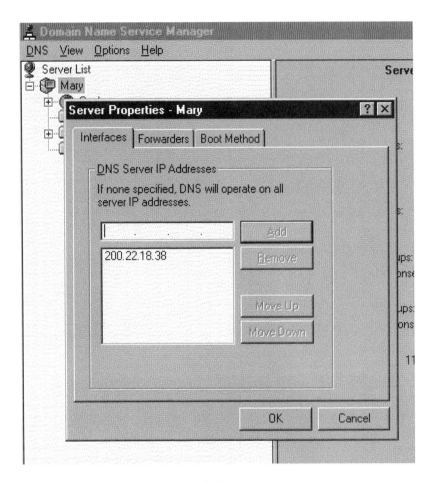

Figure 11.12 *Server Properties dialog.*

Click `Next` and `Finish` and the DNS server creates the zone and adds SOA, NS, and A records for the DNS server computer. (See Figure 11.15.) Each zone for which the machine will be authoritative creates a key in the machine's Registry. The zone we just created, for instance, will have information stored under `HKEY_LOCAL_MACHINE\System\CurrentControlSet\Services\DNS\Zones\Senate.gov`.

You can add a subdomain to your new zone by highlighting the zone, selecting `DNS` from the menu bar, and clicking `New Domain`. This reveals the `New Domain` dialog that permits you to add the name of the desired subdomain. (See Figure 11.16.)

Click `OK` and the subdomain is created (see Figure 11.17).

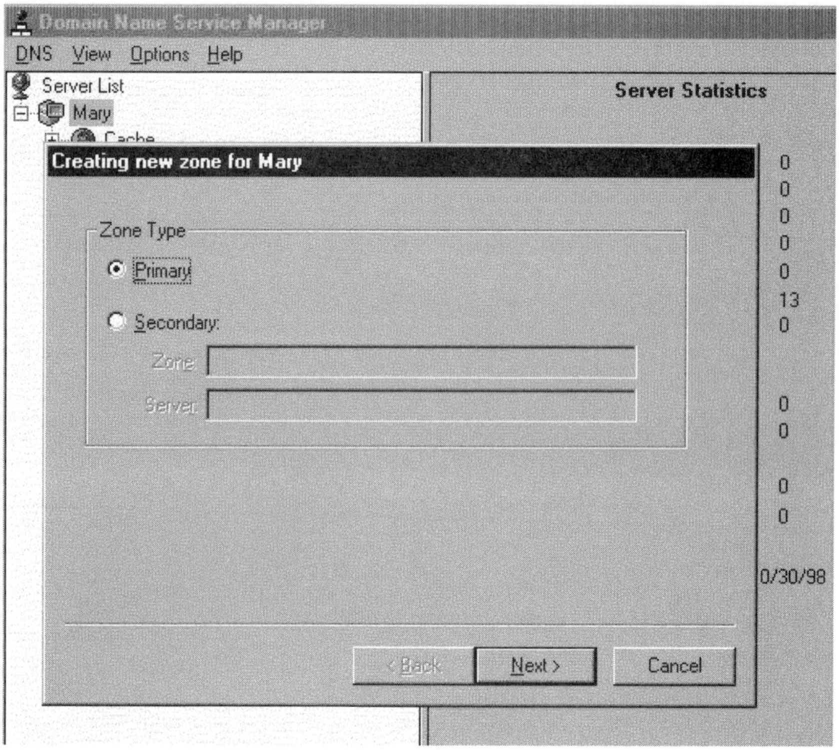

Figure 11.13 *Create primary zone.*

Figure 11.14 *Enter zone name.*

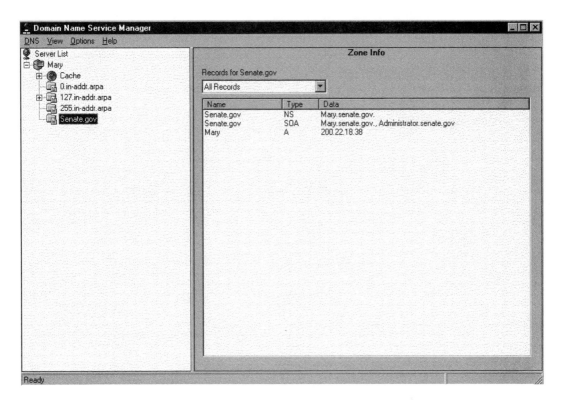

Figure 11.15 *Senate.gov zone.*

ADDING A SECONDARY ZONE

You can also include a secondary domain. To do so, select the server and `New Zone` as you did when creating a primary zone. This time, however, select `Secondary` and enter the name of the zone you want your server to administer as a secondary zone. Under `Server`, enter the name or IP address

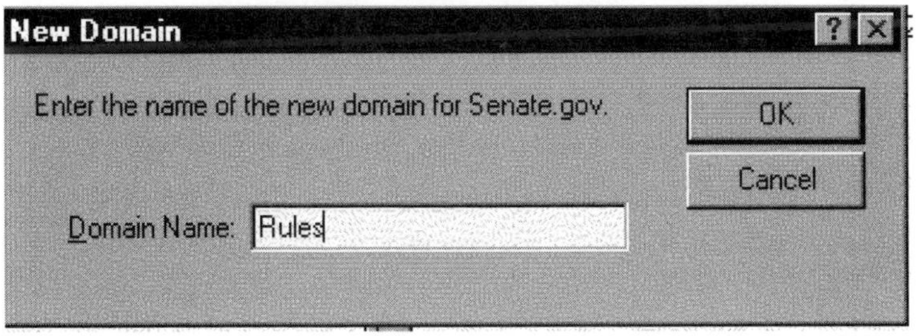

Figure 11.16 *Enter subdomain name.*

Figure 11.17 *Rules.Senate.gov subdomain.*

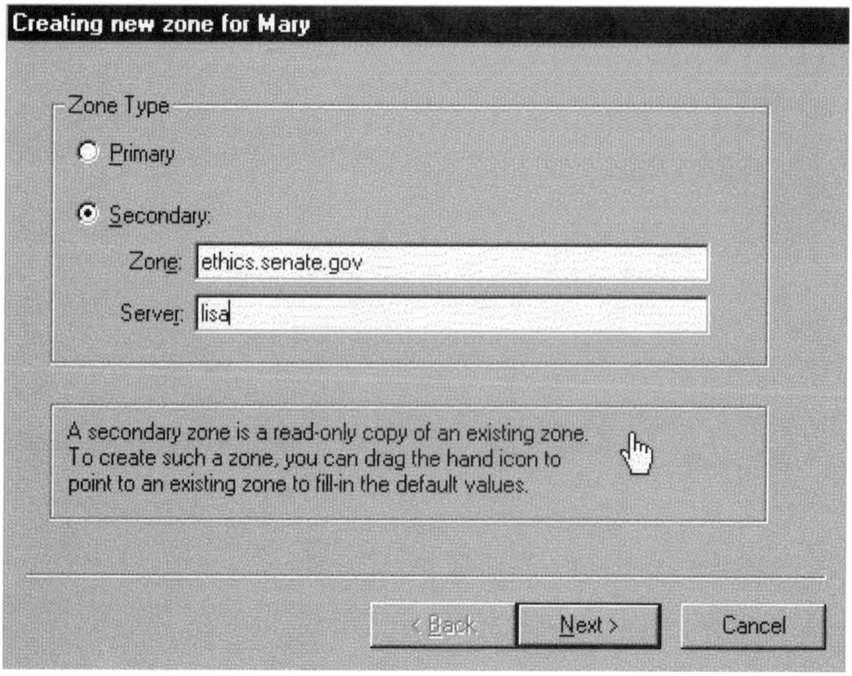

Figure 11.18 *Create secondary zone.*

of the DNS server that stores the primary zone information for the zone and click Next. (See Figure 11.18.)

The next dialog (see Figure 11.19) shows the name of the zone you selected. Pressing the Tab key will create a zone file name using the Microsoft DNS convention, just as it did when we created the primary zone. Click Next.

The next dialog (see Figure 11.20) asks you for an IP Master for the zone. This is the IP address for a master name server (as defined earlier in this chapter). Your IP master will likely be the same machine you entered as the server when you created the primary zone, but it can be any server that stores primary zone information for the zone. To enter an IP master, type the master name server's IP address in the IP Master(s) edit box and click Add. If more than one server stores primary zone information, you may add IP addresses for each.

Click Next and Finish and the secondary zone is created as shown in Figure 11.21.

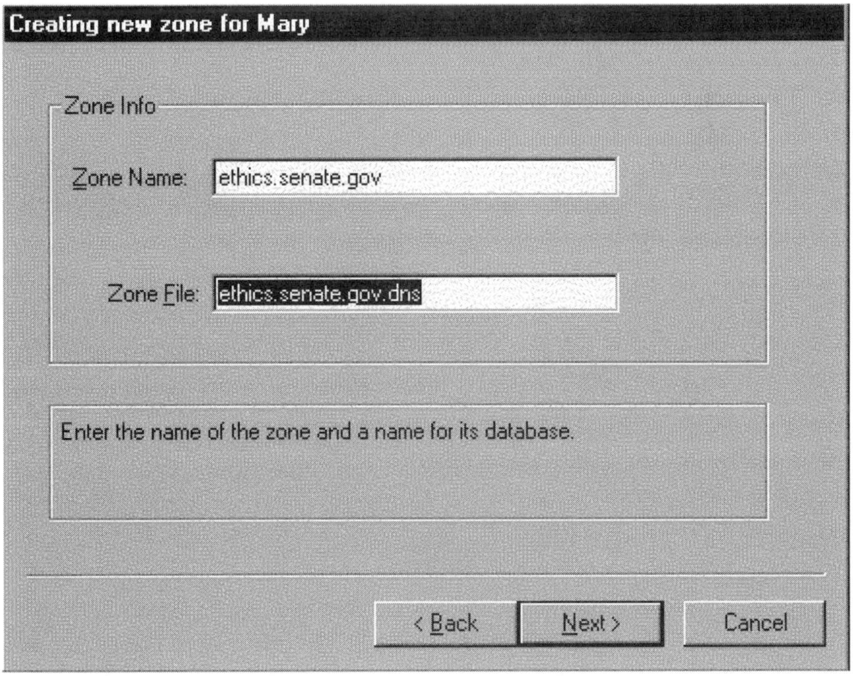

Figure 11.19 *Secondary zone name and file.*

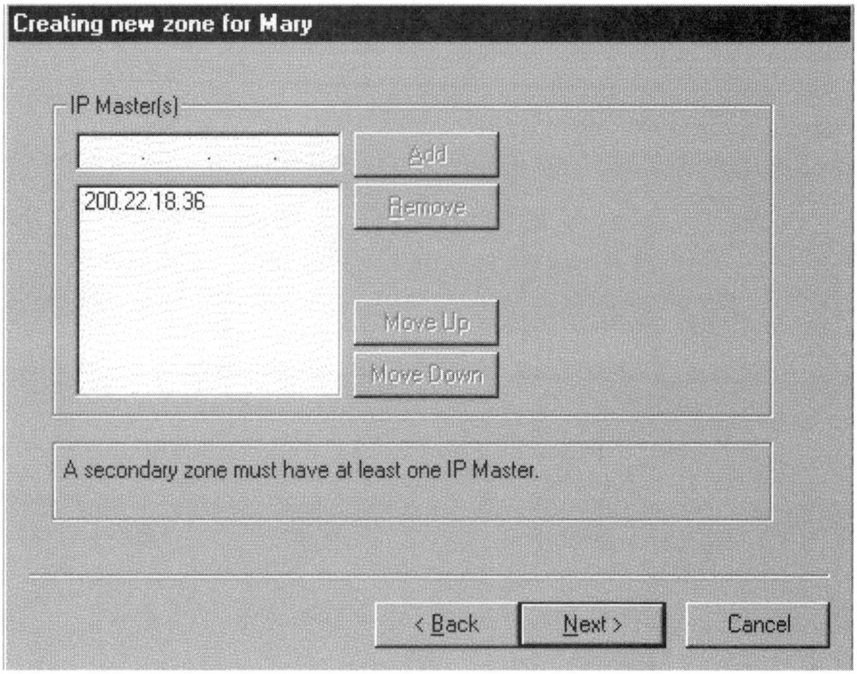

Creating new zone for Mary

IP Master(s)

[. . .]   Add

200.22.18.36   Remove

Move Up
Move Down

A secondary zone must have at least one IP Master.

< Back   Next >   Cancel

Figure 11.20 *Enter master name server.*

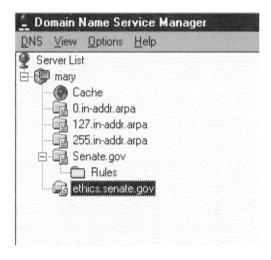

Domain Name Service Manager

DNS View Options Help

Server List
mary
  Cache
  0.in-addr.arpa
  127.in-addr.arpa
  255.in-addr.arpa
  Senate.gov
    Rules
  ethics.senate.gov

Figure 11.21 *Secondary zone ethics.senate.gov.*

ZONE PROPERTIES

You can configure zone properties by highlighting a zone and selecting `Properties` from the `DNS` menu. This reveals the `Zone Properties` dialog and its three tabs. The `General` tab (see Figure 11.22) permits you to change the zone file name and designate whether the zone is a primary or secondary zone.

The `SOA Record` tab (See Figure 11.23) permits you to configure all the zone configuration information stored in the SOA record.

The `Notify` tab permits you to identify particular secondary servers to alert when the primary server database changes. This dialog also permits you to enhance security by allowing only those secondary servers listed in the dialog to contact this server (see Figure 11.24). The fourth tab configures *WINS Lookup*, which we will discuss shortly.

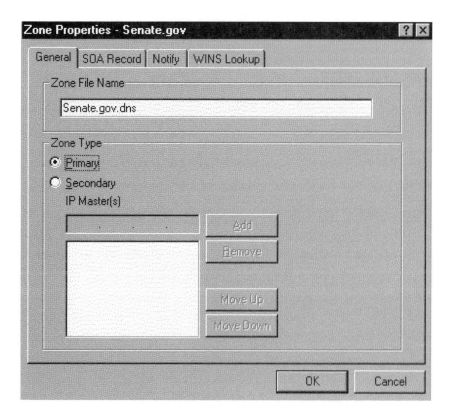

Figure 11.22 *Zone Properties/General tab.*

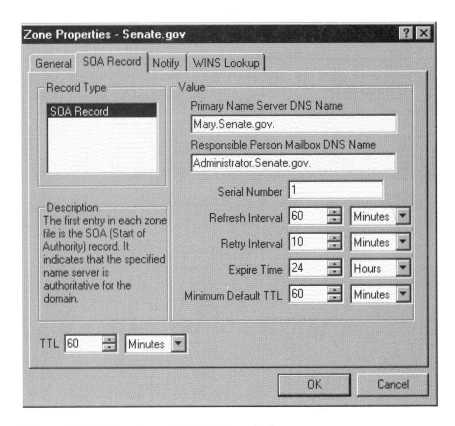

Figure 11.23 *Zone Properties/SOA Record tab.*

THE REVERSE LOOKUP ZONE

Just when you thought you had added all the zones you would need, it is time to think about reverse lookup. Reverse lookup is accomplished through the use of Pointer (PTR) records. Where do you suppose the PTR records go? We need to create a zone in which to place them. You need to create a reverse lookup zone for every network that you'll administer. In our case, we've used only the 200.22.18.0 network, so we'll need to create a reverse lookup zone for it. Remember, to create a reverse lookup zone, you reverse the octets and add the suffix .in-addr.arpa. For the 200.22.18.0 network, we'll need to create a zone called 18.22.200.in-addr.arpa. The good news is that a reverse lookup zone is created in the same way you create any other zone. See Figure 11.25.

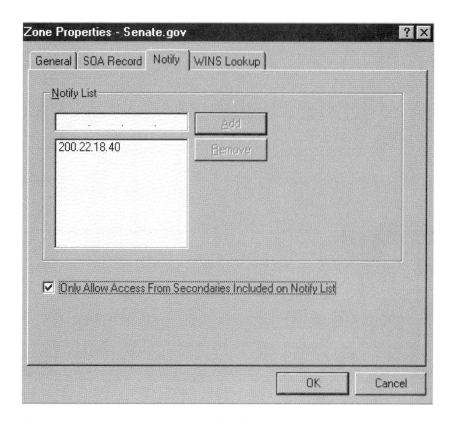

Figure 11.24 *Zone Properties/Notify tab.*

RESOURCE RECORDS

Now that we've configured a framework of zones and subdomains, we need to enter some resource records to make the system work. The most common record to add is a Host record. To add a Host record, highlight the desired zone and select New Host from the DNS menu. This will reveal the New Host dialog as shown in Figure 11.26. Enter the host name and IP address. If you check the Create Associated PTR Record check box, the server will automatically create a PTR record in the reverse lookup zone. Click Add Host and the new record is entered (see Figure 11.27).

Other records may be created as easily as the Host record. Ensure the appropriate zone is highlighted and select New Record from the DNS menu. This will bring up the New Resource Record dialog (see Figure 11.28). You can select the desired record type in the Record Type window and

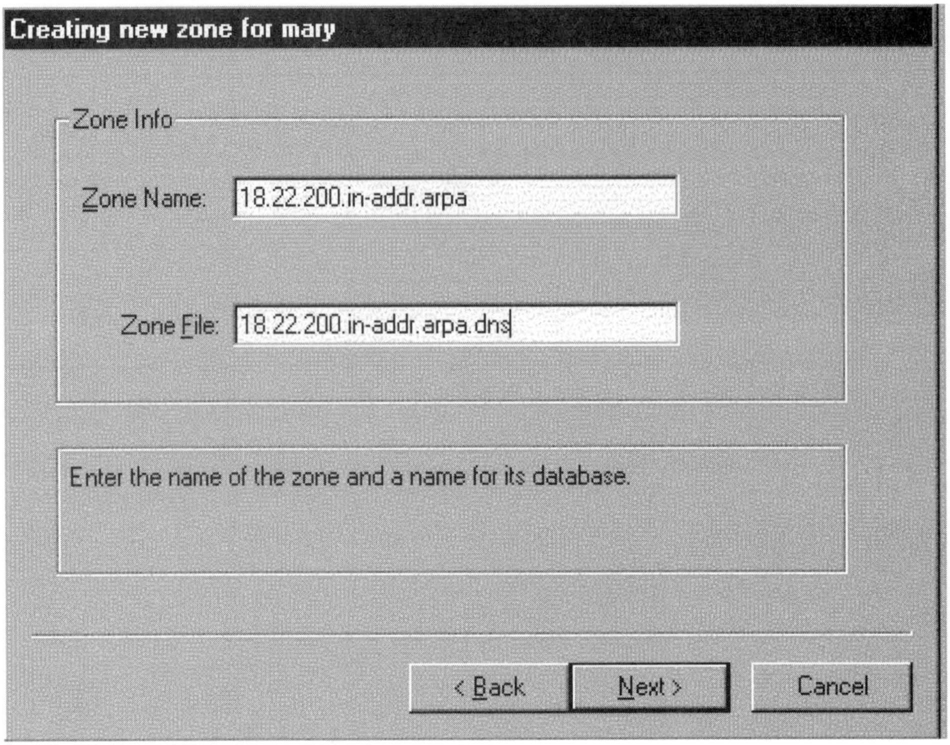

Figure 11.25 *Creating the reverse lookup zone.*

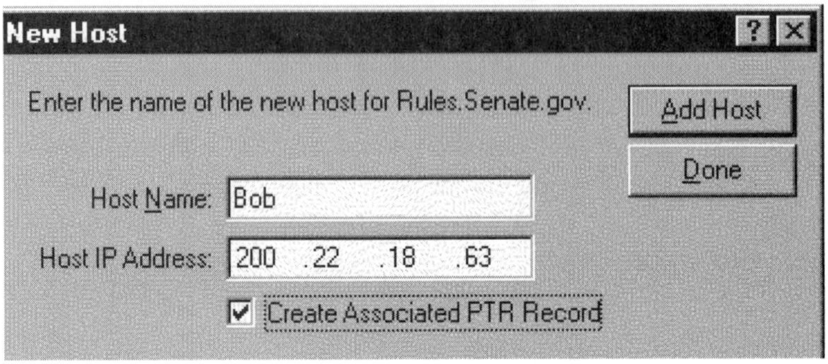

Figure 11.26 *New Host dialog.*

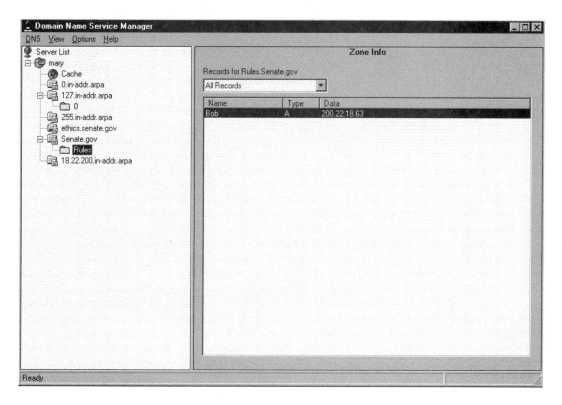

Figure 11.27 *New host record.*

enter the appropriate information in the dialog. The TTL value shown in the dialog is the default TTL set by the zone's SOA record.

You may leave it as set or enter a different value. When you click OK, the record is added (see Figure 11.29). Although the information for each particular record type differs, the procedure for adding records is the same in all cases. You may also add records by directly editing the database files found in the `<system root>\system32\dns` directory. You must stop and start the DNS service to get these manually entered changes to appear in the server.

UPDATE SERVER DATA FILES

Once you enter information into the DNS server, it is not saved in the database file immediately. The database file is written when the service stops, and is also periodically flushed during the DNS server's normal operation. To ensure your files are written to the database file immediately, select Update Server Data Files from the DNS menu (see Figure 11.30).

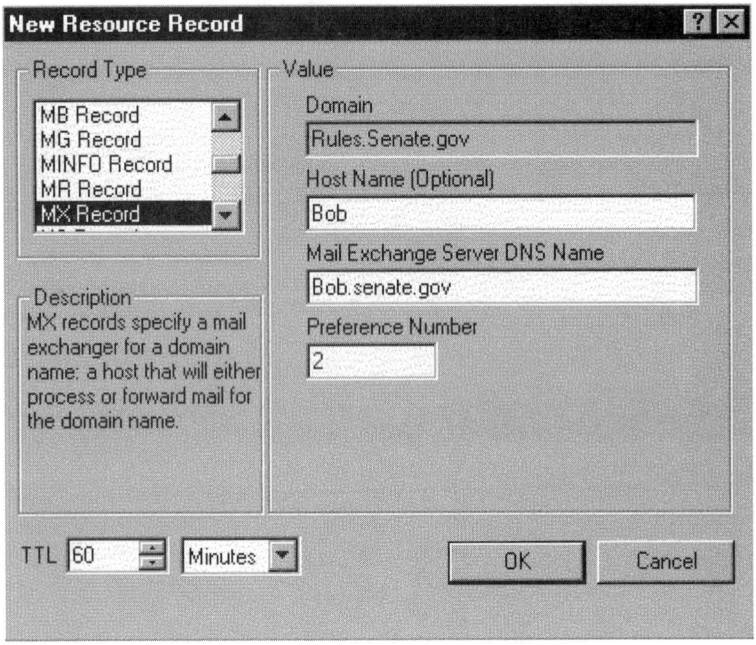

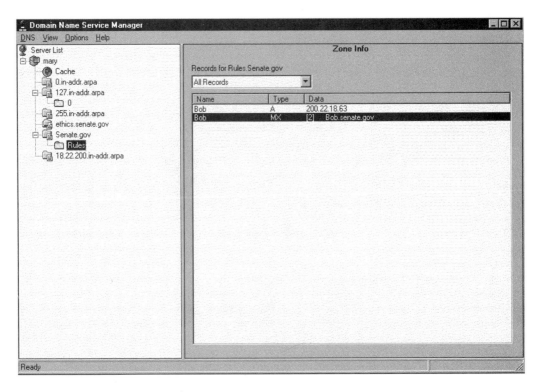

Figure 11.28 *New Resource Record dialog.*

Figure 11.29 *New MX record.*

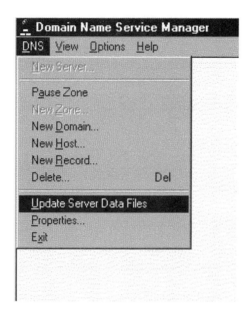

Figure 11.30 *Update Server Data Files.*

Installing and Configuring a DNS Server

If you are on an isolated network segment and not connected to the Internet, you can do just about anything. If, however, you're part of a larger network, consult with your administrator to ensure you have the correct domain name and other information. Ensure that your Windows NT 4.0 CD-ROM is in the drive so the system can copy the required files.

Install the Service
       Make sure your TCP/IP data is correct and refer to this chapter's *Installing the Service* section and follow the steps to create a DNS server on your machine. After you restart the computer, open the *DNS Manager* from the `Administrative Tools (Common)` program group and add your server as detailed in the `Configuring the DNS Server` section. Do you see the cache and reverse lookup zones?

Now that your server is running and visible in the DNS Manager, refer to the *Adding Zones and Subdomains* subsection of the *Configuring the DNS Server* section and follow the steps to create a new primary zone. If you're on an isolated network segment, you can create your own zone name (should be based on your domain name). If you're on a larger network, be sure to check with your administrator. Were SOA, NS, and A records automatically added for your server?

MCSE 11.2	**Integrating DNS with Other Name Servers**

Integration is a prime concept for DNS. We've already looked at a great deal of DNS name server integration. Recall that a DNS server will make iterative queries to several other DNS servers to "piece together" a fully-qualified domain name. We've also looked at primary and secondary servers, where DNS servers work together to share the load from DNS client queries. We've seen how to integrate DNS servers through forwarders to reach out to other DNS servers across a WAN, and we've seen how to slave DNS servers to forwarders to obtain name resolution.

Connecting DNS to a DNS Root Server

If the DNS server is to do its job in finding mappings outside its domain, it is absolutely critical that it be able to connect to a server that is authoritative for the domain that ultimately owns the host for which it seeks a mapping. Fortunately this is a simple task for the administrator. You'll remember from our previous discussion that the information required to locate an InterNIC root server is located in the `cache.dns` file. If this file is made available to your server (as we discussed earlier in the chapter), the server will be able to find a root server which will tell it where to locate the next lower level in the DNS hierarchy. If, for instance, we were attempting to locate *mary.senate.gov* from a machine in another domain, the root server would give us an address to a DNS server that is authoritative for the *.gov* domain. The *.gov* server would, in turn, help us to find the DNS server authoritative for *senate.gov*, which should give us a mapping to *mary.senate.gov*.

As you can see, without the root server information found in `cache.dns`, the DNS server would be unable to start its quest for outside information. When you install the DNS server, a `cache.dns` file with the required InterNIC root server data is installed. If you need to obtain a new Internet cache file, you can obtain one at: *FTP://rs.internic.net/ domain/named.cache*. If you are using DNS on a network that is not part of the Internet, you'll need to create a `cache.dns` file using the same format illustrated in Figure 11.5, but with information on the name servers which are authoritative for your network.

Connecting DNS to a WINS Server

While integration between DNS servers is critical for DNS to do its job, Windows NT 4.0 has an additional name server integration feature that can make the job of DNS administration *much* easier! Remember that, although the DNS server's database is static, requiring manual updating, a WINS server automatically updates its database, using input from its client machines. (Although WINS can also use static mappings, the primary purpose of the WINS server is to provide an *automated* name resolution capability.) Unfortunately, WINS does not provide the robust host name resolution capability of DNS. Combining these two systems, however, can allow us the best of both worlds: DNS in the hierarchical Domain Name Space, and WINS in the flat NetBIOS name space.

As we saw earlier in this chapter, the Microsoft DNS server can use a WINS record to permit it to find an appropriate WINS server. A DNS server equipped with a WINS record will still attempt to obtain host name resolution in the conventional manner. If the DNS is unable to find a mapping in its database for a host in a zone for which it is authoritative, it will convert the host portion of the FQDN to a NetBIOS name and query its mated WINS server. If the WINS server can resolve the NetBIOS name, it will return the IP address to the DNS which, in turn, returns the mapping to its client.

DNS servers configured to integrate with WINS servers can provide mappings for DHCP clients whose IP addresses periodically change. WINS integration relieves the DNS administrator of the burden of entering data for every computer in the network into the DNS database—provided the network computers are WINS clients.

If a zone is to provide WINS resolution, every DNS server *authoritative* for that zone must be configured for WINS resolution. Note that this applies only to authoritative servers; secondary servers and caching-only servers need not be configured for WINS lookup.

Configuring a DNS Server for WINS Lookup

Now that we're convinced of the benefits of DNS/WINS integration, just how do we go about linking these resources together? To provide your zone with a WINS lookup capability, select the appropriate zone in *DNS Manager,* select the DNS menu, and click Properties to reveal the Zone Properties dialog. From this dialog, select the WINS Lookup tab (see Figure 11.31).

Check the Use WINS Resolution check box, enter the IP address of the applicable WINS server(s) in the WINS Servers edit box, and click Add. If multiple WINS servers are entered, the Move Up and Move Down buttons may be used to alter the order in which they're queried. If your DNS server has secondary servers that are not Microsoft DNS servers, check the Set-

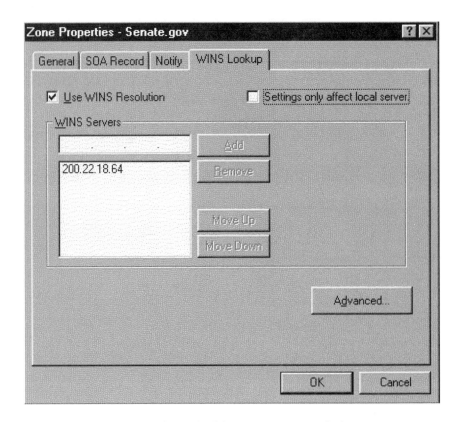

Figure 11.31 *Wins Lookup tab of the Zone Properties dialog.*

tings Only Affect Local Server check box to prevent copying WINS records to the non-Microsoft server.

WINS REVERSE LOOKUP

There is also a reverse lookup capability inherent in the DNS/WINS link-up. You'll remember we discussed a WINS-R record earlier. To enable the reverse lookup capability, select the appropriate reverse lookup (in-addr.arpa) zone in *DNS Manager*, select the DNS menu, and click Properties to reveal the Zone Properties dialog. From this dialog, select the WINS Reverse Lookup tab (see Figure 11.32).

Check the Use WINS Reverse Lookup check box and enter the host domain name that will be appended to the NetBIOS name (during a reverse resolution) in the DNS Host Domain edit box. As in the forward look-up

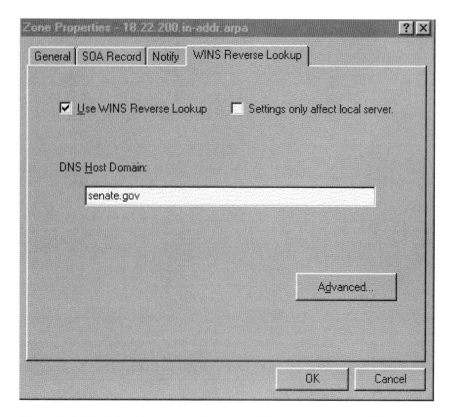

Figure 11.32 *WINS Reverse Lookup tab of the Zone Properties dialog.*

case, check the `Settings Only Affect Local Server` check box if your DNS server uses non-Microsoft DNS servers.

WINS TIME TO LIVE AND LOOKUP TIMEOUT

As with other DNS data, WINS-supplied data is associated with a Time to Live (TTL). To adjust the TTL, click on the `Advanced` button on the `WINS Lookup` or `WINS Reverse Lookup` tab of the `Zone Properties` dialog (see Figure 11.33).

When a mapping is provided by a WINS server, it has a TTL as set in the `Cache Timeout Value` (ten minutes, by default). The `Lookup Timeout Value` sets the amount of time the DNS server will wait for the WINS server to respond. Once this value is exceeded, the DNS server will give up and return an error message to the requester.

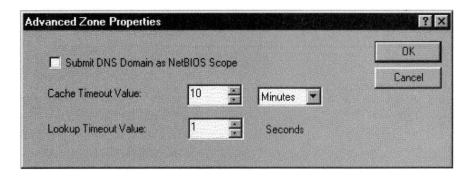

Figure 11.33 *Advanced Zone Properties.*

You may have noticed the `Submit DNS Domain as NetBIOS Scope` check box in Figure 11.33. This option is used when you are already using a NetBIOS scope in your Windows NT network. Selecting this option causes the DNS server to use both the host name and domain name in a request to a WINS server. In this case, the host name represents the NetBIOS name, while the domain name represents the NetBIOS scope. This option will work properly only if you have implemented NetBIOS scope consistently across your network.

Study Break

Reviewing DNS Integration

Let's take a few moments to see how our DNS server can integrate with the rest of cyberspace.

`cache.dns`

Go to the `WINNT\System32\DNS\Samples` directory and, using *Notepad*, open the `cache.dns` sample file. Look at the A and NS records contained in the file. With what you've learned, you should be able to create similar records for root servers in your network. (Remember that you shouldn't write your own `cache.dns` records if you'll operate on the Internet.)

WINS

Refer to this chapter's *Configuring a DNS Server for WINS Lookup* section (and set your DNS server to use the WINS server you installed in Chapter 7, "NetBIOS Over TCP/IP"). With this integration, what host names will you need to manually add to your DNS database?

MCSE 11.3   Configuring DNS Server Roles

Throughout this chapter we've discussed a myriad of DNS server roles. Let's review the roles to make sure we know how to configure each of them.

Primary Name Server

Your server becomes a `primary name server` when it is configured with a primary zone. Add a primary zone as we discussed earlier in the section titled *Adding Zones and Subdomains,* and as illustrated in Figure 11.13.

Secondary Name Server

Your server will function as a secondary name server when configured with a secondary zone. To add a secondary zone, follow the guidance in the *Adding Zones and Subdomains* section and refer to Figure 11.18.

Master Name Server

You do not actually configure a DNS server to be a *master name server.* You instead configure a secondary server to *recognize* a particular name server as a master name server. Enter this information as the *secondary* server, as illustrated in Figure 11.20.

Caching-Only Server

Since a *caching-only* server is authoritative for no zones, this is an easy configuration. To create a caching-only server, simply install the server and create no primary or secondary zones for it!

Forwarder

As with *master name servers, forwarders* are not actually configured. Instead, you decide which machines will act as forwarders and configure the rest of the DNS servers to use these designated machines. This configuration must be accomplished at each server. To configure a server to use forwarders, select the `DNS/properties` (click on `Properties` from the `DNS` menu) dialog in *DNS Manager* and click on the `Forwarders` tab. As shown in Figure 11.34, check the `Use Forwarder(s)` check box and enter the IP address(es) of your designated forwarders. The `Forward Time Out` value determines how long this server will attempt to contact a forwarder before moving on to the next one on the list.

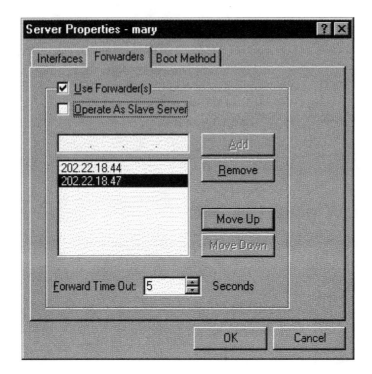

Figure 11.34 *Forwarders tab of the Server Properties dialog.*

Slave

To configure a machine to be a slave to one or more forwarders, simply check the `Operate As Slave Server` check box on the `Forwarders` tab of the `Server Properties` dialog (see Figure 11.34).

Study Break

Using DNS Server in a Secondary Role

Your DNS server is currently functioning as a primary name server. If there is another DNS server operating on your network, you can give it a secondary name server role too. Refer to the *Adding a Secondary Zone* subsection of this chapter's *Configuring the DNS Server* section to add a secondary zone. Wait a few minutes for the system to complete a zone transfer. Do you see records for the newly added zone?

Configuring a DNS Client

All this work in configuring DNS servers won't do us very much good if we don't configure some machines to act as DNS clients. Fortunately, this is an easy process. In Chapter 6, we learned how to configure clients using the Dynamic Host Configuration Protocol (DHCP). Now we'll take a few moments to learn about a static configuration.

DNS client configuration is accomplished from the DNS tab of the TCP/IP Properties dialog (Control Panel|Network). Simply enter the IP address(es) of the applicable DNS servers in the DNS Service Search Order edit box to designate the DNS servers your client will use (see Figure 11.35).

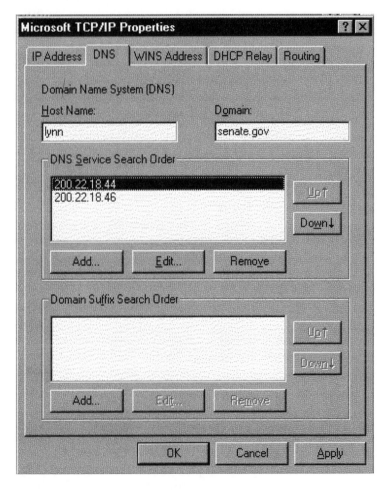

Figure 11.35 *DNS tab of the TCP/IP Properties dialog.*

Using NSLOOKUP for DNS Troubleshooting

The NSLOOKUP utility is the primary DNS diagnostic tool. In its simplest form, NSLOOKUP permits you to quickly retrieve an IP address or host name from your default DNS server. NSLOOKUP has both an interactive and non-interactive mode. Use the non-interactive mode when you need only a quick piece of data (e.g., the IP address of a particular host) and use the interactive mode when several queries are required.

The NSLOOKUP utility's syntax is:

```
nslookup [-option...] [computer-to-find | - [server]]
```

In this notation, `option` signifies one or more NSLOOKUP options; `computer-to-find` represents a host name, FQDN, or IP address to look up (if a hyphen is used here, NSLOOKUP switches to interactive mode); and `server` refers to the DNS server. If you simply type `nslookup`, you'll enter the interactive mode for the default name server. If you enter a `computer-to-find`, you'll seek that information in non-interactive mode using the default name server.

Figure 11.36 shows the result of a simple non-interactive query. The name server was the default server (in this case, `mary.senate.gov`). The non-authoritative answer simply indicates the mapping came from the name server's cache and not the authoritative server for the host's domain. This would indicate the default name server had recently resolved the mapping (TTL not expired).

To enter the interactive mode, simply type `NSLOOKUP` at the command line. You're presented with a prompt (>) from which you may enter repeated `NSLOOKUP` queries. For a detailed list of `NSLOOKUP` options, type `HELP` at the prompt. To exit the interactive mode, type `EXIT` at the prompt. (See Figure 11.37.)

```
C:\>nslookup www.house.gov
Server:  mary.senate.gov
Address:  200.22.18.36

Non-authoritative answer:
Name:    www.house.gov
Address:  143.231.86.196
```

Figure 11.36 *Simple use of NSLOOKUP.*

```
C:\>nslookup
Default Server: mary.senate.gov
Address:  200.22.18.36

>
```

Figure 11.37 *NSLOOKUP interactive mode.*

Some Useful NSLOOKUP Commands

You can learn a plethora of NSLOOKUP commands by typing HELP at the NSLOOKUP prompt. We'll point out two useful commands here, however:

DEBUG

You can turn debugging mode on or off by typing set debug or set node-bug. Debugging is off by default. When debugging is turned on, you receive much more information about the packet sent to the server and the resulting answer. To use DEBUG or NODEBUG for a non-interactive query, use them on the command line with a hyphen (e.g., nslookup -debug mary.senate.gov)

DOMAIN INFORMATION

You can retrieve domain information through use of the ls option and domain (rather than host name). This will provide the output shown in Figure 11.38.

```
C:\>nslookup
Default Server: mary.senate.gov
Address:  200.22.18.36

> ls senate.gov
[mary.senate.gov]
  senate.gov.                NS      server = mary.senate.gov
  mary                       A       200.22.18.36
  bill                       A       200.22.18.64
  bob                        A       200.22.18.44
  lisa                       A       200.22.18.46

>
```

Figure 11.38 *NSLOOKUP ls option.*

Summary

In this chapter, we saw that the rapid growth of the Internet dictated a system for the resolution of host names to IP addresses that was sufficiently robust to provide service to millions of users throughout the world. We found that the first step in such a system was the production of a hierarchical name space and the creation of Domain Name System (DNS) servers to manage the lists of hosts and IP addresses.

In DNS parlance, *resolvers* are clients, while *name servers* are the DNS servers that provide name resolution to the resolvers. Name servers are responsible for a subset of the Domain Name Space referred to as their *zone(s) of authority*. If a name server needs to resolve a name not in its zone of authority, it can contact other DNS servers to obtain the mapping. It starts with a root-level name server which will give it the IP address of the next name server in the chain and so on until the name server authoritative for the desired zone is located. When a name server obtains IP address information, it retains it in its cache for a specified *Time to Live* (TTL). When the TTL expires, the data is flushed from the server's cache. When cached data is passed to another machine, a decremented TTL is passed with it.

Name servers can function in a number of roles. *Primary name servers* are authoritative for one or more zones. *Secondary name servers* provide zone information using the data maintained on a *master name server*. The process of obtaining zone information from a master name server is called a *zone transfer*. A server with no primary or secondary zone information is known as a *caching-only server*. A caching-only server maintains only data it has obtained in querying other servers. A server designated as a *forwarder* will forward requests from local name servers to name servers operating across the Internet. A name server configured as a *slave* can only request information through its designated forwarder(s).

When a resolver makes a *recursive* query to a name server, the name server must return the requested information or an error message indicating it cannot find the desired data—it cannot return a reference to another name server. The name server responding to the recursive query may need to perform an *iterative* query to obtain the requested data. In an iterative query, the server may have to contact a series of name servers, each one providing an address to the next one at successively lower levels in the Domain Name Space until the desired host mapping is located. An *inverse query* will provide a host name when an IP address is known. Inverse queries are facilitated by records stored in the `in-addr.arpa` domain.

DNS servers utilize a number of files to operate and maintain their data. The *database file* is a text file that contains a series of records containing DNS mapping information. We discussed the *SOA, A, NS, PTR,*

CNAME, *MX*, *HINFO*, *WINS*, and *WINS-R* records. The *reverse lookup file* is a database file that contains the Pointer (PTR) records that permit DNS reverse lookups. The *cache file* contains the host information that enables a name server to find root servers in the internetwork, allowing it to resolve names beyond its authoritative domains. Finally, the *boot file* contains initialization data for the DNS server itself. Normally, a DNS server running on a Windows NT system will initialize using information in the system's Registry, but can be configured to use boot file information instead.

When planning for a DNS installation, you should first determine if your DNS services should be run within your organization or by your ISP. If you will operate on the Internet, you'll need to register a domain name with the InterNIC and will need to provide that agency with IP addresses of at least two DNS servers that service the domain (these services *may* be performed by your ISP). You should ensure you have at least a primary and secondary DNS server for each domain and will need to register your servers with a DNS server immediately above them in the Domain Name Space.

DNS is installed and configured much as any other Windows NT network service. The first installation step is to ensure the server's TCP/IP parameters are properly configured. If all TCP/IP parameters are correct, the installation will automatically create SOA, A, and NS records for your server. Once you have installed the service, you can use the Windows NT *DNS Manager* to add primary, secondary, and reverse lookup zones. Resource records for your primary zones may be entered using the *DNS Manager*.

For a DNS server to adequately function, it *must* be able to integrate with other name servers. Most basically, a DNS server must be able to locate the Internet *root name server* (or root servers on your local network if you aren't on the Internet). The root name servers provide the name server with IP addresses for other name servers that can provide information for the network's top-level domains. The name server can then contact servers at successively lower levels until it obtains the requested information. Addresses for the root name servers are contained in the `cache.dns` file. An Internet `cache.dns` file is automatically installed when DNS is installed. Alternatively, you may download an updated one from the Internet. If you will use DNS name resolution on a network other than the Internet, you must edit the `cache.dns` file to reflect the root servers in *your* network. It is also possible to integrate a DNS server with a local WINS server. DNS servers so configured are able to obtain individual host mappings from the WINS server, obviating the necessity of entering a host record for each machine in the domain.

DNS client computers may be configured automatically by the Dynamic Host Configuration Protocol or manually by supplying IP addresses for applicable DNS servers in the `TCP/IP Properties` dialog.

The `nslookup` utility provides a command line capability to retrieve information from a selected DNS server. The utility has both interactive and non-interactive modes to allow for several queries or just a single request.

▲ REVIEW QUESTIONS

1. *Sandy has configured DNS servers to perform host resolution on her company's intranet. The company has decided to access the Internet and Sandy has been tasked to install another DNS server to provide name resolution beyond the company's internal network. How can Sandy ensure the new server will be able to find Internet domain information?*

   A. By setting the IP address for the InterNIC as the server's default gateway

   B. By using the HOSTS file

   C. By using the `cache.dns` file

   D. By integrating the new DNS server with all local WINS servers

2. *Your network has four Windows NT servers, 20 UNIX machines, and 200 Windows NT workstations. Your Windows NT workstations are DHCP clients, and DHCP automatically configures them as WINS clients also. Realizing that your UNIX computers will require a host name resolution capability, you install DNS on one of the Windows NT servers. After entering the UNIX host names and IP addresses, how can you minimize additional administrative effort?*

   A. Create a HOSTS file on the DNS server to track the UNIX computers

   B. Enable WINS resolution on the DNS server

   C. Install a DHCP Relay Agent on the UNIX network segment

   D. Create an LMHOSTS file on the DNS server with an entry for each Windows NT workstation

3. *Kim is installing DNS servers in her network and wants to ensure DNS database redundancy. How should Kim configure a second WINS server to provide redundancy?*

   A. As a forwarder

   B. As a master name server

   C. As a secondary name server

   D. As a slave server

4. *Steve's network uses DHCP, DNS, and WINS services. Some of his users are complaining that IP-address-to-host name resolution is not functioning. What would you suggest Steve do to troubleshoot the problem?*

    A. Run `nbtstat` against the DHCP server

    B. Check the `cache.dns` file

    C. Check the reverse lookup file with NSLOOKUP

    D. Delete `in-addr.arpa`

5. *Bob manages a network with a mix of Windows NT and UNIX computers and has installed a primary and two secondary DNS servers to manage the* `marketing.mcseinc.com` *zone of the* `mcseinc.com` *Internet domain. Bob's boss has directed him to ensure that the DNS servers resolve names not in the DNS database through the network's WINS servers. How should Bob proceed?*

    A. Configure all three DNS servers for WINS resolution

    B. Configure the primary DNS server to use WINS resolution

    C. Configure all DNS servers for WINS reverse lookup

    D. Configure DHCP to permit WINS reverse lookup

6. *Your network consists of Macintosh and Windows 95 client computers. You have installed several Windows NT computers to function as Web servers. You want to let all clients access the Web servers through* Internet Explorer *using host names. What service should you use?*

    A. FTP

    B. DHCP

    C. DNS

    D. WINS

7. *Vicky is using two DNS servers to support the non-Microsoft computers operating in her single DNS zone network. With the addition of several more non-Microsoft hosts, she decides to add an extra DNS server for load balancing. How can she set up the new server to support this role without generating any zone transfer traffic on the network?*

    A. As a slave server

    B. As a forwarder

    C. As a caching-only server

    D. As a secondary server

8. *One of your users is complaining that he cannot connect to a particular Windows NT server using* Internet Explorer. *The server's FQDN is* `research.mcseinc.com` *and your user consistently gets the following message: "Internet Explorer cannot open the Internet site http://research.mcseinc.com. A connection with the server could not be established." Your user has no trouble when attempting to contact other sites. What would you suspect as possible causes of the problem? (Select all that apply.)*

   A. The DNS server has no entry for `research.mcseinc.com`

   B. The ARP cache on the client computer has no entry for `research.mcseinc.com`

   C. The client computer has no default gateway setting

   D. The DNS server returns an incorrect IP address for the host at `research.mcseinc.com`

9. *Linda can connect to the FTP service of a Windows NT server with* Windows NT Explorer *but cannot connect using the command* `ftp fileserver.mcseinc.com`. *What is the likely cause of the problem?*

   A. The FTP server is not WINS-configured

   B. Linda's workstation is not configured to run DNS

   C. The FTP server is a DNS secondary server

   D. Linda's workstation has a bad subnet mask

10. *Which file does a DNS root server need before it can connect to the Internet?*

    A. `cache.dns`

    B. Boot

    C. DNS database

    D. HOSTS

    E. LMHOSTS

    F. `in-addr.arpa`

11. *Your network consists mainly of Windows NT computers. What is the best way to minimize the number of static records maintained by the network's DNS servers?*

    A. List WINS before DNS on each client's name resolution configuration dialog

    B. Configure the WINS server to resolve FQDNs

C. Configure the DNS server to use the WINS server for name resolution

D. Configure the WINS server to provide the DNS server with IP address mappings for the Windows NT machines in the network

12. *Your mail server is not functioning properly. You suspect it's not visible as a mail server on the network. What DNS record should you ensure is present?*

   A. WINS

   B. MX

   C. PTR

   D. HINFO

13. *Shane has two DNS servers in his network already and plans to add a third to process DNS queries destined for the Internet. How would you tell Shane to employ the new server?*

   A. As a master name server

   B. As a slave server

   C. As a forwarder

   D. As a secondary server

Connectivity in Heterogeneous Environments

Chapter 1, "Introduction to TCP/IP," introduced the TCP/IP protocol suite as a tool to connect dissimilar systems such as UNIX and Windows platforms. In this chapter, we'll explore the connectivity options for using Microsoft TCP/IP to interoperate in a heterogeneous environment. We will look more deeply into the Microsoft TCP/IP connectivity utilities we introduced in Chapter 1, discuss how to use REXEC and Telnet, and show the features of the built-in FTP client. We'll also spend some time on TCP/IP printing support and configuring a Windows NT computer to act as a print server for UNIX clients.

At the end of this chapter, you will be able to:

- Discuss what is needed to connect to a remote host through Microsoft networking.

- Use Microsoft TCP/IP utilities to access resources on a TCP/IP-based UNIX host.

- Use the built-in FTP client to connect to the FTP server.

315

- Install the TCP/IP Print Service on a Windows NT-based computer to create a TCP/IP printer.
- Use LPR and LPQ utilities to print to a printer attached to a UNIX host.

MCSE 12.1 Microsoft TCP/IP Connectivity Utilities

Now that you're familiar with how to plan, install, and configure the Microsoft TCP/IP protocol suite, you should have no problem in building a complex TCP/IP-based network where computers can effectively share resources such as files and printers. But stop! The TCP/IP protocol only gives *connectivity* to foreign computers (such as UNIX, OS/2, or VMS) because it is a common *network* protocol. To actually access resources and accomplish something with these foreign machines, common utilities (usually client/server) must exist on both ends. In Chapter 1, we discovered that Microsoft TCP/IP includes useful TCP/IP utilities for data transfer, monitoring, and printing. These utilities, however, are specific to the TCP/IP version (Microsoft, UNIX, OS/2, etc.) in use. The question is; can you use standard Microsoft networking commands and utilities (for example, Net Use and *Windows NT Explorer)* to connect to and access data on a remote non-Windows host? The answer is yes if the following conditions are met:

- Both computers must be able to communicate using the same protocol. (This protocol actually doesn't have to be TCP/IP. Protocols such as IPX or NetBEUI will work as long as all systems use the same protocol.) This is often referred to as *transport driver connectivity.*
- The non-Microsoft host must support the SMB (Server Message Blocks) protocol. (SMB is the file-sharing protocol used on all Microsoft network products.) This requirement is referred to as *SMB connectivity.*
- If the two computers have the NetBIOS scope parameter configured, the scope ID must be the same or they will not be able to establish a NetBIOS session. (You'll remember we covered NetBIOS scopes in Chapter 7, "NetBios Over TCP/IP.")

If these conditions are met, Microsoft-based clients can easily connect to non-Microsoft platforms, and vice versa. Today, many vendors have implemented NetBIOS over TCP/IP and included SMB support in their operating systems. For example, LAN Manager for UNIX and DEC PATHWORKS on VMS both feature SMB support.

UNIX-based computers can also access Windows NT servers through the SMB protocol with the installation of an SMB-based client. Alternatively, UNIX clients can connect to Windows NT servers using their native NFS (Network File System) protocol if a Windows NT server has an NFS service installed. (Although the NFS service is not included in Windows NT Server 4.0, third-party NFS servers are available for it.)

Connectivity Using Microsoft TCP/IP Utilities

Although many third-party solutions exist, we will explore only the native Microsoft TCP/IP utilities that allow you to integrate Windows NT systems into heterogeneous environments. The Microsoft TCP/IP utilities listed in Table 12.1 provide several options for connecting to foreign TCP/IP-based hosts.

Most Microsoft TCP/IP utilities are styled after their UNIX counterparts with a command line interface. Some of the utilities, however, utilize a graphical interface.

Table 12.1 *Microsoft TCP/IP Connectivity Utilities*

Utility	Function
Remote Copy (RCP)	Allows you to copy files between a Windows NT-based computer and a server running RCP daemon (or service) without logging on.
File Transfer Protocol (FTP)	Provides bi-directional file transfers between a Windows NT-based computer and a TCP/IP host running FTP server software.
Trivial File Transfer Protocol (TFTP)	Provides bi-directional file transfers between a Windows NT-based computer and a TCP/IP host running TFTP server software. A subset of FTP.
Microsoft Internet Explorer	Allows access to documents stored on World Wide Web servers.
Remote Shell (RSH)	Permits you to run a command on a remote host with RSH server software installed. (Does not require you to log on to the target host.)
Remote Execution (REXEC)	Allows you to run a process on a remote host. (Requires you to provide a valid user name and password.)
Telnet	Provides terminal emulation to a TCP/IP host running Telnet server software.
Line Printer Remote (LPR)	Allows you to send a print job to the printer connected to a server with the LPD service.
Line Printer Daemon (LPD)	Services LPR requests and submits print jobs to the printing device.
Line Printer Queue (LPQ)	Provides the ability to view the print queue on the LPD server.

Data Transfer Utilities

Microsoft TCP/IP data transfer utilities allow you to obtain files from remote TCP/IP computers and even permit you to copy files between two remote computers. These utilities are RCP, FTP, TFTP, and Web browsers such as *Microsoft Internet Explorer*.

RCP

The *Remote Copy* command line connectivity command can be used to copy files between a Windows NT computer and a computer running *rshd* (RSH service, or daemon, as it is called in UNIX) software. Since Windows NT does not use the RSH service, a Windows NT-based computer can only participate as the computer from which RCP commands are issued.

The RCP command does not use passwords—authentication is provided by a special .rhosts file on the target computer. The .rhosts file specifies which computers and users can access a local account using RCP. The .rhosts file is a text file, each entry of which consists of a host name and possible user name. The RCP command transmits the local user name to the remote computer. The remote computer checks to see if the given user and computer from which the communication was initiated are listed in its .rhosts file. If appropriate .rhosts information is found, the file transfer is granted.

The syntax for the Windows NT RCP command is:

```
RCP [-a | -b] [-h] [-r] [host[.user:]]source
[host[.user:]]destination
```

Switch	Explanation
-a	Specifies ASCII transfer mode. This mode converts end of line (EOL) characters to a carriage return for UNIX and a carriage return/line feed for personal computers. This is the default transfer mode.
-b	Specifies binary image transfer mode.
-h	Transfers hidden files.
-r	Copies the contents of all subdirectories (destination must be a directory).
host	Host name of source or destination computer.
.user:	If the user portion is omitted, the currently logged on Windows NT user name is used. If a fully-qualified host name is used, which contains the period (.) separators, the [.user] must be included. Otherwise, the last part of the host name is interpreted as the user name.
source	Specifies the files to copy.
destination	Specifies the destination path.

Any filename that is not preceded with a forward slash (/) for UNIX computers or a backward slash (\ ) for Windows computers is considered to be relative to the current working directory (the directory from which the command is issued for the Windows NT computer or the logon directory for the remote computer).

For example, the command

```
rcp report.doc hpserv.johnm:/users/johnm/NTReport.doc
```

copies the file `report.doc` from the Windows NT local directory to `/users/johnm/NTReport.doc` on the UNIX server `HPSERV`. For this operation to successfully complete, the appropriate `.rhosts` file must exist on the `HPSERV` computer.

When `.rhosts` files are properly configured, the RCP command can be issued from a Windows NT computer to copy files *between* two computers running *rshd*. For example, you can use the following syntax to copy a file from one UNIX computer to another:

```
rcp serv1.user1:report.doc serv2.user2:reportcopy.doc
```

If your machine is part of a network, check with your network administrator before creating a `.rhosts` file. Because `.rhosts` files provide access to resources and can be created by non-administrator personnel, they are prohibited on many networks.

FTP

FTP (File Transfer Protocol) is a command line TCP/IP utility that transfers files between local and remote TCP/IP hosts. (FTP is defined in RFC 959.) In contrast to the RCP command, the FTP utility authenticates when a user name and password are supplied for the remote computer.

FTP was one of the earliest methods used to transfer files on TCP/IP–based networks and the Internet. Currently the World Wide Web

(WWW) has replaced most FTP functions, but FTP is still the only way to *upload* files from a client computer to a server over the Internet.

To use FTP to transfer files between two computers, both computers must support their respective FTP roles. In other words, one needs to be an FTP client and the other an FTP server. The FTP client can issue commands to the server (commands to download files, upload files, and create or change directories on the server). For a Windows NT-based FTP client to connect to a remote FTP host, the target (remote host) computer must have the FTP service running and the user account for the Windows NT must be user-configured.

Table 12.2 describes the most common FTP commands. The following example illustrates a typical FTP session:

```
C:\WINNT>ftp
ftp> open hpserv
Connected to hpserv.traincert.com.
220 hpserv FTP server (Version 1.7.109.2 Tue Jul 28
23:32:34 GMT 1992) ready.
User (hpserv.traincert.com:(none)): johnm
331 Password required for johnm.
Password:********
230 User johnm logged in.
ftp> get library.cpp
200 PORT command successful.
150 Opening ASCII mode data connection for library.cpp
(12500 bytes).
226 Transfer complete.
```

Table 12.2 *Common FTP Commands*

Command	Purpose
open	Connects to the specified FTP server.
delete	Deletes files on the remote computer. (Requires appropriate permissions.)
dir	Lists the remote directory's files and directories.
get	Downloads a remote file to your computer.
help	Displays descriptions for FTP commands.
put	Uploads a file from your computer to the remote computer. (Requires appropriate permissions.)
mkdir	Creates a directory on the remote computer. (Requires appropriate permissions.)
bye	Ends the FTP session with the remote computer and exits FTP.

```
12500 bytes received in 4,00 seconds (3,12 Kbytes/sec)
ftp> bye
221 Goodbye.
```

An FTP connection can also be established by using third-party utilities. Cute-FTP, for example, is an FTP utility that permits you to issue FTP commands using a graphical interface.

FTP does not encrypt user names and passwords during authentication. Using FTP through the Internet can cause a security gap.

In addition to FTP client software, Windows NT contains the FTP server software. You can install the Internet Information Server (IIS) on your Windows NT server. IIS includes the FTP server service. On Windows NT Workstation, the FTP server service is included when you install Peer Web Services (PWS). Once you have installed an FTP server, you are able to publish documents on the Internet.

TRIVIAL FILE TRANSFER PROTOCOL · The Trivial File Transfer Protocol (TFTP) is a subset of FTP. It is a fast, simple file transfer protocol that uses the User Datagram Protocol (UDP) transport, but does not support any user authentication. Files need to be world-readable and writable (UNIX permissions) on the remote system to be used by TFTP. While FTP can be used interactively, TFTP allows only unidirectional file transfer. FTP uses well-known TCP port numbers: 20 for data and 21 for connection dialog where TFTP uses UDP port number 69 for its file transfer activity. Because TFTP doesn't support authentication, the Windows NT FTP server service does not support it. The TFTP protocol is described in RFC 1350.

WEB BROWSERS

Web browsers can access documents stored on WWW servers using the Hypertext Transfer Protocol (HTTP). HTTP is an Application Level protocol that utilizes TCP to transfer data. More specifically, a Web browser acting as a client sends an HTTP request to TCP port 80 of the Web server. The HTTP request contains the name of the document to be sent, as well as some additional information such as browser version and client language. Having received such a request, the Web server responds with the status of the transaction (successful or failed) and the data for the request. The type of data varies. A client can accept text documents, images, sounds and others. After the requested document is sent, the connection is closed. If an HTTP document consists of multiple objects (for example, inline images), a separate connection is opened for each object.

A good example of a Web browser is *Microsoft Internet Explorer* (included with Windows NT). For the latest version of *Microsoft Internet Explorer,* visit *http://www.microsoft.com/ie/*.

The advantages of using a Web browser are the following:

- A Web browser can download text and graphical files and automatically display them to the screen.
- A Web browser can play sound and video clips.
- A Web browser can launch helper applications for known file types. (For example, when downloading a *Word* document, a properly configured Web browser can launch *Word* and open the file with it.)
- A Web browser can save a file of an unknown type to a local hard disk drive.
- Web browsers exist for nearly every operating system and hardware platform.
- Web browsers support multiple protocols, including Gopher, Network News Transfer Protocol (NNTP), and FTP. (You can, for example, use *Microsoft Internet Explorer* as an FTP client.)

Using a Web browser, you can easily access documents on a Web server running under different operating systems such as UNIX, Novell Netware, or Windows NT.

Remote Execution Utilities

Sometimes you don't need to download a file, but only wish to execute a command on a remote host. For example, an administrator of a mixed UNIX and NT network might want to view a list of files on a UNIX computer while siting at a Windows NT computer. This is a job for the *remote execution utilities*!

RSH

The command line connectivity utility RSH runs commands on a remote host which is running the *rshd* daemon (a UNIX daemon is equivalent to a Windows NT service). For example, you can use the RSH command to remotely compile programs. A user does not have to log on to the UNIX host to run a command—RSH security is implemented using the `.rhosts` file.

Here is the syntax of the Windows NT RSH command:

```
RSH host [-l username] [-n] command
```

Switch	Explanation
host	Specifies the remote host on which to run the command.
-l username	Specifies the user name to use on the remote host. If omitted, the logged on user name is used. (The user must be listed in the `.rhosts` file.)
-n	Redirects the input of RSH to NULL.
command	Specifies the command to run.

The following code fragment shows how to issue a command to a UNIX host from a Windows NT computer. This command sends the contents of the log file on the UNIX computer `hpserv` to the specified e-mail address:

```
C:\WINNT\>rsh hpserv cat logfile "|" mail
root@traincert.com
```

> You must use quotation marks around redirection symbols (| , > , >>) for redirection to occur on the remote host. For example, `rsh hpserv file1 ">>" file2` appends *remote* `file1` to *remote* `file2`, and `rsh hpserv file1 >> file2` appends *remote* `file1` to *local* `file2`.

REXEC

In contrast to RSH, the REXEC utility provides remote execution facilities based on a user name and password. To use REXEC, a user must have a valid account on the TCP/IP host.

The syntax of the REXEC command is the following:

```
REXEC host [-l username] [-n] command
```

Switch	Explanation
host	Specifies the remote host on which to run the command.
-l username	Specifies the user name to use on the remote host. If omitted, the logged on user name is used.
-n	Redirects the input of REXEC to NULL.
command	Specifies the command to run.

REXEC prompts the user for a password and authenticates the password on the remote host. If the authentication succeeds, the command is executed.

In the following example, we see how you could view a mailbox on a UNIX host from a Windows NT computer using a REXEC session:

```
C:\WINNT>rexec hpserv -l johnm mail
Password (hpserv.traincert.com:):*******
From Administrator@traincert.com Thu Nov 12 21:08 GMT 1998
Received: by mail.traincert.com
        (1.37.109.4/16.2) id AA23186; Thu, 12 Nov 98 21:08:39
        -0300
Date: Thu, 12 Nov 98 21:08:39 -0300
From: Administrator <Administrator@traincert.com>
Subject: Log Files
Apparently-To: johnm@traincert.com

Don't forget to clear the log files today!!!
```

You cannot run most interactive commands. For example, *vi* or *emacs* cannot be run using REXEC.

TELNET

This connectivity command starts terminal emulation with a remote host running a Telnet server service. Telnet provides DEC VT 100, DEC VT 52, or TTY emulation. You can think of a Telnet application as a utility that transfers a sequence of characters from your computer to a remote process.

When you install the TCP/IP protocol suite on Windows NT, the Telnet client utility is installed automatically. You can launch the Telnet client by selecting `Telnet` from the `Accessories` program group or by using the command prompt. To connect to a remote computer using the *Telnet* application, the remote host must be running a Telnet daemon (or service). In addition, you must have a valid user account on the remote host. When you connect to a remote host, you will be asked to input a user name and password before you can issue commands.

Windows NT does not provide the Telnet daemon. There are several third-party Telnet services/daemons for Windows NT. For more information about Telnet daemons for Windows NT, see Microsoft Knowledge Base article Q149255. The Microsoft Windows NT Server Resource Kit version 4.0 provides basic TCP/IP Telnet server functionality, but as of this writing, it is only beta software.

When you launch the *Telnet* client application from the command prompt, you can pass, as an argument, a host name or IP address for the computer to which you want to connect. (You can also use the `Remote System` command from the `Connect` menu if the Telnet client is already running.) For example, to connect to computer `hpserv`, type the following at the Windows NT command prompt.

```
telnet hpserv
```

For this command to work successfully, the host name resolution must be set up properly.

When the Telnet connection is established, you will be prompted for a valid user name and password. The following is an example of a typical Telnet session. User input is in bold typeface.

```
HP-UX hpserv A.09.01 C 9000/710 (ttys0)

login: johnm
Password:********
Please wait...checking for disk quotas
$ ls -a
.                        .sysadm_htpasswd    fp
..                       .vedrc              htpasswd
.cshrc                   .vue                index.txt
.elm                     .vueprofile         mail
.exrc
```

Using Telnet Client to Connect to a Remote Process

You can use the Windows NT *Telnet* client application to connect to the remote TCP/IP service by specifying the port number, which is used by this service. You may want to do this when troubleshooting this service. Of course, you must know the commands which are used by the service. For example, to connect to the SMTP service (TCP port 25) on computer `hpserv`, type the following at the command prompt:

```
telnet hpserv 25
```

After issuing this command, you can transfer commands directly to the SMTP service on computer `hpserv`. In the following example, `johnm` sends an e-mail message that reads `Mail server testing` to user `admin` (user input is marked in bold typeface).

```
220 hpserv HP Sendmail (1.37.109.4/16.2) ready
HELO mcse.traincert.com
250 hpserv Hello mcse.traincert.com, pleased to meet you
MAIL FROM: johnm@traincert.com
250 johnm@traincert.com... Sender ok
RCPT TO: admin@traincert.com
250 admin@traincert.com... Recipient ok
DATA
354 Enter mail, end with "." on a line by itself
Mail server testing
.
250 Ok
```

MCSE 12.2 Configuring a Windows NT Computer to Support TCP/IP Printing

One of the problems that administrators face in a mixed network is how to ensure that each client can print. Clients from different operating systems behave differently in creating print jobs, and sending those jobs to a print server and on to print devices. If your network consists of only Microsoft clients, network printing is as easy as "point and print." If, on the other hand, you are also blessed with clients running other operating systems, printing becomes more complex. This is mainly because print server services (software modules on print servers that receive print jobs) support print jobs from clients of only one type. For example, if a UNIX client wants to print a document on a Windows NT-based print server, a print service that understands UNIX-style print jobs must be installed on Windows NT. As we're about to see, however, by using Windows NT Server as your network print server, you have a seamless way to print, no matter what operating systems your networked computers use.

Let's focus on TCP/IP printing and see how Windows NT supports it. But first, let's review the overall Windows NT printing architecture. (See Figure 12.1.)

Network printing methods differ greatly depending on what type of client initiates the print job. When a Windows NT machine prints, it sends

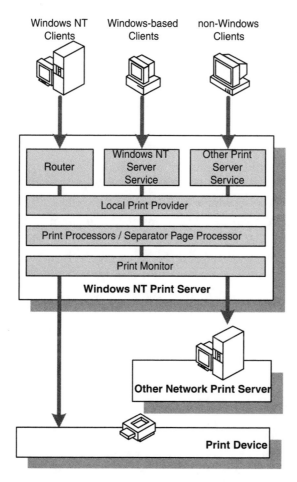

Figure 12.1 *Windows NT printing architecture.*

its print job to the server by using remote procedure calls (RPCs) to the server-side print router. If a Microsoft-based (non-Windows NT) client prints, the print job is delivered to the Windows NT Server service on the print server through client redirectors. If a non-Microsoft client prints, the print job is delivered to the corresponding print server service.

Next, the router or print server service passes the print job to the local print provider on the server (a component of the spooler), which spools the print job (writes it to disk). The local print provider can then poll the print processors and separator page processor. Finally, the job is passed to the print monitor, which transmits it to the print device or to another server over a specific communications channel.

As you can see, because each type of print client creates print jobs differently, a variety of print server services are required to receive and handle print jobs. Let's now turn our attention to just how Windows NT supports TCP/IP printing.

TCP/IP printing can be explained in terms of three applications: *Line Printer Remote* (LPR), *Line Printer Queue* (LPQ) and *Line Printer Daemon* (LPD). LPR and LPQ are client applications that communicate with the LPD application on the print server.

TCP/IP Printing Utilities

For a Windows NT computer to accept jobs from LPR clients (such as UNIX computers), the Windows NT *LPD* service (officially called *Microsoft TCP/IP Printer Server* service) needs to be installed and running. In Figure 12.1 you can consider the LPD service as the "Other Network Print Server" service.

When the *TCP/IP Printer Server* service is installed and started, it is ready to accept print jobs from LPR clients. (See Figure 12.2.) Of course, we're assuming the Windows NT computer has a print device attached with a properly installed printer driver.

Study Break

Installing Microsoft TCP/IP Printing Services

1. Go to `Control Panel`.
2. Double-click `Network` and go to the `Services` tab.
3. Click `Add` and select `Microsoft TCP/IP Printing`. (See Figure 12.3.)
4. Click `OK` to restart your computer.

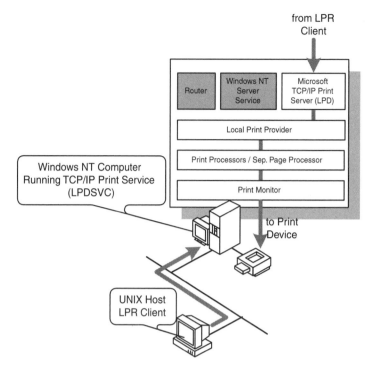

Figure 12.2 *A Windows NT computer running TCP/IP Printer Server service can accept print jobs from LPR clients.*

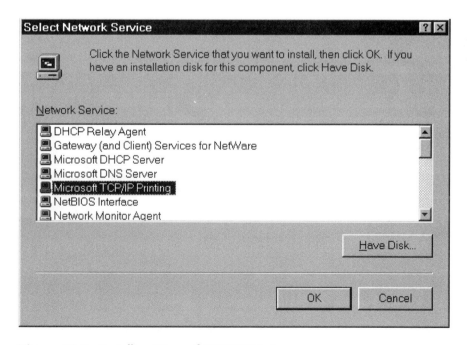

Figure 12.3 *Installing Microsoft TCP/IP Printing.*

By default, *Microsoft TCP/IP Print Server* is configured to start manually. It is recommended that the *TCP/IP Print Server* service be configured to start automatically. You can do this either through `Services` in `Control Panel` or *Server Manager:*

1. Click on `Services` to reveal the `Services` dialog (see Figure 12.4).
2. Select `TCP/IP Print Server` and click the `Startup` button.
3. Select the `Automatic` startup type and click `OK`.
4. The service will start automatically when Windows NT starts up. To ensure it is running in the current session, however, click the `Start` button and then `Close` (after the service successfully starts).

You can also use the command prompt to start the *Microsoft TCP/IP Print Server* service. To do this, type `net start lpdsvc` at the command prompt.

When LPD receives print jobs from LPR clients, it submits them to the spooler. An LPR client always sends some control information within a print job. This control information contains administrative data. LPD uses that control information to assign a data type (TEXT or RAW) to the print job. For example, if the LPR client sends the f, o, or p control command, the LPD assigns the TEXT data type to the print job. This ensures that the spooler will alter this print job before printing. If the LPR client sends the l

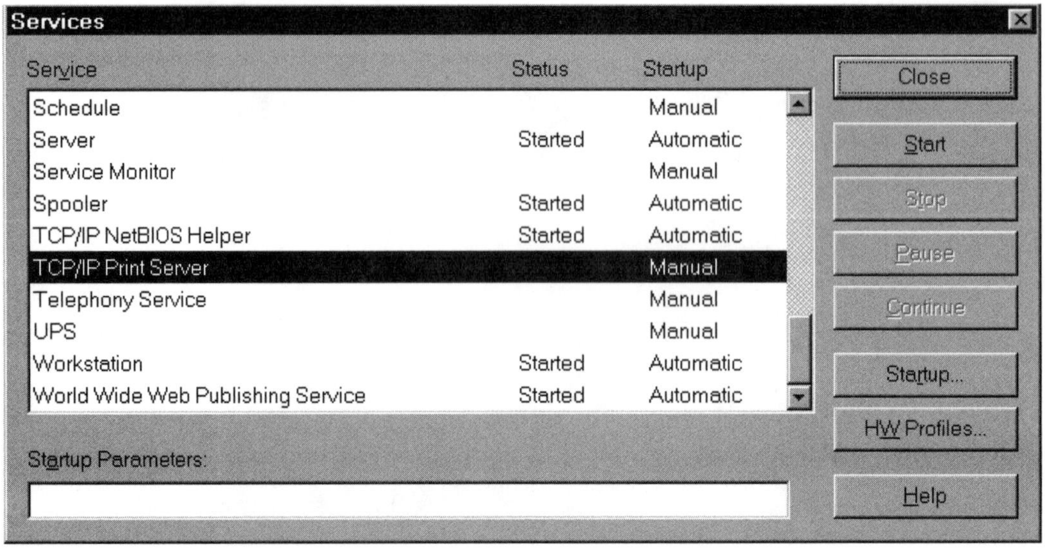

Figure 12.4 *Configure the TCP/IP Print Server service to start automatically.*

control command, the LPD assigns the RAW data type to the print job and the spooler does not modify it before printing.

The *Microsoft TCP/IP Print Server* cannot be customized using a graphical user interface. You can, however, use the Registry editor to change configuration parameters in `HKEY_LOCAL_MACHINE\SYSTEM\CurrentControlSet\Services\LPDSVC\Parameters`. You can control the maximum number of concurrent users by changing the `MaxConcurrentUsers` parameter. By setting `AllowJobRemoval` to zero, you can prevent the removal of a print job from the print queue, and by setting `AllowPrinterResume` to zero, you can prevent anyone from resuming printer operation when it is paused. These latter two parameters both default to `1`.

Most UNIX clients send the f control command within their print jobs. If your LPD print server is running, Windows NT treats these print jobs as the TEXT data type instead of the RAW data type (as they would be on UNIX). This could result in incorrect printing. To correct this problem, configure the UNIX LPR clients to send the lower-case (1) control command. (Refer to your UNIX documentation for instructions on this configuration.)

Submitting Print Jobs Using LPR

LPR is one of the protocols in the TCP/IP protocol suite. Defined in RFC 1179, LPR was originally developed as a standard for transmitting print jobs between computers running the UNIX operating system. Currently, LPR software exists for most operating systems, including Windows NT. Using the Microsoft LPR utility, you can issue print jobs to:

- UNIX computers.
- Windows NT computers with the *TCP/IP Print Server* service installed.
- Windows for Workgroups computers with a third-party LPD.
- Network printers such as HP JetDirect or Emulex NetJet.

Some network-attached print devices that support TCP/IP are not fully compliant with RFC 1179: some do not implement the entire specification, while others implement a proprietary specification. In these cases, the LPR utility may not print properly.

When you installed the *TCP/IP Print Server* service, the LPR software was installed also. You can now submit print jobs to any computer running the LPD service (or daemon). You could, for example, submit a job to a UNIX host or another Windows NT computer using the following command line syntax:

```
lpr -Sprint_server -Pprinter_name [-C class] [-J job] [-o
option] [-x] [-d] filename
```

Switch	Explanation
-Sprint_server	Specifies the name or IP address of the host providing LPD service.
-Pprinter_name	Specifies the name of the printer queue ("printer" in Windows NT terminology).
-C class	Job classification to use on the burst page.
-J job	Job name to print on the burst page.
-o option	Type of the file (by default, assumes a text file; use -o l to indicate binary [e.g., Postscript] files).
-x	Compatibility with SunOS 4.1.x and prior.
-d	Send data file first.
filename	Specifies the name of the file to be printed.

Note The LPR options are case-sensitive and must be typed using the correct case. In a Windows environment, you will be mostly concerned with the -S, -P, and filename arguments; optional arguments are included here for completeness.

For example, the following command, issued on the WKS computer, submits the file c:\boot.ini to the printer queue named LASER3D attached to the UNIX computer hpserv. (See Figure 12.5.)

```
lpr -Shpserv -PLASER3D c:\boot.ini
```

For this command to work successfully, host name resolution must work properly.

Additionally, computer WKS can issue a print job to the printer attached to computer MCSE:

```
lpr -SMCSE -PNTPrinter c:\boot.ini
```

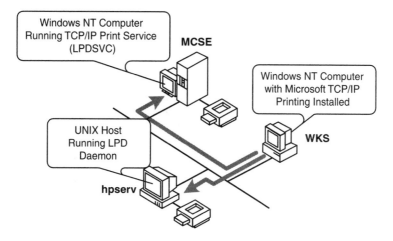

Figure 12.5 *Computer with LPR software can submit print jobs to LPD servers.*

To send a print job, the LPR software under Windows NT 4.0 makes a TCP connection to the LPD service using any available port between 512 and 1023. Windows NT 3.5× sent all TCP/IP print jobs using TCP ports 721 through 731. If enough jobs were sent in Windows NT 3.5×, this often produced a bottleneck and caused delays.

Using LPR, you send a print job directly to the LPD service or print device and bypass the spooler. The print job is neither spooled nor modified. The LPR utility sends the control information along with the print job so that the server-side LPD software knows how to handle the print job. By default, the LPR command sends the f control command. You can use the -o switch to override this behavior.

Unfortunately the LPR protocol does not support detailed error status information. Therefore, if anything goes wrong, LPR reports only a generic error condition.

USING LPQ TO CHECK THE PRINT STATUS

Once a file has been sent to the printer using LPR, you can examine the status of the printer queue by using the LPQ command. To use the LPQ command from the Windows NT command prompt, you must first install the *Microsoft TCP/IP Print Server* service. The syntax of the LPQ command is the following:

```
lpq -Sprint_server -Pprinter_name [-1]
```

Switch	Explanation
-Sserver_name	Name or IP address of the host providing LPD service.
-Pprinter_name	Name of the print queue.
-1	Verbose output.

The following sequence of commands submits a print job and then displays the status of the print queue (user input is in bold typeface):

```
C:\WINNT>lpr -SMSCE -PNTPrinter c:\boot.ini
C:\WINNT>lpq -SMCSE -PNTPrinter -1
                       Windows NT LPD Server
                       Printer NTPrinter (Paused)
Owner    Status    Jobname    Job-Id  Size  Pages Priority
-------------------------------------------------------------
JOHNM    Waiting   c:\boot.ini    9    404     0      1
```

Configuring Print Manager with LPR

Although LPR works fine from the command line, you may want to take advantage of Windows applications. You may be wondering if you can print from *Microsoft Word* or *Excel* to a TCP/IP printer. The answer is: yes, you can! You simply configure the Windows NT *Print Manager* to use the LPD print server—known as the *LPR Print Monitor*.

The *LPR Print Monitor* redirects a spooled print job from the local computer to the LPD service running on another computer. To take advantage of the *LPR Print Monitor,* you must add an LPR port in the Add Printer wizard. You will need to supply the name or IP address of the server running the LPD software, as well as the name of the printer on that server.

Let's look at how Windows applications can print to the TCP/IP printer through the *LPR Print Monitor.* (See Figure 12.6.)

When a Windows-based application prints, the application calls the graphics device interface (GDI). GDI renders the print job in the printer language of the print device. Then the print job gets passed to the spooler. The router, being part of the spooler, passes the print job to the local print provider, which spools it to disk. After being altered by the print processor and separator page processor, the job is despooled to the LPR print monitor, which sends the print job to the TCP/IP host running the LPD service. The entire process is transparent to the application, which thinks that the printer is connected locally.

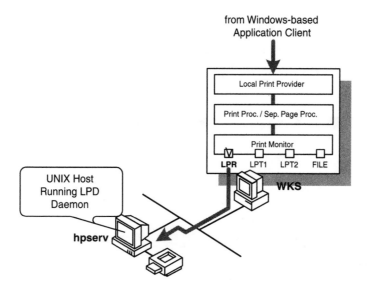

Figure 12.6 *Printing using the LPR Print Monitor.*

  If the target LPD server is Windows NT-based, the printer should have the `Everyone/Print` permission set so that **LPR** clients can print.

Study Break

Configuring a Windows NT Printer to Use LPR Software to Submit Print Jobs to LPD

1. Ensure that *Microsoft TCP/IP Print Server* is installed (completed in the previous exercise).
2. In `Control Panel`, double-click `Printers` and launch the `Add Printer` wizard.
3. Select `My Computer` and then click `Next`.
4. Click `Add Port` and select the LPR port.
5. Type the name or IP address of the computer running the LPD software and type the name of the printer created on that server. (See Figure 12.7.)
6. Click `OK` and follow the `Add Printer` wizard instructions to configure specific printer properties.

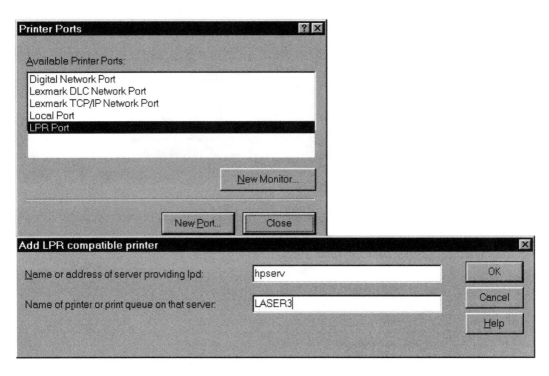

Figure 12.7 *Configuring Print Manager to use the LPD print server.*

Once you have created a printer that uses the LPR port, you can submit print jobs to this printer and they will be automatically redirected to the computer running the LPD service.

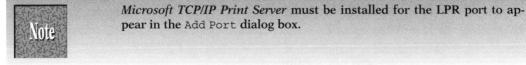

Microsoft TCP/IP Print Server must be installed for the LPR port to appear in the `Add Port` dialog box.

Using Windows NT as a Print Gateway

In some cases, you may want to consider configuring a print gateway on a Windows NT computer. Windows NT with *Microsoft TCP/IP Print Server* services installed can be configured to provide the following gateway functions:

1. Act as a gateway for Microsoft-based clients to forward their print jobs to print servers running LPD software.

2. Act as a gateway for LPR clients such as UNIX-based computers to automatically forward these print jobs to another printer.

PRINT GATEWAY FOR MICROSOFT-BASED CLIENTS

You can configure a Windows NT computer as a print gateway so that Microsoft-based clients can print documents on printers attached to computers running the LPD service. The entire printing process is transparent to Microsoft clients—client computers do not have to run LPR software or even the TCP/IP protocol (clients must use a protocol that is also in use on the print gateway server).

Study Break
_____

Enabling Your Windows NT Computer to Provide Print
Gateway Services for Microsoft-based Clients

1. Install *Microsoft TCP/IP Print Server* (accomplished earlier in this chapter).
2. Using the `Add Printer` wizard, create a new printer and add the LPR port (as accomplished in the previous exercise).
3. Provide an address of the print server with LPD service and a name of the print queue on that server.
4. Once the *LPR Print Monitor* is configured, share this printer.
5. Connect your Microsoft-based clients to the shared printer.

Once you have completed the preceding steps, the printing process will be patterned after that shown in Figure 12.8. Microsoft-based clients connect to the shared printer and issue their print jobs as if the printer were attached directly to the NT-based print server. After receiving the print job from the network client, the print server spools it as a regular print job. In the final stage, however, when the print job gets to the print monitor, the print monitor transfers it to the UNIX host running LPD.

PRINT GATEWAY FOR LPR CLIENTS

Suppose that you have several UNIX clients that need to print documents, but all printers are attached to the Microsoft-based computer with no LPD software installed. A Windows NT server configured as a print gateway can solve this problem. In this situation, Windows NT LPD (*TCP/IP Print Server*) receives a print job from a UNIX client and forwards it to any printer visible to the Windows NT computer.

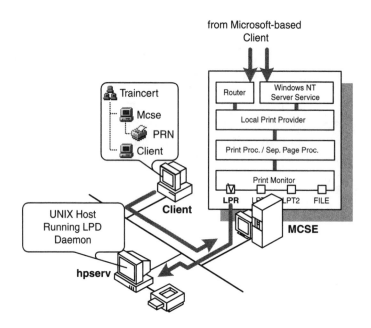

Figure 12.8 *Windows NT server as a print gateway for Microsoft-based clients.*

Study Break

Providing Print Gateway Services for LPR Clients

1. Install Microsoft *TCP/IP Print Server*.
2. Using the `Add Printer` wizard, create a new local printer and add a new local port.
3. Map the new local port to any visible network printer. (See Figure 12.9.)
4. Install the appropriate printer driver with the `Add Printer` wizard.
5. Give a name to the printer. (This name will also be used by the LPR clients.)
6. In `Control Panel`, configure the *TCP/IP Print Server* service to start automatically.

Now your Windows NT computer can accept print jobs from LPR clients and automatically forward them to the network printer. The only requirement is that this network printer be visible to the Windows NT print gateway. (See Figure 12.10.)

MCSE 12.3 Configuring a RAS Server and Dial-up Networking for Use on a TCP/IP Network

In addition to conventional networking, Windows NT permits dial-up connectivity through its dial-up networking and Remote Access Service (RAS)

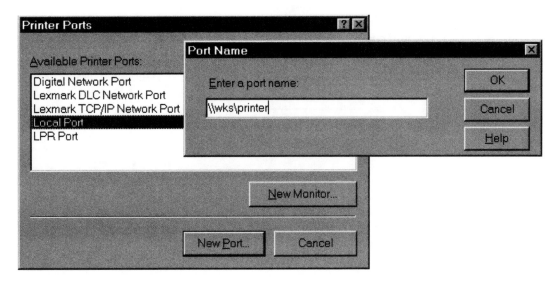

Figure 12.9 *Creating a new local port and mapping it to the existing network printer.*

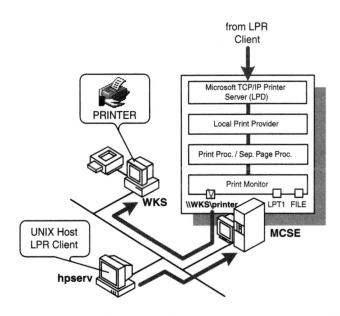

Figure 12.10 *Windows NT server as a print gateway for UNIX-based clients.*

features. With the RAS server feature installed, a Windows NT server is able to provide connections for users at remote locations through dial-up networking or other point-to-point (PPP) protocols. After the connection is established, remote links become transparent and a remote client can use the network resources as if it were directly connected to a local network segment.

Installing and Configuring RAS Server

Installing and configuring RAS differs from configuring dial-up networking clients. Dial-up clients are configured primarily to dial to remote locations, and RAS servers are configured to provide access to network services for those clients. RAS can be installed either during the initial Windows NT setup or after the installation of Windows NT.

Study Break

Installing RAS Server after Windows NT Is Set Up

1. In `Control Panel`, double-click `Network` and go to the `Services` tab.
2. Click `Add` and select `Remote Access Service`.
3. Provide the path to the distribution copy of Windows NT if needed.
4. If your machine doesn't already have a configured modem, you'll be given the opportunity to invoke the `Modem Installer` to install one—respond `Yes`.
5. If you have a modem, you may allow it to autodetect, otherwise check the `Don't Select my modem, I will select it from a list` checkbox and click `Next`.
6. Under `Standard Modem Types`, select `Dial-Up networking serial cable between 2 PCs` (you don't need to have a serial cable, but this will "trick" the system into thinking it is using a modem) and click `Next`.
7. Select an available port, click `Next`, and then click `Finish`.
8. When the `Add RAS Capable Device` dialog appears, verify the appropriate modem (or serial cable) is showing in the `RAS Capable Devices` window and click `OK`.
9. In the `Remote Access Setup` dialog, click `Configure`, select `Dial out and Receive Calls`, and click `OK`.
10. Click `Continue` and you are ready to configure the TCP/IP features of your RAS server. (See Figure 12.11.)
11. At the top of the dialog, you can limit remote clients running TCP/IP to connect only to the RAS server or to the entire network—select the option you desire.

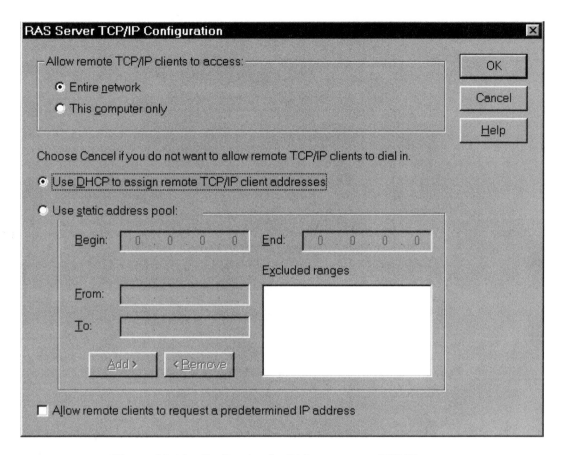

Figure 12.11 *Configuring the RAS server to use TCP/IP.*

12. If your server is in a DHCP environment, you may allow it to obtain IP addresses for its dial-in client from a DHCP server, or you can enter your own range of IP addresses under the static address pool (consult with your network administrator for the DHCP status or for the appropriate IP addresses, if required). If you select the DHCP option, ensure the DHCP scope has enough IP addresses for dial-in clients. Remember that each RAS connection requires *two* IP addresses: one for the client side and one for the server side. If you select your own IP address range, remember that the range must be valid for the subnet the RAS server is in.

13. You may allow dial-up networking clients to request a predetermined IP address by checking `Allow remote clients to request a predetermined IP address`. If this box is checked and the client is configured to provide an IP address, this will be the address assigned to the client for the session.

14. When you're satisfied with the configuration settings, click OK to close the Network dialog.
15. After the system resets the bindings, you're given an opportunity to restart the computer. Accept the restart and your RAS server is installed.

If you use a static pool of IP addresses for RAS clients, create this pool such that it includes at least the maximum number of simultaneous dial-in TCP/IP clients plus one addresses. The RAS server always uses the first IP address in the defined static pool for the address of its own RAS interface. Make sure RAS clients aren't configured to request this first address, or they will not have connectivity to the remote network once the RAS connection has been made.

Installing Dial-up Networking

Dial-up networking (a client-side version of remote access) is automatically installed during Windows NT installation if Remote access to the network is selected during setup. Dial-up networking can also be installed manually by double-clicking the Dial-Up Networking icon in My Computer. After installing dial-up networking, you must also configure phone book entries, dialing properties, and protocol settings.

Study Break

Installing and Configuring Dial-up Networking From My Computer

1. Select My Computer and double-click Dial-Up Networking.
2. If dial-up networking is not currently installed, this will launch the installation wizard, which will ask for a phone book entry. Click OK and follow the instructions of the wizard to enter a phone number (if you will not actually be calling a server, you may make up any telephone number).
3. Click More from the Dial-Up Networking dialog and select Edit Entry and Modem Properties.
4. Click the Server tab on the Edit Phonebook Entry dialog that is now visible.
5. If you will be connecting to a RAS server, ensure PPP is selected in the Dial-up Server Type window.

6. Ensure `TCP/IP` is selected under `Network Protocols` (other protocols may be used, but this is a book on TCP/IP).
7. Click on the `TCP/IP Settings` button and note that you can accept an IP address assigned by the server or specify your own (this is the client side to the predetermined IP address request described in the previous section).
8. Still in the `TCP/IP Settings` dialog, note that you may accept name server addresses from the server or request your own.
9. Click `OK`, `OK`, and `Close`. Dial-up networking is installed. The next time you double-click `Dial-Up networking` in `My Computer`, the `Dial-Up Networking` dialog will appear, permitting you to make connection through the entry you configured above by clicking `Dial`.

Using RAS for Routing IP Packets

Microsoft Windows NT RAS server includes routing capabilities that can be used to connect local area networks together and to the Internet. Let's discuss a typical situation when you are using a dial-up connection to an Internet Service Provider (ISP) to connect a small network to the Internet. (See Figure 12.12.)

To implement this structure, you must fulfill the following requirements:

1. Install TCP/IP on the Windows NT computer that will act as the dial-up client. When configuring the LAN adapter, it is very important that its IP address is from a different subnet than the IP address the dial-up adapter is using. (The IP address of the dial-up adapter is assigned when the connection to the RAS server is established. The ISP can configure its RAS server to assign a predetermined IP address for your dial-up adapter.)

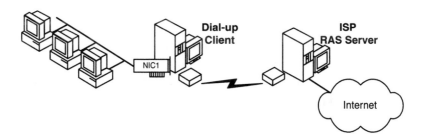

Figure 12.12 *Connecting a small network to the Internet using Microsoft RAS server.*

2. Install TCP/IP on all computers inside your LAN that will gain access to the Internet. Use unique, valid IP addresses for this. You may need to obtain a single class C network from the ISP for this purpose. This block of IP addresses must be from a different subnet than the one the ISP is using for its modems/routers.

3. Modify the `HKEY_LOCAL_MACHINE\System\CurrentControlSet\ Services\RasArp\Parameters` Registry key on the dial-up client computer by setting the `REG_DWORD` value of `DisableOtherSrcPack- ets` to `0`. (By default, the header of each IP packet sent though the RAS computer uses the IP address of the RAS server as the source. Because the packets that come from the internal LAN are not originated by the RAS server, you must make this change to permit the internal LAN packets to traverse the RAS server.)

4. Enable IP forwarding on the dial-up computer in the `Advanced TCP/IP Properties` dialog box.

5. Ensure that the ISP has created a route that forwards all packets for your LAN to your Windows NT dial-up client computer.

(More information about using RAS for routing IP packets is available in the Technet knowledge base article Q121877.)

Summary

In this chapter, we discussed Windows NT TCP/IP connectivity issues. We spoke about various connectivity utilities and identified when to use each one. Data transfer utilities (RCP, FTP, TFTP, Web browser) allow you to obtain files from remote TCP/IP computers. Remote execution utilities (RSH, REXEC, Telnet) allow you to execute a command or a program on a remote host. Some of the TCP/IP connectivity utilities require additional configuration on remote computers. UNIX hosts, for example, must maintain the `.rhosts` file for RSH and RCP to work.

We also explored TCP/IP printing and what is required to support it under Windows NT. The LPR utility lets a Windows NT computer print on a printer attached to a UNIX host, while LPQ allows you to view the status of the printer queue. Windows NT also provides the *TCP/IP Print Server* (also known as LPD), which allows a UNIX host to print on Windows NT printers. We also discovered that the Windows NT *Print Monitor* could be configured with an LPR port to permit Windows-based applications to take advantage of TCP/IP printing.

Finally, we discussed how the Windows NT RAS server and dial-up networking are configured in the TCP/IP environment and worked through an example where we connected a small LAN to the Internet using RAS and dial-up networking. Here we discovered that it was particularly important to ensure the dial-up adapter was assigned an IP address on a different subnet from that of the LAN on which the dial-up server was operating.

▲ REVIEW QUESTIONS

1. *Which of the following Microsoft TCP/IP utilities have password protection? (Select all that apply.)*
   A. FTP
   B. LPR
   C. LPD
   D. REXEC
   E. RSH

2. *To use the RCP utility, which configuration file must be set up on the target computer?*
   A. LMHOSTS
   B. HOSTS
   C. .RHOSTS
   D. SERVICES

3. *Which utility do you use to print files on printers connected to UNIX hosts?*
   A. LPD
   B. RCP
   C. LPR
   D. NET

4. *Which TCP/IP connectivity utility can you use to check the printer queue on a UNIX host?*
   A. LPR
   B. Control Panel
   C. LPQ
   D. LPD

5. *Which of the following utilities are used for TCP/IP printing?*

    A. Telnet

    B. RCP

    C. LPD

    D. REXEC

    E. LPQ

6. *Can you establish a Telnet session with a remote host without supplying a valid user name and password?*

    A. Yes

    B. No

7. *Which one of the following uses TCP protocol?*

    A. FTP

    B. TFTP

8. *Windows NT can connect with a foreign host when the host*

    A. Has a unique NetBIOS name

    B. Has TCP/IP installed

    C. Is configured with appropriate TCP/IP services

    D. Is a member of a Windows NT domain

9. *Which of the following encrypts passwords?*

    A. FTP

    B. TFTP

    C. RCP

    D. Telnet

    E. RSH

    F. None of the above

10. *Which of the following statements must be fulfilled to permit a Windows NT computer to communicate with a foreign host using Microsoft networking commands?*

    A. The non-Microsoft host must support the SMB protocol

    B. NetBIOS scope parameters for the Windows NT computer and the remote host must be the same

    C. Both computers must be able to communicate using the same protocol

    D. Both computers must be members of the same Windows NT Domain.

11. *You want to compile a program on a remote UNIX host. Which utility are you going to use for this?*

    A. RCP

    B. REXEC

    C. LPR

    D. Web browser

12. *You are the administrator of a mixed network that consists of a Windows NT server computer, several Windows NT Workstation computers, Windows 95 computers, and UNIX computers. UNIX computers have printers attached. How can you provide Windows-based computers the ability to print on UNIX printers? (Select all that apply.)*

    A. Install *TCP/IP Printer Server* service on a Windows NT Server computer

    B. Instruct Windows-based computer users to use the LPR utility to send their print jobs to a Windows NT computer

    C. Install a new printer on the Windows NT Server computer, create an LPR port, and map this port to the UNIX computer with the printer attached

    D. Share the printer on the Windows NT Server computer

    E. Instruct Windows-based computer users to connect to the shared printer on the Windows NT Server computer

13. *What is the right syntax for using the LPR utility?*

    A. `LPR -Sserver_address -Pprinter_name filename`

    B. Type `filename > LPR -Pprinter_name`

    C. `Net send LPR://server_address/printername filename`

    D. `LPR C:\Boot.ini`

14. *You are going to connect your company's network to the Internet. To do this, you configure a Windows NT Server computer with a network adapter and a modem. You connect the network adapter to the network hub and to the rest of your company LAN. You set up dial-up networking* *on the Windows NT Server computer and configure the dial-up client to obtain an IP address from your ISP. What IP address should you assign to the network adapter on the Windows NT Server computer?*

A. Any IP address

B. Any IP address from the same subnet as that of the dial-up adapter

C. Any IP address from a different subnet as that of the dial-up adapter

D. No IP address assignment is needed; when the RAS connection is established, both the dial-up adapter and network adapter will receive IP addresses from the ISP

15. *From where can a TCP/IP dial-up client obtain an IP address when connecting through a RAS server?*

A. DHCP

B. IP list on the RAS server

C. Predetermined IP address, selected by the client

D. All of the above

Simple Network Management Protocol

In this chapter, we'll describe the *Simple Network Management Protocol* (SNMP), cover its terminology, and learn how to install and configure it on a Windows NT 4.0 system.

At the end of this chapter, you will be able to:

- Describe SNMP.

- Install and configure SNMP on a Microsoft Windows NT 4.0 computer.

- Explain how to test the SNMP installation.

SNMP Overview

While the Simple Network Management Protocol was originally designed to provide monitoring and troubleshooting for network bridges and routers, the use of SNMP has expanded to most hardware and software in modern business communications. With SNMP, you can monitor workstations and servers on your network, mid-

349

range systems that may be attached, and the routers, gateways, and other connection devices that are SNMP-enabled.

SNMP uses a distributed system of network management systems and agents. The required components are SNMP Managers (termed *management systems* in the RFCs) and SNMP Agents. The Microsoft SNMP service consists of SNMP Agent software that provides information to applications like *Microsoft Systems Management Server, HP OpenView,* and other third-party management systems.

Network management stations perform polling to collect information about network elements. They monitor and control network elements through the use of management applications. Network elements are devices such as hosts, gateways, terminal servers, and some software components. These elements have built-in management agents that are responsible for obtaining and reporting information required by the network management stations.

SNMP operates at the OSI Application Layer and uses Windows Sockets (WINSOCK) and UDP to communicate between network management stations and the Agents in the network elements. Figure 13.1 provides an overview of SNMP network architecture.

The SNMP management system directs SNMP Agents to alter (set) or inspect and retrieve (get) variables present in the network elements. Management stations run specialized software not included in the Microsoft TCP/IP suite to direct the Agents' activities. To do this, the stations use three commands: set, get, get-next. The set command is not as widely used as get or get-next because most hardware does not provide a mechanism to set parameters remotely.

The SNMP Agent performs work as directed by the SNMP management stations. The Agent functions on a particular machine and takes orders from and reports information to the management system, which normally operates on a remote system. The SNMP Agent can issue traps to provide the management system with information about unexpected events or error conditions on the SNMP Agent's system. Password violations or exceeded threshold values would be likely candidates for an Agent trap.

When installed on a Windows NT 4.0 server, SNMP Agent software permits you to use the Windows NT *Performance Monitor* to chart TCP/IP values such as packets sent and received or the number of TCP/IP transmission errors on a network.

SNMP Communities

SNMP communities are groupings of computers running SNMP services. The communities are given a "community name," which they use for primitive security and context checks to validate Agents and Managers in setting

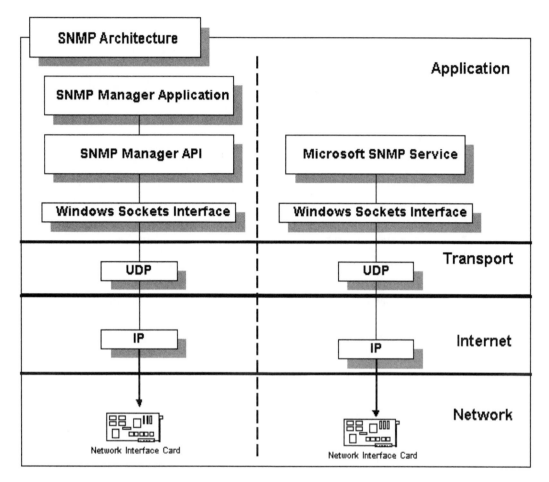

Figure 13.1 *SNMP network architecture.*

traps and issuing commands. Although an SNMP Agent can be a member of more than one community, it will only respond to requests made by SNMP Managers in its configured communities. Because SNMP Managers can get sensitive information about your network, keeping communications within a community is a good thing. Communities help to prevent unauthorized people from installing their own SNMP Managers and Agents to compromise someone else's network. The default community name given during the installation of an SNMP Agent is "Public." Multiple communities can be helpful if you wish to divide network monitoring responsibility among several administrators.

The SNMP Service on Microsoft Windows NT 4.0

Any machine running Microsoft Windows NT 4.0 with the SNMP service installed can provide its status to an SNMP management system over TCP/IP. Microsoft's SNMP service is SNMP Agent software that sends its status whenever it is polled by a management system or whenever the system handles some type of significant system event (such as running out of disk space). Microsoft's SNMP Agent service is able to support requests from and report traps to multiple SNMP management systems. The service supports the use of IP addresses OR host names to identify management hosts and provides for monitoring the TCP/IP protocol in the Windows NT *Performance Monitor*.

Management Information Base

A Management Information Base (MIB) outlines what information can be collected about a particular network resource. An MIB is a database that contains a set of objects representing a wide variety of information about network devices. One example of this might be the version of the software that is running on a host computer. Another more specific example can be found in the LAN Manager MIB, which has objects to permit collection of user and logon statistics. MIB objects appear in the Windows NT *Performance Monitor*.

To do their jobs efficiently, the SNMP management systems and agents must share a common understanding of MIB objects. Microsoft's SNMP service supports Internet MIB II, LAN Manager MIB II, DHCP MIB, and WINS MIB. The DHCP and WINS MIB objects are Microsoft-specific and are automatically added when DHCP and WINS are installed.

The Internet MIB II defines 171 objects that are required for fault or configuration analysis. (MIB II is an expansion of the earlier Internet MIB I standard and is defined in RFC 1212.) The LAN Manager MIB II defines objects, including such items as statistical, share, session, user, and logon information.

MIB NAME SPACE

MIB objects are defined in a hierarchical tree, which has been compared to the Windows NT Registry. Each manageable object has a unique identifier that consists of a location in the tree and the object name. The InterNIC assigns authority for different parts of the name space to individual organizations so they can provide information and track their own objects. Each organization defines its own object names and does not have to register each new name or expanded function with the InterNIC. The name space represents a named value pair such that an object name and object number are paired in an MIB database. Any object can be identified in this way, either by its name or number. The information on standard MIB object types can be found in RFCs 1155, 1157, and 1213 (you may find the RFCs at www.cis. ohio-state.edu/htbin/rfc). Information on Microsoft MIB object types can be found in the Microsoft Windows NT Server 4.0 Resource Kit.

To better understand the MIB name space, refer to Figure 13.2, as we look at two examples. The first example is the MIB structure for an object called sysDescr (system description), taken from RFC 1155:

```
iso org dod internet mgmt mib system sysDescr
 1   3   6    1     2   1    1      1
```

The number for sysDescr becomes 1.3.6.1.2.1.1.1 and its full name is iso.org.dod.internet.mgmt.mib.system.sysDescr.

Once sysDescr is registered, the owner can assign names to objects anywhere below it. For instance, 1.3.6.1.2.1.1.1.0 is the first object under sysDescr and returns information about the hardware and software used on the host. The object name would be: iso.org.dod.internet.mgmt.mib.system.sysDescr.0. We'll revisit sysDescr at the end of this chapter when we use it to find computer information.

In another example, we see in Figure 13.2 that Microsoft has registered the LAN Manager MIB II as 1.3.6.1.4.1.77.

Warning

Don't confuse MIB names or numbers with FQDNs or IP addresses. They may look similar, but they represent totally different things.

MCSE 13.1 Installing and Configuring SNMP on Windows NT 4.0

Microsoft's SNMP service can be installed on any Windows NT-based system that is running the TCP/IP protocol. The Microsoft SNMP service is supported by the WINSOCK interface, which uses UDP to send and receive communications. It does not require authentication between Managers and Agents beyond the verification of configured community names.

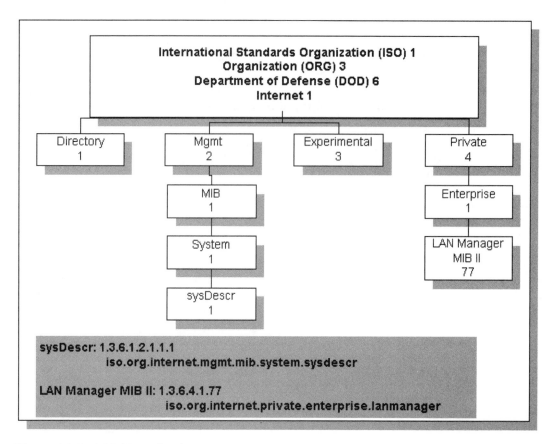

Figure 13.2 *MIB hierarchical name space.*

Before you install the Microsoft SNMP service, make sure you know the following information:

- Host name or IP address of the computer on which you will install the Agent service.
- Host name or IP address of the SNMP Manager(s) to which your machine will report.
- Name of the community in which your computer will function.

Once you have this information you can install SNMP as a service as follows:

1. Right-click on `Network Neighborhood` and select `Properties` or go to `Start|Settings|Control Panel|Network` and double-click.

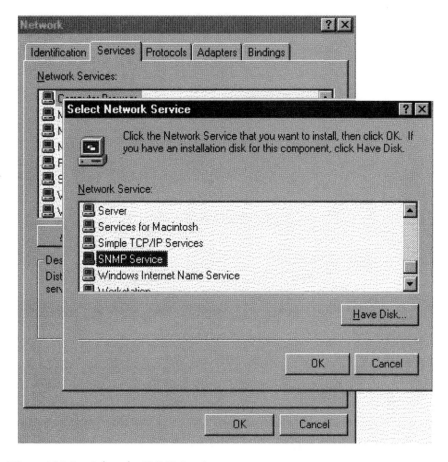

Figure 13.3 *Select the SNMP Service.*

2. Select the `Services` tab, click on the `Add` button and select `SNMP Service` as shown in Figure 13.3 (remember to have your Windows NT CD or installation files available as new software will be needed).
3. Once the files are loaded, you are shown the `SNMP Properties` dialog box. Select the `Traps` tab as shown in Figure 13.4. Table 13.1 defines the options on this tab.
4. Under the `Traps` tab, enter the community name by clicking the `Add` button. Remember the default name is `Public`. If your network has a prevailing SNMP community, you may use that name. In the figure, we assumed a name of `Private`.
5. Enter the host name or IP address of the machine(s) to which you want the SNMP service to send traps by clicking the `Add` button. (If you will

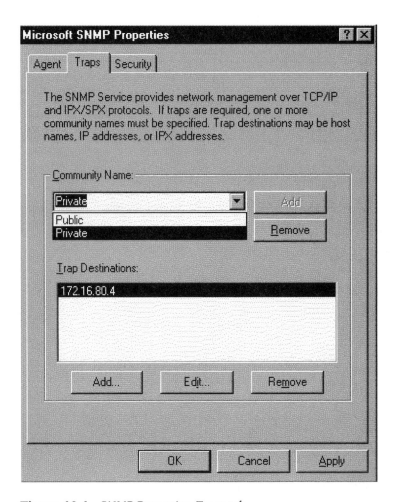

Figure 13.4   *SNMP Properties, Traps tab.*

Table 13.1 *SNMP Service Configuration Parameters: Traps*

Parameter	Explanation
Send Trap with Community Names	Used to identify the community name for the SNMP Agent. If you define a community name, you must identify a management system by host name or IP address. The default community name is `Public`.
Trap	Used to identify the IP address or host name of the SNMP management system(s) that will receive traps.

only use SNMP to provide information to your machine's own *Performance Monitor,* you may enter just the identification of your own computer, or you may leave this blank.)

6. When you close the `Network` dialog, you are asked if you wish to restart the computer—accept the restart and the SNMP installation is complete.

With SNMP now installed and running, let's take a look at the rest of the configuration opportunities. We'll start with SNMP security:

1. Open the `Network Dialog,` select `Services|SNMP Service,` and click the `Properties` button.

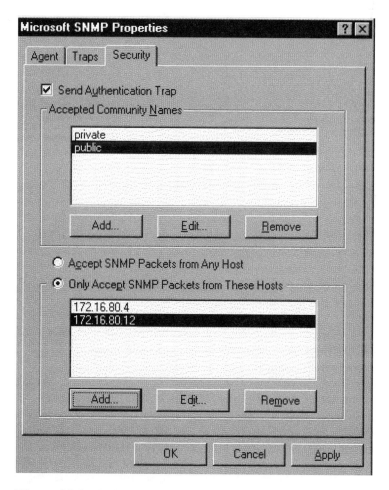

Figure 13.5 *SNMP Properties Security tab.*

Table 13.2 *SNMP Security Configuration Options*

Parameter	Explanation
Send Authentication Trap	When the SNMP Agent receives a request for information with an incorrect host or community name, it can send a failed request trap to the SNMP Manager.
Accepted Community Names	Permits configuration of one or more community names. By default, all Managers and Agents belong to the `Public` community.
Accept SNMP Packets From Any Host	Enables this SNMP Agent to accept SNMP Manager requests from any SNMP Manager in its community.
Only Accept SNMP Packets from these Hosts	Permits the Agent to respond to only the specified SNMP Managers.

2. Select the `Security` tab to reveal the dialog shown in Figure 13.5.
3. Using Table 13.2 as a guide, you may set security as desired for the SNMP Agent on your computer.

The `SNMP Properties` dialog box also permits you to configure the Agent services for SNMP by selecting the `Agent` tab (shown in Figure 13.6).

You can enter the name of the person who uses the computer running the SNMP Agent in the `Contact` field of the SNMP `Agent` dialog box. In the `Location` field, enter the physical location of the computer. (Name and location information permit you to locate a particular machine and the person responsible for it when information concerning the machine is intercepted.) You can configure the SNMP Agent services in the `Service` area of the dialog as detailed in Table 13.3. This will control the services performed by the SNMP Agent on the local computer.

Study Break

Installing SNMP to Provide an Extension to Windows NT Performance Monitor

Since Windows NT comes with Agent software but no management software, there is a limit to how much you can do with SNMP in a constrained environment. In this exercise, we'll install SNMP and use it to provide an extension to the Windows NT *Performance Monitor*. If you are on a large network, you may want to check with your network administrator to see if there is a machine in

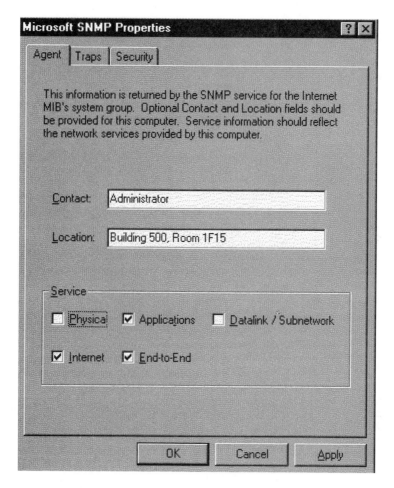

Figure 13.6   *SNMP Properties Agent tab.*

Table 13.3 *SNMP Agent Configuration Options*

Parameter	Explanation
Physical	Used if host is a `physical` device such as a repeater.
Applications	Used if host uses any TCP/IP applications. (This should always be selected.)
Datalink/Subnetwork	Used if host is a bridge.
Internet	Used if host is an IP router or gateway.
End-to-End	Used if host is an IP host. (This should always be selected.)

the environment running SNMP management software to permit you to set traps to monitor your machine.

1. Launch the Windows NT *Performance Monitor* from the `Administrative Tools (Common)` program group.
2. Select `Edit|Add to Chart` and inspect the available objects in the `Object` window. Can you find the ICMP, IP, TCP, or UDP object? (This exercise assumes SNMP has never run on your machine and that the listed objects are not available. If SNMP or some other service that installs those objects has previously run on your machine, the objects will be present. You can still accomplish the exercise, but the results will be far less dramatic.)
3. Close *Performance Monitor* and follow the steps at the start of this section to install and configure SNMP. (If you will only use *Performance Monitor* in conjunction with the service, any configuration you accomplish after installation will be only for your training and experience.)

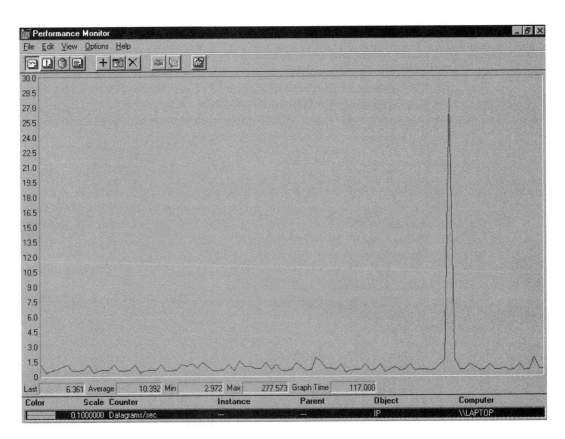

Figure 13.7 *Performance Monitor showing Datagrams/Sec.*

4. Once SNMP is installed, return to *Performance Monitor* and check for the presence of the ICMP, IP, TCP, and UDP objects.
5. Select the IP object and add `Datagrams/Sec` in *Performance Monitor*. Minimize *Performance Monitor* and perform some network activity such as using `Network Neighborhood`. Return to *Performance Monitor* and note the activity caught by SNMP. (You may need to reduce the size of the vertical maximum in *Performance Monitor* to easily view the activity.) Figure 13.7 shows the *Performance Monitor* screen set to a vertical maximum of 30 and displaying datagrams per second. The `net use` command was used to generate the activity spike.

Testing the SNMP Configuration

After you have successfully installed SNMP on Microsoft Windows NT 4.0, it's a good idea to test the system and verify that you have set the parameters properly. Errors will be logged in the `Event Viewer/System Log` if they originated from SNMP. Installation of the SNMP service will copy an outdated version of the `inetmib1.dll` file to your system, so you MUST reapply Service Pack 2 or greater to ensure the updated MIB gets on your system.

Although Microsoft's SNMP service on Windows NT 4.0 is an Agent and not a management system, the `SNMPUTIL` command line utility, which is found in the Microsoft Windows NT 4.0 Resource Kit, enables your machine to act like a management system for the purpose of testing. SNMPUTIL uses case-sensitivity and the use of the wrong case in the community name, for example, will cause the utility to fail.

The syntax for the SNMPUTIL command is:

```
snmputil <command> <agent> <community> <object_ID>
```

- The values for `<command>` are very similar to the standard SNMP command set:
  - `get`—retrieves the value of the requested object.
  - `getnext`—retrieves the value following the requested `object_ID` in the base.
  - `walk`—steps through the MIB branch specified by `object_ID`.
- Replace `<agent>` with the host name or IP address of the machine running the Agent service.
- Place the name of the SNMP community in the `<community>` field.
- Enter the name or number of the SNMP object in the `<object_ID>` field. There is information both in the resource kit instructions and in RFCs 1212 and 1213 on how to construct object IDs. This is beyond

the scope of this course, so we'll just use the object ID we used in the MIB example.

To obtain information about the hardware and software used on our host, we could use the following:

```
snmputil get 172.16.80.4 Public .1.3.6.1.2.1.1.1.0
```

We could also use the object name:

```
snmputil get 172.16.80.4 Public
   .iso.org.dod.internet.mgmt.mib.system.sysDescr.0
```

You may have noticed that the object IDs in the examples are preceded by a dot (.). The preceding dot is required in this syntax. You may also have noticed that typing the entire object name in the latter example appears quite tedious ... it is. To make life easier, the `iso.org.dod.internet.` `mgmt.mib.system` branch of the Internet MIB can be shortened to `system` (note that we don't use the preceding dot in this instance). The resulting call would then be:

```
snmputil get 172.16.80.4 Public system.sysDescr.0
```

Summary

This chapter dealt with the facility for monitoring the activity of TCP/IP on the network: the *Simple Network Management Protocol* (SNMP). We saw that SNMP is used by both Windows and non-Windows systems and that it functions through *Managers* and *Agents*. The Agent resides on the machine to be monitored and reports to the Manager. Agents can set traps to detect unusual activity and report these traps to Managers. We learned that Windows NT doesn't supply any SNMP management software, but it does have an installable SNMP Agent which can report to third-party Managers and which provides additional objects for the Windows NT *Performance Monitor*.

You saw that SNMP security can be enhanced by placing SNMP systems within communities. Agents can be directed to report only to Managers within their configured community. We saw the default community name was *"Public"*.

We took a brief look at the construction of the *Management Information Base* (MIB), which stores the definitions of the objects used by SNMP to monitor network activity. We also developed an understanding of the hierarchical MIB name space.

We discovered that SNMP is installed as a service, much as the other TCP/IP services, and that SNMP configuration permits us to select the communities and Managers that will receive trap information and allows us to restrict responses to only specified Managers. We can also enter identification information for the operator and location of the Agent machine, and can configure the Agent service for the particular role(s) our computer will function under.

Finally, we saw that the Windows NT 4.0 Resource Kit can provide the SNMPUTIL utility which can perform as a simple SNMP Manager to permit us to test our SNMP Agent installation.

▲ REVIEW QUESTIONS

1. *Which of the following utilities is used to verify that SNMP is properly configured:*
   A. IPCONFIG
   B. WINIPCFG
   C. *Network Monitor*
   D. SNMPUTIL

2. *Sandy wants to be able to monitor hosts on her network using SNMP. What does she need to install? (Select all that apply.)*
   A. SNMP Agent software
   B. SNMP management software
   C. *Network Monitor* tools and agent
   D. TCP/IP

3. *Tim wants to be able to monitor a Windows NT server in his TCP/IP network from the UNIX computer at his desk. What must he install to permit this?*
   A. *Network Monitor* on both computers
   B. SNMP management software on the UNIX computer and the SNMP service on the Windows NT computer
   C. *Performance Monitor* on the UNIX computer and the SNMP service on the Windows NT computer
   D. You cannot monitor a Windows computer from a non-Windows platform.

4. *Vicky was directed by her IT manager to make sure her Windows NT computer sends SNMP trap information to a central SNMP management system. What information must Vicky know to do this? (Select all that apply.)*

    A. The management system's community

    B. The management system's platform type

    C. The management system's host name

    D. The management system's object ID

5. *You need to monitor TCP/IP statistics on your Windows NT server using* Performance Monitor. *What must you set up? (Select all that apply.)*

    A. *Network Monitor* tools and agent

    B. SNMP service

    C. DHCP

    D. SMTP service

6. *Linda is concerned that unauthorized management stations may be obtaining SNMP data from her computer. What is the best way for Linda to prevent this?*

    A. Remove the SNMP service from her computer

    B. Enable the `Only Accept SNMP Packets from These Hosts` option on her machine

    C. Disable her SNMP traps

    D. Run the SNMPUTIL utility with the `-r` option

Troubleshooting Microsoft TCP/IP

This is the last chapter in the book. By now you should have learned how to plan and deploy TCP/IP networks. You should also have discovered that TCP/IP services and parameters can be very knotty. This chapter will help you determine what to do if something goes wrong. We will combine a review of the most important TCP/IP topics with some helpful troubleshooting guidelines. We will cover the major TCP/IP troubleshooting utilities and discuss how to use them most efficiently. Topics covered in this chapter summarize common TCP/IP-related problems, symptoms, and possible causes, as well as the concrete steps required to troubleshoot them.

At the end of this chapter, you will be able to:

- Describe major TCP/IP-related problems.
- Choose utilities to diagnose a TCP/IP problem.
- Search for the problem source.
- Troubleshoot TCP/IP-related problems.

365

MCSE 14.1   General Considerations

When something goes wrong, we often try to choose a tool that can immediately solve our problem. Before deciding which utility to use, however, you should determine the source of the problem. A number of problems turn out not to be TCP/IP-related (for example, a network interface card malfunction) and need to be solved by other methods. In this chapter, however, we will speak only of TCP/IP-related problems.

TCP/IP problems can be grouped by category, as shown in Table 14.1.

When a problem occurs, you might want to ask yourself these simple questions:

- What should work?
- What does work?
- What does not work?
- What has changed since it last worked?

Answering these questions will help you choose the right tool to isolate the problem. For example, suppose that Mary complains that she is unable to connect to remote NetBIOS hosts by their computer name. After speaking with her, you find out that recently she accidentally deleted some files from the `%systemroot%\drivers\etc\` folder on her computer. Knowing what set of actions has resulted in this problem, you will not waste time in low-level connectivity checks, but can go directly to the folder to check for an LMHOSTS file.

Table 14.1 *Major TCP/IP-related Problems*

Problem Source	Symptoms
TCP/IP Configuration	Host initialization fails, services fail to start, communication to all (some) other hosts is impossible.
Address Resolution	Although you can ping your workstation, you cannot access some local or remote hosts.
NetBIOS Name Resolution	You can access a host by its IP address, but cannot connect to it by its *computer name.*
Host Name Resolution	You can access a host by its IP address, but cannot connect to it by its *host name.*

Windows NT Diagnostic Tools Overview

Microsoft Windows NT Server and Workstation have many useful utilities to diagnose and troubleshoot TCP/IP. Many powerful utilities are included in the Windows NT Resource Kit (for example, *Browstat* (a command line utility that can be used to force the browser elections for a specified domain), *Browmon* (a graphical utility that can be used to view browsers for selected domains), *Wntipcfg* (a graphical utility with the same functionality as IPCONFIG). In addition, as you may already know, Microsoft Systems Management Server includes an advanced version of *Network Monitor*–a great program to trace and monitor your network at the packet level. Table 14.2 lists common diagnostic utilities that are included in Microsoft TCP/IP.

Each utility may be used to diagnose only one part of a problem. None will solve an entire problem alone. Later in this chapter, you will be introduced how to use these utilities together to troubleshoot your network.

Table 14.2 *Microsoft TCP/IP Diagnostic Utilities*

Utility	Function
Address Resolution Protocol (ARP)	Displays and modifies the cache of locally resolved IP addresses to Media Access Control (MAC) addresses.
PING	Verifies the availability of the remote host by sending the echo request and analyzing replies.
TRACERT	Traces the route for packets from local hosts to the specified remote host.
IPCONFIG	Displays current TCP/IP configuration, including IP address(es), DNS, and WINS addresses.
ROUTE	Views and modifies the local routing table.
NBTSTAT	Displays protocol statistics and current TCP/IP connections using NetBIOS over TCP/IP. This utility is also used to determine the registered NetBIOS name and to view the local name cache.
NSLOOKUP	Displays information from Domain Name System (DNS) name servers about a particular host or domain. You can also use this utility to check the availability of the domain name across the Internet.
NETSTAT	Displays protocol statistics and current TCP/IP network connections.
Event Log	Standard Windows NT tool used to track events, warnings, and errors. (While the Event Log can be used for TCP/IP troubleshooting, its primary function is to track overall health of the system.)
Network Monitor	Captures and displays packets.
Performance Monitor	Displays performance counters.
Microsoft SNMP service	Supplies information to SNMP management systems.

MCSE 14.2   TCP/IP Troubleshooting Guidelines

There is no fixed sequence of steps to troubleshoot TCP/IP-related problems—everything depends on the particular scenario. There are, however, some basic guidelines that fit most situations.

The first thing you should do is to ensure the physical connection is functioning. It's useless to employ a host of troubleshooting utilities if the office hub is malfunctioning. When link reliability is in question, for example, when the WAN link is malfunctioning, you may want to ping various remote hosts to check connectivity.

Once you're sure the links are functioning properly, you should start testing the local host's configuration parameters, then examine routing configurations, and finally check name resolution issues. The hierarchy of troubleshooting steps is illustrated in Figure 14.1. Note that you test the lower layers of the TCP/IP stack first. Once the low-level TCP/IP functions are working correctly, move to the higher levels.

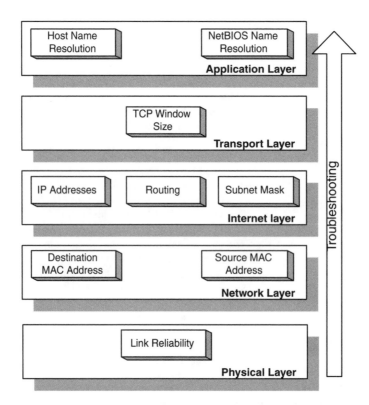

Figure 14.1   *TCP/IP troubleshooting guidelines.*

Identifying the TCP/IP Configuration

Checking the TCP/IP configuration is the most basic troubleshooting step. You might want to ensure the TCP/IP parameters have been entered without mistakes or that DHCP has set them correctly. You should begin by checking the TCP/IP configuration on the computer that appears to be experiencing problems.

A good starting point is the IPCONFIG command line utility. IPCONFIG displays the IP address, subnet mask, and default gateway, as well as other advanced TCP/IP parameters, such as WINS server, IP address, and node type.

You should use the IPCONFIG utility with the /all switch because it produces a *detailed* report concerning the current TCP/IP configuration. The following is an example of the output from IPCONFIG:

```
C:\WINNT>ipconfig /all
Windows NT IP Configuration
        Host Name . . . . . . . . . : mcse.traincert.com
        DNS Servers . . . . . . . . : 172.20.0.10
        Node Type . . . . . . . . . : Hybrid
        NetBIOS Scope ID. . . . . . :
        IP Routing Enabled. . . . . : No
        WINS Proxy Enabled. . . . . : No
        NetBIOS Resolution Uses DNS : Yes
Ethernet adapter Elnk31:
        Description . . . . . . . . : ELNK3 Ethernet
                                      Adapter.
        Physical Address. . . . . . : 00-20-AF-AC-3A-76
        DHCP Enabled. . . . . . . . : No
        IP Address. . . . . . . . . : 172.20.0.10
        Subnet Mask . . . . . . . . : 255.255.255.0
        Default Gateway . . . . . . : 172.20.0.1
        Primary WINS Server . . . . : 172.20.0.10
```

In some cases, just reviewing this report can resolve the problem. For example, if the DHCP client could not obtain the IP address, running IPCONFIG returns the IP address and subnet mask of 0.0.0.0.

```
C:\WINNT>ipconfig
Windows NT IP Configuration
Ethernet adapter Elnk31:
        IP Address. . . . . . . . . : 0.0.0.0
        Subnet Mask . . . . . . . . : 0.0.0.0
        Default Gateway . . . . . . :
```

This listing could indicate that the DHCP server is down or that there are no free IP addresses in the DHCP server's scope.

Incorrect IP Address Assignment

To determine if a computer has been assigned a valid IP address, you can use the following guidelines:

- Check that the IP address is from the correct subnet.
- Check that the IP address is not duplicated.
- Check that the IP address is not a broadcast address for the given subnet (host ID is all-ones).
- Check that the IP address is not the subnet address (host ID is all-zeroes).

Figure 14.2 shows a network where computers have IP addressing problems. Computer 1 and Computer 3 have duplicate IP addresses. Computer 2 has the IP address that is the broadcast address for subnet 172.20.0.0, mask 255.255.255.0. Computer 4 has an IP address from another subnet.

Subnet Mask Problems

Subnet mask problems are very hard to diagnose and isolate. This is mainly because, depending on the actual numbers, an invalid subnet mask can have no negative impact or can make the entire network unreachable for a particular computer. In some cases, an incorrect subnet mask could cause some comput-

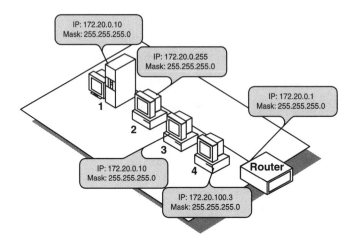

Figure 14.2 *IP addressing problems.*

ers to become unreachable, while the rest of network remains operational. In Figure 14.3, `Computer 2` has an incorrect subnet mask (displayed in bold). Although it can successfully establish a connection with `Computer 1`, `Computer 3`, and the `default gateway`, it fails to communicate with `Computer 4`.

There are two common problems with subnet masks:

- The configured subnet mask is shorter than needed (too many bits are reserved for network and subnet ID).
- The configured subnet mask is longer than needed (too few bits are reserved for network and subnet ID).

Improper subnet mask configuration is often the result of inaccurate planning or of mistyping the subnet mask during manual TCP/IP parameter assignment. These problems are particularly prevalent when we implement custom subnet masking. (You'll remember the tediousness in counting ones and zeroes in Chapter 4 and can appreciate how easy it is to make a mistake in doing so.)

Let's look at some symptoms that can indicate these two problems. Suppose we have the class C network 192.168.18.0. We divide it into eight subnets using the subnet mask 255.255.255.224. (See Figure 14.4.) Now, what happens if we assign a particular computer a shorter subnet mask: 255.255.255.192 (arrow 1). That computer would think: "The shorter my subnet mask, the more other computers I recognize to be inside my subnet". If the subnet mask is 255.255.255.0, this computer will think the network is not divided into subnets at all.

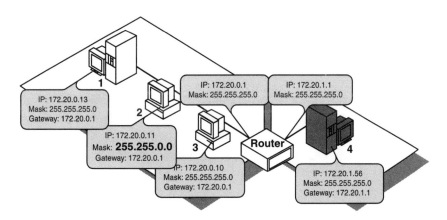

Figure 14.3 *An incorrect subnet mask may prevent your computer from communicating with one or more other machines.*

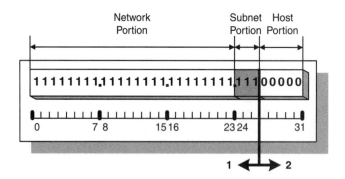

Figure 14.4 *Subnet mask problems.*

On the other hand, if we assign the computer a longer subnet mask (arrow 2), let's say 255.255.255.240, it will think some computers on the local network segment are outside its subnet.

The following example illustrates both of these subnet masking problems. Figure 14.5 shows a properly planned and configured network. Let's

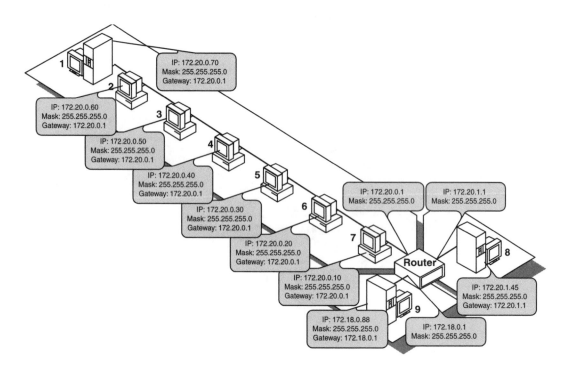

Figure 14.5 *Network without subnet mask problems.*

introduce some subnet masking errors to demonstrate how they affect network communication.

If we begin to enlarge the subnet mask of Computer 6, simulating a data entry error, the computer starts experiencing connectivity problems. Computers inaccessible to Computer 6 hosts are dimmed in Figure 14.6.

With a subnet mask of 255.255.255.192, Computer 6 thinks that Server 1 is located on a remote network. (You might remember that the computer determines whether the target host is located in the local or remote network by ANDing the IP addresses with its subnet mask and comparing the results.)

	Computer 6	Server 1
IP address	172.20.0.20	172.20.0.70
Subnet Mask	255.255.255.192	255.255.255.192
AND operation	**172.20.0.0**	**172.20.0.64**

Since the ANDed results do not match, Computer 6 will send all the packets for Server 1 to the router instead of making a direct connection. The larger the subnet mask grows, the more computers jump out of reach of Computer 6. Finally, when Computer 6's subnet mask is 255.255.255.240, even the router is outside Computer 6's subnet and communications to remote networks are impossible.

	Computer 6	Default gateway
IP address	172.20.0.20	172.20.0.1
Subnet Mask	255.255.255.240	255.255.255.240
AND operation	**172.20.0.16**	**172.20.0.0**

Note that an incorrect subnet mask of 255.255.255.128 causes no apparent problem. Although this incorrect subnet mask changes Computer 6's conception of the network, it will not prevent communication with neighboring computers.

If the subnet mask is too short, we are likely to experience problems in trying to contact remote computers. (See Figure 14.7.)

When Computer 6's subnet mask is 255.255.0.0, it recognizes Server 8 as the local computer.

	Computer 6	Server 8
IP address	172.20.0.20	172.20.1.45
Subnet Mask	255.255.0.0	255.255.0.0
AND operation	**172.20.0.0**	**172.20.0.0**

Since both ANDed results match, Computer 6 tries to send IP packets to Server 8 directly without using a router and fails. If the subnet mask is shorter, more remote computers are considered to be directly reachable.

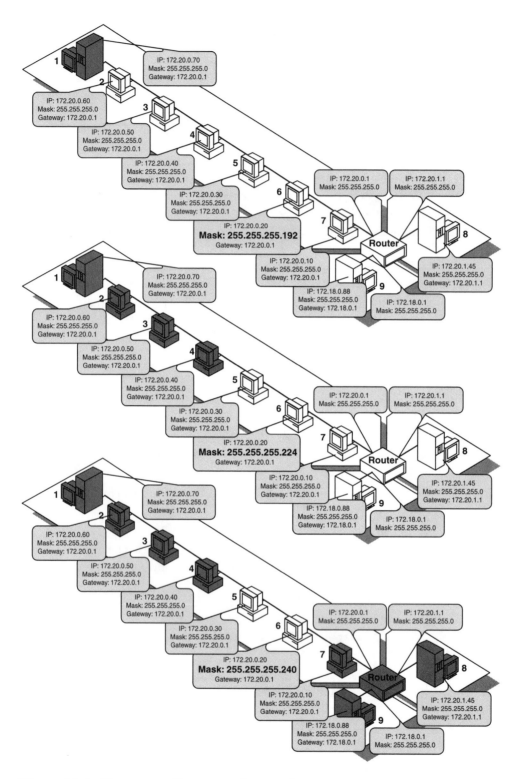

Figure 14.6 *Three stages of improper subnet masking.*

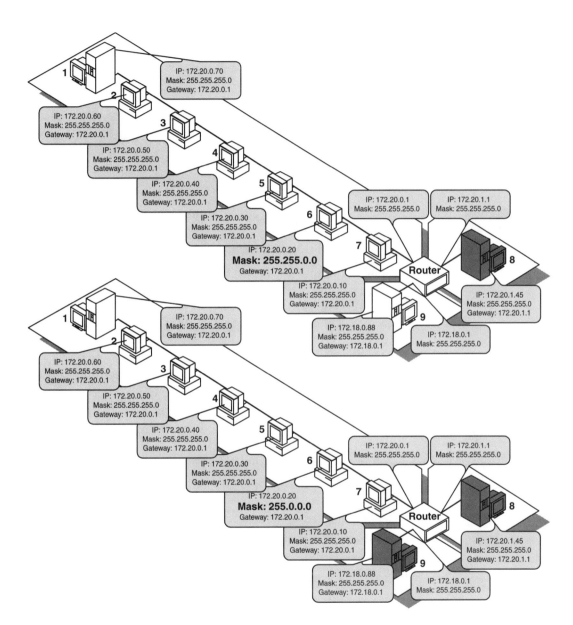

Figure 14.7 *Network with short subnet mask problems.*

```
                    Computer 6        Server 9
IP address          172.20.0.20       172.18.0.88
Subnet Mask         255.0.0.0         255.0.0.0
AND operation       172.0.0.0         172.0.0.0
```

When you troubleshoot your IP network, it might be beneficial to have a copy of your subnetting plan close by. This enables you to look up the broadcast addresses and the subnet masks, and check that they are not assigned to hosts.

MCSE 14.3   Testing IP Communications

Once your computer has obtained an IP address and a subnet mask, you should test the IP communications. PING is the utility that can be used for verifying IP-level connectivity. As you may remember, PING sends the ICMP echo request to the destination host and analyzes ICMP echo replies.

The recommended sequence of pings is the following:

1. Ping the loopback address. (If you are unable to ping the loopback address, it may indicate the computer has not been restarted after TCP/IP was installed and configured—restart and try again.)
2. Ping the IP address of the local computer. (If you cannot ping the local IP address, check to ensure your computer has a valid IP address that is not duplicated elsewhere on the network.)
3. Ping the IP address of the default gateway. (If this step is unsuccessful, check the subnet mask on your computer.)
4. Ping the IP address of the remote host. (If this step is unsuccessful, check the default gateway address configured on the local computer, the functionality of the link between routers, and the remote computer's availability.)
5. Ping the remote host by name. (If this step fails, check host name resolution.)

The PING utility has many switches that can be used to expand its functionality. To view the available command line options, type PING -?

```
C:\WINNT>ping -?
Usage: ping [-t] [-a] [-n count] [-l size] [-f] [-i TTL] [-v TOS]
            [-r count] [-s count] [[-j host-list] | [-k host-list]]
            [-w timeout] destination-list
```

```
Options:
  -t             Ping the specified host until interrupted.
  -a             Resolve addresses to hostnames.
  -n count       Number of echo requests to send.
  -l size        Send buffer size.
  -f             Set Don't Fragment flag in packet.
  -i TTL         Time To Live.
  -v TOS         Type Of Service.
  -r count       Record route for count hops.
  -s count       Timestamp for count hops.
  -j host-list   Loose source route along host-list.
  -k host-list   Strict source route along host-list.
  -w timeout     Timeout in milliseconds to wait for each reply.
```

For example, you can specify the size of the packets to use, how many packets to send, and how much time to wait for a response. There are some more advanced options of the PING utility such as specifying the type of service (TOS), the initial TTL value, and the source route. These options directly affect the header of the IP packet in which the ICMP message is encapsulated. For example, the command

```
PING -v 12 -j 194.226.192.33 194.85.165.169 194.85.36.30
www.runnet.ru
```

will cause the following ICMP packets to be sent (note that by specifying the PING options -v and -j we set the values of some fields in the IP header–printed in bold typeface):

```
+ FRAME: Base frame properties
+ ETHERNET: ETYPE = 0x0800 : Protocol = IP: DOD Internet Protocol
IP: ID = 0x2155; Proto = ICMP; Len: 76
    IP: Version = 4 (0x4)
    IP: Header Length = 36 (0x24)
    IP: Service Type = 12 (0xC)
        IP: Precedence = 0x0C
        IP: ...0.... = Normal Delay
        IP: ....1... = High Throughput
        IP: .....1.. = High Reliability
    IP: Total Length = 76 (0x4C)
    IP: Identification = 8533 (0x2155)
  + IP: Flags Summary = 0 (0x0)
    IP: Fragment Offset = 0 (0x0) bytes
```

```
IP: Time to Live = 252 (0xFC)
IP: Protocol = ICMP - Internet Control Message
IP: Checksum = 0xF92C
IP: Source Address = 193.232.80.66
IP: Destination Address = 194.226.192.52
IP: Option Fields = 131 (0x83)
   IP: Loose Source Routing Option = 131 (0x83)
      IP: Option Length = 15 (0xF)
      IP: Routing Pointer = 16 (0x10)
      IP: Route Traveled = 194 (0xC2)
         IP: Gateway = 194.85.36.30
         IP: Gateway = 194.85.165.169
         IP: Gateway = 194.226.192.33
   IP: End of Options = 0 (0x0)
 IP: Data: Number of data bytes remaining = 40 (0x0028)
+ ICMP: Echo Reply, To 194.226.192.52 From 193.232.80.66
```

By using the above PING command, we've checked whether the target host is available by specific type of service (high throughput and high reliability) and the selected route (`194.226.192.33`, `194.85.165.169`, `194.85.36.30`).

Routing Problems

Even when your computer is properly configured, a malfunctioning router can cause difficulties. An improperly configured route typically causes the problem (in this case, *improperly configured* could also mean *not configured*). Remember, if the Windows NT router does not have an interface on a given subnet, it will need a route there. You can do this by adding a static route or by using a multi-protocol router (MPR). If a router is implemented on a Windows NT computer, you can check the existing routes by using the ROUTE utility. If inconsistencies are found in the routing table, you can correct them by using the ROUTE ADD and ROUTE DELETE commands.

Note

Having multiple network adapters on a Windows NT computer allows you to add a default route for each network card. Although it will create several 0.0.0.0 routes, only one default route will actually be used. You should configure only one card to have a default gateway—this will reduce confusion and ensure the results you intended.

THE TRACERT UTILITY

The TRACERT command can be used to determine where a packet stopped on the network because of an improper router configuration or link failure. In the following example, the second router has determined that there is not a valid path for host 172.21.0.55. There is probably a router configuration problem or the 172.21.0.0 network does not exist (a bad IP address).

```
C:\>tracert 172.21.0.55
Tracing route to 172.21.0.55 over a maximum of 30 hops
1. <10 ms  <10 ms  <10 ms 172.20.0.1
2. 172.18.6.54 reports: Destination net unreachable.
   Trace complete.
```

TRACERT is useful for troubleshooting large networks where several paths can be taken to arrive at the same point, or where many intermediate systems (routers or bridges) are involved.

If you can ping across the router, but cannot establish a session, check to see if the router is able to pass large packets. The PING utility sends its data in 74-byte blocks, but NET requests can be significantly larger. You can use the PING –1 command to use a larger packet size. To correct this problem, you may want to edit the Registry to specify a smaller packet size. This must be done on every problem computer.

Note

Although we said PING sends its data in 74-byte blocks, you'll see PING indicate that it's using only 32 bytes of data. This is because PING reports only its data block length. The actual ICMP packet is 74 bytes: 32 byte data block + 14 bytes for the Ethernet header + 20 bytes for the IP header + 8 bytes for the ICMP header.

Study Break

Editing the Registry to Specify a Smaller Packet Size

All of the TCP/IP parameters are Registry values located under HKEY_LOCAL_MACHINE\ SYSTEM\CurrentControlSet\Services \Tcpip\Parameters or HKEY_LOCAL_MACHINE\SYSTEM\ CurrentControlSet\ Services\ <Adapter Name>\Parameters\tcpip. In this case, <Adapter Name> refers to the subkey for a network adapter that is bound to the TCP/IP protocol.

There are two Registry entries that can affect TCP/IP packet size. The first one is found in the `Tcpip\Parameters` subkey and is called `EnablePMTUDiscovery` (`REG_DWORD`). This entry can be set to `0` (False) or `1` (True); its default is `1`. When set to `1`, it directs TCP/IP to attempt to discover the Maximum Transmission Unit (MTU—largest packet size) over the path to a remote host. This permits TCP/IP to eliminate fragmentation at routers along the path that connect networks with different MTUs. If you set this value to `0`, an MTU of 576 will be used for connections to all machines that are not on the local subnet.

The other Registry entry is found in the `<Adapter Name>\Parameters\Tcpip` subkey and is called `MTU` (`REG_DWORD`). MTU can be set anywhere between `68` and the actual MTU of the underlying network. (The `68` minimum is required to provide space for the transport header—using a value less than this will result in an MTU of 68.) Setting this parameter overrides the default MTU for the network interface.

MCSE 14.4   Testing TCP/IP Name Resolution

Once IP-level connectivity has been checked, you should examine name resolution. Most name resolution problems occur because the computer cannot resolve the host name or NetBIOS name into the IP address.

NetBIOS Name Resolution Problems

If you can ping a computer by its IP address, but not its NetBIOS name, you may want to check that the target host is NetBIOS-enabled and ensure that the scope ID on the source and target computers is the same. If scope IDs don't match, you probably have a NetBIOS name resolution problem.

Verify that the NetBIOS name-to-address mapping is available through broadcast, WINS, or the LMHOSTS file. If you have a WINS server, check that it is operational and that the local computer has been assigned the proper WINS server address.

If you suspect trouble with the LMHOSTS file, check that it is located in `%systemroot%/system32/drivers/etc`. Check that the file format matches the sample format originally installed with TCP/IP. Check for spelling errors, invalid addresses, and identifiers. (Remember, the LMHOSTS file is parsed from the beginning, so if duplicate entries exist, only the first one is considered.) Check for capitalization errors (although the NetBIOS names in the LMHOSTS file are not case-sensitive, entries like `#PRE` and `#DOM` are). Finally, ensure that LMHOSTS file has no extension. It is easy to edit and save the LMHOSTS file with the default .txt extension (especially when using an editor like *Notepad*). If you do this, the file will NOT be recognized as an LMHOSTS file.

Note The LMHOSTS file does not support aliases for NetBIOS names. You must provide the actual NetBIOS name of each computer.

In some cases, NetBIOS name resolution works but is extremely slow. This could be caused by the large number of #INCLUDE tags and other entries in the LMHOSTS file. To correct the problem, place the most commonly used names closer to the beginning of the LMHOSTS file. Optionally you can use the #PRE tag to force entries to be pre-cached.

You can use the NBTSTAT utility to check the state of current NetBIOS over TCP/IP connections, update the LMHOSTS cache, and determine the registered name and scope ID.

The NBTSTAT utility has many switches, which can be viewed by typing NBTSTAT without arguments.

```
C:\WINNT>nbtstat
NBTSTAT [-a RemoteName] [-A IP address] [-c] [-n] [-r]
[-R] [-RR] [-s] [-S] [interval]]
-a                       (adapter status) Lists the remote
                         machine's name table given its name
-A (Adapter status)      Lists the remote machine's name
                         table given its IP address.
-c (cache)               Lists the remote name cache includ-
                         ing the IP addresses
-n (names)               Lists local NetBIOS names.
-r (resolved)            Lists names resolved by broadcast
                         and via WINS
-R (Reload)              Purges and reloads the remote cache
                         name table
-S (Sessions)            Lists sessions table with the des-
                         tination IP addresses
-s (sessions)            Lists sessions table converting
                         destination IP addresses to host
                         names via the hosts file.
-RR (ReleaseRefresh)     Sends Name Release packets to WINs
                         and then, starts Refresh
RemoteName               Remote host machine name.
IP address               Dotted decimal representation of
                         the IP address.
```

```
Interval                        Redisplays selected statistics,
                                pausing interval seconds between
                                each display. Press Ctrl+C to stop
                                redisplaying statistics.
```

For example, you can type NBTSTAT -n to display the names that were registered locally on the system by applications, such as the server and redirector. Typing NBTSTAT -c shows the NetBIOS name cache, which contains name-to-address mappings for other computers. Typing NBTSTAT -R purges the name cache and reloads it from the LMHOSTS file.

Host Name Resolution Problems

If you can ping a computer by its IP address, but not by its host name, you have a host name resolution problem. In this case, you should check that host name-to-address resolution is possible by means of a DNS server, a HOSTS file, or through NetBIOS methods.

If a HOSTS file is your primary method of host name resolution, check that the entries use the proper sequence and delimiters. If you use DNS, verify that the DNS server is operational.

Even if other methods of host name resolution are available, you should check that the DNS server is on-line and functioning. A DNS client (resolver) has a certain timeout before passing control to other methods. If the client is configured to use DNS, but the DNS server is unreachable, the client may experience long delays in host name resolution.

You can use NSLOOKUP to check records, domain host aliases, domain host services, and operating system information by querying the Internet domain name servers.

Another problem can occur when a TCP/IP connection to a remote system appears to be "hung." In this case, you can type NETSTAT-a to see the status of all activity on TCP and UDP ports on the local system. Good TCP connections usually appear with 0 bytes in queues. Large data blocks in either send or receive queues may indicate a connection problem or network delay. NETSTAT has several command line switches:

```
C:\>netstat -?
Displays protocol statistics and current TCP/IP network
connections.NETSTAT [-a] [-e] [-n] [-s] [-p proto] [-r]
[interval]
```

-a	Displays all connections and listening ports. (Server-side connections are normally not shown). (SP 3 only)
-e	Displays Ethernet statistics. This may be combined with the -s option.
-n	Displays addresses and port numbers in numerical form.
-p proto	Shows connections for the protocol specified by proto; proto may be tcp or udp. If used with the -s option to display per-protocol statistics, proto may be tcp, udp, or ip.
-r	Displays the contents of the routing table.
-s	Displays per-protocol statistics. By default, statistics are shown for TCP, UDP and IP; the -p option may be used to specify a subset of the default.
Interval	Redisplays selected statistics, pausing interval seconds between each display. Press CTRL+C to stop redisplaying statistics. If omitted, netstat will print the current configuration information once.

For example, the following command displays the IP protocol statistics:

```
C:\WINNT\>netstat -s -p ip
IP Statistics
  Packets Received                    = 4383117
  Received Header Errors              = 4154
  Received Address Errors             = 311
  Datagrams Forwarded                 = 0
  Unknown Protocols Received          = 0
  Received Packets Discarded          = 0
  Received Packets Delivered          = 4378963
  Output Requests                     = 4865242
  Routing Discards                    = 0
  Discarded Output Packets            = 0
  Output Packet No Route              = 0
  Reassembly Required                 = 0
  Reassembly Successful               = 0
  Reassembly Failures                 = 0
  Datagrams Successfully Fragmented   = 0
  Datagrams Failing Fragmentation     = 0
  Fragments Created                   = 0
```

Session Communications Problems

Sometimes you can ping a target computer by an IP address and by name, but you cannot establish a session. For example, you are unable to ftp the target host. In this case, you probably have a session problem. You may want to check that the correct services are running on the target computer and that you have the proper permissions to access it. Sometimes you are unable to connect because the maximum number of licenses is reached on the target computer. If the remote host is a UNIX-based machine, check that the appropriate daemon is configured and running.

Other Tools

EVENT VIEWER

You can use Windows NT *Event Viewer* to browse system information about TCP/IP. Important TCP/IP events, such as duplicate IP address, are recorded to the Event Log. (See Figure 14.8.)

PERFORMANCE MONITOR

The Windows NT *Performance Monitor* has many TCP/IP-related counters and also can be used to troubleshoot TCP/IP networks. Since it accesses statistics that have been gathered by the SNMP Agent, the SNMP service must be installed on computers that are to be monitored. Performance counters are available for the IP, ICMP, UDP, TCP, and other protocols of the TCP/IP suite. You can observe TCP/IP counters and thus monitor the overall health of your system. One of the features of *Performance Monitor* is that it allows counters from various systems to be monitored from a single management window. It also permits you to set alerts for the counters being monitored. For example, you can set an alert when the number of TCP connection failures exceeds a predefined value.

NETWORK MONITOR

If you are unable to solve your problem using the tools discussed, you may want to try *Network Monitor* to capture the network traffic and analyze it at the packet level. If the problem is beyond your capability, you can send the capture to a network analyst or support organization.

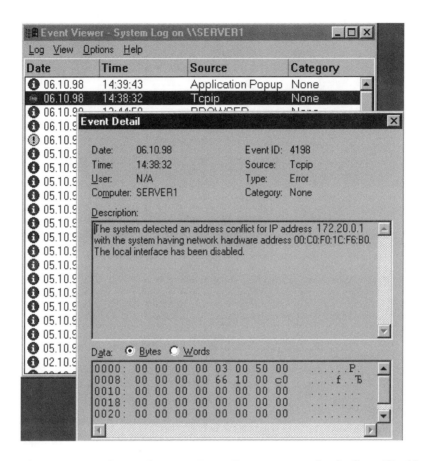

Figure 14.8 *The Windows NT Event Viewer can reveal a duplicate IP address.*

Summary

This chapter summarized common TCP/IP-related problems. We learned quite a bit about major TCP/IP faults and the methods of correcting them. You learned to troubleshoot a TCP/IP network by checking lower-level functions such as link reliability first and then to progress to IP connectivity checks, and routing and name resolution tests. We discussed the typical symptoms of some TCP/IP-related problems. Understanding the symptoms, you can frequently solve network problems without even touching a machine.

▲ REVIEW QUESTIONS

1. *You run IPCONFIG on your Windows NT Server computer and get the following output*

```
C:\WINNT>ipconfig
Windows NT IP Configuration
Ethernet adapter Elnk31:
        IP Address. . . . . . . . . : 0.0.0.0
        Subnet Mask . . . . . . . . : 0.0.0.0
        Default Gateway . . . . . . :
```

What is the most likely cause of this?

A. Duplicate subnet mask

B. TCP/IP is not installed on this computer

C. Default gateway is missing

D. This computer was unable to get the IP address from the DHCP server

2. *Which utility is used to identify the subnet mask?*

A. *Network Monitor*

B. IPCONFIG

C. PING

D. Event Log

3. *Which address symbolizes the loopback address?*

A. 127.0.0.1

B. 255.255.255.255

C. 255.255.0.0

D. 0.0.0.0

E. 176.20.0.10

4. *Your computer is configured to use WINS, DNS, HOSTS, and LMHOSTS files for name resolution. You launch a command prompt and try to ping your neighbor's computer (located in the same subnet) by using its Net-BIOS name (*ping mctcomp*). The ping command hangs for about a minute and then gives you four successful pings. What is the most likely reason on such delay?*

A. DNS server is unreachable

B. WINS server is unreachable

    C. The broadcast name resolution is a very slow method

    D. PING cannot use NetBIOS names

5. *You are the administrator of the network illustrated in Figure 14.9.*

Using FTP client software, your workstation cannot connect to the FTP server in the remote subnet. You can, however, connect to the FTP server by using Windows NT Explorer. *What is the most likely reason for this behavior?*

    A. The computer running the FTP server is down

    B. Your workstation does not have the default gateway

    C. Your workstation is not configured to use DNS

    D. Your workstation has a duplicate IP address

6. *You can successfully ping all workstations in your subnet and most remote subnets in your intranet. You cannot, however, ping* all *remote subnets in your intranet. All other computers are able to ping each other. What is the most likely reason of this problem?*

    A. You computer has an invalid subnet mask

    B. You computer has a duplicate IP address

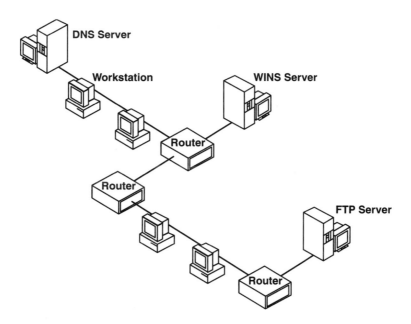

Figure 14.9 *Network example.*

C. The router is down

D. Your computer is not using WINS

7. *Which utility would you use to check how your computer registers its Net-BIOS name?*

A. NBTSTAT

B. NETSTAT

C. NSLOOKUP

D. IPCONFIG

8. *You use Microsoft* Network Monitor *and you discover that your computer sends an ARP request for the default gateway address every time it attempts to contact another machine. What could be the problem?*

A. Your workstation is not TCP/IP-enabled

B. Your workstation does not use DNS

C. Your workstation has an invalid subnet mask

D. There is no problem, this is normal

9. *Your computer has an invalid subnet mask. Which statement(s) is (are) true?*

A. Your computer cannot communicate with all other computers

B. Your computer can only communicate with remote computers

C. Your computer can only communicate with local computers

D. Your computer possibly cannot communicate with some or all computers

10. *You try to map a network drive to the computer named RED that is located on the remote subnet, but you fail. Your computer is not WINS-enabled, but it uses an LMHOSTS file. You check the TCP/IP configuration and discover that your computer has received valid TCP/IP parameters from the DHCP server. What should you check next?*

A. Check that the DHCP server is turned on and functional

B. Check that an entry for RED is present and has the correct mapping in the LMHOSTS file.

C. Check that your computer is NOT using broadcasts for name resolution

D. Check if RED is WINS-enabled

11. *A user is complaining that she is not able to connect to the corporate file server with* Windows NT Explorer. *From her computer you check that you are able to ping the corporate file server. What else should you check?*

    A. Check that the route to the corporate file server is configured

    B. Check that the user's computer is configured to use WINS

    C. Check that the user's computer has a valid LMHOSTS file

    D. Check that the user's computer has a valid subnet mask

12. *You are the administrator of the network shown in Figure 14.10. You are sitting at the computer named WKS1. You are able to access all computers in your intranet, but you are not able to access Server RED. What is the most likely reason for this?*

    A. DHCP server is in another network segment

    B. WINS server is in another network segment

    C. No route configured to the subnet with Server RED

    D. File LMHOSTS is corrupted

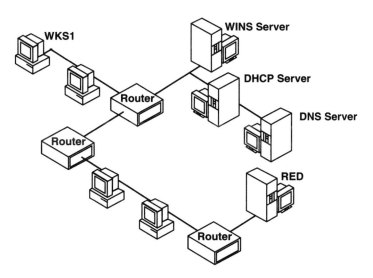

Figure 14.10 *Network example.*

13. *You can successfully ping Mary's computer, but when you use the* net use *command to connect to it you fail. You check that you are able to FTP her computer by name. What should you check next?*

    A. Check that Mary's computer is NetBIOS-enabled

    B. Check that your computer uses DNS

    C. Check that both computers are using the same scope ID

    D. Check that the link between these two computers is not broken

14. *You suspect that your computer has a duplicate IP address. Which application can you use to check it?*

    A. *Network Monitor*

    B. *Performance Monitor*

    C. *Event Viewer*

    D. *Server Manager*

15. *When you type the command* net use z: \\SRV\Public *on your Windows NT computer, you connect to the computer named SRV. But, when you use* ftp SRV *you connect to a computer named RED. What is the most likely reason of this problem?*

    A. LMHOSTS file is missing

    B. HOSTS file has an invalid entry

    C. LMHOSTS file has duplicate entries

    D. Server SRV is not a WINS client

16. *You've decided to build an intranet server for your organization. Your users use* Microsoft Internet Explorer *on a mixture of Windows 95, Windows 98, and Macintosh-based computers and will access your server using its host name. What service(s) should you install for efficient name resolution? (Select all that apply.)*

    A. WINS

    B. SNMP

    C. DHCP

    D. DNS

17. *Linda is installing a Windows NT server on her network to act as a print server for a TCP/IP network printer. What should Linda install to permit users to send their documents to the server and have it forward their documents to the printer?*

A. LPR utility

B. SNMP service

C. *TCP/IP Print Server*

D. DHCP

18. *Jim has just built a Windows NT network consisting of seven subnets, each with its own domain controller. He wants to ensure each machine can browse every other machine and make a peer-to-peer connection. He wants the network to automatically register and resolve computer names and to maintain them in a central database. What should Jim install on the network?*

A. SQL servers

B. DNS servers

C. WINS servers

D. DHCP servers

E. SNMP servers

19. *You decide to use the Windows NT* Performance Monitor *to monitor TCP/IP network activity on your computer. What should you install?*

A. *Network Monitor* tools and agent

B. SMTP

C. DHCP

D. SNMP

20. *Sandy's TCP/IP network has grown significantly in recent months and the job of managing TCP/IP configuration on all the network computers has taken valuable time from her other network management duties. What should Sandy install to reduce her workload?*

A. Netmon

B. DHCP

C. SNMP

D. WINS

E. A default gateway

21. *Vickie has just added a second subnet to her network and finds her DHCP server doesn't service clients on the new subnet. She creates a DHCP scope for the new subnet but still cannot get DHCP information to the new subnet. What should she add to the new subnet to solve this problem?*

A. WINS proxy service

B. DHCP Relay Agent service

C. DNS forwarders

D. SNMP service

22. *Your LMHOSTS files are becoming difficult to manage because of frequent changes in your network. You decide to implement something to reduce the administrative workload of maintaining these files. What should you install?*

A. HOSTS files

B. WINS

C. DNS

D. DHCP

E. A b-node

23. *You want to allow some of your users to dial in to your network from home. What service should you install?*

A. DNS

B. RAS

C. FTP

D. LPQ

Answers to Chapter Review Questions

Chapter 1

1. C
2. B, D
3. C
4. A
5. A, C
6. B
7. C
8. B, D
9. D
10. C
11. A, B
12. A

Chapter 2

1. B
2. B, C
3. D
4. B
5. A

Chapter 3

1. C
2. C
3. C
4. C
5. A, B, C
6. A
7. C
8. B
9. D
10. C
11. B
12. A
13. B
14. B
15. C
16. A
17. A, C
18. D

Chapter 4

1. C
2. C, D
3. C
4. B, C
5. E
6. A
7. B, C
8. B
9. A
10. B
11. A, B, C
12. B, C
13. B
14. C

Chapter 5

1. C
2. B

3. A
4. B
5. Metric is the number of hops to the destination. Metric determines the best route.
6. C
7. C
8. A
9. A, C
10. C
11. A, B, C
12. A, B, C
13. A
14. B
15. A
16. B
17. D
18. B, D
19. A, C
20. A, B

Chapter 6

1. Exclude the 130.110.5.70 through 130.110.5.82 range in the `Scope Properties` dialog of *DHCP Manager*.
2. No DHCP server on the new subnet, no DHCP Relay Agent to forward IP requests to another subnet's DHCP server, and/or available DHCP servers do not have a valid scope for the subnebt the client was just moved to.
3. Use the global option.
4. WINS/NBT node type.
5. `ipconfig /all`.
6. Implement a client reservation for each server under *DHCP Manager's* `Scope` menu.
7. Client hardware address and desired IP address.
8. Configure three scopes, one for each subnet. Set the `Lease Duration` at 60 days for the subnets containing the Windows NT machines, and set a five-day `Lease Duration` for the laptop subnet.
9. Place Relay Agents on subnets B and C or on the routers between Subnet A and Subnets B and C.
10. Configure DHCP to use the hybrid node type.
11. IP address(es) of DHCP server(s).

12. Place two scopes on each DHCP server, one for each subnet. Ensure the networks have a DHCP Relay Agent to forward IP requests to the other DHCP server if the primary doesn't respond within a reasonable time.

Chapter 7

1. C
2. B
3. A
4. C
5. C
6. B
7. C
8. C
9. C, E
10. D

Chapter 8

1. D
2. Since a T1 provides a relatively fast WAN link, configuring both machines as push-pull partners will provide fast, reliable replication.
3. C
4. Configure the `Primary WINS Server` field of the computer's WINS `Address` tab with the desired server's IP address.
5. B
6. E
7. D

Chapter 9

1. B
2. A, B
3. B
4. B, C
5. A
6. D
7. C
8. C
9. A, B, C
10. A, B
11. E

12. A
13. A, B
14. D
15. C

Chapter 10

1. A, C, D
2. C
3. D
4. C
5. B
6. C

Chapter 11

1. C
2. B
3. C
4. C
5. B
6. C
7. C
8. A, D
9. B
10. A
11. C
12. B
13. C

Chapter 12

1. A, D
2. C
3. C
4. C
5. C, E
6. B
7. A
8. C
9. F
10. A, B, C

11. B
12. A, C, D, E
13. A
14. C
15. D

Chapter 13

1. D
2. A, B, D
3. B
4. A, C
5. B
6. B

Chapter 14

1. D
2. B
3. A
4. A
5. C
6. A
7. A
8. C
9. D
10. B
11. B,C
12. C
13. A, C
14. C
15. B
16. A, D
17. C
18. C
19. D
20. B
21. B
22. B
23. B

INDEX

WHAT DOES CBT SYSTEMS HAVE THAT OTHERS DON'T? SCHOLARS STANDING BY.

At Scholars.com our certified Learning Advisors are available for online personalized mentoring when your students need it most — 24-hours-a-day, 7-days-a-week.

OPENING MINDS WITH PERSONAL SUPPORT.
Scholars.com introduces flexible self-paced study with the added benefits of expert help. With CBT Systems' award-winning courseware, Scholars.com works closely with students for personalized assistance through every step.

OPENING THE DOOR TO ONLINE LEARNING.
As Microsoft and Novell's largest online training provider, Scholars.com offers the only 24-hour online support in the world. Our team of Learning Advisors assists through online chats, discussion groups and help desk scenarios. Proactive mentoring also provides daily e-mail and answers to students' questions within 6 hours.

OPENING THE SECRETS TO CERTIFICATION.
CBT Systems courseware is Microsoft and Novell approved, and Scholars.com Learning Advisors are Microsoft and Novell certified. So you get help from mentors who know firsthand what it takes to pass certification exams.

Our dedication to the most effective I.T. training keeps us up nights. So don't let another 24 hours pass without online mentoring, visit our web site today.
Scholars.com — A new way to learn.

cbt systems

Try a FREE course — Microsoft: Administering Windows NT 4.0: Managing Users and Groups. Or Novell: Introducing Novell Netware 4.11. Register now at **www.scholars.com**

scholars.com™
A CBT Group Company

©1998 CBT Systems USA Ltd. CBT Systems and Scholars.com are trademarks of CBT Group, PLC. All other trademarks are the property of their respective owners.

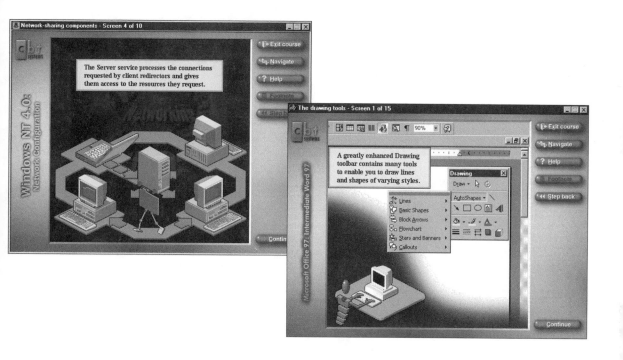

Other curricula available from CBT Systems:

- Cisco
- Informix
- Java
- Marimba
- Microsoft
- Netscape
- Novell

- Oracle
- SAP
- Sybase
- C/C++
- Centura
- Information Technology/
  Core Concepts

- Internet and Intranet
  Skills
- Internetworking
- UNIX

CBT SOFTWARE LICENSE AGREEMENT

IF YOU DO NOT AGREE WITH THESE TERMS AND CONDITIONS, DO NOT INSTALL THE SOFTWARE.

This is a legal agreement between you and CBT Systems Ltd. ("Licensor"), the licensor ("Licensor") from whom you have licensed the CBT Group PLC courseware (the "Software"). By installing, copying or otherwise using the Software, you agree to be bound by the terms of this License Agreement (the "License"). If you do not agree to the terms of this License, the Licensor is unwilling to license the Software to you. In such event, you may not use or copy the Software, and you should promptly contact the Licensor for instructions on the return of the unused Software.

1. **Use.** Licensor grants to you a non-exclusive, nontransferable license to use Licensor's software product (the "Software") and accompanying documentation in accordance with the terms and conditions of this license agreement ("License") License and as specified in your agreement with Licensor (the "Governing Agreement"). In the event of any conflict between this License and the Governing Agreement, the Governing Agreement shall control.

You may:

a. (if specified as a "personal use" version) install the Software on a single stand-alone computer or a single network node from which node the Software cannot be accessed by another computer, provided that such Software shall be used by only one individual; or

b. (if specified as a "workstation" version) install the Software on a single stand-alone computer or network node from which node the Software cannot be accessed by another computer, provided that such Software shall be used only by employees of your organization; or

c. (if specified as a "LAN" version) install the Software on a local area network server that provides access to multiple computers, up to the maximum number of computers or users specified in your Governing Agreement, provided that such Software shall be used only by employees of your organization; or

d. (if specified as an "enterprise" version) install the Software or copies of the Software on multiple local or wide area network servers, intranet servers, stand-alone computers and network nodes (and to make copies of the Software for such purpose) at one or more sites, which servers provide access to a multiple number of users, up to the maximum number of users specified in your Governing Agreement, provided that such Software shall be used only by employees of your organization.

This License is not a sale. Title and copyrights to the Software, accompanying documentation and any copy made by you remain with Licensor or its suppliers or licensors.

2. **Intellectual Property**. The Software is owned by Licensor or its licensors and is protected by United States and other jurisdictions' copyright laws and international treaty provisions. Therefore, you may not use, copy, or distribute the Software without the express written authorization of CBT Group PLC. This License authorizes you to use the Software for the internal training needs of your employees only, and to make one copy of the Software solely for backup or archival purposes. You may not print copies of any user documentation provided in "online" or electronic form. Licensor retains all rights not expressly granted.

3. **Restrictions**. You may not transfer, rent, lease, loan or time-share the Software or accompanying documentation. You may not reverse engineer, decompile, or disassemble the Software, except to the extent the foregoing restriction is expressly prohibited by applicable law. You may not modify, or create derivative works based upon the Software in whole or in part.

1. **Confidentiality**. The Software contains confidential trade secret information belonging to Licensor, and you may use the software only pursuant to the terms of your Governing Agreement, if any, and the license set forth herein. In addition, you may not disclose the Software to any third party.

2. **Limited Liability**. IN NO EVENT WILL THE LICENSOR'S LIABILITY UNDER, ARISING OUT OF OR RELATING TO THIS AGREEMENT EXCEED THE AMOUNT PAID TO LICENSOR FOR THE SOFTWARE. LICENSOR SHALL NOT BE LIABLE FOR ANY SPECIAL, INCIDENTAL, INDIRECT OR CONSEQUENTIAL DAMAGES, HOWEVER CAUSED AND ON ANY THEORY OF LIABILITY, REGARDLESS OF WHETHER LICENSOR HAS BEEN ADVISED OF THE POSSIBILITY OF SUCH DAMAGES. WITHOUT LIMITING THE FOREGOING, LICENSOR WILL NOT BE LIABLE FOR LOST PROFITS, LOSS OF DATA, OR COSTS OF COVER.

3. **Limited Warranty**. LICENSOR WARRANTS THAT SOFTWARE WILL BE FREE FROM DEFECTS IN MATERIALS AND WORKMANSHIP UNDER NORMAL USE FOR A PERIOD OF THIRTY (30) DAYS FROM THE DATE OF RECEIPT. THIS LIMITED WARRANTY IS VOID IF FAILURE OF THE SOFTWARE HAS RESULTED FROM ABUSE OR MISAPPLICATION. ANY REPLACEMENT SOFTWARE WILL BE WARRANTED FOR A PERIOD OF THIRTY (30) DAYS FROM THE DATE OF RECEIPT OF SUCH REPLACEMENT SOFTWARE. THE SOFTWARE AND DOCUMENTATION ARE PROVIDED "AS IS". LICENSOR HEREBY DISCLAIMS ALL OTHER WARRANTIES, EXPRESS, IMPLIED, OR STATUTORY, INCLUDING WITHOUT LIMITATION, THE IMPLIED WARRANTIES OF MERCHANTABILITY AND FITNESS FOR A PARTICULAR PURPOSE.

4. **Exceptions**. SOME STATES DO NOT ALLOW THE LIMITATION OF INCIDENTAL DAMAGES OR LIMITATIONS ON HOW LONG AN IMPLIED WARRANTY LASTS, SO THE ABOVE LIMITATIONS OR EXCLUSIONS MAY NOT APPLY TO YOU. This agreement gives you specific legal rights, and you may also have other rights which vary from state to state.

5. **U.S. Government-Restricted Rights**. The Software and accompanying documentation are deemed to be "commercial computer Software" and "commercial computer Software documentation," respectively, pursuant to DFAR Section 227.7202 and FAR Section 12.212, as applicable. Any use, modification, reproduction release, performance, display or disclosure of the Software and accompanying documentation by the U.S. Government shall be governed solely by the terms of this Agreement and shall be prohibited except to the extent expressly permitted by the terms of this Agreement.

6. **Export Restrictions**. You may not download, export, or re-export the Software (a) into, or to a national or resident of, Cuba, Iraq, Libya, Yugoslavia, North Korea, Iran, Syria or any other country to which the United States has embargoed goods, or (b) to anyone on the United States Treasury Department's list of Specially Designated Nationals or the U.S. Commerce Department's Table of Deny Orders. By installing or using the Software, you are representing and warranting that you are not located in, under the control of, or a national or resident of any such country or on any such list.

7. **General**. This License is governed by the laws of the United States and the State of California, without reference to conflict of laws principles. The parties agree that the United Nations Convention on Contracts for the International Sale of Goods shall not apply to this License. If any provision of this Agreement is held invalid, the remainder of this License shall continue in full force and effect.

8. **More Information**. Should you have any questions concerning this Agreement, or if you desire to contact Licensor for any reason, please contact: CBT Systems USA Ltd., 1005 Hamilton Court, Menlo Park, California 94025, Attn: Chief Legal Officer.

IF YOU DO NOT AGREE WITH THE ABOVE TERMS AND CONDITIONS, DO NOT INSTALL THE SOFTWARE AND RETURN IT TO THE LICENSOR.

About the CD

The enclosed CD contains the following computer-based training (CBT) course module:

Introduction to TCP/IP and IP Addressing

The CD can be used on Windows 95, Windows 98, or Windows NT systems. To access the CBT course, launch the SETUP.EXE file. For further information about installation, read the README.TXT file on the CD. At the Start menu, select Run and type in D:/readme.txt (where D is your CD-ROM drive).

Technical Support

If you have a problem with the CBT software, please contact CBT Technical Support. In the US, call 1-800-938-3247. If you are outside the US, call 3531-283-0380.

Prentice Hall does not offer technical support for this software. However, if there is a problem with the media, you may obtain a replacement copy by e-mailing us with your problem at: disc_exchange@phptr.com